Students of Revolution

Students of Revolution

Youth, Protest, and Coalition Building
in Somoza-Era Nicaragua

CLAUDIA RUEDA

University of Texas Press ❧ *Austin*

Requests for permission to reproduce material from this work should be sent to:
   Permissions
   University of Texas Press
   P.O. Box 7819
   Austin, TX 78713–7819
   utpress.utexas.edu/rp-form

♾ The paper used in this book meets the minimum requirements of
ANSI/NISO Z39.48–1992 (R1997) (Permanence of Paper).

Library of Congress Cataloging-in-Publication Data

Names: Rueda, Claudia P., 1984–, author.
Title: Students of revolution : youth, protest, and coalition building in Somoza-era
Nicaragua / Claudia Rueda.
Description: First edition. | Austin : University of Texas Press, 2019. |
Includes bibliographical references and index.
Identifiers: LCCN 2018054095
      ISBN 978-1-4773-1930-7 (cloth : alk. paper)
      ISBN 978-1-4773-1931-4 (library e-book)
      ISBN 978-1-4773-1932-1 (non-library e-book)
Subjects: LCSH: Student movements—Nicaragua—History—20th century. |
Students—Political activity—Nicaragua—20th century. | Youth—Political activity—
Nicaragua—20th century. | Nicaragua—History—1937-1979. | Nicaragua—Politics
and government—1937-1979.
Classification: LCC LA463.7 .R84 2019 | DDC 378.1/98109728.5—dc23
LC record available at https://lccn.loc.gov/2018054095

doi:10.7560/319307

Contents

Acknowledgments

This research would not have been possible without the generosity of the many Nicaraguans who opened their doors to me when I was a graduate student. The community at the Instituto de Historia de Nicaragua y Centroamérica was welcoming and supportive, especially María Ligia Garay, María Auxiliadora Estrada, Miguel Ayerdis, Juan Pablo Gómez, Aura Torres, and Yessica Rivas. Yuridia Mendoza, Tania Ordoñcz, and Eimeel Castillo were friends and colleagues. I am especially thankful for Eimeel's intellectual generosity and wise counsel. Father Fernando Cardenal, Israel Lewites, and Camilo de Castro Belli shared their wide network of contacts with me. Thank you to the many people who took the time to share their stories with me.

Numerous scholars have helped shaped this book. I am especially grateful to Virginia Garrard-Burnett for her guidance while I was a graduate student at the University of Texas at Austin. I thank Tanalís Padilla for her insightful comments on the many chapter drafts. Jaime Pensado read the entire manuscript and provided suggestions at a critical point in the writing. John McKiernan-González, Seth Garfield, Jonathan Brown, Charles Hale, Susan Deans-Smith, Arturo Arias, Anne Martínez, Ann Twinam, and Laurie Green provided valuable feedback both on this project and during my time in graduate school. I am lucky to have been in the graduate program at the University of Texas at Austin at the same time as Juandrea Bates, Renata Keller, Kristin Cheasty Anderson, Lauren Hammond, María Sofía Corona, Julia Ogden, Sarah Steinbock-Pratt, Susan Zakaib, and Valerie Martínez. I am grateful for the wisdom of Fernanda Soto Joya, Heather Peterson, Bonar Hernández, José Barragán, Claudia Carreta Beltrán, and Matt Gildner. Kency Cornejo, Takkara Brunson, Shennette Garrett, Veronica Martínez-Matsuda, and Cristina Salinas have been critical role models and friends. The amazing staff at the Benson Latin American Collection in Austin made my life and research so much easier. I thank Jorge Salinas, A. J. Johnson, Margot Gutiérrez, and Adán Benavides for their assistance.

Texas A&M–Corpus Christi provided a supportive climate for finishing this book. I am especially grateful for my colleagues in the Humanities and English Departments. Peter Moore and Mark Hartlaub helped facilitate research leave. Beth Robinson, Sandrine Sanos, Jennifer Sorensen, Kathryn Vomero Santos, Chrissy Lau, Sarah Salter, Lucy Sheehan, Mara Barbosa, Melissa Galvan, and Jennifer Brown provided a vibrant intellectual community. Adam Costanzo, Dawson Barrett, and Patrick Carroll gave feedback on portions of this book and on the publishing process. I owe a special debt of gratitude to Beth Robinson and her knowledge of the literature on US social movements. Thank you to Andrea Zelaya for being an able research assistant. I could write volumes on the ways Brenton Day and the interlibrary loan department at the Bell Library made this book possible.

Funding for this research came from the Ford Foundation, the American Association of University Women, and the History Department at the University of Texas at Austin. At TAMU-CC, the Franz Endowment, the Haas Professorship, and the Office of Research, Commercialization, and Outreach funded research and travel. The Woodrow Wilson Career Enhancement Fellowship Program enabled me to complete this book. I am grateful for the assistance of Shana Sabbath, Marilyn Lehman, Dan Reichers, Rayna Truelove, and Marti Beck.

Kerry Webb and the team at the University of Texas Press have been patient with my many questions. I thank Kerry especially for supporting this book project and shepherding it through the publication process.

A number of people I met as an undergraduate have continued to support me over the years. Tanalís Padilla has been a commiserator extraordinaire, mentor, and close friend. I am grateful for her wisdom and solidarity. Lourdes Gutiérrez Nájera has been a vital source of encouragement and advice. Craig Wilder's class on US history sparked an abiding interest in the puzzles of the discipline. I thank Katherine Harrington, Carolyn W. Lee, Joanna Lau, Wendy and Paul Manganiello, and Robert Herr for their friendship, advice, and comments on this and other works.

Many people have made my life better simply by being present. Ottoniel Argüello, Esa Westmann, and Kim de Haan were my surrogate family as I researched this book. I do not know where I would be without Tara Lehew, Camilla Figueroa, Keith Kachtick, and Lindsay Breithaupt. I thank Eduardo Canales, Raul Alonzo, Lacy Sanders, Isla Lara, and Gilbert Gonzalez for their friendship. The Days welcomed me into their family. The Lozanos and the Ruedas taught me to work hard and laugh harder. Emma Lozano has been a lifelong source of encouragement. I am especially grateful for the support of Michelle Gould, Christina Garza, Katiuska Flynn, and Melissa Phillips. I am lucky to have Gabriel Rueda, Meghan Guzman, Jaime Rueda, and Anna Rueda in my life.

Juandrea Bates has been there from day one. Colleague, friend, and sister, she has given me more pep talks than I can count. Our long conversations keep me going. I cannot thank her enough for her friendship, brilliance, kindness, and sense of adventure.

Brent Day is a big deep breath of calm. His sense of wonder inspires me; his quiet discipline motivates me. Thank you for your patience, encouragement, and love. Thank you for the thoughtful conversations. Thank you for helping me establish balance in my life. Thank you for being part of it.

Finally, I am deeply grateful to my parents, Jaime and Laura Rueda, for their support and love. My dad is my role model. He taught me to value curiosity and courage. My mother taught me how to make a life in this world. As I child, I watched her volunteer and organize. As an adolescent, I saw her learn a new career. As an adult, I have marveled at her resilience. I dedicate this book to her and to my grandmother, Emma G. Lozano—two amazing women who have known what it is to persist.

List of Acronyms

AES	Asociación de Estudiantes de Secundaria (Association of Secondary Students)
BECATs	Brigadas Especiales Contra Actividades Terroristas (Special Antiterrorist Activity Brigades)
CAP	Comité de Acción Popular (Committee for Popular Action)
CEJIS	Círculo de Estudios Jurídicos y Sociales (Juridical and Social Studies Circle)
CEUUCA	Centro Estudiantil Universitario de la Universidad Centroamericana (University Student Center of the Central American University)
CIVES	Comités Ciudadanos de Vigilancia Electoral y Defensa del Sufragio (Citizen Committees for Electoral Vigilance and the Defense of Suffrage)
CSUCA	Consejo Superior Universitario Centroamericano (Higher Council of Central American Universities)
CUUN	Centro Universitario de la Universidad Nacional (Student Center of the National University)
ENAG	Escuela Nacional de Agricultura y Ganadería (National School of Agriculture and Animal Husbandry)
FDC	Frente Demócrata Cristiano (Christian Democrat Front)
FEL	Frente Estudiantil Liberal (Liberal Student Front)
FER	Frente Estudiantil Revolucionario (Revolutionary Student Front)
FSLN	Frente Sandinista de Liberación Nacional (Sandinista National Liberation Front)
FSMN	Federación Sindical de Maestros de Nicaragua (Nicaraguan Federation of Teachers' Unions)

FUN	Federación Universitario de Nicaragua (Federation of Nicaraguan University Students)
GN	Guardia Nacional (National Guard)
GPP	Guerra Popular Prolongada (Prolonged People's War)
IHNCA	Instituto de Historia de Nicaragua y Centroamerica (Institute for Nicaraguan and Central American History)
INEP	Instituto Nacional Eliseo Picado (Eliseo Picado National Institute)
ISC	International Student Conference
IUS	International Union of Students
JDN	Juventud Demócrata Nicaragüense (Nicaraguan Democratic Youth)
JEC	Juventud Estudiantil Católica (Catholic Student Youth)
JPN	Juventud Patriótica Nicaragüense (Nicaraguan Patriotic Youth)
JRN	Juventud Revolucionaria Nicaragüense (Nicaraguan Revolutionary Youth)
JS	Juventud Somocista (Somocist Youth)
JSN	Juventud Socialista Nicaragüense (Nicaraguan Socialist Youth)
JUC	Juventud Universitaria Católica (Catholic University Youth)
MCR	Movimiento Cristiano Revolucionario (Revolutionary Christian Movement)
MES	Movimiento Estudiantil de Secundaria (Secondary Student Movement)
MPU	Movimiento de Pueblo Unido (United People's Movement)
OSN	Oficina de Seguridad Nacional (Office of National Security)
PSN	Partido Socialista Nicaragüense (Nicaraguan Socialist Party)
UCA	Universidad Centroamericana (Central American University)
UDE	Unión Democrática de Estudiantes (Democratic Union of Students)
UNAN	Universidad Nacional Autónoma de Nicaragua (National Autonomous University of Nicaragua)
UNAP	Unión Nacional de Acción Popular (National Union of Popular Action)
UNN	Universidad Nacional de Nicaragua (National University of Nicaragua)
UNO	Unión Nacional Opositora (National Opposition Union)
USIS	US Information Services

Introduction

In the early morning hours of Saturday, September 26, 1970, a group of forty young men and women, students at the Universidad Centroamericana (UCA), accompanied by several priests, entered the National Cathedral in Managua, Nicaragua. After waiting patiently for the mass to end, they informed the priest that they were there to take over the church. The youths ushered out the last remaining worshippers and locked the doors behind them. They were protesting a wave of arrests that had rocked Nicaragua in recent days as the regime of Anastasio Somoza Debayle cracked down on the rising tide of dissent. By 7:45 a.m., the National Guard had encircled the cathedral, which was next door to the National Palace. Cutting off the water and electricity to the church, the soldiers seemed to prepare for a siege.

Then something remarkable happened. César Aróstegui, one of the students protesting that day, remembered, "The Guard surrounded us, but the pueblo surrounded the Guard."[1] People began filling up the streets and paralyzing traffic. There they remained as military planes and helicopters circled overhead and as soldiers carrying rifles tried to push them away from the cathedral.

The 1970 occupation of the National Cathedral was the first of its kind in Nicaragua and significant for many reasons. First, the protesting students were not the usual suspects from the national public university, which had a long history of opposition to the regime. Instead, they were the children of Nicaragua's upper classes who attended the Catholic university. The Managua daily, *La Prensa*, covered the protest almost as they would a social event, albeit one with a strong undercurrent of tension and violence. A reporter wrote that Marina de Lacayo Fiallos, whose daughter was holed up in the church, was "dressed in pink and demonstrated a serene concern" for her child.[2]

Second, the students had won some very important allies: Archbishop Miguel Obando y Bravo negotiated on their behalf with General José Somoza, the president's half brother. Twenty-two Jesuits signed a letter of support condemning the regime for its mistreatment of political prisoners. The church was not only willing to work with the protestors, it also worked around them. The following day, after students took over several other churches, the priests happily gave their Sunday masses in the streets. Finally, parents like Sra. De Lacayo were in the crowd that day, returning the *V* for victory signs their children were making from the windows of the cathedral. The youths proclaimed from megaphones that their mothers should not worry "because the authorities of the university and Christ are with us." They had other unexpected supporters. One of the National Guard soldiers took a megaphone on Saturday night to declare his support for the protestors. No doubt remembering the Somozas' long history of repression, a sixty-year-old laborer, crying in fear, predicted a massacre was about to occur. Despite the legitimacy of his concern, there was no violence that Saturday.[3]

To the contrary, the student strike was enormously successful. Within hours, the National Guard had released one of the student prisoners, William Hüper Argüello, with apologies for torturing him, and General Somoza promised to reveal information about the prisoners.[4] Students throughout the country began occupying churches in solidarity, and by Sunday afternoon, Somoza agreed to permit a human rights committee to visit the prisoners and investigate the allegations of mistreatment.[5] Meanwhile, Nicaraguans rallied to the youths' side. An editorial in *La Prensa* extolled the students for "opening a non-communist and non-violent door of hope for Nicaragua, as the civic, peaceful and Christian protest they are now engaged in."[6]

The student occupation of the cathedral is emblematic of the unexpected development of the student movement in Nicaragua. During the Cold War, students in the university emerged as the most consistent and vocal opponents to the Somoza regime, which had been in power since the 1930s. The trajectory of this movement, its class, religious, and political dimensions, all belie common stereotypes of student activism in this period. Observers of student protest in Latin America in the 1960s and 1970s were quick to label the participants as communists and leftists, as radicals eager for "quick solutions," and vehement enemies of the "rightist United States."[7] Such rhetoric permeated US embassy reports, the discourse of nation-states under attack, and even some academic and newspaper articles that appeared across the continent.

Yet, as the cathedral occupation shows, student protest in Cold War-era Nicaragua is not so easy to characterize. For one, those students were not necessarily communists or Marxists. Second, religious, as well as democratic, ideals drove their protest, which won the support of various sectors of their society. Third, they represented a cross section of that society: men and women, scholarship students and the distant relatives of former presidents, priests and irreverent teenagers. Finally, the activism and organizing they engaged in the early 1970s was not a new development, but instead a legacy of decades of student political engagement.

That last point is critical. In recent years, studies of student protest have focused on the "Long Sixties," the era of mass mobilization that rocked countries around the world. Yet, the qualities that made the sixties a particularly heady period for youth elsewhere — the mass protests in the streets, the challenges to political authority, the violent encounters with the state, and the irreverent attacks on traditional hierarchies — were not new developments in Nicaragua, but rather consistent parts of student protest since at least the 1930s. In fact, Nicaragua did not experience mass student mobilizations in 1968, but there had been many before then and there would be many after.[8]

The factors that triggered discontent in Mexico, Brazil, Uruguay, and elsewhere (rising inequality, authoritarian regimes, deteriorating social services, and underfunded educational systems) had been present in Nicaragua for several decades and had been catalyzing student unrest for just as long.[9] Indeed, if we accept the argument made by scholars that the mobilizations of the sixties were, in part, a response to the unfulfilled promises of the Depression and postwar-era push to modernize via industrialization and democratization, then it makes sense that the 1960s would look very different in Nicaragua, where such experiments were severely limited and, in fact, curtailed by the dictatorship that began in the 1930s.[10] Scholarly understanding of the era, though, has been shaped by the literature on student protest in larger and/or wealthier Latin American countries. The view from smaller nations with lengthier histories of authoritarian regimes, like Nicaragua, suggests that the hallmarks of the Long Sixties actually characterized much of the Cold War period.[11]

This expanded time frame is important because it helps explain Nicaragua's revolutionary trajectory. As one of only two countries in the hemisphere to experience a successful social revolution during the Cold War, Nicaragua's long history of protest and repression under the Somozas meant successive generations learned from the experiences of their predecessors. The dictatorship forced students and other dissidents to develop innovative strategies for building coalitions and destabilizing the state, which culminated in the successful Sandinista Revolution in 1979.

This book thus argues that it is more useful to understand student protest across the Cold War era instead of in the isolated realm of a single decade, albeit one with flexible boundaries. The historian Gilbert Joseph and others have argued that the Cold War in Latin America was more than a struggle between two superpowers and their surrogates. Instead, Joseph proposes that the conflict was more broadly a reactionary effort "by the United States (and its local clients) to contain insurgencies that challenged post- (or neo-) colonial social formations predicated on dependent economies and class, ethnic and gender inequality" and traces its origins to the Mexican Revolution.[12] In Nicaragua, students constituted a key part of the insurgencies that challenged the Somoza regime, which was a long-time US ally and a dictatorship whose policies deepened the country's inequality.[13] Joseph's definition underscores the uniquely local manifestations of the Cold War: Latin American insurgencies were not directed by foreign superpowers; rather, the impetus for rising up came from local grievances. Examining student protest over the long period of the Cold War reveals that Nicaraguan students had been part of domestic demands for redress much longer than the sixties. Indeed, they were invigorating revolutionary struggles for much of the twentieth century, and their ideologies and strategies help us understand when and why these movements failed or succeeded.

Young people not only contributed to the success of the Sandinista Revolution, they are also part of a much bigger story that traces how diverse sectors of society come together and fall apart in the struggle for democracy and social justice. Drawing on student archives, state and university records, and oral histories, I uncover the political conditions, demographic shifts, and confrontations with the state that politicized university students during the Somoza era (1937–1979). Throughout the dictatorship, state corruption, repression, and mismanagement politicized new generations of students who resented the limitations such practices placed on their behavior, their university, and their nation. Student political participation ebbed and flowed with the Somozas' inconsistent authoritarianism, but at key moments in the dictatorship, students took public action that earned them a degree of legitimacy and ultimately helped overthrow the regime. Their increasing moral authority, derived from their historical record of action, meant people paid attention when they protested, and wide swaths of the public took action when they endured violent repression. *Students of Revolution* thus illuminates the role students play in raising broader political consciousness and furthers our understanding of the most enduring familial dictatorship in Latin America and the revolution that ended it.

Somoza, Sandinistas, and Students

From 1937 to 1979, the Somozas, first the father and then his sons, ruled the country, accumulating vast sums of wealth and property for themselves and their allies. Anastasio Somoza García came to national prominence as the director of the US Marine-trained National Guard (GN) in 1933. At that time, the Marines were departing Nicaragua after intermittently occupying the country since 1909. In their place, they left behind the National Guard with Somoza at its head. The self-designated general actually had very little military experience, but he was a savvy political actor who had befriended US Secretary of State Harry L. Stimson and other US agents, including several Marine officers. After his North American friends lobbied hard on Somoza's behalf, President Juan Bautista Sacasa appointed him chief of the new national military. Almost immediately, Somoza set about building a loyal army and neutralizing his opponents, whether they be Sacasista officers or General Augusto César Sandino, who had led the guerrilla war against the US occupation in the late 1920s and early 1930s. Benefitting from the new non-interventionist US policies as well as the internal weakness of the Nicaraguan state, Somoza staged a coup d'état in 1936, overthrowing Sacasa and paving the way for his own presidency. With the support of an odd coalition of Liberals, Conservatives, workers, and peasants, Somoza won the presidency in 1936. He would maintain his hold over the country for the next twenty years.[14]

If Somoza came to power with the aid of a broad cross section of society, his sons did not enjoy such support. After an erstwhile student assassinated Anastasio Somoza García in 1956, his eldest son Luis, who had been president of the National Assembly, came to power. Luis Somoza Debayle initiated a small democratic aperture, but his administration was still characterized by the ready use of force against dissidents. During this period, his younger brother, Anastasio Somoza Debayle, commanded the National Guard and was all too willing to deploy his forces against critics, which now included armed revolutionaries. The Frente Sandinista de Liberación Nacional (Sandinista National Liberation Front, or FSLN) started to come together in the early sixties, and the guerrilla organization would prove to be the family's enduring adversary. Luis Somoza stepped down in 1963, in favor of his chosen successor, René Schick, and for the next four years, non-Somozas occupied the nation's highest office. Nevertheless, the two brothers remained active behind the scenes, with Anastasio continuing as head of the Guard. The family returned to the public sphere in the lead-up to the 1967 presidential election, which Anastasio Somoza won handily, if not honestly. However, his brother did not live to see him inaugurated. Luis

Somoza died of a massive heart attack in April, a few weeks before the new president was sworn in.

The Somoza family dominated Nicaraguan political life throughout the Cold War period to the chagrin of the growing opposition. As the decades wore on, the family held tight to the reins of power and grew enormously wealthy from their government connections. Gradually, larger and larger sections of the population began expressing their opposition. The 1972 earthquake that devastated Managua, and the regime's corruption in its aftermath, contributed to the opposition's coalescence. After recovering from several debilitating defeats in the 1960s, the FSLN pulled off stunning attacks against the government that humiliated Somoza and illustrated the regime's vulnerability. The state's violent response radicalized campesinos, who were the primary victims, as well as the middle class, which previously had been neutral or passive opponents but whose children now became targets of regime repression. In early 1978, the prominent opposition journalist Pedro Joaquín Chamorro, was assassinated, and a mass uprising in the indigenous community of Monimbó was brutally quelled. Such spontaneous rebellions would continue to destabilize the government and fuel FSLN revolutionary efforts. Somoza finally fled the country in July 1979, and the Sandinistas marched triumphantly into Managua.[15]

Since the 1980s, Nicaragua has elicited much scholarly attention, and the bulk of it has focused on the dynamics of the Somoza regime and the struggle to overthrow it. Like other countries in Central America, Nicaragua has a long history of guerrilla struggle that began most famously with Sandino in the 1920s. In the decades following, individuals from across the political spectrum took up the strategy in their battle against the regime. These rebels often worked with other Latin American nations and movements that, at varying times, sought to resist the US imperial interests that propped up dictators throughout the region.[16] Most famously, the Cuban revolutionary government played a decisive role in the formation of the FSLN as it shaped the ideology of the Front's founder, Carlos Fonseca. From the late 1950s until his death in 1976, Fonseca blended the ideology of the Cuban revolutionaries and Nicaragua's own historical legacy of struggle to craft a nationalist and socialist revolutionary project.[17]

The FSLN and other anti-Somocista movements made many mistakes, chief of which was underestimating the political consciousness of the peasant and working classes. Anastasio Somoza García had won their loyalty in the 1930s and 1940s with promises of labor reform and land redistribution, and his limited efforts to enact such policies ensured their continued support. His sons' fitful and ineffective attempts to replicate their father's populism ultimately turned labor away from the regime and radicalized their politics.[18] The revolutionary coalition that formed in the 1970s still faced a formidable opponent in the National Guard, which remained loyal to the regime. Yet, even in the most violent period of the dictatorship, divisions within the military, combined with its corruption and brutality, weakened its efficacy and contributed to its ever-deteriorating reputation.[19] Each of these factors help explain the breakdown of the Somozas' support base and the rise of a broad opposition movement under the direction of the Sandinistas.[20]

Largely missing from these accounts are the young people, and specifically students, who constituted an important part of the opposition.[21] Yet, youth played a critical role in the success of the Sandinista Revolution in 1979. The nation's universities had been a bastion of anti-Somocismo for much of the regime's history, and by the 1970s, college and secondary students were organizing barrios, spreading information, and staging dramatic protests that highlighted the regime's brutality and brought together various sectors. In this regard, student participation in the revolutionary movement in Nicaragua paralleled events throughout Latin America, where a significant number of young people joined or supported the guerrilla movements battling military regimes. Scholars have yet to fully examine the role of youth in the revolutionary unrest that marked the region's Cold War experience.

That said, the history of student and youth movements in Latin America is increasingly becoming a topic of great interest to historians. For several decades, academics were most interested in excavating the university reform struggles that rocked the region in the 1910s and 1920s. Their studies shed light on the new meaning that youths assigned to their institutions as they fought for autonomy from the Catholic Church and the state, a more professionalized faculty, a culturally relevant education, and a greater role for themselves in the administration. In particular, these studies have shown how the reform struggles cemented students' commitment to a socially oriented university, one that offered programs for workers and prioritized solutions for the nation's problems.[22] Scholars of student movements in the 1930s and early Cold War era showed how states, and, in particular, repressive regimes, responded to the students' newfound freedoms. They highlighted the politicization of student movements as young activists began prioritizing the transformation of their society over changes within their university.[23]

The bulk of research on student mobilization, however, has focused heavily on the great upheavals of the Long Sixties. These studies have gone a long way toward explaining the rise of student protests in this period, their countercultural and international influences, and state and societal responses.[24] Scholars of the mid- to late Cold War period, in particular, have focused on the cultural ascendency of youth and the role of memory in building and sustaining student movements and how consumer patterns explain the emergence of distinct youth identities in the 1960s.[25] My study of student protest in Nicaragua draws on many of the conclusions these academics have reached and makes several critical interventions.

For one, this is a study of the mechanics of the Nicaraguan student movement. It shows how university students fought for and won political legitimacy and how they used that cachet to intervene in national political struggles. As Victoria Langland found in Brazil and Heather Vrana in Guatemala, student political authority was premised on the relatively elite nature of the student body and its high level of organization. Additionally, students' own claims about their future role in society, their willingness to sacrifice, and their moral purity buttressed their demands for political inclusion.[26] As is true for all social sectors, student political engagement in Nicaragua was a messy and complicated process. Young people in the anti-Somoza student movement subscribed to conflicting ideologies and fought bitterly over strategy, often in the context of severe censorship and repression. Recent scholarship has shown that similar divisions marked the student movements in Uruguay and Mexico in the Long Sixties.[27] Like these works, *Students of Revolution* uncovers the complicated networks, competing ideologies, and changing loyalties that marked the student movement in Nicaragua, but it is most interested in examining how students reached out to and worked with other sectors not only in the sixties but also across the Cold War era.[28] This book then is not just about student activism, but about students' efforts to organize their society.

As a study of students' organizational and rhetorical strategies, *Students of Revolution* argues that young people in the university, and in their society, relied on an understanding of student exceptionalism to both legitimize and protect their political activities. Students and their supporters articulated a firm belief that young people studying in the university (and in secondary schools, to a lesser degree) deserved special privileges and protection due to their youth and their future status as professionals and political leaders. This notion would enable students to take risky political actions and win freedoms denied most other sectors. Arguably, the most important freedom they won was university autonomy, the legal and administrative separation of the university from the state. Nicaragua's National University was one of the last in Latin America to gain autonomy, and it held on to its independence for the duration of the Somoza regime. The freedom from government interference enabled the National University to become a seedbed of resistance and was the most visible manifestation of students' privileged status. It was not, however, a magic shield, and by the end of the 1970s, student exceptionalism meant little to National Guardsmen who seemed to be especially targeting youth.

As elsewhere, the meaning of "youth" and "student" in Nicaragua thus changed over time, and both young people and their society helped construct these notions. In this way, my work on student organizing further clarifies the ways in which young people, especially those in the universities, as well as in the secondary schools, played with the idea of "youth" and the category of "student," subtly redefining these terms to suit their needs. Likewise, it examines how the society around them, from Somoza to their parents, interpreted ideas of youth to delegitimize or support their protests. This kind of discursive analysis has become increasingly popular in the field of youth studies. Scholars of student movements in Argentina, Guatemala, Mexico, and elsewhere have excavated the ways in which various groups, from conservative politicians to psychologists, have shaped the meaning of youth to suit their own purposes.[29] In analyzing these shifts, they have helped explicate the rise and repression of student movements in the Long Sixties.

This book mainly focuses, however, on the political history of student protest and the nitty-gritty of student organizing in order to reveal critical aspects of revolutions in general and Nicaragua under Somoza specifically. Key to this story are the many young women who defied traditional gender norms to organize against the regime. Scholars have long observed that revolutionary movements can be contradictory spaces for women, whose interests are often subordinated to the larger struggle. At the same time, women's participation in revolutionary movements upends traditional notions of gender in ways that can be liberating. Building on the work of Margaret Randall, whose oral history collections illustrate the critical role women played in the guerrilla movement, this book highlights the myriad ways that young women participated in the Nicaraguan student movement.[30] As was true elsewhere in the sixties, young women's political activism generally avoided questions of gender equality while simultaneously challenging gendered expectations.[31] Their work in organizing communities, leading student organizations, and marching in the streets transformed their lives and their society, and young women were central players in the student movement for much of the Somoza era.[32]

Studying student protest in Nicaragua helps explain both the longevity of the Somoza regime as well as its moments of weakness. By uncovering the ways in which the regime dealt with young protestors, this book examines how Anastasio Somoza García managed to spin their dissent in ways that legitimized his rule. Likewise, it reveals the ways in which the regime of his sons violently overreacted to student demonstrations and, in so doing, alienated important sectors of their base. Finally, it further uncovers what everyday life was like during the dictatorship, the censorship that curtailed people's activities, and the fear that permeated quotidian routines as well as the lingering spaces where protest and dissent were still possible.

This is a story about Nicaragua, but the dynamics of youth protest, repression, and dictatorship extend to regimes and revolutionary movements in other places. In highlighting the critical role students and their schools played in mobilizing opposition, this study also sheds light on the process of revolution. While scholars have looked at the role of campesinos, labor unions, elites, and guerrillas in the success of the Sandinistas, none have examined in detail how students contributed to the revolution.[33] This is part of a larger lacuna in the literature on revolution—one that is only now starting to be addressed.[34] Young people disproportionally joined the ranks of the guerrilla movements in Latin America, and many a revolutionary movement emerged from or found a fertile recruiting ground in the university.[35] Yet, few studies have analyzed the role that young people play in fomenting revolution. My work argues that youth were key to creating the cross-class alliances necessary for revolution to occur. With the privileges and protections provided by their status as students, young people throughout the Somoza era organized inside and outside the university, promoting first reform and later revolution. Their actions catalyzed the wider political engagement of their society.

Civil Society and Political Consciousness

As a study of student protest, this book shows how student goals and strategies changed over time, as well as when and why students garnered mass support and thus built mass resistance. These questions are critical to understanding the key role students play in mobilizing their society. Of late, it has become popular to use the notion of civil society to evaluate the democratic health of a community or nation, and the term has its utility. When studying social and revolutionary movements, however, it is more useful to analyze mass mobilization through the lens of consciousness.

Although there are many ways to define the term, "civil society" really centers on two key provisions: it is made up of voluntary organizations and it is separate and largely independent from the state.[36] At several points during the Somoza era, students attempted to mobilize civil society through, for example, organized and voluntary groups that effectively spread information and enlisted broader support. However, under a decades-long dictatorship, there were few organizations completely autonomous from the state. Not even students and student organizations were completely independent from the regime. Under Anastasio Somoza García, the regime appointed administrators and faculty and could close universities at will. This would change somewhat in the 1960s and 1970s after the National University was granted autonomy, but even then, the government still controlled the school's budget. The dictatorship's extensive reach meant that civil society was rarely truly independent and separate from the state.

Moreover, the term "civil society" elides significant class divisions that are important to consider and whose implications this book seeks to examine.[37] The term suggests that all voluntary organizations are on a level playing field, when, in fact, some have significantly more resources and access to power. Student activists realized this early in the 1940s, and their attempts to mobilize civil society were, upon closer analysis, actually efforts to attract elite benefactors and working-class followers. These differences are significant if we are to understand the ways in which cross-class coalitions come together and fall apart.

The lens of consciousness, in contrast, offers a more valuable way to explore students' role in mobilizing wider society, while still paying attention to different sectors. Indeed, to understand how any group is mobilized, we must examine the sparks that prompt political engagement. Marxist scholars perceive consciousness to come from the interchange of thought and action, and many have sought to understand how consciousness is transformed and the process through which critical consciousness is developed.[38] The unique ability students have to act as catalysts between thought and action helps us better understand their capacity to promote change.

One of the fundamental arguments of this book is that students had a special ability to spark wider mobilization in Nicaragua. The unique capacity to spread dissent came from a few characteristics unique to students. For one, throughout the Somoza years, students were often one of the few sectors willing to take action against the regime, whether that meant protesting, striking, or taking up weapons. Their willingness to act was a byproduct of their understanding of what it meant to be a student.[39] Second, students were particularly well positioned to spread information. Student participation in various networks—family, school, work, church, and neighborhood, among others—meant they possessed many "weak ties," or passing relationships with people from different sectors. This meant that students were uniquely suited for spreading information among diverse groups of people. Moreover, in Nicaragua, where very few had the privilege to go to school, students enjoyed a symbolic status that protected them from violence and garnered them widespread support when they did suffer any kind of state repression. That symbolism centered not only on their youth, but also on their potential—they were the future political and economic elite, and as such, their safety was vital to the nation's interests.⁴⁰ Combined, these factors meant that students enjoyed the political space to mobilize and to protest and encourage others to do the same. In so doing, they provided their elders (and juniors) with a reason and a venue in which to act.⁴¹

The students' ability to catalyze wider political consciousness is directly tied to their relative privilege in their society as well as to their diverse backgrounds. It is hard to characterize the class origins of the university student body because it changed over time. In the early decades of the Somoza era, higher education was largely the domain of Nicaraguan elites, who often sent their children abroad for school, and the small middle class. In later years, however, students came from a wide swath of society. In 1958, for example, the rector of the National University noted that his students were the "children of school teachers, washerwomen, artisans, small business owners and workers."⁴² Urbanization combined with the expansion (albeit still inadequate) of education meant that the number of young people who moved past secondary school into the university rose steadily throughout the twentieth century. By the 1970s, these youths came from increasingly diverse backgrounds. Many would have been the children of recently displaced peasants, tradespeople, and small business owners.⁴³ That means that, as the twentieth century wore on, students increasingly had ties to multiple sectors of society.

Regardless of their class origins, students were in a unique position in a society that badly needed doctors, engineers, and other trained professionals. When their progress was halted, because of a strike or repression, people generally took note. This meant the students could resist Somoza through acts of aggressive defiance. The wider society might not always agree with their ideology or tactics, but they noticed them. Further, they often felt compelled to protect the students, a sentiment that is not inevitable. Jaime Pensado has shown that in Mexico, for example, a concerted effort by the state to delegitimize student protest in the 1960s earned young activists the enmity of a diverse sector of society.⁴⁴ Such was not the case in Nicaragua, however. For most of the Somoza era, students enjoyed widespread support. To understand why, this book traces their political strategies, the state's response, and the wider society's reaction.

Students drew on a variety of tactics to challenge the state. Most of these can be classified under the rubric, "weapons of the relatively privileged." In his study of peasants, James Scott coined the phrase "weapons of the weak." Like peasants, students lack the power and the political legitimacy to alone threaten the regime's existence. What they do possess is a special capacity to create disorder. They can also promote outright defiance, a power that, Scott would argue, peasants and other subalterns usually do not enjoy because the potential consequences are simply too great.[45] For much of the Somoza era, though, students were relatively safe. They might suffer the consequences of unemployment or a lost scholarship, but their family's survival rarely hung in the balance. They could thus resist the regime through overt and aggressive defiance. These perhaps are not tactics that can directly overthrow the state, but they do shine a light on its failings and, under certain circumstances, can catalyze wider civic action that threatens the stability of the dictatorship.

The regime in turn drew on a wide repertoire of repressive tactics to silence students. The Somozas were more than willing to use the power of the state against their critics, which frequently included young people, and often sent the National Guard to censor opposition publications, break up protests, and physically harm dissidents. This lengthy and variable history of repression would shape student strategies throughout the dictatorship. That said, it is important to note that the regime hesitated to use the kind of extreme and indiscriminate violence against students that neighboring military regimes deployed more regularly in the later decades of the Cold War. Soldiers did fire on peaceful protestors, kill student prisoners, and disappear activists, but until the end of the 1970s, such actions were not the norm and the wider society vehemently denounced this kind of repression. The regime seemed to understand that such overt brutality against young demonstrators might unify the opposition; instead, it selectively deployed violence to threaten opponents and suggest the power of the state. Most often, it pursued measures that sought to coopt, divide, or delegitimize their young critics. Although it must be emphasized that these norms changed under the tenure of Anastasio Somoza Debayle (1967–1979), students nonetheless enjoyed greater liberty to protest than any other sector for the bulk of the Somoza era.

Finally, Nicaraguan society was remarkably tolerant toward student organizing. Reactions to student protests varied over the *longue durée* of the Somoza years, but for the most part, a broad cross section of the population showed up at their demonstrations, supported their efforts, and spoke out when the students suffered any retaliation or repression. Even when adult allies condemned student tactics, they still generally supported their right to protest. In part, the widespread acceptance of the notion of student exceptionalism contributed to such lenience, but also many leading anti-Somocistas had themselves once been student activists. This book traces that genealogy of dissent to show how generations of activists remained engaged in the struggle against Somoza, promoting and supporting the political engagement of their successors in the university.

The narrative of this book and the focus on student protagonists build toward the ultimately successful 1979 revolution. It argues that students were central to creating a culture of insurrection that inspired wide swaths of society to embrace the legitimacy and necessity of armed rebellion.[46] But to make that argument, the majority of the book is dedicated to uncovering the long history of student organizing that compelled other sectors to defy the regime. If students are a unique group because they have the privilege to protest and speak out, what, if anything, does doing so accomplish in the context of a decades-long dictatorship? How are students able to generate change and what kind of change is produced? *Students of Revolution* argues that the students' everyday acts of defiance and the support they garnered opened up spaces for political mobilization that future generations of students and dissidents would be able to deploy in the revolutionary struggle that toppled the dictatorship.

A Note on Sources

Natural disasters, dictatorships, and budgetary constraints are only some of the problems that have limited the preservation of archives in Nicaragua. Researchers must think creatively and broadly about sources, searching a multiplicity of archives in both Nicaragua and the United States. Luckily, given the relatively recent nature of the revolution, oral history provides an additional source for excavating the decades that led up to it.

This book relies heavily on student-authored sources and other records that emanated from the nation's universities under Somoza. The primary sources of analysis for this study are the flyers, publications, and correspondence from the Centro Universitario de la Universidad Nacional (CUUN), which is the main student governing body at the National University, and various other student organizations.[47] These documents shed light on students' changing politics, their strategies, and the structure of their organizations. They also reveal elements of the larger student movement that encompassed the nation's universities, secondary schools, and barrios. Student newspapers like *El Universitario* and *El Estudiante* describe aspects of the movement's politics and worldview. University records and publications convey what life was like in the university. The Universidad Nacional Autó-noma de Nicaragua (UNAN) preserved some of the reports and studies that charted the institution's growth and development, especially in the 1960s and 1970s. These institutional documents help contextualize the student movement within the larger changes happening in the university.

Oral histories shed further light on the experiences of young people during the dictatorship. To get a variety of perspectives on the student movement, I interviewed students, advisors, parents, and university administration and staff. Published memoirs and oral history collections, including Mónica Baltodano's magisterial four-volume collection of interviews with participants in the Sandinista revolution, have been especially valuable for uncovering the role that students, and especially young women, played in fomenting revolution in the 1970s. Combined, these sources detail the day-to-day functioning of the student movement—how young people drafted and distributed flyers, how they evaded the Guard, and how they balanced (or did not balance) their studies and their activism. The documents also offer the students' perspectives and their memories of key events and developments that did not necessarily make it into the student archives, like the 1952 medallion incident when students spat on a bronze plaque of Somoza in the university or the meteoric, but short-lived, rise of the Christian Democrat Front in the 1960s.

Nicaraguan and US government documents add to the picture of the conditions in which students acted. Official Nicaraguan government correspondence and spy reports disclose the mechanisms the state deployed to contain student dissenters. Ministry of Education reports, in particular, illustrate how the regime responded to the waves of student strikes in the 1970s. The limited collection of documents from the Oficina de Seguridad Nacional (OSN) held at the Instituto de Historia de Nicaragua y Centroamerica (IHNCA) likewise reveals elements of the regime's repressive apparatus in the 1950s and early 1960s.[48] Because so many Nicaraguan government records are missing, I turned to the archives of the US State Department to understand some of the challenges facing the regime and how it dealt with them. These sources contextualize the socioeconomic, political, and cultural structures that constrained protest and shaped student strategies. The US government was particularly interested in threats to internal order and specifically those emanating from the left. Consequently, they closely monitored the student movement, especially in the 1960s and 1970s. US embassy reports thus recorded information about student government elections, as well as protests and other more mundane activities. These records fill in some of the structural and chronological gaps in the student records.

Relying so closely on US State Department documents poses several interesting methodological and conceptual challenges. For one, these documents are (quite obviously) always written from the perspective of the US embassy in Nicaragua. For much of the Cold War, the embassy agenda was to appear neutral, while simultaneously supporting and advising an authoritarian regime the US government relied on to ensure political and economic stability. That contradictory mission means historians must be particularly skeptical of embassy analyses of Nicaraguan motives and behavior, including those of students and the Somozas. Various ambassadors worked closely with the ruling family, and their advice and the material support they facilitated are some of the many factors that help explain the regime's long tenure. These ambassadors' interpretations of the opposition were often colored by their relations with the Somozas and/or US geopolitical imperatives.

Further, because Nicaragua has a long and entangled history with US imperialism, these documents provide valuable insight into the deeply complex relationship between Nicaraguans and the United States that the historian Michel Gobat has illuminated for the late nineteenth and early twentieth century.[49] Throughout the Cold War, Nicaraguans, from statesmen to students, regularly visited the US embassy to chat, vent their frustrations, ask for advice, and sometimes request US intervention. At the same time, some of the visitors were also public critics of US hegemony. These documents thus shed further light on the ambivalent relationship between the United States and Nicaragua, and that is part of the story of the student movement told here.

Finally, this book draws on Nicaraguan newspapers to further contextualize student activism and illuminate their society's broader response. National newspapers, such as the conservative *La Prensa*, provide a window into how various sectors of society perceived student protests. Labor newspapers from the 1940s reveal how the left viewed student activists and why their efforts to forge a coalition failed. Combined, all these sources help recreate the world the students inhabited and the ways in which they understood it.

Book Organization

This book traces the instrumental role of students in fostering a culture of insurrection—one in which many in society, from elite housewives to manual laborers, came to perceive the idea of armed revolution as not only legitimate but also necessary. To do that, it examines the process in which university students fought for political legitimacy and then used that authority to shape the society around them. Their actions drummed up support first for reform and then later for revolution.

Students of Revolution focuses on youth in higher education. Most of the chapters center on student activities at the nation's largest university, the National University in León, where the student government left behind an extensive archive. However, as a study of how young people mobilized their wider society, the book is necessarily interested in examining the interactions between students at various schools and levels. The chapters thus also analyze the activities of young people in secondary and vocational schools, as well as those at other Nicaraguan universities.

To uncover the origins of student frustration with the regime, chapter 1 traces the development of a specific oppositional student political consciousness to Nicaragua's tumultuous history in the first quarter of the twentieth century. This chapter contextualizes Somoza's rise to power while also examining the emergence of students as national political actors in the 1940s. Although previous generations had been politically active, their numbers were too small and their politics too divided to make any significant mark on the country's politics. That would change under Somoza when the regime's authoritarianism united students across political persuasions.

Chapter 2 highlights the key role students played in the postwar democratic movement in Nicaragua. Between 1944 and 1948, students helped organize and maintain a cross-class national opposition movement that fought against Somoza's reelection plans. Capitalizing on the privileges that came with being students in a society where higher education was off limits to the majority, these youths organized acts of defiance that compelled other sectors to add their voices to the students' calls for democracy and social justice. Indeed, their youthful audacity impressed wide swaths of society, from staunch Conservatives to domestic workers. These groups were particularly outraged when the regime targeted students for repression, and they took to the streets to protest the abuse of innocent and idealistic youth. However, as this chapter shows, their youth proved to be a double-edged sword: they received considerable support when they endured repression, but at the same time, their allies and enemies could more easily dismiss their political aspirations.

The book then turns to student activism in the final years of the Somoza García regime. Reeling from the imprisonment, exile, and even murder of their friends in the late 1940s, students retreated into the university, where they continued agitating against Somoza in less direct ways. At a time when the regime appointed the rector and key faculty members, many students came to resent the porous divide between the National University and the state, and the generation of young people starting college in the 1950s prioritized the struggle for university autonomy, agitating for the official separation of their school from the government. Chapter 3 thus examines how the student movement changed tack: instead of attacking the regime head on, students lobbed their critiques at the administrators and professors who were the face of Somocismo in the university. Surprisingly, they often appealed to the dictator for help in their battles with the university administration. This chapter argues that students, freshly aware of the limitations of political activism, sought to benefit from the patrimonial nature of Somoza's rule, while Somoza attempted to use the conflict to further reinforce his personalistic regime and its hold on the university. What seemed to be narrow, university-based protests actually constituted struggles against the way life was organized during a dictatorship.

After Anastasio Somoza García's assassination in 1956, his elder son ascended to the presidency. To solidify his hold on power, Luis Somoza undertook limited reforms to open up the democratic process. These reforms included granting the university its autonomy. But at the same time as the regime promised greater liberties, it continued to operate a vast repressive military apparatus that censored free speech and abused, arrested, and murdered dissidents. Chapter 4 explores how students and faculty tested the limits of the National University's newly awarded autonomy in this increasingly unstable context. The rector, Mariano Fiallos Gil, began experimenting with new programs and plans that would modernize the school and solidify its status as the nation's premier intellectual institution. Students sought to turn the university into a bastion of democracy, and they worked hard to mobilize secondary students, parents, and community members in their campaigns against the regime. The July 23, 1959, massacre of peaceful protestors would test their organizing capacity and ultimately underscore the growing moral authority and political significance they had come to enjoy. This chapter argues that a combination of Mariano Fiallos Gil's humanist policies, student activism, and the state's repression contributed to the cohesion of the university, unified the student body against Somoza, and promoted the wider society's civic engagement.

The sixties is the era most associated with radical youth activism, but the student movement in Nicaragua tells a much more complicated history. Committed to stepping down at the end of his term, Luis Somoza passed the presidency to his chosen successor, René Schick, who instituted a small democratic aperture that lasted from 1963 to 1966. As the Cold War intensified throughout the world, various entities—from the US embassy to the nascent Frente Sandinista de Liberación Nacional—vied to influence a generation they believed to be either the problem or the solution to both global and local conflicts. With such a wide array of allies and options, the anti-Somoza movement fractured, and participation in the student government at the National University fell to all-time lows. Chapter 5 examines the ideological diversity of the 1960s and the growing popularity of moderate politics. It argues that at a time when the economy seemed to be flourishing and the Somoza stranglehold loosening, student political participation waned even as the conflict between moderate and revolutionary students intensified. In tracing this history, this chapter uncovers the many terrains on which the Cold War was fought: for Nicaraguan students, this was a conflict not just between capitalism and socialism, but also between dictatorship and democracy, nationalism and imperialism, reform and revolution.

The final two chapters explore the student movement under the regime of the last Somoza. Anastasio Somoza Debayle's campaign for president in 1967 unified the students across the political spectrum against their common enemy. The violence, corruption, and mismanagement of his regime, combined with the organizing efforts of both the FSLN and a growing progressive sector of the Catholic Church, helped radicalize a new generation of students. Chapter 6 shows how university youths turned their campuses into vibrant centers of dissent that provided key support to other sectors challenging the state. In the process, students began forging connections across classes and parties. Chapter 7 looks at how they moved beyond their campuses to continue organizing their society. As the political and economic situation became increasingly critical, more and more students left the university to join the guerrillas in the mountains, work in the urban underground, or organize Christian Base Communities. They played varied roles in the revolution, and their activism, and the repression they endured, generated wider support for the Sandinista struggle. In the final years of the dictatorship, young people organized massive nation-wide student strikes and participated in urban insurrections that destabilized their society. This chapter studies these actions to detail the precise ways in which young people contributed to Somoza's overthrow.

In exploring the history of student protest in Nicaragua, my research emphasizes the critical role urban youth played in the success of the revolution, but more generally it looks at how students carved out a space for themselves in the national imagination and political sphere. For much of the Cold War period, students actively fought to foster the idea that their status as budding intellectuals and future professionals merited special considerations and privileges, including the right to protest (sometimes impertinently) and the right to agitate freely against the regime. In illuminating how they made these claims and persuaded the general population of their exceptional status, my work traces the process by which students came to be associated with political militancy and thus demystifies the ways in which they became activists. There is nothing immutable about the idea of ideal-istic and radical youth. My work shows that this conceptualization was an image students fought hard to cultivate precisely because it could legitimize their political participation.

If, as scholars like Greg Grandin have argued, the Cold War was a battle between competing visions of what the state and society should look like, it is critical to examine in earnest what those visions were and how different groups put them on the table.[50] By illuminating students' dreams for a more democratic world and their strategies for creating it, my work brings youth, who constituted much of the fodder for the guerrilla battles throughout Latin America, to the fore, and we can begin to understand how revolution-ary ideas spread among ordinary men and women on the ground.

CHAPTER 1

The Origins of Student Anti-Somoza Consciousness, 1937–1944

Nicaraguan students have a contentious history with the Somoza regime's portraiture. In 1939, a small group of students at the university in León, led by Octavio Caldera and Eligio Álvarez Montalván, doused a painting of the president with sulfuric acid. More than a decade later, students spat on the newest icon installed in the university auditorium in León, an iron medallion bearing Somoza's profile. Both times, they faced harsh punishment. In the 1930s, they were imprisoned and tortured for their disrespect. In the 1950s, the entire student government, most of whom had not been present the day of the expectorate demonstration, was expelled.

As a form of protest, desecrating the likeness of the dictator may not be the most threatening to the state, but these actions exemplified student anti-Somoza activism in the 1930s and 1940s. For the first few years of his tenure, such contemptuous displays of political theater constituted the only overt challenge to Somoza's rule, and until around 1944, students were the sole sector protesting the dictator.

Their opposition presents a paradox: as children of the middle and upper classes, they benefitted from the expanded state the regime created, yet they were also his earliest and most vocal opponents. Several historians of Latin America have noted the close connection between the region's middle class and the government bureaucracy that offered steady, well-paid employment and, in some places, expanded the educational system to reach their children.[1] In Nicaragua, Somoza enacted similar policies that provided the country's small but growing middle class with government jobs and increased access, albeit still quite limited, to higher education. So why were these relatively privileged youth so opposed to a regime that apparently benefitted them?

Their anti-Somocismo was rooted in a specific political consciousness that had been forged by Nicaragua's tumultuous recent history. Born into a US-occupied Nicaragua, these students were on the cusp of adolescence when Augusto César Sandino began a guerrilla war against the US Marines stationed in their country. As teenagers, they witnessed Somoza's ascension and observed the US policy of non-intervention. As students in the university, they grappled with the cognitive dissonance caused by the Allies' war rhetoric of World War II and their own government's authoritarianism.

These events shaped their understandings of their world, and the privileged status students occupied in their society framed their political aspirations. Because successive regimes had not prioritized education, only a tiny minority of young people could afford to attend the nation's two universities in Granada and León. Consequently, Nicaraguan society depended heavily on the small number of professionals its school system produced, and youth who could pursue higher education held an important symbolic place in the nation. They constituted Nicaragua's future and as such deserved special protection and consideration. This notion of student exceptionalism enabled their political participation and specifically their protests. However, their liminality, temporarily stuck between youth and adulthood, dependency and independence, was a mixed blessing that simultaneously spurred a sense of student invulnerability but also could be used to delegitimize their protests.

Although most Nicaraguan students held liberal sympathies, they resented the party's standard-bearer, President Somoza, because his political practices threatened their own class interests. Somoza's populism jeopardized their place in the social hierarchy, and state repression threatened their ability to participate in political debates. This chapter shows that as the regime's authoritarianism became more apparent and as the country's poverty deepened during the World War II era, young activists attempted to use the privileges associated with their status as students to protest the regime and promote a different vision of Nicaraguan politics.

The Student Liberal Tradition and the US Occupation

Nicaragua's institutions of higher education were not above the deep political factionalism that historically had wracked the country. The nation's politics were bitterly divided between the Liberal and Conservative Parties, which had been fighting for power almost since Nicaragua's emergence as an independent nation in 1838.[2] So intense was their rivalry that each faction had its own university in their respective capitals, León and Granada. Families tended to send their children to study at the school that corresponded with their political ideology, and, perhaps reflective of the nation's political climate, the Liberal university in León was the country's largest.[3] Consequently, most of the university students had at least Liberal sympathies, and this orientation marked their politics for much of the late nineteenth and early twentieth centuries.

Founded in 1812, the University of León did not flourish until the decades of Liberal rule that marked the end of the century. Advocating for a strong and engaged central state, Liberal presidents in the 1870s slowly began expanding the nation's educational system, building secondary schools and pushing for greater government regulation. Despite these efforts, the number of schools remained relatively small for many of the next fifty years, and only the children of the elite and middle class could pursue higher education in Nicaragua. During the final decades of the nineteenth century, around seventy students—the sons and a few daughters of the rising coffee-grower and merchant classes—enrolled in the University of León each year.[4]

Their political background placed these youths at odds with the US-sponsored governments that took power after 1909. That year, the United States, allied with Conservative elites, helped overthrow the Liberal dictator, José Santos Zelaya. In the sixteen years of his tenure, Zelaya's administration had overseen the expansion of Nicaragua's transportation and communications systems, much to the ire of his party's traditional opponents. Conservatives objected to the use of government funds to promote export development. They preferred a small state and a society organized around the patron-client system. Zelaya's harsh repression of dissidents culminated in the Conservatives' decision to request foreign intervention.[5] Troubled by Zelaya's economic nationalism and particularly his desire to build a trans-oceanic canal to rival the Panama Canal, the US government readily obliged and, in 1909, ousted the president and installed a new Conservative-led coalition government.[6]

For the next twenty-five years, the United States played an outsized role in Nicaraguan affairs. From 1909 to 1933, the country became a virtual US protectorate. North American diplomats instituted measures to promote political and economic stability, while simultaneously protecting their citizens' business interests. With their help, the new government obtained loans and established repayment plans that prioritized servicing the debt before funding public services. Several state-owned industries, like the railroad and bank, were handed over as collateral to US corporations. Meanwhile, US officials oversaw transparent elections and advocated for laws that institutionalized bipartisan politics. If all else failed, the Marines were on hand to quash any unrest, as they did several times. Unsurprisingly, US bureaucrats and corporations amassed considerable power in this period and, in conjunction with the ruling Conservatives, created a very limited government, beholden to North American interests.[7]

As the occupation wore on, sectors of the population bristled under US control, and by the 1930s, students were taking an active role in the resistance. Specifically, the militarization of the country alienated many Nicaraguans. Tasked with ensuring "order," soldiers, both foreign and domestic, became powerful figures, mediating disputes, intervening in party politics, and controlling municipal governments.[8] Even the university was affected. During their annual carnival in 1932, a student speaker sharply denounced the occupation. Many resented the Marines' efforts to limit student political activism, and when soldiers tried to arrest the speaker, a group of students, including the future professor and university rector Mariano Fiallos Gil, blocked them. Student opposition was so great that they raised funds for Augusto César Sandino's guerrilla war against the Marines.[9]

A Liberal general, Sandino fiercely opposed the occupation and the Nicaraguans, both Liberal and Conservative, who supported it. In 1928, he and one hundred and fifty men began using hit-and-run tactics against the Marines. His movement bitterly divided the country, as some sectors, including youth in the university, rallied to support his anti-imperialist agenda, and others, including many politicians, dismissed him as a bandit.[10]

These events shaped student politics. Although most students identified as Liberal, the party was increasingly divided in the 1930s. Some Liberals supported Sandino, while many others believed US intervention was the only way to maintain stability and forge a workable peace with the Conservatives. Surprisingly, given Nicaragua's history, few students in the 1930s and 1940s exhibited overt anti-American sentiments. Instead, many sought to work with the hemisphere's hegemon.[11] Meanwhile, another Liberal general, Anastasio Somoza García, was preparing his own bid for power.

The Origins of the Somoza Regime

To understand student anti-Somocismo, it is necessary to trace the dictator's rise to power. In the 1920s, the United States created the Guardia Nacional (National Guard, or GN), a supposedly apolitical military to help guarantee stability. Trained and led by the Marines, however, the new army served the imperial interests of the United States. Moreover, its mission to "impose democracy by force," to use historian Michel Gobat's memorable phrase, meant that the GN took on a wide variety of tasks, from policing to local governance. The military thus wielded considerable power and would provide a launching pad for Anastasio Somoza García's long career.[12]

The creation of the GN intensified the country's unrest and set up the conditions for Somoza's ascendency. Sandino and his supporters expanded their targets to include the new Nicaraguan forces. Their increasingly successful guerrilla struggle, combined with a growing domestic interest in isolationism, finally persuaded the United States to recall the Marines in 1933. The US withdrawal heralded the Roosevelt administration's Good Neighbor policy, which called for strict non-intervention in Latin American affairs. In a final overt act of influence, however, the departing US officials lobbied for the nomination of Anastasio Somoza García to head the military. With the backing of President Juan Bautista Sacasa, his wife's uncle, Somoza assumed command of the Guard in 1932.[13]

That year was a difficult one for Nicaragua. The global depression was decimating the demand for its exports and aggravating social tensions. Financially strapped and facing an interminable guerrilla war, President Sacasa decided to negotiate with Sandino and promised him nominal control over the north in exchange for disarming. Somoza refused to accept such generous terms for the man who had been attacking the GN and their allies for the past six years, and, in 1934, he arranged Sandino's assassination. The military then instigated a wave of repression that effectively crushed the guerrilla movement.[14]

Somoza had his sights on the presidency and began building popular support. Like the populists then coming to power in the United States, Brazil, and elsewhere, he promised to use the powers of the state to promote the general welfare. Specifically, he advocated for limited land redistribution, infrastructure development, and expanded labor rights. A wide spectrum of Nicaraguans stood to benefit from such measures, and Somoza attracted supporters from both the Conservative and Liberal camps, as well as workers, artisans, and, of course, soldiers, who embraced him as their own.[15]

The general needed such a broad base because he could not legally run for the nation's highest office. The constitution barred relatives of the sitting president and military officers from holding the position. In May 1936, Somoza staged a coup and took power from his own party. To bolster his legitimacy, he held elections later that year and won in a landslide. The United States, in keeping with its new non-interventionist policy, stayed out of the fray, but many Nicaraguans perceived its neutrality to be a sign of support for Somoza.[16]

Upon taking office in January 1937, Somoza began expanding the state and his influence within it. Congress passed laws that gave the president the power to name banking officials and audit their activities. Consequently, the president exercised unprecedented control over the nation's financial system: he had a say in everything from who could acquire loans to the national exchange rate. The government needed revenue to initiate any substantive policy changes, so Somoza raised taxes and made their collection more efficient. As the bureaucracy grew, the president placed Guard officers in key positions and slowly took control of municipal governments. These changes created thousands of jobs, which Somoza personally doled out in exchange for loyalty. Finally, in 1938, Somoza pushed through a constitutional reform that promised limited land redistribution, worker protections, and freedom of expression.[17]

At the same time, the president laid the foundation for an enduring authoritarian regime. For one, when the constituent assembly rewrote the constitution, they suspended all elections until 1947, essentially giving Somoza a ten-year term. Moreover, the document promised freedom of expression while sharply limiting it—prohibiting, for example, any speech that threatened the government. That measure institutionalized what had become the norm as the Guard silenced dissidents with threats of exile. The GN was quickly becoming a repressive force as the regime militarized the government and gave officers control over everything from the national communications system to dispensing visas. From these positions, they could deny public employment, services, and even bank loans to the government's critics. Citizens grew to fear the Guard. Others resented policies that benefitted the oligarchy and hurt the poor. For example, early on, Somoza devalued the national currency in order to help merchants pay off debts. Consequently, basic staples became more expensive, a change that disproportionately affected the lower classes. Meanwhile, the president and his allies grew rich from bribes and the misuse of state funds, while the promised labor and land reforms were slow to materialize.[18]

Somoza's record helps explain why, despite widespread discontent, there was very little open opposition in the early years of his rule. The president had amassed enough control over the state to benefit loyalists and punish dissidents. Indeed, the absence of protest was a product of both repression and Somoza's willingness to negotiate with and/or coopt the opposition when necessary. These tactics contributed to the longevity of his regime, which lasted until his assassination in 1956.

Students and the Regime

Unexpectedly, the main opposition to the regime emerged from the hallowed halls of the university. In this primarily agricultural society, very few youths had the opportunity to go to school, much less to pursue an advanced degree. Throughout the 1930s, the annual enrollment at the universities totaled around two hundred.[19] These were the children of the upper and middle class who had the resources to pay for books and boarding. With the requisite free time to pursue political activities, these youths possessed a sense of privilege associated with their status as students that propelled them to act when the regime threatened their collective interests.

A unique student political consciousness emerged in the 1930s. College youth united to demand university autonomy—an official administrative separation between the state and their schools. In so doing, they followed their peers throughout Latin America who had burst onto the political scene demanding greater freedoms for both the university and their wider society in the 1920s. Inspired by the movement in Argentina to reform higher education and create more democratic universities, young Latin Americans were committed to creating an engaged institution, one that pursued both national development and social justice. In 1931, student representatives from each of Nicaragua's universities founded the Federación Universitario de Nicaragua (Federation of Nicaraguan University Students, or FUN) to do the same. The organization lobbied for the universities' expansion and independence from the state, sought alliances with labor, and offered their professional expertise to the public at a discounted rate. Its mission was hampered, however, by its small membership and internal political squabbles. Nonetheless, the Federation's goals signaled the emergence of a student self-consciousness—that is, an understanding of themselves as a unique sector of the population with certain responsibilities and privileges. This student identity solidified in the early years of Somoza's rule.[20]

University students had a complicated relationship with the regime. On one hand, they benefitted from many of its reforms: the expanded bureaucracy provided jobs for students and their families that enabled them to continue their education. On the other, the regime severely limited basic freedoms and threatened their class interests, as illustrated by the protests surrounding the Ley Armijo. In July 1939, Somoza's minister of public education, Modesto Armijo, decided to grant professional titles to pharmacists who had more than twenty-five years of experience but no formal training. The law was meant to endear the regime to its supporters, but instead it gained the enmity of much of the university population.[21]

Perceiving the decree as an encroachment on their professional privileges, more than three hundred students took to the streets of León in August 1939 to demand its repeal. Arguing that the Ley Armijo "made a mockery of the legitimate rights and aspirations of the university student body," the demonstrators articulated a notion of student identity that revolved around their yet-to-be-obtained title and the class position it promised.[22] That identity was thus both liminal and aspirational—it was based on their current transitional position as trainees and on their future status as credentialed professionals—and it was powerful. Many of the students were children of Liberals, and Somoza was still striving to unify the party, which remained divided between those who supported the deposed president and those who backed Somoza. Moreover, as the nation's future professionals, these young demonstrators would one day be an economically and politically powerful social group. In the end, Somoza relented, quietly repealing the law.

Students also resented the regime's growing authoritarianism, which punished even the most abstract of protests. On October 27, 1939, during their annual social, several young men from Managua's law school staged a play in which they proclaimed solidarity with France, declared war on Nazi Germany, and obliquely critiqued their own government. In response, the regime arrested nine of the actors for violating Nicaragua's neutrality. Somoza, an early sympathizer of fascism had grown silent on the issue as US opposition to the Axis became apparent, and, as its response to the play indicates, his regime took very seriously any threat to the nation's neutrality pact.[23]

The incident and its aftermath highlighted the growing cohesiveness of the student body. For one, the detained activists held beliefs from across the political spectrum. Reportedly, two belonged to the Conservative-reactionary movement, which had fascist leanings; the rest were Liberals. Further, a local newspaper noted that a "generous student fellowship" compelled several students, including one young woman, who were not involved with the play to turn themselves in for arrest as well. Moreover, when six students denounced the performers in the press, the student law society called an assembly to expel them from the organization.[24] Collectively, these actions indicated that university youth considered themselves a unified body that closed rank against exterior and interior threats.

They were also a sector that enjoyed unique privileges. The detained students received some surprising amenities while in prison: their jailers permitted visits from friends, a radio, a billiards table, and beer.[25] Such luxurious treatment speaks to the students' elite status and the regime's hesitancy to mistreat the scions of fellow Liberals. It also exemplified the regime's contradictory reactions to student protest in its early years. Arresting youths for denouncing Adolf Hitler at a social event betrayed the regime's sensitivity to any kind of criticism—in this case, against its foreign policy toward Europe and, more subtly, against the regime's growing authoritarianism. Nonetheless, if jailing the students because they threatened Nicaragua's neutrality was a farcical overreaction, then supplying them with billiards and other comforts was likely the regime's way of preempting further criticism.

Their status as students did not always shield them from state violence. In February 1939, university administrators hung a portrait of Somoza in the main hall in the University of León. In protest, anti-Somoza students doused the painting with sulfuric acid. The GN arrested five students and held them for more than four months under extreme conditions that included torture. Two, Eligio Álvarez Montalván and Octavio Caldera, were ultimately expelled from the university.[26] The regime also came down hard on those who kept Sandino's memory alive. In 1940, the police arrested several students for distributing fliers that accused Somoza of murdering the guerrilla leader. Charging them with subversion and insulting the government, the state exiled eight of the students to Little Corn Island and sentenced nine others to hard labor.[27]

The government's violent reaction to these isolated student protests reflected a growing hemispheric fear of student activism. Latin American governments had watched as students everywhere assumed a greater role in national politics and become a driving force for social change. In Cuba and Peru, young people had helped organize political parties and overthrow dictatorships.[28] By the end of the 1930s, these governments were taking measures to curtail the militancy brewing in higher education. Several countries rolled back some of the reforms that had given the university in Latin America a privileged position.[29]

Somoza took a different tack: he dealt with the students' unrest by building a new university in Managua, inaugurating the Universidad Central de Nicaragua (Central University of Nicaragua) in September 1941. As some historians have argued, locating the university in the capital would also increase Somoza's control over its affairs.[30] However, his decision to build the Central University was not just a power play. Well aware of the university's symbolic value, the president was actively courting its young charges. The regime repeatedly emphasized the role of higher education in nation building. The act of creating the Central University declared that universities constituted the "essence of each country" because along with their mission to create professionals, they also "forge the national soul" and ensure the nation's "distinguished place among civilized societies."[31] A commemorative booklet from the ceremony exalted the function of the new school, which "will form men who, tomorrow, will be the pride of the country and elevate the cultural level to a plane where it will win the admiration of all."[32]

The regime's rhetoric had significant consequences. In extolling the virtue of the university, Somoza promoted the public profile of its pupils. They too celebrated the school's function in the nation but envisioned a more proactive role. In his speech at the ceremony, law student Manuel Zurita declared that the "university should completely reform and change the cultural foundation of the nation."[33] He criticized its predecessors for merely manufacturing professionals, "who get their degrees by regurgitating texts and lectures" and excoriated the other universities for being "exclusively contemplative, speculative and expectant."[34] His harsh assessment of the country's higher education foretold the active presence the Central University students expected the institution to have on the national stage. Zurita's speech heralded a much more activist orientation for the institution, one that would flourish in the climate of World War II.

As Somoza laid the foundations for decades of authoritarian rule in the last few years of the 1930s, students begin pursuing more organized political activism. Before this period, their actions had been largely individualized and uncoordinated, but the creation of the FUN, the protest against the Ley Armijo, and the increasing number of anti-Somoza demonstrations reveal the way in which students were beginning to think of themselves as a cohesive group with unique privileges and responsibilities. The war era solidified this notion of student exceptionalism.

Catalyzing Nicaragua's Democratic Effervescence

Although Central America's participation in World War II was negligible, the financial and human cost of the conflict had a large impact on the region's citizens and governments. The Allies' emphasis on democracy provided activists throughout the region with a compelling language of rights that they deployed against repressive regimes at home. From Guatemala to Costa Rica, students rose up to demand an end to the dictatorships that had dominated their countries since the Great Depression.

As other sectors joined their protests, authoritarian regimes fell and more democratic governments emerged. These were the early eruptions of what the historian Gilbert Joseph has called Latin America's "democratic effervescence."[35] From 1944 to about 1948, leftists, workers, students, and other groups worked together to fight for economic and social justice. For a brief time, they forced a small democratic opening. In Nicaragua, a student protest in June 1944 set in motion a chain of events that nearly toppled Somoza and initiated a short-lived democratic aperture. The students' tactics, their society's response, and the state's repression illuminate the various factors that forged student consciousness in this period and enabled them to spur their wider society to action.

Paradoxically, World War II both strengthened and weakened the Somoza regime. The conflict provided the government with a pretext to further clamp down on dissent and bolster Somocista control. After the bombing of Pearl Harbor, Nicaragua formally entered the war and the president declared martial law—ostensibly to prevent any instability that the Axis powers might exploit. For the anti-Somoza opposition, these measures illustrated the regime's increasing authoritarianism. Their fears grew in 1943, when Somoza drafted a constitutional reform bill that permitted the reelection of a president during wartime. Officially, the amendment provided for consistency during crises, but, considering Nicaragua's nominal participation in World War II, it was a thinly veiled attempt to ensure Somoza's hold on power for another term.

Somoza likely believed he had the support necessary to enact the law. The economy had grown in recent years as factories began manufacturing previously imported products, adding thousands of jobs and turning workers into a significant political force. Moreover, with the revenue from his tax reforms and the financial assistance of the United States, Somoza had begun improving the nation's infrastructure and schools.[36] Indeed, as a direct result of his policies, the number of university students doubled between 1942 and 1946, from around six hundred to more than twelve hundred. The construction of schools also doubled the number of secondary students from 1,725 in 1944 to 3,445 in 1945.[37]

While the war-era economic boom facilitated these reforms, it also underscored the contradictions inherent in the country's uneven development. Many of these improvements meant little to the vast majority of Nicaraguans who endured extreme poverty. The cost of living rose significantly between 1939 and 1943, and prices for essentials like beans and rice shot up by almost 130 percent.[38] Because wages did not keep pace with inflation, hunger was widespread, and few poor children had the opportunity to go to school.

The country's destitution did not deter Somoza's avarice. He used state money to develop his ever-expanding personal portfolio, which, by 1942, included a dairy farm; several coffee *fincas*; sugarcane fields; banana plantations; cattle ranches; shoe, soap, and match factories; a newspaper; and various other holdings. Amid rising prices for basic staples, Somoza enjoyed a monopoly on many of these products and freely used government resources on his private investments.[39]

The contrast between Somoza's expanding personal wealth and the declining fortunes of the masses, combined with his reelection plans, engendered widespread criticism in early 1944. Angry citizens scrawled the word "hunger" on paper córdobas featuring Somoza's notoriously pampered daughter Lillian.[40] The country's largest newspaper printed a statement opposing reelection on the front page and was promptly shut down.[41] Prominent members of Somoza's own party denounced his plans to run again, and when he retaliated by having the National Bank recall their debts, their protests grew louder.[42] Under pressure to respond to his critics, Somoza announced in mid-June that he too was anti-reelection. He planned to step down before his term was over, so that he could run as a regular citizen.[43]

His logic did little to reassure the opposition, which was eagerly watching political developments in neighboring countries. Inspired by events in El Salvador, Guatemala, and Honduras, where students were initiating strikes that threatened long established dictatorships, the youth of Managua's Central University decided to take action.[44] On June 27, 1944, they left their campus carrying banners that proclaimed solidarity with their Central American peers and opposition to Somoza. Characterizing the protest as a "true expression of youth," the writer for the Conservative newspaper *La Prensa* observed, "Alongside the son of a conservative family were the descendants of legitimate and old-guard liberals, as well as sons of public officials, of known re-electionist leaders and even the descendants of secretaries of state and high functionaries within the government."[45] Despite the marchers' elite status, hundreds of workers immediately joined, as did large numbers of Conservatives and dissident Liberals. Many more watched from the sidelines.[46] This cross-class uprising would reverberate throughout society.

The students' speeches and signs reveal the ways in which both the regional struggle against authoritarian regimes and the global battle for democracy shaped their political consciousness. The posters they carried highlighted their emerging political importance: "Nicaraguan students are one with those of Central America," "The blood of the students murdered by [the Guatemalan dictator] Ubico demands vengeance," "We will win Central America's liberty at whatever cost," and "Honduran students will overthrow the tyrant Carias." Such slogans celebrated students' role in creating political change and made it clear that these youths were beginning to see themselves as part of a wider movement working to promote democracy. The regional student uprisings had reinforced a new understanding of the political capabilities of students, and young Nicaraguans were assuming a more proactive place for themselves in the nation, one that would require sacrifice and vigilance.

They justified this vision of youthful civic engagement with allusions to the global conflict. Thanks in part to Somoza's strategic devotion to Franklin D. Roosevelt, ordinary Nicaraguans were very familiar with Allied declarations. Early on, Somoza realized that he would need to maintain favorable relations with the United States if he was going to continue to secure economic assistance. Such aid made it look like the United States supported the regime, and, despite the Good Neighbor policy, the embassy's approval remained important to many Nicaraguans who had lived through multiple US interventions. Consequently, Somoza took great pains to publicize his positive relationship with the United States. In his first years as president, he inaugurated a school and built a road, both named after Roosevelt. Indeed, the rhetoric the Allies employed to justify the war provided students with compelling language to defend their own struggle for democracy at home. In their June 27, 1944, speeches, students declared that Nicaragua was not free and demanded the four freedoms that Roosevelt had promised at the beginning of the war when he declared that all people were entitled to freedom of speech, freedom to worship, freedom from want, and freedom from fear.[47]

The students used the context of the war to highlight the many problems facing Nicaragua and its neighbors. One student, Pedro Joaquín Chamorro, standing in front of the US embassy, declared that the countries of Central America, including his own, lacked even the last of Roosevelt's liberties: "the right to live without fear."[48] Another, Francisco Frixione, demanded "an end to the dictatorial regimes in Central America because our impoverished states cannot sustain armies that only serve to choke liberty and maintain dictatorships."[49] Student political activism thus was rooted in both national concerns and the regional struggles against authoritarianism.

The violent end to the march further underscored the contrast between the regime's democratic rhetoric and reality. A little after seven that evening, a tear gas bomb stunned the protestors as they passed by the barracks of the military academy. Soldiers descending from the academy and the president's residence up the hill quickly surrounded them, brutally beating marchers before arresting more than four hundred. The detained included prominent student leaders as well as dozens of workers and opposition politicians.[50]

The war loomed large in the discourse that followed the repression. Somoza referenced the tense global climate to chastise students, denouncing the protests for "occur[ing] at the exact moment when all Nicaraguans should be united to aid in whatever way possible the United Nations that are today fighting on the battlefield for the freedom of the world."[51] Where Somoza saw the students' protest as undermining the war effort, young people and their supporters directly linked their demands to the Allied cause and the Central American mobilizations. In a June 29 statement, they explained that as "citizens of the republic . . . appreciating the value of the heroic blood our generation is pouring on the battlefield and which will give rise to the universal rule of the principals of the Atlantic Charter," they were compelled to declare their solidarity with "our heroic brothers of Guatemala and El Salvador" as well as their peers in Managua.[52] This language was particularly ironic and powerful given Somoza's paeans to Roosevelt.

As one of the first civilian protests the regime had endured, the student mobilization posed a significant threat to Somoza. He immediately went on the defensive. The day after the march, the president accused the protestors of provoking the military, attempting to start a riot, and encouraging sedition. The charges were obviously overblown, but the consequences were very real. The capital looked like a war zone as armored cars roamed the city, while police and military cadets patrolled the streets. Rumors circulated that the detainees would be taken to the military jail in León, which was notorious for its brutal conditions.[53] The day after the arrests, female relatives of the detained organized a demonstration. *La Prensa* described the protest: "an enormous number of mothers, wives, daughters, girlfriends and sisters, dressed in mourning, marched through the streets, walking between thousands of spectators." Bystanders applauded as they passed.[54]

As the protests continued, Somoza abruptly changed course. Always eager to appear as the nation's benevolent patriarch, he made a show of treating the imprisoned youth leniently. On the night of June 30, Somoza invited prominent opposition politicians to the Presidential Palace to pick up their sons, who had participated in the demonstration. In front of their fathers, Somoza lectured the young men for insulting him when "he considered himself their spiritual father, because he had done so much for the university." Despite his hurt feelings, he was letting them go free because of their youth. Released into the custody of their parents, the young men were chauffeured home in presidential cars.[55] In the end, the majority paid a fine of 12.40 córdobas each and were released.[56] It was a small price to pay for their alleged crimes of sedition and rioting.

The episode was a masterpiece of political theater and earned front-page coverage. In portraying the protestors as misbehaving schoolboys, Somoza delegitimized their critiques and reinforced his paternalistic benevolence. The young men were students in the university, many with full-time jobs and families, but by treating them like children, Somoza reminded both the young activists and the nation that he was sole judge of their fate and their future. By casting himself as their "spiritual father," Somoza was personally responsible for any gains they made. As such, he believed himself to be above their reproach and considered any criticism to be evidence of their ingratitude. In this view, students were not full-fledged democratic actors; rather, they were recipients of Somoza's largesse and were expected to behave with appropriate deference. When they did not, Somoza was justified in punishing or pardoning them as the ungrateful children he perceived them to be. Students were not the only sector to endure such treatment: Somoza felt organized labor was also beholden to him for his support.[57] In such a paternalistic atmosphere, the freedom to protest was tenuous at best.

Undeterred, young people throughout the country rose up to defend their peers in the university, and the repression they suffered catalyzed further action. After solidarity strikes planned for July 4 were quashed, youth in many major cities deserted their secondary schools en masse.[58] On July 5, 1944, young people attempting to organize a protest in León were arrested, triggering a solidarity demonstration later that night with ten thousand people in attendance. The mass of protestors spanned several blocks and was heading toward the jail when news spread that the detained would be released.[59] The students' initial demonstration had tapped into a deep vein of discontent with the regime's policies.

In the midst of the greatest crisis he had faced so far, Somoza took measures to both appease and punish the opposition. On July 5, he officially renounced his intention to run again for president.[60] It was a significant concession to the power of widespread public dissent, but many were not satisfied. The following day, rumors circulated of an impending general strike in León and Granada.[61] *La Prensa* reported that business had ground to a halt in the capital as shopkeepers closed their doors and citizens deserted the streets.[62] To weaken the budding opposition movement, Somoza exiled several of its leaders, including high-profile political figures Eduardo Conrado Vado and Salvador Buitrago Ajá and students Francisco Frixione and Luis Andara Ubeda to Corn Island.[63] Octavio Caldera, who had destroyed Somoza's portrait in 1939 and participated in the 1944 protests, was deported. The Ministry of Education shuttered the Central University, the epicenter of the protests, for most of July.[64] Finally, Somoza made several important concessions to the country's burgeoning labor movement, which had participated in the initial protest. Promised a long-awaited labor code and the right to organize a socialist party, workers did not join the solidarity demonstrations and strikes in July.[65] Thanks to these measures, the regime weathered the crisis.

Debating the Role of Students in Society

Although they had won their most prominent demand, no reelection, student activists faced a subsequent wave of repression. In mid-July, a young Costa Rican in his fifth year of medical school at the Central University was expelled from the country for participating in the June 27 protest. Soon after, students from Granada and León went on strike to demand the return of their exiled peers, and in late July, several were arrested for trying to coordinate a solidarity demonstration.[66] The repression sparked a debate in the nation's newspapers over the place of politics in the university and the role of students in politics. At stake for the participants was not only the very future of the nation, but also the character of the citizens the university produced.

The regime's ready use of force indicated where it stood on the issue. Somoza defended his stance in his July 28 declaration reopening the Central University in Managua. He explained that while students could organize around university issues, he "would never allow them to be manipulated by politicians." He went on to say that "outside of the university, in the street, the students have the freedom to organize whatever kind of demonstration," but within campus, he "demand[ed] order and study above all."[67] For Somoza, the danger of allowing political organizing in the university lay in the students' vulnerability to outside forces and the potential for disorder that might result.

His comments sparked a flurry of impassioned rejoinders in several newspapers. For Gabry Rivas, the editor of *La Nueva Prensa*, the very nature of the university was at stake. Should the university be a home for students that is "free from fear?" Otherwise, he went on:

> If a student has to hide his views and even . . . refrain from freely express-
> ing his beliefs within school, because that is a right he only has outside of
> the classroom . . . if it is necessary or essential that a university student, who
> is a citizen, renounce his political rights in order to drink the milk of culture
> from an inflexible nurse, then it is and always will be preferable that those
> fountains run dry, that the university's doors be closed and sealed.

If universities are to be free of politics, the author pointed out, then those who enter are expected to give up basic rights in exchange for an education. Such a bargain, Rivas claimed, would create "a bloated youth, lacking ideals, without concerns, without questions, and aimless, dutifully converted into a slavish, contemptible and servile class."[68]

There is a fascinating contradiction embedded in this defense of student political activism. For one, the editor is demanding free speech for students, a basic right that in Somoza-era Nicaragua was denied to citizens. In the aftermath of the students' June protest, Somoza had severely limited dissent and implemented new restrictions on freedom of speech.[69] Why then did students especially deserve to enjoy these rights? The metaphor of students suckling at the breast of the university is telling: students are infants whose development depends on the nature of the parent, here the university. These students deserve special consideration because they are citizens in formation, and the years spent in the university are preparing them for the duties of engaged members of society. The language Rivas uses to defend students' political rights, though, is embedded in the image of them as infants—a common, but ironic, trope given their ultimate desire to enter the adult world of politics.

On the other end of the spectrum was the Somocista newspaper, *Novedades*, which firmly believed the university was no place for politics. Its editor envisioned the university as an "uncontaminated laboratory" that operated in a political and social vacuum. The pure pursuit of apolitical scientific knowledge, however, required students to give up certain rights, such as the right to express political ideas and beliefs. According to the editor, Somoza was actually defending the university's liberty by keeping politics off campus.[70] It was a sleight of hand common among regimes that prized stability above all else. In this view, it was only by defending order that they could create an environment in which people could enjoy their rights. To create order, though, the government had to deny certain freedoms.

The students, who had begun to view their struggle as rooted precisely in the circumscription of their rights, did not agree. They were not convinced that democracy ended at the doors to the university. Condemning conditions on the campus in Granada, the student Edguardo Buitrago explained: "They don't allow us to speak, they deny us permission to publish journals that express the way we feel and think, and now they prevent us from having meetings in our own university? I ask the president, is this democracy?"[71] Like the editor of *La Nueva Prensa*, Buitrago believed that the denial of those rights would create a generation of "non-individuals who lack moral values, men who will later bring shame and dishonor to Nicaragua."

For the students, the repression they endured not only confirmed their disillusionment with Somoza-era democracy, but also underscored the critical role they had in improving the nation. Political activism was central to their education.

These debates reveal the origins of the special treatment and considerations students would enjoy throughout the Somoza era. They were not immune to repression, but there existed both among the student body and the wider population the firm belief that these youths were the nation's future. Although relatively few citizens actually attended the university, those who did emerged members of the country's small professional class. Consequently, many believed they were destined to have an outsized role in politics, and the university was their training ground. It was where they learned to debate, write about politics, and hold meetings. These were traditional modes of middle-class and elite political engagement, yet they were regularly denied to most Nicaraguans. The notion of student exceptionalism thus maintained that their future responsibility meant they especially deserved the basic civil liberties denied most everyone else. Moreover, these debates reveal how students' activism spurred the larger society to think about what democracy and democratic institutions should look like. The conversation playing out in the nation's newspapers was, at root, about citizenship and civil rights. Even if that conversation was only about students, the essential freedoms required for a nation to function smoothly were a clear subtext.

Students believed that their youth was central to their ability to catalyze wider civic engagement and legitimize their political participation. They celebrated "the role that we represent as youth, to awaken the national conscience towards a better future."[72] They believed they could fulfill this function precisely because their youth afforded fresh perspective. Responding to a wave of repression that took place at the end of July and targeted the university in León, students proclaimed their duty to participate in national politics. Edguardo Buitrago, for example, wrote that it was precisely the students' uncorrupted nature that legitimized their protests and their opinions. "Students," he declared, "should be heard and should be taken into consideration because the voice of youth, still uncontaminated by the vices and defects of professional politicians, represents a true ideal, a sincere desire for liberty and justice."[73] Claiming to represent youth, students were assuming a leadership role for themselves that was primarily based on their innocence and the fresh perspective it provided.

The students' negative view of politicians was both a critique of Somoza's control and a response to the factionalism that had plagued the country for most of their lives. This was a generation born around 1926—that year, the

Conservative caudillo, Emiliano Chamorro, refused to honor his 1924 presidential defeat to a joint Conservative-Liberal ticket and staged a revolution to take power. Twenty years later, young activist Ismael Reyes Icabalceta noted that his rejection of the traditional politicians was based on this history, which "left me an orphan."[74] Party leaders had failed Nicaragua, and students now demanded their right to participate in the national political conversation. For these writers, youth provided political legitimacy. Their age and political inexperience placed them above party politics, as, in Buitrago's words, "independent men," unswayed by factional loyalties.

Conclusion

In the first years of Somoza's rule, students asserted themselves as a new and unique group in Nicaraguan politics. The general had come to power in the midst of a hemispheric surge in student organizing, as youth in universities across Latin America began to take on an active role in national politics. Organizing likewise, young Nicaraguans used their status as professionals-in-training to make demands on the state, first for themselves and later for their wider society. The symbolic power they had as the nation's future intensified the significance of their actions to sympathetic adults, who had watched as students across Central America rose up to demand an end to the dictatorships plaguing the region. After Nicaraguan youth did the same and suffered the regime's repression, their adult allies rushed to defend their foray into politics and to demand they receive the basic freedoms denied the rest of society.

Being a student in a small, predominantly agricultural nation carried with it special privileges. Nicaragua badly needed the professionals coming out of the university not just for their technical expertise but also because they were the nation's future decision makers. Students' political activism was closely linked to their current and future class status, a connection that would have profound implications for their efforts to build coalitions with the working class.

Nonetheless, by the mid-1940s, students had come to see themselves as a galvanizing force in the country's politics, which they believed to be beset by apathy. The debates over politics in the university convinced these young activists that they needed to secure the institution's independence from state interference. In July 1944, they began to demand university autonomy. At the time, this meant apolitical hiring, the inviolability of the campus, and legal status for all the associations that operated within the universities.[75] By creating a space outside the reach of the state, university autonomy would institutionalize student exceptionalism. That struggle would continue in the 1950s.

What began as a specific political conflict—a protest against Somoza—had turned into a fight for students' political rights. Throughout the rainy season of 1944, these young activists had never articulated a concrete vision of a Somoza-less Nicaragua; they merely wanted him gone. After the president promised not to run for reelection, however, they suddenly found their right to participate in politics questioned. They did not let these debates stop them.

CHAPTER 2

Protest and Repression during the "Democratic Effervescence," 1944–1948

By August 1944, Somoza's hold on the country was secure. That did not mean, however, an end to political persecution, as Francisco Frixione's experience illustrates. An avowed communist, the twenty-three-year-old middle-class law student was one of the most visible activists of the mid-1940s. While holding down several part-time jobs, Frixione also worked with labor organizers, led the student law association, and wrote paeans to the USSR.[1] He represented a small but increasingly radical segment of the student body, and his activities placed him squarely in the government's crosshairs.

On October 7, 1944, Frixione mysteriously disappeared. Ten days later, he reappeared, badly wounded. He initially told the press that "unknown persons" had kidnapped and beaten him while moving him between prisons, but by the end of the month, he was refusing to give more details. The US embassy, which kept tabs on the story, suspected that the regime had bought his silence. The ambassador expressed uncertainty over who orchestrated Frixione's disappearance, whether it was the National Guard or the government, but distinguishing between them was an impossible exercise.[2] The Guard had repressed a high-profile anti-Somoza dissident, and in so doing, the regime sent the message that students were not immune to violent reprisal.

Frixione's kidnapping demonstrates the extreme measures the regime used to intimidate its enemies, including its young opponents in the universities. The June 1944 demonstration initiated a cycle of protest and repression that continued until a frenzy of arrests in 1948 silenced many of the democratic movement leaders. This period coincided with an uptick in protests and organizing that marked Latin America's democratic effervescence. Although these movements did not last long—the rising tide of anti-communism in the late forties and the repression it engendered fractured coalitions—the burst of popular mobilization forced states throughout the region to take seriously the demands of the working class and, at least briefly, to expand the democratic process.[3] While historians have emphasized the primacy of the left in organizing these demonstrations, few have paid attention to the role of students in catalyzing dissent. As the last chapter explored, students initiated the mass protests that toppled dictators and demanded reform in Central America. In Nicaragua, young people continued to agitate against the Somoza regime, organizing compelling acts of defiance that stimulated civic engagement and wider protest.

Along with labor strikes, student activism lent this period its effervescent quality. Students demonstrated not only a unique capacity to catalyze wider activism but also the sheer difficulty of building an opposition movement in a repressive climate. University youth organized mass demonstrations and initiated national dialogues. Between 1944 and 1948, they founded their own newspaper, created their own university, organized an opposition block, and, even ran for political office. During this period, students, more than any other group, took to the streets to protest the regime's abuses, corruption, and malfeasance, and the violence they endured sparked wider opposition to the regime.

However, their capacity to mobilize various sectors of their society did not translate into an ability to build effective coalitions. While their suffering could rally the wider society to action, students alone could not build a social movement capable of overthrowing Somoza. This chapter argues that the very qualities that made their acts of disorder compelling to the wider society—their youthful innocence and idealism—made it hard for them to claim the legitimacy necessary to be taken seriously by their adult allies and opponents. Moreover, student politics disparaged the working and campesino classes while simultaneously presuming their unconditional support—a recipe for conflict. These problems were exacerbated by the regime's ready use of repression to silence critics and its willingness to make deals to neutralize opponents. Ultimately, this period witnessed the consolidation of Somoza's rule.

Agents of Effervescence

Students were the most visible anti-Somoza protestors throughout Nicaragua's democratic effervescence. Whether they were planned or spontaneous, private or public, at home or abroad, student demonstrations kept the opposition in the public eye. Although severely constrained by the state's repressive apparatus, student protest revealed Somoza's vulnerability and helped open a space for democratic activists to maneuver.

Students in the first wave of exiles after the June 1944 protests continued agitating from abroad, where they helped connect the regional democratic movements. In early September, Octavio Caldera, one of the students who had spoken at the initial rally in June and who had taken shelter in Costa Rica, shot at the Nicaraguan chargé d'affaires and was deported to Panama. There he reportedly drew the government's attention after he made contact with "radical student groups" and was exiled to Mexico.[4] Mexico at that time had become a haven for dissidents from abroad, and Nicaraguan students found a vibrant community there. For example, Pedro Joaquín Chamorro organized efforts on behalf of students in Nicaragua at the Universidad Nacional Autónoma de Mexico, where he was studying in exile.[5] Exiled students thus linked the democratic movements in different countries, building solidarity and sharing news.

Meanwhile, the June 1944 student demonstration had catalyzed both a democratic movement and a small political opening at home. The mass protests had forced the regime to offer significant concessions to the opposition in order to maintain its hold on power. In August, as a show of strength, Somoza gave exiles amnesty, and political dissidents trickled back into the country over the next few months. To further stabilize his regime, he pushed through a labor code that legalized unions and permitted the organization of a socialist party in late 1944. The result was a boom in labor organizing: within a year, more than seventeen thousand workers had been unionized, and they had organized several major strikes. Socialist organizers spearheaded much of this activity. Such measures not only bolstered his base but also gave the regime a sheen of legitimacy. The historian Knut Walter has argued that by allowing some opposition organizing, Somoza fended off charges that his government was a budding dictatorship.[6] Appeased by these changes and Somoza's withdrawal of his reelection plans, the opposition atomized.

Somoza's dogged ambition soon brought them together again. Once the political situation stabilized, the president began scheming to extend his tenure. In July 1945, an editorial in Somocista newspaper *Novedades* declared that because Somoza had been appointed to head the government by a constituent assembly in 1938, he had not technically been elected. Consequently, he could run for president without violating the constitution's prohibition against reelection.[7] Other newspapers immediately denounced the proposal.[8] Various government functionaries criticized Somoza's latest ploy for power, and one resigned in protest.[9] Socialists also condemned his machinations and began to talk of allying with the Independent Liberals, the Conservatives, the Central American Unionists, and, significantly, the students of the Central University.[10]

The youngest members of the opposition quickly proved to be the most aggressive opponents of the regime, earning both persecution and the respect of various sectors of society. For example, in September of that year, students in Granada staged a satirical play that lampooned Somoza and his ministers. The National Guard stopped the performance and forced several actors to walk from Granada to Nandaime, almost twenty-four kilometers. Days later, the student who played Somoza was given a hero's welcome at an elite wedding in Granada.[11] Spontaneous demonstrations also showcased students' growing militancy. In December, two hundred baseball players at a tournament in Managua staged an impromptu protest when a soldier attacked one youth for disobeying an order. In response, the young people marched off the fields and into the streets of the capital, demanding democracy and death to Somoza.[12]

Such actions carried considerable risk, and this period was marked by the regime's inconsistent response to student activism—a sign of the tricky nature of dealing with protest when an authoritarian regime has claimed itself to be populist. At times, the government gave students permission to hold protests weakly disguised as cultural celebrations. At other times, it forbade demonstrations that were not overtly political, such as a celebration marking the end of World War II.[13]

On occasion, the regime responded to relatively private protests with outright violence. In late October 1945, the National Guard opened fire on a student-organized farewell banquet for Andrade Guzman, the Guatemalan foreign minister, wounding one youth and compelling forty others to seek asylum in the Guatemalan Legation. Students from the universities in León and Managua had organized the dinner, which turned into a vehement denunciation of Somoza. At one point, the Guatemalan minister declared that "liberty could be achieved only by blood in the streets and not by a president imposed upon Nicaragua by a foreign government."[14] The next morning, October 17, Somoza shut down the Central University. Days later, the National Guard attempted to arrest Francisco Frixione in order to forestall a student demonstration protesting the closure. When the GN realized he was not home, they arrested his two brothers instead. Frixione was forced to take asylum in the Mexican embassy.[15]

Students reacted aggressively to the assault on the university, and their response to the repression rallied their adult allies and younger peers. A few days after the school's closure, thirty young people attempted to storm the doors and were blocked by more than fifty soldiers guarding the university.[16] In solidarity, several leading oppositionists planned a general strike that would begin with secondary schools in Managua and then gradually spread to those in other major cities.[17] Activating the thirty-five hundred youths studying in the nation's secondary schools would significantly extend the protest—their numbers more than doubled the universities' population at this time.[18] Students hoped labor would then join. Within days of the failed attempt to arrest Frixione, the strike was underway, and students in Managua and Granada were skipping class to protest.[19]

The regime marshalled various mechanisms to preserve its stability. There were reports of police abuse in all the major cities. In Granada, the National Guard confiscated documents and files from the university student center, and the minister of public instruction punished secondary students who participated in the protest.[20] In addition, several students and professors were exiled for participating in a demonstration against Somoza.[21] The state even shaped the media's portrayal of these events. Members of the regime called foreign journalists to ensure that they reported the official version of the incident. They also forbade the telegraph companies from delivering any messages from the opposition. Finally, the government harshly clamped down on free speech. The National Guard closed anti-Somoza presses and arrested people printing their own pamphlets.[22] In this climate, the general strike failed, but the protests had again showcased the students' capacity to energize the opposition.

The multi-layered repression suggests the regime's vulnerability. The impending Allied victory in Europe was energizing democratic movements worldwide. Meanwhile, the US government had refused to endorse Somoza's reelection plans.[23] While Somoza acted "as cocksure as ever" and displayed delusions of mass popular support, the US embassy observed that the regime was actually at its weakest point since the 1944 protests.[24] The population seemed to perceive Somoza's readiness to rely on brute force, via the National Guard, as evidence of his waning power.[25] Perhaps for these reasons, in November 1945, Somoza finally lifted the state of siege enacted at the beginning of World War II.[26]

By keeping dissent visible, student activism helped maintain Nicaragua's democratic effervescence. Their 1944 protest and the solidarity demonstrations it triggered had forced the regime to allow a small political aperture, which tolerated labor organizing and minor opposition activity. Throughout this time, students were at the forefront of the anti-Somoza opposition, organizing acts of defiance that embarrassed the regime and revealed both its violence and vulnerability.

Building the Opposition

Almost immediately after Somoza loosened the wartime restrictions, students began organizing a movement to beat him at the polls. During the democratic effervescence, they published an aggressive anti-Somoza newspaper, drafted a surprisingly progressive political agenda, spearheaded the creation of an opposition coalition, and became nationally recognized symbols of democratic activism. These activities helped build a broad opposition movement, as students brought together long-time political enemies in a joint effort to defeat the dictatorship.

The student newspaper, *El Universitario*, promoted the wider political consciousness of their society. One of the most vociferously anti-regime newspapers of the era, the periodical celebrated Somoza's most famous adversary, Augusto César Sandino, relentlessly exposed the regime's corruption, and at times even threatened revolution. Founded in December 1945, after Somoza lifted the state of siege, the paper featured a regular satirical column that chronicled the antics of a fictional politician, Kakaseno (roughly translated: Full-of-shit), a not-so-veiled caricature of Somoza. By the time it stopped printing in 1947, *El Universitario* was a biweekly periodical with a circulation that at its peak reached ten thousand, double the circulation rate of *Flecha*, one of the country's major daily newspapers.[27] The paper thus provided university youth with a national platform, and their aggressive coverage of the regime lent their perspective particular authority. Labor papers, the mainstream press, and even the US State Department reprinted and reported on their articles. [28] Their writings clearly resonated with the public.

Although it was the official paper of Managua's University Student Center, *El Universitario* focused on national politics and, specifically, on highlighting the dictatorship's failures. Articles described the regime's disregard for the constitution, denounced state corruption, and condemned the self-interest of its bureaucrats. Student journalists shone a light on the regime's repression and inefficiency: they interviewed peers who had been tortured, publicized arbitrary detentions, and reported on the lack of social services. An early edition, for example, critiqued Somoza's annual Christmas message, condemned his control over judicial appointments, discussed the consequences of the capital's inept sanitation services, and featured a first-person prison account.[29] During a time when newspapers were shuttered for vaguely implying corruption, *El Universitario* became an important source of anti-regime news and commentary.

The paper also promoted the budding opposition movement. Some columns highlighted the lives of exiled dissidents, while others demanded their return. Over time, the paper became even more aggressive. Several articles were directed to soldiers in hope of extinguishing their loyalty to Somoza. When the election of 1947 drew near, students wrote voting instructions, advertised protests, and called for revolution if the ballots were not honored.[30]

Despite its militant anti-Somocismo, *El Universitario* stayed in print for almost two years—its longevity testament to the students' growing standing in the national political sphere. Somoza did attempt to shut them down on several occasions. In February 1946, just two months after *El Universitario* began publishing, the government closed the paper on charges that its editors had misrepresented the periodical as a student publication when it was actually a political journal. A huge outcry followed. The editor of the labor newspaper, *Ahora*, wrote that the "suspension has distressed all those who fight to secure our liberties" and demanded that Somoza rescind the order.[31] Both Conservatives and Liberals supported the students, and eventually the Supreme Court canceled the suspension.[32] The regime continued trying to suppress the periodical, but each time, prominent political figures took up the cause and the paper continued publishing. Significantly, their defense of *El Universitario* was not based on the authors' youthfulness, but rather on freedom of the press—rhetoric that indicated the students' credibility in the larger society.[33]

With a growing national profile, students turned their attention to revitalizing national politics. In January 1946, the newly organized Federación Universitario de Nicaragua (Federation of Nicaraguan University Students, or FUN) proposed the creation of a new political party. In their initial statement, students pointed out that, in contrast to traditional parties, this new organization would unite people behind not a caudillo but a concrete agenda. The party would be driven by a desire to build a "dynamically democratic" government. The students envisioned an interventionist state that would provide social services, redistribute land, set prices for basic food stuffs, and even initiate a literacy campaign. They demanded a decentralized government with a reorganized military and an anticolonial foreign policy. This fairly progressive platform exemplified the regional demand for a more expansive democracy that promised both economic and political freedoms.[34]

Their plan immediately drew the support of leftist labor organizers, who popularized it with their much larger base. The Socialist Party effusively praised the students' concrete action plan. Workers especially were eager to join the new "party for the masses" that they hoped would open up the political system to historically marginalized sectors.[35] It is not a coincidence that the Socialists and the FUN were the two organizations most dedicated to organizing a coalition. Both were relatively new actors in Nicaragua's political sphere. They seemed aware of the vulnerability this entailed and appreciated the power of coalitions. Moreover, both saw themselves as the political vanguard. In a January 1946 article, a Socialist labor leader celebrated the growth of the university student movement and indicated that both workers and students, as new political actors, had a duty "to orient the new consciousness" that desires democracy.[36] Recognizing the numerical value of the growing working class, students saw them as key members of the opposition coalition.[37] Finally, both were eager to participate in a political sphere that had long been limited to the traditional parties.

A massive protest in late January 1946 showcased the potential power a united opposition could marshal and illustrated the students' prominent place in the movement. On stage before an audience of more than one hundred thousand people, student leaders sat beside opposition politicians and labor activists who celebrated their role in creating the political opening. One Conservative politician mentioned two of the students by name when he proclaimed, "This manifestation was achieved through the blood of Guillermo Sánchez Arauz, of Francisco Frixione, . . . and hundreds of others."[38] Another politician, Octavio Pasos Montiel, offered a special welcome to the students who "with one single leap have incorporated themselves into the glorious global student tradition," and "have thrown themselves into [the struggle] without fear."[39] His words illuminated the potent symbolism of student politics: their actions, marked by bravery and patriotism, were part of a larger global tradition.

Student efforts to unite anti-Somocistas crested in May 1946 when a surprising array of political actors—including socialists, Conservatives, Independent Liberals, Central American Unionists, and students—met to discuss the students' proposal for a new party.[40] A month later, workers, students, and Unionists officially formed the National Liberation bloc.[41]

However, long-held class and ideological divisions had not disappeared, and they loomed over the discussions. Conservatives and Independent Liberals were considering joining the new bloc, but they may have hesitated over the progressive tenets of the platform. Conservatives likely balked at the strong interventionist state the students had envisioned: the platform promised a central government that would diversify the economy, modernize agriculture, and promote industrialization. Independent Liberal leaders like Carlos Pasos, a mill owner with a reputation for strike busting, probably took issue with the platform's labor protections.[42] These points of contention underscored the difficulty of coalition politics.

Class biases also threatened the unity between students and workers.

Many young activists did not seem to view the working class as equal partners in the quest to reform the country.[43] They criticized workers and campesinos for being passive victims of state manipulation or, worse, being duped by the regime. An article in *El Universitario*, for example, condemned the "low passions of the masses and the passivity that permitted Somoza to ascend" to the presidential palace.[44] Another student concluded, "We cannot allow our poor campesinos to continue serving as the stepping stones for upstart dictators."[45] The blame was clear: it was on the backs of campesinos that Somoza had risen to office.

Such sentiments betray the class assumptions that undergirded student politics. Students expected to lead the new movement for social justice and took for granted that workers would follow their command. They based their claim to leadership on their education. As one wrote, students were "heroic, disinterested and intelligent. They did not follow caudillos … they were not moved by their stomach, but by the beauty they had absorbed through their books."[46] Such rhetoric produced a sharp divide between students and the lower classes and recreated class hierarchies within the democratic movement.[47]

Despite these problems, by mid-1946, students had brought these disparate groups and interests to the table—a significant achievement in Nicaraguan politics. These were groups that historically had been staunchly opposed to each other—had even taken up arms against each other. Moreover, it was the dawning of the Cold War. Conservatives were vehemently anticommunist, but here they were talking with socialists. This feat was one of many students managed to accomplish during the democratic effervescence, as they publicized the regime's corruption and galvanized wider civic engagement through their newspaper, their protests, and their organizing efforts. In these ways, they helped build an active opposition movement.

The Opposition Coalition Dissolves

The budding coalition fell apart before its differences could be resolved. In late June 1946, students organized a dramatic anti-Somoza demonstration. The resulting repression effectively splintered the opposition. Once more, the regime went into overdrive to covertly and overtly suppress the protest, and the tension widened the fractures among students, socialists, and the traditional political parties. The opposition movement's dissolution highlights the ways in which the students' very youthfulness both helped and hurt their political efforts.

The demonstration's organization reveals the contradictions that pervaded Somocista "democracy." In the lead-up to the second anniversary of the June 27, 1944, protest, students requested permission from Managua's *jefe político* to hold a demonstration in honor of the "Day of the University Student." The date plainly indicated that the event would commemorate the repression the students had endured two years earlier. Surprisingly, the regime acquiesced.[48]

Its decision can be understood as part of its larger erratic execution of democracy. In the months leading up to the protest, the government permitted several opposition demonstrations while covertly sabotaging them. For example, in March 1946, the state permitted protests in Juigalpa and Masaya and even ordered the National Guard to its barracks during the rallies as a "good faith" gesture. However, newspapers reported that the train schedules (owned and operated by the government) had changed abruptly, and demonstrators were unable to reach the Masaya protest.[49]

The actions of the university rector, Captain Benjamín Argüello, on the day of the protest suggest that the regime similarly hoped to thwart the student event. When a group of students arrived at the university to obtain the school flag, which they planned to fly at the demonstration, they found that Argüello had called in troops to surround the campus. The protestors somehow managed to acquire the flag and made their way to the plaza in front of the National Cathedral where the demonstration was to take place. Several trucks filled with soldiers soon caught up and attacked the young men, beating them and leaving several wounded. Undeterred, the injured youth, including Orlando Montenegro, Octavio Caldera, and Ernesto Flores García, continued to the plaza, and the protest began at four o'clock.[50]

The violence that students had endured and their continued activism earned them the enthusiastic support of their society. Under the watchful eyes of the armed Guardsmen stationed at the nearby National Palace, more than eight thousand people showed up for the demonstration.[51] Illustrative of the students' national prominence, politicians and labor organizers sent representatives to participate in the protest. Their speeches and the subsequent media coverage celebrated the students' protest and the democratic movement it catalyzed. Alluding to important dates in the history of Latin America and Nicaragua, Representative Octavio Pasos Montiel proclaimed that history would regard June 27 as the "Grito de Dolores of a new independence."[52] *La Prensa*'s reporter celebrated the second anniversary, writing:

> For the first time in Nicaragua, students gave a cry of protest and liberty against the dictator. . . . That historic day, the students were beaten, threat-

ened, taken prisoners ... that day marked the beginning of that great journey that has culminated in these days with the union of the entire country against Somoza.[53]

Just two years after the students' initial protest, anti-Somocistas were rhetorically enshrining their actions in the annals of Nicaraguan history.

Sure of their vanguard position, students demanded action. Francisco Frixione declared: "The tyranny has continued past June 27, 1944, because we all believed that attending protests was enough." Two years of erratic repression and the restriction of civil liberties had convinced them that it was time for more radical measures: a general strike.[54] Students were confident that the pueblo was behind them. Orlando Montenegro declared that Somoza would eventually have to exile everybody if he hoped to defeat the opposition.[55] Their certainty that the masses were against the regime would hinder their efforts to build an anti-Somoza coalition.

The regime violently suppressed the commemorative demonstration, again triggering a mass outcry over the repression of students. After the speeches ended, the young demonstrators marched to the university to return the school flag. A crowd followed, and as they traveled along Roosevelt Avenue, the National Guard attacked, launching tear gas and beating protestors and bystanders, male and female, young and old, alike. The normally understated US ambassador reported that the repression was "a revelation of unrestricted *guardia* brutality."[56]

Although many innocent people were wounded that day, the *La Prensa* journalists fixated on the violence the young protestors suffered. According to a reporter, the group of students carrying the flag continued on through the chaos to the university. At one point, the Guard launched a tear gas canister at the student activist César Carter Cantarero, described as "one of the heroes of this day of suffering and heroism." According to the reporter, "César carried the flag, and, wounded, marched with it, receiving punches from all sides. When they shot the tear gas bomb, he picked it up to throw it back, but with such bad luck, it exploded in his hands." Upon reaching the university, students stormed the locked doors. The Guard followed and, in a "spectacle of savagery," beat the students and shot at them with bullets and tear gas. The paper's rendering of the students' actions and the violence inflicted on them maximized the emotional effects of the brutality.[57]

Perceptions of the students' martyrdom grew with Somoza's decision to close the university in Managua. Accusing the young activists of subverting public order, Somoza and his minister of education permanently shuttered most of the Central University departments.[58] The students and their allies erupted in anger. Politicians condemned the National Guard's attack on the students.[59] An editorial in *La Prensa* lamented the way in which the regime's actions had disillusioned students whose "youthful heads had been filled with democratic ideals."[60] The repression of the innocent provided a ready justification for more protest.

Students hoped to capitalize on this outrage by organizing a general strike. That strategy had precipitated the overthrow of the dictator, Maximiliano Hernandez Martinez, in El Salvador in 1944, so students had reason to be hopeful. The pretext for the strike would be the removal of the university rector, Benjamín Argüello, who had called the soldiers in the first place. Declaring that Argüello's presence in the university jeopardized their "personal security and their dignity as university students," they demanded his resignation and declared a strike.[61] By July 1, the nation's three universities were participating, and they were soon joined by secondary students across the country.[62] Rumors of a strike in the military academy compounded a general sense that the regime might again be on the verge of collapse.[63]

Somoza responded with a dramatic show of force. National Guardsmen patrolled the city, and, according to many accounts, were beating students without provocation.[64] Amid reports of a student-planned protest on July 4, the regime prepared as if for war. Somoza ordered the air force to be in the air and ready for duty.[65] With the capital on virtual lockdown, the day passed without incident. Armed with machine guns, soldiers patrolled the streets waiting for any sign of protestors. They even blocked the roads into and out of several major cities.[66]

Despite the participation of three thousand students, the strike ultimately failed because they were unable to convince workers to join them. In an editorial in the main Socialist paper, the writer harshly criticized the students' "passionate and careless actions," writing that "Nicaragua cannot save herself if her children allow their emotions to carry them away." Underneath the denunciation of reckless youth, the author hinted that students were being manipulated by the traditional political parties and required more thorough "ideological orientation" from their leaders.[67]

Student presumptions that labor would act when called upon revealed a substantial rift between the young activists and their leftist allies. It is not clear why Socialist Party leaders did not support the strike. Perhaps calling for such a massive action just when their party was gaining control of the national labor movement seemed a risky maneuver. Moreover, the reason for the strike, removing the university rector, was likely too narrow to galvanize their base—perhaps even too narrow to galvanize wider societal action. Even if Socialists had been willing to strike, no official deal was yet in place to guarantee labor's political position vis-a-vis the traditional parties. Should Somoza fall, there were no guarantees that the next government would respect labor rights. The historian, Jeffrey Gould, who interviewed student activists from the era, concluded that the class divides among the labor left and the middle class and elite opposition members doomed the alliance: "Whereas the Socialists assessed the middle and upper classes in terms of their attitude and behavior toward labor, the opposition could only conceive the political world in terms of the somocista/anti-somocista antinomy."[68] The rhetoric labor leaders employed to criticize students bolsters this analysis, while also highlighting the ways in which adult opponents could quickly dismiss the political pretensions of young activists. On July 3, Argüello voluntarily resigned, declaring that the dramatic reduction of the Central University's departments meant it no longer required a rector. A few days later, the engineering students announced that they would return to class, and the Federation of Nicaraguan University Students called the strike off.[69]

The failure to draw support for the strike turned students off coalition politics. After the Socialists had refused to strike, students withdrew from the National Liberation Block. Representatives from the student federation explained that their organization was too divided politically to act as a unified block, declaring that "they were made up of Liberals and Conservatives … that, in sum, they did not constitute a numerical force outside of the traditional groups in Nicaraguan politics."[70] Their anti-Somoza enmity may have helped them set aside ideological differences in 1944 at the beginning of the democratic movement, but it was not enough to unite them behind a single course of action, especially as the emerging Cold War intensified the animosity between anti-communist Conservatives and leftists.[71] The opposition block dissolved quickly as various groups and individuals found they could not agree on strategy and ideology.

Having given up on the coalition, students now tried to work through the traditional parties. In September 1946, more than one hundred Conservative students petitioned the director of the Conservative Party to consider nominating Arsenio Álvarez Corrales and Eduardo N. Matus Vargas, two student leaders, as candidates for deputy positions in the national congress, thus sidestepping the traditional nomination procedure. Both had long histories of opposition to the regime. Álvarez Corrales had been one of the editors of *El Universitario*. Matus Vargas, a pharmacy student, also wrote for the student paper and had only recently returned from exile in Guatemala.[72] These credentials framed their request, and the petitioners argued that the party could not question the students' dedication to national liberation for they had been "the first to give the cry of rebellion against the dictatorship."[73] Later that month, Liberal students tried to nominate Francisco Frixione, Octavio Caldera, and César Carter Cantarero to be deputy candidates, again on the basis of having initiated the "virile campaign . . . against the dictatorship."[74]

Party leaders were unconvinced that their record of activism qualified them for office and used the students' youth to discredit their ambitions. In a subtly scathing editorial, the editor of *La Prensa* wrote that students were "embryos of the men of tomorrow," and as the "brains of tomorrow" are today "all heart and sentiment," spoiled by "societies that love them as their hope and tolerate them as youth." Comparing students to "larva that wants to fly before it has wings," the editor recommended they focus on their education; politics would come later.[75]

Their youthfulness was now a mark against them in their quest to enter the political sphere. What had once helped legitimize their political participation now justified their exclusion. Their youth had alternately earned them praise, attention, repression, and scorn. After the failure of the general strike, students learned that their status as politically active students was not enough to earn them real political power—and the parties' response to their electoral ambitions only further drove home the message.

La Universidad Libre de Nicaragua

If the opposition coalition fractured along class lines, the students' newest project deepened those divides. After Somoza closed the Central University in July 1946, students and politicians discussed the need for autonomous universities. One deputy introduced a bill that would create free universities, funded by the government but beyond its control. While the proposal languished, students took matters into their own hands. In the days after their school was shuttered, they founded the Universidad Libre de Nicaragua (Free University of Nicaragua). Creating a university from scratch, though, required considerable financial support, and the school's founding best illustrates the class hierarchies that undergirded student politics and limited the democratic movement.

Spearheaded by students, the Free University got off the ground with the help of some of Nicaragua's most illustrious politicians. On July 7, 1946, more than one hundred students met to determine the university's directory board. They unanimously elected the former rector of the Central University, Dr. Salvador Mendieta, to head the new school. In addition to being a noted educator, Mendieta was also a well-established politician and leader of the movement to unify Central America.[76] He drew on his extensive contacts to finance the school, aided by a wealthy anti-Somocista landowner, José Argüello Cervantes, who invited eleven businessmen and professionals to form a corporation to fund the school.[77] Initially, they planned to sell six thousand shares at 50 córdobas each to start the school off with a three hundred thousand-córdoba budget. The members purchased 202 shares themselves and enlisted students, a local women's organization, the Frente Femenil, and others to help sell the shares.[78] In this way, Nicaragua's elite came together to support the university students and ensure their continued education.

Thanks to these efforts, the Free University was operational within weeks of its creation. By the end of July, the board had rented a palatial three-story home in the center of Managua for the university, hired two permanent employees, and several porters.[79] The new university managed to retain the services of many of the professors formerly employed at the Central University. By September, there were seventy-two professors teaching 170 students.[80]

The inaugural ceremony for the Free University celebrated the key role that students and their school were to play in national renewal and highlighted the class biases that continued to plague that effort. Intellectuals and politicians were particularly proud that the students had taken the initiative to found their own university and that the school would stand as a counterpoint to the regime. Dr. Gerónimo Ramírez Brown explained that while "the government can extinguish the lantern of the university momentarily, the *pueblo* will light it, as they are doing now."[81] Ramírez Brown was clearly pleased that the Free University had been a community effort, but, given the fact that most of the funds came from the business and political elite, his speech, perhaps inadvertently, revealed a limited understanding of the *pueblo* that continued to haunt the opposition movement and its efforts to reform national politics.

The student speakers that day exalted the university's critical role in molding citizens and, by extension, their society. Joaquina Vega declared that "only the university ... can inculcate a love of truth, of freedom, of tolerance, of ... Social Service and of a democratic spirit."[82] Rafael Córdova Rivas similarly laid out a vision of the university as an "orienting" force that would "raise the civic condition" of "demoralized" and disinterested citizens.[83]

This vision, which shaped the school's mission, was remarkable for both who was included and who was excluded. Vega's participation in the ceremony underscored the school's commitment to women's education. In her speech that evening, she proclaimed that women had finally found a space where they could exercise the "political rights that even today are denied."[84] She spoke on behalf of ten other female students. The following year, twenty-seven of the 172 students enrolled were women.[85] Though their numbers were small, women played an active role in the university, representing the school at off-campus functions and serving as class representatives. In 1946, for example, one of the five representatives from the pharmacy school was a woman, Alicia Morales. She also represented the pharmacy students on the college's board, and, in the law school, one representative was a woman.[86] The wider student body also supported women's rights, as evidenced by the 1946 statutes for the University Center of Managua, the city's student organization, which expressed a commitment to women's suffrage.[87]

If women's participation in the university hints at the student movement's inclusivity, then the school's daily operations and outreach efforts illustrate its limitations. From its inception, the Free University was an elite-led project. Dr. Mendieta's inaugural speech said as much: "Here we are forming one single body, businessmen, professors, and students, and here we are conquering the destiny of Nicaragua with science, morality, and public spirit."[88] Workers and peasants were to be their targets. Early on, students and faculty declared a commitment to cultural and social uplift. For the former, they organized cultural events, in which guests lectured on topics ranging from indigenous folklore to the women's movement in Latin America.[89] The school publicized these events in newspapers, suggesting they were directed at local luminaries and the students themselves.[90] An illustrative example of the university's myopic good intentions comes from the meeting minutes of one of their general assemblies. One of the deans proposed opening the university's library to the public, and the measure was accepted. But its brief hours—from ten to twelve in the morning and three to five in the afternoon—must surely have limited workers' use.[91]

Students also reached out to the workers, but their efforts to raise civic consciousness were hampered by their inability to acknowledge working-class politics. In late December 1946, the university rector suggested that students organize talks in Managua's neighborhoods to help "the people struggling for their redemption."[92] Students embraced the idea, noting in their meeting minutes that such outreach projects were important because among the urban poor, "civic confusion/ disorientation was overwhelming, especially among women who we can classify as anti-civic."[93] The gendered dimension likely reflected a lingering bitterness toward the working-class women who had supported Somoza during the 1944 student protests.[94]

The students hoped to address this "civic ignorance" through their outreach program in the capital's working-class and poverty-stricken barrios. They offered health and legal services and planned civic workshops that would teach families to place the needs of the country above loyalty to political parties. The moral of their talks would be that the "bad government that has plagued Nicaragua has many causes, the most important of which is the ignorance of the people and their lack of knowledge about civic rights."[95]

These harsh charges indicate more about student politics than the lack thereof among workers and campesinos. The blanket assumption that members of the working class were "disoriented" betrays the limits of the students' social uplift: they could not imagine that these men and women were indeed political, but with a politics oriented to their own class interests.[96] In fact, it is striking that the student outreach effort did not appear to include a discussion of labor rights, a topic that would have been at the forefront of many workers' minds during this period. As discussed earlier, Nicaragua was experiencing a boom of labor activity. By mid-1945, union membership had swelled to seventeen thousand. Many of these workers—especially those in urban areas, the very sector students suspected of civic confusion—had been organized by Socialist Party militants who were fighting for systemic reforms.[97] In contrast, traditional party politicians had a long history of working against the interests of workers and campesinos. These groups had no reason to trust that the situation had changed. By blaming the rise of Somoza on the "common people," students missed an opportunity to reflect on the political structure of the day. The rise of Somoza had just as much to do with the corruption and ideological flexibility that characterized the traditional party system and its leaders who frequently cut backroom deals as it did with absent or bought voters.[98] These contradictions reveal the limits of Nicaragua's student-led democratic effervescence. Students hoped to lead alongside traditional political elites and in that way improve the lot of the poor and working class. Workers apparently were not going to be full partners in this endeavor.

The establishment of the Free University highlights the aspirational nature of the student movement. Many of these young people were members of the newly expanding middle class and occupied positions in its lowest echelons, working part-time or full-time as teachers, law clerks, lab assistants, low-level bureaucrats, or shop clerks.[99] Their class status was thus somewhat tenuous, and students seemed to have possessed an acute class consciousness. They were particularly interested in the trappings associated with their status as soon-to-be professionals. For example, in one meeting, students debated wearing jackets to class. The assembly was divided, but the motion lost for reasons related to the tropical heat. At that same meeting, students requested the university offer classes on money management ("how to make money, save it and use it honorably") and intellectual morality.[100] Such conversations hint at the students' hopes for class advancement.

As a manifestation of Nicaragua's democratic effervescence, the Free University reveals the limits of the students' democratic politics. Their activism had the potential to mobilize various sectors of society, but often along class lines. As their outreach efforts reveal, students envisioned themselves at the forefront of a democratic movement, supported by elites, that would shepherd Nicaragua and its lower classes into a new, more just era.

The End of the Democratic Effervescence

The Free University closed amid the repression that followed Somoza's May 1947 coup when he seized power from his chosen successor. Students again sprang into action, but the opportunism of the political elite, severe repression, and widespread apathy ultimately doomed their efforts. As the Cold War dawned, fears of communist subversion justified escalating repression, and many of the students' most active leaders were forced into exile.

The 1947 elections reunited the regime's opponents—including students, Conservatives, and Independent Liberals—behind the candidacy of Dr. Enoc Aguado. A long-time Liberal, Aguado was running against Leonardo Argüello, the candidate of Somoza's National Liberal Party.[101] Although both candidates had similar platforms, anti-Somocistas viewed Argüello as a regime puppet. Students mobilized to support his opponent. They used the extensive reach of *El Universitario* to promote Aguado and organize anti-Somoza protests.[102] More than a thousand people gathered to participate in a student demonstration against the regime in León. One of the students, Aquiles Centeno Pérez, encouraged the public not to turn over their arms, as the law stipulated before elections, because "we will need them to defend our homes."[103]

In the end, there was election fraud, but no uprising. Voter registration irregularities discriminated against Conservatives, ballot boxes disappeared, and votes were incorrectly tallied.[104] Yet, there was little outcry when Argüello was announced the winner. Emboldened, the regime went after the student opposition in force. First, Colonel Julio Somoza, the dictator's brother, sued Reinaldo Antonio Téfel and Rodolfo E. Fiallos, two of the students behind *El Universitario*, for libel and won. The court fined each 300 córdobas.[105] Then in late February, the minister of the interior shut down the paper for being "subversive, contrary to the interests of the republic and defamatory to the person of the president." He further charged the paper's four editors, Carlos Santos Berroterán, Arsenio Álvarez Corrales, Octavio Caldera, and Eduardo Pérez Valle, with "the crimes of contempt for authority, acts against the internal security of the state, inciting public disorder, and, no less grave, sedition."[106] Boldly flouting the regime, students created a new newspaper, *Avanzada*, and published their first issue on March 11.[107] Three days later, the minister of the interior sued the *Avanzada* editors for "libeling the president . . . and civil and military authorities."[108]

Meanwhile, Somoza found himself under attack from surprising quarters — the presidential palace. Prevented from pursuing reelection by popular will, Somoza had chosen Leonardo Argüello because he believed he would be easily manipulated. The new president, however, immediately took measures to curtail Somoza's power. Argüello replaced Somocistas in key government positions and extended an olive branch to students and labor. When he ordered Somoza's resignation from the National Guard and exile on May 25, the dictator staged a coup. Within a week, Argüello was forced to flee the country, and Congress appointed a new executive. Somoza would rule for the rest of the decade through more acquiescent puppet presidents.[109]

Won over by Argüello's willingness to defy Somoza, students were ready to take up arms to defend him in the days before the coup. They made contact with anti-Somocistas in the Guard, but, in the end, Somoza moved too quickly. Within hours of the coup, he rooted out the disloyal officers who were to supply the students with weapons. Their arrest thwarted any chance of an armed uprising.[110] Moreover, the regime sent a clear message when the National Guard detained the brother of Francisco Frixione, one of the former editors of *El Universitario*, in his place on May 30. The regime's persecution of a well-known dissident like Frixione contributed to widespread fear.[111]

Undeterred, students attempted to rally the opposition. They helped organize a new coalition, the Nicaraguan Democratic Union, that brought together Socialists, Independent Liberals, and others to fight for Argüello's restoration, and they organized demonstrations in favor of the deposed president. They also continued publishing *Avanzada*, which remained as virulently anti-Somocista as ever. On June 21, the government ordered *Avanzada*'s closure and confiscated their papers.[112] Defiant, students published another issue on June 24. In it, they called for armed uprising and raged against the politicians and foreign capitalists who had benefitted from keeping Nicaragua in a state of "political backwardness."[113] Again, the police seized the edition, but this time no more issues appeared.[114]

The opportunism of the political elite hindered students' efforts. High-profile oppositionists were more interested in brokering a deal with the regime than in participating in a democratic movement. A few days before the coup, Somoza had approached prominent Independent Liberals and Conservatives to test their interest in forcing out Argüello and redistributing power. Although they initially rejected his plan, opposition leaders like Carlos Pasos and Emiliano Chamorro spent the next few weeks negotiating with Somoza.[115] Eventually, both parties decided not to cooperate with the regime, but those weeks of inaction cost the opposition momentum.

State repression severely limited those who were trying to organize. Throughout June, students, Socialists, and elite women were virtually the only sectors willing to take to the streets, but the GN blocked their actions, shutting down meetings and demonstrations.[116] Undaunted, students began organizing their annual June 27 protest against the regime, allying again with Socialist Party members. Rumors spread that demonstrations would be held throughout the city. On the morning of the planned protest, bombs exploded at the homes of high-level Somocista functionaries. Blaming students, the Guard moved in and squashed the protest before it began.[117]

The budding Cold War justified the escalating repression. In the wake of the coup, Somoza sought to attract support by accusing his many enemies of being leftists. The regime even tried to brand President Argüello a communist to justify his overthrow.[118] Claiming the bombings to be the work of communist agents, Somoza went after student activists and the left in full force, imprisoning many and eventually exiling several to the island of Ometepe.[119] According to the US embassy, the repression was so complete that by early July, "practically all leaders of the Socialist Party and of the University Student group are now under arrest, in asylum or hiding."[120]

With much of their leadership in exile, the student movement retreated into the university. During this time, the Free University permanently closed; the school was in serious financial straits and the government refused to recognize its degrees. Its director, Salvador Mendieta, and many of its students joined the waves of exiles fleeing repression. In April 1947, Somoza renamed the University of León, although its designation as the National University did not seem to mean much. The following year, its students were hoping to convince the president to complete the stalled construction on their campus.[121] Their peers in the capital, meanwhile, urged the president to reopen the Central University in Managua. To persuade the government, they declared that the students who led the political movement had now graduated or fled the country and promised that if the university was reopened they would not allow any kind of political activity on campus.[122] Those who continued agitating against the regime would do so through the political parties.

The murder of a high-profile student activist cemented the danger of dissenting under Somoza. On the night of December 17, 1948, Uriel Sotomayor Ramírez, a politically active law student and the son of a well-known

Liberal family, was meeting with fellow students at a bar. They were drawing up a petition to get the Organization of American States (OAS) to investigate a border dispute between Nicaragua and Costa Rica when a group of Guardsmen arrived to arrest them. The soldiers forced the youths out of the bar and began beating them. One soldier, Braulio Meneses, struck Sotomayor on the head with his rifle so hard that the weapon broke, and Sotomayor fell to the ground. He was forced to stand and taken to the jail with the other students. The next day, the National Guard notified his family that their son had died, claiming that Sotomayor had fallen from his bunk.[123]

An autopsy contradicted the Guard's story and triggered a public outcry. A physician, Sotomayor's brother, traced the cause of death to a skull fracture and trauma to the chest.[124] Students from Managua and Granada gathered in León to plan their response, but the National Guard immediately arrested them. During Sotomayor's funeral a few days later, thousands of men, women, and children marched through the streets of León with handkerchiefs covering their mouths, likely a reference to the regime's violent silencing of dissent.[125] Condolences and denunciations poured in from throughout the country and as far away as Chile as students and their families mourned the first student martyr under Somoza.[126] In a rare semblance of justice, the regime court-martialed his killer and found him guilty. He was sentenced to five years in prison but was allowed to live at home. Not three months later, he fled to Honduras.[127]

Sotomayor's murder was just one example of the regime's increasing brutality. The National Guard did not hesitate to torture dissidents, and prisoners died mysteriously in detention. Commenting on the regime's penchant for violence, the US embassy noted, however, that "killings in rural areas of politically unimportant people usually do not receive much attention."[128] In contrast, the murder of students garnered significant coverage. Just a few months after Sotomayor was killed, the body of another student, Ernesto Flores García, was found beaten and stabbed to death. Flores García, a medical student and member of the Independent Liberal Party was a well-known activist who had had run-ins with the regime before: he had been among the students beaten during a protest in June 1946. In November 1948, he was detained for his political activities and imprisoned for several months, during which time he was tortured. He was murdered soon after his release. While many suspected his death was politically motivated, the regime seems to have covered it up as a crime of passion.[129] These killings outraged Nicaraguans, but the population had been driven into quiescence by the repression, the loss of its most politically active leaders, and the compromises made by those who remained.

Conclusion

In the postwar period, students became key members of the opposition. Their defiant protests and willingness to shed their own blood drew significant public attention and earned them a place at the opposition table. However, while their allies celebrated their sacrifices and their ability to compel wider activism, they did not see students as mature, autonomous political actors. Students mirrored such attitudes in their perceptions of the working class. In the postwar zeal for expanded democracy, activists and organizers were still figuring out how to form effective partnerships. Their biases undermined these efforts, and when combined with the regime's repression, alliances splintered.

The regime's ready use of violence indicated an important shift in the government's relations with its critics, especially those in the university. Gone was the paternalism that characterized Somoza's approach to student protest in the first half of the decade. Unable or unwilling to placate its youthful opponents, the regime turned to more brutal ways of eliminating their protests: kidnapping, torture, exile, and, sometimes, murder.

Faced with the regime's heavy hand, the inefficacy of the traditional political system, and the bankruptcy of the nation's democracy, students retreated into the halls of the university, reluctant to participate in national politics. By the end of the decade, a new generation of students eschewed overt political activism. In the 1950s, they would focus their energies on reforming a smaller arena: the university.

CHAPTER 3

Defending Student Dignity, 1950–1956

The students entering the university in the early 1950s had a very different understanding of the risks associated with political organizing. This cohort had come of age in the 1940s. They had witnessed the repression of a generation of student leaders who had opposed the Somoza regime. Many surely heard about the kidnapping of Francisco Frixione, the young activist who mysteriously disappeared and then reappeared badly beaten in 1944. They read in the news about the exile of César Carter Cantarero, the student dissident who nearly died during a hunger strike while in jail in 1947.[1] Some might have even marched in the 1948 silent protest that took place after the murder of the prominent student activist, Uriel Sotomayor Ramírez. The GN claimed the youth died after "a fall from his prison cot," but his crushed temple and battered body told a different story.[2] The violence sent a clear message that dissent was dangerous, and a generation of youth absorbed the lesson.

In the early 1950s, few took to the streets to criticize the dictator. Instead, students remained ensconced in the university and absorbed in campus conflicts. These young men and women worked out deals with politicians behind closed doors. They threw corncobs at substandard teachers. These are not the images associated with Cold War–era student protests, which usually involved mass marches and violent confrontations with state agents. Yet, the former forms of protest were just as common, if not more so. Mass protest was a powerful tool for challenging political authority, but it was not the only weapon in students' arsenal. In the 1950s, state repression bred innovation.

In the aftermath of the increasing violence that marked the onset of Nicaragua's Cold War, students may have retreated into the university, but they did not remain quiescent. Having witnessed firsthand the limitations of traditional political activism and experienced the political discrimination of their elders, students turned their attention to fighting the representatives of Somocismo most present in their daily lives: the faculty and staff of the university, many of whom were Somoza appointees or loyalists.[3] In part, this decision may have been based in self-preservation—Sotomayor's murder and the exile of several student activists were powerful deterrents—but their strategy was also pragmatic: if students were not welcome (or safe) in the political sphere, they would turn their campus into their own political stage. If they could not make Nicaragua more democratic, they would make the university more responsive to their will.

This was an approach that did not threaten the regime's hold on the nation, but it did limit Somoza's control over their school. In his groundbreaking study, *Weapons of the Weak*, James C. Scott lays out a two-pronged vision of resistance: "Where institutionalized politics is formal, overt, concerned with systematic, de jure change, everyday resistance is informal, often covert, and concerned largely with immediate, de facto gains."[4] This chapter examines the political activities between those two poles. Students in the early 1950s generally shied away from national politics—their experience with state repression and party bankruptcy in the 1940s had discouraged those efforts, but they also did not embrace "passive non-compliance, subtle sabotage, evasion" or any of the other "weapons of the weak."[5] They did not have to. Their class background and status as students usually protected them from the worst of the regime's excesses, which meant they had more room than peasants or workers to resist authoritarianism.

This relative privilege meant students could safely deploy more aggressive tactics, so long as they did not overtly challenge Somoza. Students drew on a range of actions, including strikes, political theater, declarations, and spontaneous displays of contempt to criticize the dictator's representatives, but they rarely directed their ire toward him. Indeed, they often requested Somoza intervene on their behalf. In this way, students hoped to claim the university as a privileged and protected space, and they understood only Somoza could make that happen. Focusing on student activism at the National University in León, this chapter shows how students both resented and sought to benefit from the patrimonial nature of Somoza's rule, while he himself managed to spin their protests and pleas for assistance in ways that benefitted his personalist regime.

Nicaragua in the 1950s

Understanding the changing nature of student opposition to the dictator requires a closer look at the state under Somoza. In the early 1950s, the regime was stronger than it had been in years. Somoza freely used the power of the state to shore up his base and consolidate his rule. Force alone, however, does not explain his longevity. Somoza held on to power for so long because when he was not enriching himself from the state's coffers, he was undertaking moderate reforms, developing infrastructure, and promoting economic development. As members of a growing middle class, students and their families benefitted from these policies, but, at the same time, state repression fueled their opposition to the regime.

The 1950 presidential election illustrates the mechanisms that the regime deployed to stay in power. Promising economic advancement, expansion of social services, and infrastructure development, Somoza campaigned widely in April and May 1950. Conservatives made similar promises, but their campaign suffered from a lack of concrete policy suggestions and blatantly biased electoral procedures. Because voting was public, intimidation was rampant. Government employees, including soldiers, "asked" small businesses to donate to Somoza's campaign or risk losing their licenses to operate. The regime also distributed small cards that would be stamped at the polls if they voted for Somoza. If they did not, state employees would lose their jobs.[6] A stamped card also enabled ordinary citizens to pass military checkpoints and even avoid some charges.[7] In this climate, Somoza won easily; his party claimed 153,297 votes out of 202,698 cast.[8] While those numbers were surely inflated, many believed Somoza had won a majority of the electorate.

His victory testified to the general perception that his regime promised stability and development. The postwar economic boom, coupled with rising prices for coffee and cotton in the 1950s, fueled unprecedented economic growth. The price of coffee nearly quadrupled between 1946 and 1956. Government income rose from nearly 53 million córdobas in the 1945–1946 fiscal year to more than 282 million in 1955–1956. US aid and international loans subsidized various infrastructure projects. New roads and bridges along with expanded access to electricity were all tangible signs of development. Somoza also founded a national development institute that provided private companies with loans and technical advice. These measures created jobs and opened up pathways for advancement, and such developments pacified political opponents.[9]

The country's economic growth also led to the expansion of the middle class and the appearance of what the US embassy called "an upper-lower class."[10] Some of this could be attributed to the government: the number of state employees increased by 60 percent between 1945 and 1956, so that by 1956, nearly sixteen thousand people were employed by the state. With the increase in government income, their salaries likewise rose. The historian Knut Walter has argued, however, that the growth in the bureaucracy did not keep pace with the country's increasing budget or growing needs.[11]

The country's educational system best illustrates this phenomenon. While the amount of money for public education increased in this period, the number of children attending school grew along with it, and the increasing funds were not enough to affect the growing population. By 1956, 139,896 children were attending primary school, an increase of more than 10,000 from 1950, but in that same period, the number of school-aged children had grown from 229,700 to 291,416. Thus, by 1956, well more than half of the children in Nicaragua did not attend school.[12] The percentage of illiteracy hovered around 63 percent in the early 1950s.[13] As Walter concludes, the regime "barely held its own, if at all, in social programs."[14]

At the same time, the state continued to closely monitor and repress dissent. Throughout this period, the regime heavily censored any stories that might disrupt public order, a charge they interpreted quite loosely; punished criticism of its international allies; and prohibited any links between publishers and international organizations.[15] In a report on the country's political conditions, a US foreign services officer noted, that "there is little room for effective political organization or expression."[16]

Such tactics weakened an already enervated opposition. The leftist labor movement had been crushed in the aftermath of Somoza's 1947 coup, and campesinos had their hands full dealing with the devastating effects of the rapid expansion of cotton cultivation, which displaced many from the land.[17] Somoza had successfully co-opted Conservatives in 1950 by offering the party limited representation at all levels of government.[18] Frustrated with the bankruptcy of the traditional political structures, some dissidents tried to form new political parties, but their efforts were hamstrung by state repression and an inability to form effective alliances. Others embraced more violent measures. A bipartisan rebellion, organized in exile, attempted to overthrow the regime in 1954, but the Guard quickly thwarted it.[19]

This was the context in which students acted in the 1950s. For many, the ability to pursue higher education was a result of the economic boom. In 1951, Somoza ordered the university in Granada to close—evidently, to consolidate resources for the National University—and by 1956, more than a thousand students were studying in León.[20] Because elites traditionally sent their children abroad for their education, those who pursued higher education in Nicaragua came from middle-class families that directly benefitted from Somoza's development policies.[21]

That did not necessarily mean they supported the regime. It is hard to characterize student politics not only because little documentation from this period has survived but also because, with the exception of one group, the Juventud Somocista (Somocista Youth, or JS), students were not allowed to organize along political lines at the National University.[22] Newspapers suggest that Conservative students were a small minority who sometimes faced reprisals from faculty and staff.[23] Few students were leftists. The government had banned the Partido Socialista Nicaragüense (Nicaraguan Socialist Party, or PSN) in 1950, and the exile and repression of its leadership hindered the organization's growth in this decade. In 1956, Carlos Fonseca, Tomás Borge, and Silvio Mayorga founded a student branch of the PSN, but the party did not seem very interested in organizing students at this time, and the cell did not last long.[24]

A significant portion of the student body was allied with the Liberal party, and many apparently supported the regime. In 1955, Juventud Somocista leaders told researchers from the International Student Conference that they had about four hundred members. While the number seems quite large, it is not unlikely that membership was required to receive scholarships and other favors—a time-honored Somocista practice. In fact, Somoza's National Liberal Party funded the organization, and it was well known that one had to be a "favorite of the government in order to enjoy a scholarship."[25]

That said, there were certainly ardent Somocistas within the ranks of the student body, and the main source of political conflict was between those students who were against the regime (Conservative, Liberal, Socialist, or otherwise), and those who supported it. The former was the larger group. Given the advantages that came with membership, it seems safe to say that students who were not in the Juventud Somocista probably opposed the regime. Moreover, judging from the nature of their activism, the elected leadership of the student government at the university in León, the Centro Universitario, seems to have been fervently anti-Somoza in this period, and the levels of participation in their demonstrations indicate that this stance was widespread.

If, in the 1940s, anti-Somocista youth had learned how difficult it was to challenge the regime in the streets, then their successors would narrow their focus and take their fight to the classroom. They hoped to create a more democratic campus that respected student voices. Their battles against authoritarian Somocista administrators constituted one of the most visible forms of resistance to the regime in this period.

Defending Student Rights

Somoza may not have played a direct role in the university's day-to-day operations, but he selected the men who did. These appointments created a porous divide between the state and the university in León as Somoza wielded political influence in the school via surrogates who policed student politics. Not surprisingly, the university reflected the state's growing authoritarianism. Supporting the interests of the dictator, administrators censored students and promoted regime loyalists. Resisting the efforts to control them, students in the early 1950s fought for the right to use university space, to exercise free speech, and to fire well-connected but incompetent professors. They framed these protests as a battle for student rights, but the close connection between the state and the university meant that even these narrow demands constituted a subtle form of resistance to the regime.

University dissidents most often bumped up against the two most powerful representations of Somocismo on campus: the minister of public education, a Somoza appointee, and the Junta Universitaria, the school's governing board, which consisted of the state-appointed rector, or university president, his handpicked general secretary, and the heads of each faculty. Because the regime often handed out teaching positions, the board was typically stacked with ardent Somocistas.[26] These men controlled the use of campus spaces as well as the university's budget and other quotidian activities, and their decisions provoked some of the most intense protests of the era.

A 1950 conflict over the use of a school building exemplifies the struggle for student rights. In early November, the Centro Universitario, the student government at the university in León, learned that the Junta had denied them permission to hold their inauguration ceremony on campus. In response, the student center declared a strike. The administration was unmoved. The minister of education, Dr. Emilio Lacayo, told reporters that he supported the board and warned that if students missed more than fifteen days of class they would not be allowed to take their final exams, "even if that meant that the entire student body of the university of León would fail the current school year."[27] The strike leaders doubled down. They formed a vigilante committee to prevent strikebreakers from entering the building and encouraged students from across the country to join them. By November 4, 90 percent of university students were striking to demand the removal of the university board.[28]

Students leveraged their identity in the struggle against the board. Representatives of the strike committee told *La Prensa*:

The minister would not dare to fail all of the students in all of the faculties because that would mean paralyzing student life in Nicaragua since [students] in Granada have declared their solidarity with us in León if that happens. Moreover, that unprecedented act ... would provoke protests from university students throughout the American continent.[29]

Despite their small population, students believed that the critical function of the university meant that their strike (and any punishment they endured) was of national and even international importance. They were certain their peers throughout the hemisphere would take up their cause. International solidarity, and the publicity it would engender, was yet another tool students could draw on.

Aware that the dictator's word mattered most in an authoritarian regime, the protestors sent a delegation to plead their case to Somoza. In a letter they planned to present to him, the students decried "the damage to student dignity that results from requiring them to sign a document in which the university board imposes on them a series of conditions required to use the building." Such oversight quashed student autonomy and insulted their integrity. They explained that this incident was one of many where "the board systematically refuses to give permission to use the building anytime the student body wants to hold an event that is independent of the university's official authorities."[30] Students clearly believed they had the right to use campus space without undue administrative oversight.

In a dictatorship, such a demand had significant political undertones. The Junta had probably denied the students' request to use the building in order to prevent extemporaneous denunciations of the regime. In response, students felt the board was infringing on their rights as members of the university. They argued that the board's consistent refusal to allow them use of the building "converts the university board into a dictatorship."[31] It was an intrepid strategy: they were writing a dictator to ask him to stop the regime-appointed board from working like a dictatorship.

The students' tactics read like performance art, and their later actions underscored the heavy symbolism they used to critique the university and, by extension, the regime. As part of their protest, they planned a funeral march for their defunct liberties. At four in the afternoon on Monday, November 6, the student body, dressed in mourning, would leave the university from the stalled construction site for the new auditorium—a subtle critique of the regime, which had promised to complete the building. From there, *La Prensa* reported, they would walk through the streets of León, ending up at the cemetery where they planned to bury "their rights and liberties as students" as represented by "a liberty cap and the university insignias." Students expected members of Leonese society to join them in "solidarity with their ambitions for university autonomy or for liberties in the current university regime."[32]

If, at first glance, it seemed as though the students had inflated a relatively minor issue, the journalist's reference to the struggle for university autonomy clarified the stakes. The fight over university space and the students' desire to limit the board's authority were key elements of the university autonomy movement, which emphasized the principle of co-governance and the school's separation from the state. Indeed, the confident assumption that other students on the continent would support their protests made sense if they were framing their actions in terms of university autonomy—a struggle for which recent generations of students in the Americas had fought.[33]

As one of the first major student protests after the end of the democratic effervescence, this episode highlights a shift in goals and strategy. For much of the 1950s, students struggled to obtain the institutional independence that had been systematically denied in the 1940s when universities were closed and students punished at the whims of the dictator.[34] That said, the struggle for university autonomy was not apolitical. As this protest shows, student activism in the university often contained the seeds of a critique of the regime even if the students never overtly criticized Somoza. In fact, they often asked him to intervene on their behalf. However, the thrust of their protest was directed at the very way in which their university reflected the larger Somocista state, specifically in terms of the lack of free speech and the administration's authoritarianism.

Student confrontations with an overbearing university board were not uncommon in the early 1950s. For example, in late June 1951, weeks after Somoza had closed the university in Granada, students in León planned an event in honor of the Day of the University Student, which commemorated the 1944 Central University student protest. The board decided that the students could use a campus hall only if they submitted their speeches for review beforehand. The organizers balked, replying that "they are not under martial law that would require them to do what the board wanted." Again, students drew on the language of authoritarianism to critique the school administration. This time the board discreetly covered up the conflict. After the students cancelled the event in protest, the school organized its own day in honor of the students.[35]

The public response to this and similar incidents suggests a widespread belief that students had a special right to freedoms that were denied to the rest of society. Covering the canceled student event, leading newspapers *La*

Prensa and *Excelsior* protested the board's violation of the "freedom of expression within a cultural center."[36] A few months later, Dr. Carlos Cuadra Pasos, the Conservative intellectual, gave a speech in favor of university autonomy. He argued that the university "should, before and above all, be a stimulus of culture, open to all knowledge" and free of the nepotism that determined who won scholarships or faculty positions.[37] Such pronouncements were predicated on the idea that the university deserved to be above the political machinations that touched every aspect of Nicaraguan life, and Cuadra Pasos, as head of the loyal opposition, would have been very familiar with such maneuvers.

In addition to free speech, young Nicaraguans also believed they were entitled to a well-equipped and well-staffed university and they sharply condemned the state of their school. In late September 1951, an open letter, written under the likely pseudonym, Román Latino, criticized the minister of education and his hollow promises, writing that "the students are tired of waiting . . . our hopes and ambitions have been defrauded upon finding that the comfortable university residencies were nothing more than an ancient mansion full of bugs, that the famous libraries are really four cabinets with old moth-eaten books." The author further lamented the shortage of basic furniture, like chairs, and chronically absent professors.[38] The article's palpable frustration and detailed knowledge of the campus suggested a student author.

The university did not let such critiques go unpunished. A few days after the article appeared, university officials threw a student, Pedro Rafael Gutiérrez, out of the dormitory for criticizing the school in a newspaper. Threatened with expulsion, Gutiérrez refused to back down, telling reporters, "I protested because of the failure to comply with various orders, in our favor, that the minister gave to the student leaders." Moreover, Gutierrez claimed, students resented the many incompetent professors who were appointed for political reasons. When asked why Gutiérrez was expelled from the dorm, the minister of education replied, "The professors also have the right to defend themselves."[39] The university's denial of free speech was so complete that students could not even criticize their professors or the state of the university.

In these struggles, student activists could rely on some influential allies. The generation of dissident alumni, which had come out of the university in the mid-1940s, were now in a position to provide support. Pedro Joaquín Chamorro, the former student activist who had finished his degree in exile, was now the director of his family's newspaper, *La Prensa*, where he took up their cause. Chamorro wrote an impassioned open letter to the university rector, Juan de Dios Vanegas, denouncing his authoritarianism. Chamorro declared that a university without freedom of thought is "not a true center for professional study, but a political school, created for political convenience."[40]

Students also fought to have a say in hiring decisions, and they agitated aggressively against mediocre professors whose political ties ensured their employment. Sometimes they did so in ways that highlighted their immaturity. That was the case in late July 1953, when students revolted inside the classroom of a law professor they judged incompetent. *La Prensa* reported that "he left the classroom under a rain of corncobs."[41] Most demonstrations, however, were highly disciplined. In August 1954, law students called for the resignation of another ineffectual professor. After the faculty sided with their colleague, the student center voted unanimously to strike.[42] Writing to the university-wide community, the strike committee declared that their protest was "framed within the most basic rights of the university student."[43] Entitled to quality teachers, students felt they had a right to protest incompetent ones. This time, they rejected the idea of appealing to the state for support, telling reporters "they would not visit [the minister of education] because their problem is currently before the university board of the National University and not the Ministry of Education."[44] In so doing, students underscored their limited agenda—this was strictly a university-based struggle for student rights.

The regime and its loyalists in the university drew on an arsenal of repressive tactics to force the students back into the classroom. The head of the pharmacy school threatened to expel strikers in his faculty. In response, students called for his resignation as well. Other professors attempted to discredit the protest by implying that the students were being influenced by opposition politicians.[45] Then, the minister of education delayed the release of student pensions, ostensibly because of budget cuts, but the timing suggested otherwise.[46] Additionally, at least one professor announced that he would mark students absent for the days they were on strike, a move that jeopardized their ability to pass the class.[47] These strategies punished students on a variety of levels, and at least some youths left town to avoid political retaliation.[48]

The strike failed in the face of the administration's intransigence. Even though the protestors had won the support of some members of the faculty and larger society, the two professors refused to resign and the fifth-year law students who had initiated the protest called off the strike. In a final statement, they lambasted the professor who started it all for his "outrageous egoism" and argued that his "family relationship" with the secretary of the board ensured his continued employment in the university. The students also backtracked on their earlier declaration to not request government intervention: they blamed the minister and the president's refusals to get involved for the strike's failure.[49]

The students' statements emphasized the contradictions of their university-based politics. Products of their political system, they both challenged the regime's control (and the corruption it bred) and hoped to benefit from it in their struggle against the university administration. Because state violence had made traditional forms of political protest too risky, they challenged the regime in indirect ways. They drew on a variety of tactics to critique Somoza's representatives and wrest some control of the university away from them. In these efforts, young activists benefitted from the notion of student exceptionalism. They and their supporters relied on the idea that, as students of the National University, they were entitled to certain privileges, freedom of speech, freedom of assembly, the right to a decent education—all rights that the regime systematically denied the rest of society. A broader political critique was thus embedded within their demands, but students tempered that message by appealing to the dictator himself. Somoza, however, did not directly intervene in such university-based matters, that is, not until they jeopardized his own image.

Spitting on the Dictator

It is not a coincidence that the single largest protest in the university during the early 1950s occurred in response to an administrative decision that literally placed Somoza at the heart of the university. In mid-November 1952, students walking by the auditorium of the National University spotted a new addition to the hall's portrait gallery. Beside the paintings of the poet Rubén Darío and other illustrious national intellectuals hung a bronze plaque with the profile of the dictator, Anastasio Somoza García. An outraged crowd of students broke down a door, spat on the medallion, and denounced its presence. Later that day, the student government issued a declaration criticizing the board members responsible for placing the medallion in the auditorium.[50]

The university board in conjunction with the military acted quickly to repress the protest. They immediately suspended the eight student officers who had signed the declaration. Students responded by declaring a university-wide strike, and more than five hundred occupied their campus on November 16.[51] The next day, the state sent Guard reinforcements to León.[52] While the commander of the unit worked to suppress news of the activities, other soldiers moved against the students' leaders. In the pre-dawn hours of Tuesday, November 18, the Guard arrested the expelled students and put them on the first train to Managua, bound for the notorious El Hormiguero prison.[53] Although they were released soon after their arrival, their detention only heightened the already fraught atmosphere in León.

The tension brewing in the university city boiled over on November 18. The National Guard had cordoned off the university, isolating the one hundred students who still occupied the building and preventing others from joining them. All afternoon, the protestors threw firecrackers at the soldiers. At about six in the evening, the soldiers responded with disproportionate force. Somebody shouted, "Fire," and several Guards shot at the protestors, wounding at least two.[54] By the next morning, the university was empty, and soldiers stood guarding its locked doors.

What had happened? How had the conflict escalated so quickly? In the span of five days, the students had initiated an innocuous if provocative protest, the Guard had intervened, and blood was spilled. A closer examination of the failed negotiations, the public response, and the authorities' actions sheds light on the students' motives. What began as a protest against the presence of Somoza's portrait quickly turned into a rejection of the university's servility, its administrators' draconian tendencies, and the country's lack of representative democracy. The medallion incident demonstrates how the porousness that existed between the state and the nation's sole institution for higher education could both suppress student liberties and also protect them.[55] It also highlights the way in which Somoza managed to spin dissent to his own advantage.

Somocistas inside and outside the university attempted to defuse the threat through rumors and coercion. Administrators drew on a tested repertoire to repress the students. Low-income students receiving aid from the government were particularly at risk. The day after the expulsions, two Somocistas—a student and a professor—visited scholarship students to request that they sign a declaration in support of Somoza, threatening them with the revocation of their financial aid if they declined. The loss of their monthly stipend would have been devastating as it covered a third of their monthly expenses.[56] Academically weak students were also vulnerable to coercion, and the two Somocistas offered to let those who had failed the recent exams retake them if they signed the petition. Finally, regime supporters blamed the protest on the Conservative transfer students from Granada, who, they alleged, were trying to get the National University shuttered so that their school would be reopened. In this way, the regime's adherents exploited the vulnerabilities of the young people, whose poverty, politics, or academic record made them a target for the regime.[57]

The Somocistas had reason to be proactive—the student protest was attracting considerable support, especially after the shooting. Suggestive of larger societal displeasure, members of León's Social Club debated sanctioning two prominent Somocista professors who were members of the university board.[58] While some newspapers criticized the students' methods, most condemned the administrators' servility and the violence to which it led.[59] Pedro Joaquín Chamorro, the former student dissident who was now the director of *La Prensa*, again emerged as the students' most ardent defender. In an impassioned editorial, he declared that "depriving a person of their right to free expression is detestable, but to do so specifically in the university indicates with much more violence and truth the evils of capriciousness." He argued that "the University does not belong to Gen. Somoza nor does it belong to the Government" and should not be managed "as if it was a hacienda or a government dependency" where they "remove those whose opinions the government does not like." In essence, Chamorro was outraged with the regime's efforts to censor students simply because they attended a state-funded institution. However, the reality was that the regime denied most everybody those very rights. Chamorro declared that by suppressing student opinion, the regime was attempting to "mold minds by force."[60] For him, the freedoms of thought and expression were critical for the effective functioning of a university.

Other alumni who had marched with Chamorro in 1944 also rallied behind the new generation of dissidents. Many had helped found a new political party, the Unión Nacional de Acción Popular (UNAP), and they published an editorial on November 19, 1952, proclaiming their solidarity with the youthful protesters. Referencing their own history of struggle, they critiqued the expulsions and the censorship in the university and argued that "the future of the New Nicaragua is tied to the student youth. . . . The redemption of our pueblo depends on their dignified struggle for liberty."[61] Considering that the student protests of 1944 had garnered enough support to seriously threaten Somoza's hold on power, it is not a surprise that the protagonists of that struggle would see student activism as a galvanizing force for wider change. The difference, however, was that this generation of students was not trying to overthrow the regime.

The students' reactions to the Guard's violence underscored their relatively limited agenda. Surprisingly, they did not remonstrate the soldiers or even the state. Instead, they focused their ire on the university administrators, whom they blamed for calling in the soldiers. A law student, Alfredo Castro, described the attack in epic terms:

> Yesterday, the directors of the highest house of culture in Nicaragua became the directors of the most cowardly abuse, with their age on their backs, faint-

> hearted, numb with their primitive fear, they descended the steps of the university temple to beseechingly implore those from the barracks to rise up, [and] taking refuge behind the violent glare of the blade, in the plain light of day, they attacked the spirit and flesh of the university with bullets.

Castro and the other students made it clear that blame did not lie with the "Guardia who lacked the right to deliberate [the order]"; instead, it was on the backs of the board members who had called in the soldiers.[62]

Whoever was to blame, the Guard's rapid arrival exemplified the way in which the state and the university administrators operated in collusion. The Guard's presence and the violence that ensued showcased how even very narrow disputes, when rooted in the university, had the potential to quickly turn into a national political conflict because of the close connection between the school's administration and the state. Those links were precisely what the students objected to: if their initial protest was rooted in their anti-Somocismo, their mass mobilization in the aftermath of their leaders' expulsions was a response to the structural organization of their institution. They vehemently condemned the administration's subservience before the dictator and the way the board had come to mirror the dictatorship's authoritarian tendencies.

The students' declarations highlight these frustrations. Throughout the strike, the protestors only professed two demands: that their leaders be reinstated and that the board take responsibility for the violence. In essence, they wanted the board to respect their right to protest and to recognize some kind of limit to their power to expel students at will and call the Guard in to repress dissent. The students' struggle to be heard lay at the heart of the conflict. Moreover, they resented the partisanship the board promoted at the university, exemplified by the plaque. The presence of the plaque, as well as the draconian punishment inflicted on the protestors, betrayed what the students called the "servile and groveling attitude" of the board.[63]

In the wake of the shooting, several youths emphasized to the press that this was a struggle for student dignity. They told a reporter that "the events that have occurred at the national university are the result of the virile protest of the university against the members of the university board" and not, they implied, against the state. Moreover, they added, the protestors came from across the political spectrum, included Somocistas, and were united by their desire to defend "*la dignidad universitaria*."[64] They did not elaborate on how that dignity had been threatened, but it can be extrapolated from previous protests that students understood it to be based on the university's autonomy from the regime and students' ability to act unfettered within it.

As the strike wore on, it became clear that the porous divide between the university and the Somoza regime was exacerbating the situation. Students, at the urging of several professors, had drafted a pardon request that would have given the expelled leaders a one-year suspension. But when the professors received their petition, they told the young people that they needed to direct the request to Minister of Education Crisanto Sacasa. The students rushed to revise the document. Later that night more than one hundred students met with Sacasa at his home, where they received word from the board that only Somoza could grant an official pardon because "he represents the only authority with the power to revoke the decision of the university authorities." The students expressed their consternation. Why would they need an official pardon from Somoza? *La Prensa* reported that students "consider the Minister of Education qualified to resolve the issue of the pardon and see no reason at all that they are making them petition the president of the Republic." Sacasa explained that the ministers "are nothing more than clerks of the president." Things turned even more Kafkaesque when, at the end of the night, Sacasa said that, at any rate, the students could not introduce the request for pardon; legally, their expelled companions had to file it, but nobody knew exactly where those students were after the GN arrested them and took them to Managua. When student representatives requested that Sacasa ask for the return of their peers, he declined, saying "it is not necessary for them to come, they can sign the petition wherever they are."[65]

The efforts to revoke the expulsions reveal some of the difficulties of living under the regime. For one, the right hand seemed not to know what the left was doing, as evidenced by the confusion over who had the power to absolve the student leaders. In all likelihood, nobody wanted to issue the pardon because to do so might have risked offending Somoza. These kinds of machinations had inspired the students' initial protest and were now perpetuating the conflict.

As tensions continued to rise, all parties concluded that the only person who could end the conflict was the president himself. The spreading protests likely encouraged Somoza to intervene. The Guard had arrested two secondary students in Diriamba after they were caught promoting an impending solidarity strike at their school. In Matagalpa, where Carlos Fonseca, who later founded the Sandinista National Liberation Front, was finishing up his education, armed soldiers from the National Guard surrounded the secondary school after its students went on strike.[66] As repression grew, the situation appeared to grow increasingly out of control.[67] Newspapers began demanding that Somoza intervene.[68] Juan Ramón Avilés, the director of *La Noticia*, ran an editorial titled "Nicaragua Will Lose a Thousand Years"—a reference to the very real danger that the university's thousand students would fail the school year because of the absences accruing while they were on strike. The editorial implored Somoza to act. Carlos Tünnermann, who attended the university at that time, remembered the editor pleading, "You cannot allow one thousand students to fail, go and remove the medallion. Only you can."[69]

The regime was much stabler in the 1950s than in the previous decade. Somoza, though, likely recalled well the upheavals that had occurred in 1944 and 1946 when student protests against the lack of civil liberties had catalyzed wider mobilizations that destabilized his regime. Thus, it is no surprise that once the university strike threatened to turn into a national protest, he decided to act. Explaining to supporters that the medallion had been placed there without his knowledge, he declared he would resolve the problem himself.[70]

On November 27, 1952, the president arrived in León. Entering the hall with his military retinue, and under the astonished eyes of the Guard, local supporters, and dozens of schoolchildren, he took down the medallion.[71] Tünnermann recalled the awkward ceremony:

> He didn't greet anybody. He came in and went straight to the medallion, but it was a little too high, so he requested a chair. He got on top of the chair, grabbed the medallion, and tried to take it off with his own hands. Of course he couldn't. He requested a chisel and a hammer. They ran to find a chisel and a hammer, and he began to pound, Anastasio Somoza García, pounding, pounding, loosening it and when it was loose, he pulled it off and passed it to his son.[72]

They left immediately, *La Prensa* reported, "without saying a single word, leaving all of the local supporters and university authorities completely disconcerted."[73]

The episode was rife with humiliations and symbolic significance. Tünnermann's recollection collapsed the removal of the medallion and the 1939 removal of a portrait of the general that also hung in the auditorium. It was the portrait that required a chair to stand on, and it was Somoza's son who, at his father's request, removed it. The discrepancy matters less than the vivid memory of the ceremony's awkwardness. One can imagine the silent, uncomfortable crowd watching the powerful general remove his medallion.

Somoza's participation in such an embarrassing public spectacle gave him a chance to prove his presidential beneficence. By intervening in a way that seemed to highlight his humility, he portrayed himself as a benevolent leader, willing to humble himself to mollify the students. Moreover,

"When Somoza Took the Hammer." *La Prensa*, November 29, 1952.

he could reestablish order. The strategy apparently worked. According to the US embassy, the local reaction to the president's visit "was immediately favorable," and a raucous celebration awaited him at the train station when he arrived and left León.[74] While the regime likely organized the show of public support, it still indicated how Somoza capitalized on the situation to his political advantage.

The students' narrow agenda helped him do so. They took great pains to establish that their protest was not against the president himself. When they heard he would remove the medallion, they debated sending somebody to tell him that their opposition was "more than anything a response to the junta's treatment."[75] In this way, they attempted to distance themselves from any public critique of Somoza.

It was a savvy move on their part, for they hoped to capitalize on Somoza's benevolence to win their actual demands: the reinstatement of their peers and the removal of the board. After his trip to León, Somoza was visited by a delegation of students looking to plead their case. This time, with the threat of the strike's continuation, they won significant concessions. Somoza promised to reinstate the expelled youth and replace the present board. He even told the students that he agreed that the university administration and local authorities had responded poorly to their protest.[76] By December 6, classes had resumed, and while most of the old board remained in place, its members publicly declared their desire to cooperate with students.[77] The dictator had exercised his power on behalf of the students, and, in so doing, he ensured their compliance—for the time being.[78]

The conflict's resolution highlights one of the most surprising characteristics of student activism in the 1950s: the youths' ready appeal to Somoza for help. Indeed, what at first may appear to be a contradictory decision betrays their narrow agenda as well as their political shrewdness. Their disgust over the placement of his portrait and all that it represented may have started the conflict, but they understood well that, in a patrimonial style of government, he was the only person who could intervene on their behalf. For anybody else, taking down the portrait or pardoning the students would have risked insulting the dictator. Finally, the students could appeal to Somoza for help because they really were not making any larger political critiques or claims, as they said repeatedly. This was an issue between them and the board, and who better to solve it than the man to whom the majority of its members pledged loyalty? In this way, students managed to extract some concessions, but, along the way, they shored up the regime.[79]

The medallion incident highlights General Somoza's political skill. Reading the writing on the wall, he took the necessary measures to neutralize the threat to his regime that a nationwide strike might generate. Moreover, by intervening on behalf of the students and reprimanding his appointed officials, even if they were acting to protect his image, Somoza could portray himself as the benevolent and humbled peacemaker, a move that drummed up public support and reaffirmed the legitimacy of his rule.

In the strike's aftermath, the opposition press praised students as democratic heroes. Pedro Joaquín Chamorro valorized their protest in an editorial: "The students' firm and virile protest forced in our heavy climate a democratic solution. The determination of 1000 young men, later joined by the majority of the university's professors, resulted in General Somoza's effective correction in an area where we have never seen him or his government concede in any way." Chamorro was hopeful that the event would set a precedent, and that, from now on, the government would listen to public opinion. Strikingly, Chamorro neglected to mention the Junta's draconian response to the students' actions, which had been at the heart of their protest.[80] In his zeal to take the medallion incident as a teachable moment, Chamorro erased the protestors' central demand—the reinstatement of their expelled leaders and not the removal of the portrait.

Future generations made a similar mistake. Vilma Núñez, who moved to León for school in 1958, recalled the upperclassmen recounting "the struggles of the older people, like when they removed the medallion that Somoza tried to put in the university auditorium."[81] Alejandro Serrano Caldera, who also entered the university in 1958, remembered the incident: Somoza "had a conflict with the students ... it was a tense crisis situation between students and the dictatorship."[82] The crisis was actually brought on by the board, which represented the regime and was one of its daily manifestations in the students' lives, but it is significant that in the memory of these students, it was between their predecessors and the dictatorship.

The moment marked a significant student victory. Some fifty years after the protest, Carlos Tünnermann vividly recalled how they relished their triumph: "The holes [from the plaque] were there because the university authorities were so afraid that they did not dare fill in the holes, and we were happy. . . . Those holes marked the location of Somoza's medallion, which the students made him remove."[83]

In the early 1950s, students fought for a voice in the school's affairs. But what on the surface may have looked like narrow university-based protests, actually constituted struggles against the way life was organized during a dictatorship and, in particular, the blurry line between state and university. Yet, just as that blurry line was the source of the problem, it also provided the students a chance to exploit their connection to the regime and vice versa. Indeed, the medallion incident illuminates the nature of the political game in 1950s Nicaragua, as students sought to protect their own rights and role in the university, no matter the means, and Somoza sought to co-opt the opposition to bolster his legitimacy. Realizing their vulnerability, students would spend much of the decade seeking the solidification of that line that separated the state and the university.

The Legislative Struggle for University Autonomy

The medallion incident underscored the need for institutional autonomy, and from then on, students prioritized that struggle. Reduced to its most essential elements, university autonomy meant both political separation between the state and the university and student participation in its administration. The movement is most famously associated with Córdoba, Argentina. In 1918, students there rebelled against a university system they felt to be archaic, authoritarian, and isolated from its society. After months of protests, they won several major demands, many of which are hallmarks of today's modern university, including academic freedom, merit-based hires, co-governance, research, and community engagement. A wave of Latin American countries subsequently adopted what became known as the Córdoba reforms, and by mid-century, most had autonomous public universities.[84] In the 1950s, Nicaraguan youth worked hard to join their ranks, even drafting their own legislative bill that would give the National University autonomy. In so doing, they sought to protect and institutionalize the privileges associated with being a university student and the role they hoped to play in the nation.

During the medallion protest, a group of law students, working with faculty advisors Mariano Fiallos Gil and José Pallais Godoy, founded the Círculo de Estudios Jurídicos y Sociales (Juridical and Social Studies Circle, or CEJIS), which was dedicated to promoting student engagement with the university.[85] In July 1953, the student government tasked CEJIS with writing an autonomy bill. Members researched the laws that had given other Latin American universities their autonomy, held conferences on the subject, and sought to drum up public support for the project.[86]

In 1955, CEJIS unveiled a bill that would create a democratic and democratizing university. Advocating for the creation of a school of humanities, research-oriented departments, and academic freedom, the authors articulated a vision of a university capable of creating an engaged citizenry. Graduates, they insisted, must emerge from the university with a sense of "national responsibility," ready to act as "agents of cultural democratization." To do this, the university needed to go to the people, whether by offering extension classes for workers or making it easier for students who had to work full time to attend classes.[87]

The bill also democratized administrative and hiring decisions. Critiquing the system of clientelism that awarded faculty positions to regime loyalists, the authors proposed a competitive hiring process and demanded higher salaries for professors so that they could dedicate themselves exclusively to teaching. The rector would be elected by a body composed of students and faculty members instead of by the minister of education as in recent years. Combined, these changes removed Somoza's control over university employees. Finally, the bill called for elected student representatives to serve at each level of the university's administration, from the governing council to the electoral committee, and even on each faculty's governing board. These positions, the authors argued, would help students become more responsible and more invested in the life of the institution.[88] It would also help safeguard their rights, as students would now be part of the committees granting permission to organize events and establishing policies.

The bill would create a modern university that produced citizens and not just professionals—a refrain repeated often in the 1950s.[89] The school was to be a training ground: a place to experiment with ideologies and methodologies and practice bureaucratic administration and civic engagement. The bill thus protected the students' freedom to express themselves, to assemble, and to participate as equals with their elders—precisely because these practices would create the kinds of socially conscious citizens the nation required. This vision was in keeping with the messages students had been hearing since the 1940s—that they played a vital role in the nation's future and as such deserved resources and privileges denied other sectors. Somoza himself had said so. His opponents said so. Now students were merely requesting that the rhetoric of student exceptionalism be institutionalized.

Their proposed legislation clearly jeopardized Somoza's hold on higher education, and the regime would not take such an assault lightly. Bolstering the university's independence from the state would take away Somoza's discretionary power over the school and its students, one of the more powerful tools the regime had to ensure student quiescence. No longer would students have to maintain deferential relations with the dictator in hopes of winning his support for their struggles with the administration. Nor would they have to call on Somoza to defend their rights, which would now be enshrined in the law. In October 1955, their bill was introduced to Congress, where it was soundly defeated twenty-five to five.[90] Once again, students learned that their lack of real political power meant their ability to push through legislation was negligible.

The Dictator's Assassination

The effort to win legislative autonomy thrust students back into the political scene. Around the time that they were finalizing their proposed legislation, it became clear that Somoza had no plans to relinquish power. In 1955, he proposed a constitutional change that would allow him to run again for president and began campaigning.[91] The prospect of continued Somocista domination galvanized the opposition, including many students, and the regime greeted the protests with escalating repression.

Students drew on a variety of tactics to challenge the regime and organize the opposition. In August 1955, anti-Somocista students began trying to forge an opposition coalition, bringing together Conservatives and Independent Liberals both inside and outside the university.[92] That year, during the annual fiesta, which often commented on national politics, their queen magnanimously declined efforts to "reelect" her.[93] Students also made more direct protests: the night before León was to host a parade in honor of Somoza's bid for his party's nomination in February 1956, unknown persons threw rotten eggs all along the planned route. The National Guard suspected the students' involvement and arrested several. The day of the event, students slipped into the university and unfurled a black flag over part of the building as a sign of mourning. In fact, the authorities had feared precisely such actions and had taken preventative measures against several prominent anti-Somocista students, whom they arrested without specifying a cause on the night before the president's arrival.[94] The students' tactics might seem minor, but they disrupted any sense of consensus that the president hoped to capitalize on. The young protestors, after all, were operating in León, the Liberal stronghold, and these public displays of opposition highlighted the divide within the president's own party.

To many, it appeared that the general was settling in to rule for life, and a small group of anti-Somocistas in exile decided to take more extreme measures. In early 1956, a former student, Rigoberto López Pérez, made contact with Nicaraguan exiles in El Salvador and volunteered to assassinate Somoza.[95] Late in the evening of September 21, as the city's elite celebrated Somoza's official nomination for the presidency, López Pérez entered the party and shot the dictator four times at close range. After an observer wrestled him to the ground, a soldier shot him twenty times, killing him. Somoza died a few days later, on September 29, in the Panama Canal Zone, where President Dwight Eisenhower had arranged for him to be treated by his personal physician. His son, Luis, as president of the National Assembly, was next in line for the presidency and was sworn into office later that day. His younger son, Anastasio Somoza Debayle, commanded the National Guard.[96]

The second generation of Somozas unleashed a wave of repression. The US embassy recorded that, "as precautionary measures," known dissidents were arrested, including "some 60 key communists and most of the leaders of the two opposition parties." The small Socialist Party bore the brunt of the initial blame for the assassination, with the regime assuming early on that communists must have been involved.[97] In addition, the Guard arrested key staff members from the major opposition papers, and the state imposed severe censorship on those that continued printing.[98] Historians have reported high numbers of arrests: anywhere from hundreds to thousands of civilians were detained, including members of both the opposition and the president's own party.[99]

The regime did not hesitate to torture suspects. Clemente Guido, a student who had been in contact with Nicaraguan exiles in El Salvador, described the brutal beatings as well as the water torture he endured while confined.[100] Pedro Joaquín Chamorro, the director of *La Prensa*, was reportedly held in a cage next to those that housed the lions in the Somoza family's zoo. He later wrote about the "electro-therapy" the Guard administered to the prisoners and other forms of severe psychological and physical torture.[101]

Students were not spared the repression. The Guard targeted prominent leaders. They ransacked the offices of the Centro Universitario and confiscated the organization's archives.[102] More than twenty youths, from the president of the student center to the editor of its newspaper, were detained.[103] These were visible student leaders and political activists. Arnulfo Dolmus, the president of the university student center, was an outspoken Independent Liberal who had denounced Somoza's reelection bid.[104] Carlos Fonseca, who edited a reincarnated *El Universitario*, and Tomás Borge were also well-known dissidents, and their organizing extended beyond university-based activities and into the circles that apparently orchestrated the attack.[105]

By the end of the military trials in January 1957, sixteen men were behind bars and the country had settled into a fragile peace.[106] The state had released many of the prisoners, including several students. They returned to their classrooms and began preparing for their final exams, with the knowledge that at least one of their peers and a few of their professors were still in jail.[107]

Conclusion

In the early 1950s, student resistance was not overtly concerned with national politics. They did not explicitly condemn Somoza's authoritarianism or comment on the bankruptcy of the two-party system. They did not demand social justice or land reform. Yet, in pursuit of narrower goals, they openly refused to cooperate with the regime's surrogates in their university. In so doing, they still managed to destabilize their society. This form of resistance lies somewhere between the institutional political organizing and the "weapons of the weak" James Scott has described. Student protests in this era highlight some of the creative ways that youth managed to demand concessions and contest authoritarianism in the face of repression.

Their focus on protecting student privileges challenged the agents of Somocismo most present in their daily lives: university administrators and faculty. To push back against the "dictatorial rule" of these Somoza surrogates, students demanded full membership in the university: they wanted control of common space, quality teachers, and better resources. These rights, they argued, were essential to their dignity as students. On the surface, their demands might have seemed driven by self-interest, but the struggle for university autonomy sought to create a university removed from the influence of the state, one that might be a civic bastion. Moreover, their demands highlighted the regime's failings—the denial of basic liberties, incompetent political hires, and inadequate infrastructure. Young activists drew on a repertoire of tactics that challenged the regime's rule without directly confronting Somoza. They went on strike, lobbied the dictator, visited the press, and organized acts of political theater.

They could deploy these tactics precisely because their status as students provided them a ready network of protection. They relied on the backing of both international students and notable alumni. Many of the leaders of the mobilizations in the 1940s had become prominent public figures. Pedro Joaquín Chamorro at *La Prensa*, the former student activists who founded UNAP, and others used their position to call attention to student struggles. The students' supporters recognized their collective potential and demanded they be given the privileges the regime denied everybody else. In this way, students and their complaints about the quality of the university became a convenient and relatively safe vehicle to criticize the regime.

If their status as students gave youth a relatively privileged place in their society, it also hampered their ultimate political efficacy. Students may have been able to make overt demands on the state for the sake of their education, but in so doing, they also paid homage to the power of its ruler.

CHAPTER 4

"La Pequeña Gran República," 1956–1959

In June 1958, when Vilma Núñez arrived in León for her first year as a law student, the National University had just won its autonomy. The administrative and legal separation of the school and the state, which President Luis Somoza Debayle had decreed a few months before, meant that the university had become one of the few public spaces beyond the regime's control. For students, this was an incredibly exciting time, and Núñez recalled the vibrant sense of possibility that filled the university:

> I believe I lived the most beautiful epoch of the university. We were enjoying autonomy for the very first time .... I felt like it was a shield that as long as you had it ... nothing could happen to you. That from within the university it was possible to propel the struggle and that more than that ... it was invulnerable to the attacks of all and that we could do so many things.

Núñez decided to join the Centro Universitario de la Universidad Nacional (CUUN), the university's student government, where she met students who had embraced a variety of political ideologies from communists to Christian Democrats.[1]

León in the late 1950s had become Nicaragua's cultural and intellectual center with the university at its heart. Under the guidance of Mariano Fiallos Gil, a Somoza appointee, the National University became a tightly knit community, offering cultural, scientific, and other programming open to all. The public, in turn, embraced the school and its young charges as their own. Núñez recalled how the family from whom she rented a room adopted her as one of their own, watching her more closely than her own mother.[2]

The modernization of the university and the emergence of a cohesive community around it were possible in part because of the ascendance of a new Somoza. When Luis Somoza took power after his father's death, he initiated some democratic reforms. Hoping to improve Nicaragua's image abroad, the new president took measures to open up the country's political sphere. For university students, the greatest manifestation of the state's new orientation was Somoza's decision to grant the university autonomy in March 1958. A newly independent administration, led by Mariano Fiallos Gil, set about remaking the National University. Students responded to their new freedom with a burst of mobilization, lobbying for the release of Tomás Borge, a peer who had been in prison since Somoza's assassination, and organizing a nation-wide protest movement when the regime refused.

At the same time as the regime promised expanded freedoms, the Somozas continued to operate a vast military apparatus that abused, arrested, and murdered dissidents. Thus, while students experienced a level of freedom previously unknown, which enabled their militant criticism of the regime, they soon bumped up against the limits of university autonomy. The school's administrative independence from the state ensured that students' freedoms were protected on campus, but such liberties did not extend to the streets or to the people, including the many secondary students, who joined their protests. Outside the hallowed halls of the university, the National Guard continued to crack down on protestors, as epitomized by the 1959 shooting of peaceful student demonstrators that left four dead.

The students' response to the attack illuminates both their organizing skills and the ways in which they drew on gendered perceptions of masculine honor and feminine vulnerability to protect their privileges. Women played a key role in mobilizing outrage, and they relied on traditional notions of chivalry to protect them as they crossed the city to organize other sectors. Scholars have examined the challenges facing the generation of young women who became politically active in the sixties, but Nicaraguan women were already risking their reputations and their safety to challenge the state in the late fifties.[3] The male-dominated student leadership meanwhile deployed notions of masculine dignity to legitimize their struggle against the regime. In so doing, however, they elided the presence of a cohort of young women who were actively working to garner wider support for the movement.

The dawning of the era of university autonomy highlights the contradictions of the regime under Luis Somoza and the limitations of the students' strategies. The official separation of the university from the state meant that the school could finally become the civic bastion that students had been envisioning since the 1940s. However, in practice, the dictatorship severely circumscribed the students' ability to organize beyond their campus. Moreover, the regime did not fully respect the sanctity of their school. Somoza openly acknowledged the presence of spies, and armed soldiers studied alongside students.

University autonomy, youth and their supporters learned in the 1950s, would not be enough to protect student political liberties or turn the university into a democratizing force, but it did cement notions of student exceptionalism. Their membership in an elite institution, one of the very few beyond the regime's control, instilled in students a sense of privilege and possibility. They used their newfound freedoms to mobilize their wider society. When those privileges were violated, as they were in the 1959 massacre, students embraced a level of militancy not yet seen in Nicaraguan history.

Luis Somoza's "Representative" Democracy and University Autonomy

In 1956, when Luis Somoza assumed the presidency, he faced a variety of challenges. Considerable opposition to his family's rule fueled a period of intense political tension. Discontent even came from within his own National Liberal Party, where dissidents threatened to run their own candidate or ally with the Conservatives. Rumors of their late father's wealth, estimated as high as $50 million, made the Somozas targets of popular and elite anger, and the regime faced a growing number of attempts to overthrow it.[4] In light of the many threats to his legitimacy and the regime's instability, the new president instituted some democratic reforms, which included granting the university its autonomy.

In the 1950s, Latin America was entering into a period of revolutionary upheaval, and the new president likely understood that popular support at home and abroad would be necessary to maintain political stability. In Guatemala, a US-sponsored coup overthrew the democratically elected government of Jacobo Arbenz in 1954, initiating an era of violence and unrest. The success of the Cuban Revolution in 1959 inspired a new generation to adopt armed struggle. In Nicaragua, between 1956 and 1959, there were at least five insurgent attempts as various sectors, radicalized by the repression that followed Somoza Garcia's assassination, took up arms. Conservatives, military officials, leftists, and others organized guerrilla movements in this period, sometimes working together but just as often not. The Somozas' deep unpopularity throughout the region ensured support from abroad: both the Honduran president and the Cuban government, for example, provided logistical assistance for an insurgent force that was later massacred at

El Chaparral in Honduras in 1959.[5] In the end, however, these movements lacked the popular support and urban organizing that could sustain what was sure to be a prolonged conflict with Somoza's well-trained military.[6] Nonetheless, repeated invasions, even if short-lived, jeopardized the image of stability Somoza hoped to project.

Neither was Somoza helped by the economy. Nicaraguan elites in the early 1950s had dedicated more and more land to cotton cultivation, which had become increasingly profitable. However, in 1956, the prices for cotton began to fall steadily, and the Nicaraguan economy entered into a brief recession. Hardest hit were the peasants, who had been driven off the land in the rush to plant more cotton, and the poor in general because food prices had risen as growers had replaced grain fields with the more lucrative fiber.[7]

In the face of these political and economic tensions, Somoza enacted several reforms that professionalized the bureaucracy and distributed power, at least somewhat. For example, he forced many state employees to quit their second and third jobs so that they could devote their attention exclusively to the state institutions that employed them. He also delegated some tasks to close associates like his brother Anastasio, whom he placed in charge of the National Guard, and his brother-in-law and ambassador to the United States, Guillermo Sevilla Sacasa.[8] These small attempts at spreading power suggest the kind of representative democracy Somoza envisioned, one where loyal Somocistas, if not Somozas, shared power.[9]

The president's decision to grant university autonomy reflected this new context. Nicaragua's status as one of the last countries in Latin America without an autonomous national university reinforced the country's undemocratic image. Moreover, abdicating the right to intervene in the affairs of the school fell in line with Somoza's professed desire to open up the government. As part of that effort, he had reorganized his cabinet, appointing Dr. René Schick and Dr. Pedro J. Quintanilla to head the Ministry of Education. Tasked with revamping the national educational system, these men looked to one of their former professors, Mariano Fiallos Gil, to help modernize the National University.

They offered the position of university rector to Fiallos Gil, a respected intellectual, a lawyer who had studied at the University of Michigan, and a professor popular with his students. He was, however, not easy to convince. A long-time Liberal, Fiallos Gil had taken several state positions in the 1940s—career moves he grew to regret once the regime's authoritarianism became apparent. According to his biographer, he feared becoming a pawn of the newest Somoza. Eventually, he accepted the position with several conditions: total freedom to hire employees and control the budget, university autonomy within a year, and more resources. To his surprise, Somoza agreed, and Fiallos Gil became the rector of the National University of Nicaragua on June 6, 1957.[10]

Somoza's acquiescence makes sense when we consider his interest in modernizing Nicaragua. Carlos Tünnermann, a former student who became Fiallos Gil's secretary, suggests that the decision was related to Somoza's plans for the country.

> Central American integration was occurring at that time, the economic integration. And Luis Somoza, who was a businessman and the brightest of the Somozas, the most prepared, realized that Nicaragua was going to need professionals who were better qualified, was going to need to prepare at a higher level, and that the university needed to be radically transformed.[11]

In this context, then, Somoza, ever the astute businessman, was thinking of the quality of the university's graduates, and Mariano Fiallos Gil had a supremely qualified resume. He had worked in the Ministry of Public Instruction and Physical Education under Somoza García in the early 1940s and had been the rector of the Central University in 1944 during the student protests that nearly toppled the regime. During those upheavals, Fiallos Gil had not hesitated to shut down the university, and his hard line, which he later explained as a move to protect the students, may have helped convince Luis Somoza that, as rector of the new university, he would keep the students under control.[12]

Somoza granted the university autonomy in March 1958, ushering in an era of relative freedom for the student body. However, because university autonomy was an executive decree, it could be repealed by the president at any time.[13] Consequently, even this long-wished-for gain remained susceptible to the whims of the dictatorship. Just as his predecessor had wielded the carrot and the stick, so too did the new president, balancing the repression that followed in the wake of his father's assassination with gestures toward a more democratic opening. Students and faculty would seize the opportunity.

Building "A Small Great Republic"

Upon assuming the leadership of the National University, Fiallos Gil began building an intellectual community, one dedicated to the nation and its people. His great refrain was that the university should not merely produce professionals; it should mold an engaged citizenry. To do this, he sought to turn the university into "la pequeña gran república," complete with entitlements for members and outreach to non-members.

If he could not do much about the ramshackle state of the buildings, the run-down classrooms, the dated equipment, and the poorly stocked library, then Fiallos Gil would recreate the spirit of the university. As part of his Liberal humanist philosophy, the rector believed the institution should place the development of humanity at the center of its mission, and, in this pursuit, it had an obligation to address the most pressing issues facing the nation.[14] In a letter to students he handed out on the first day of classes after the autonomy announcement, Fiallos Gil spelled out his vision of a humanist university upon which the health of the entire nation depended. The institution, he said, should be "on a permanent state of alert to serve and defend mankind."[15] Significantly, he believed higher education should empower students to take an active role in the world around them, including in contemporary debates and struggles.

To cultivate this vision, Fiallos Gil took measures to professionalize the university's staff and create a modern academic faculty. Wanting professors who were "exclusively dedicated to the scientific life and to teaching," he requested that all teachers submit a document listing their educational history, teaching experience and curricula, attendance at professional conferences, and publications.[16] The request sent a message that the new rector expected faculty to meet certain professional and pedagogical standards. He set an even higher bar for himself: he followed a punishing schedule of international meetings and organized more than fifty local conferences in his first year alone.[17]

Clearly, Fiallos Gil set a premium on the exchange of ideas. Sergio Ramírez, who entered the university in 1959, has written that, under the rector's direction, "the university became for the first time a public place for debates, where one heard the most varied and contradictory theses, and it was a beautiful way that the university could affirm its status as the nation's conscience, as a living being, active and awake."

Students occupied a firm place within the university's administration and services. While they had previously held a single seat on the university assembly, under Fiallos Gil, they enjoyed representation on the university board and on the boards of the individual faculties. In practice, however, the principle of co-governance was more about representation than sharing power—after all, there was only one student on each board, which was made up of anywhere from six to twelve members.[18] That said, students did enjoy decision-making power in other areas. For one, the administration placed students in charge of several university publications.[19] For example, the student representative on the university board, Denis Martínez Cabezas, also served as the director of the new biweekly *Gaceta Universitaria*, which would keep the general population abreast of the university's activities.[20] The university also began printing a monthly literary magazine, *Cuadernos Universitarios*, which featured works by students, professors, and national writers.[21] These publications not only brought together faculty and their pupils in a joint intellectual endeavor, but also publicized the kind of work and research the institution produced and, in this way, helped root its place in the nation.

In a move that promoted community and student identity, Fiallos Gil prioritized student services. In his first year, he moved the single student dorm from its dilapidated building to a better location and then opened another dorm to ease overcrowding. Combined, both housed nearly one hundred students.[22] More students could now live near campus, where previously many had rented rooms in the more inexpensive barrios on the outskirts of town.[23] To further integrate students and faculty, the university founded the University Club in 1958, complete with a gymnasium and fitness classes. Although the administration complained that not as many professors used it as they would like, the club provided students with a central meeting space. It held the offices of the CUUN and was a place where students met to relax and unwind, meet up, and organize.[24] Finally, the administration turned its attention to the pupils' well-being: it organized a system where local doctors saw students for free, funded a theater troupe, and offered intramural basketball, baseball, and weightlifting teams.[25] Hallmarks of today's universities, such services and activities ensured that students were spending more time together, exchanging ideas, and enjoying leisure time. These interactions and the privileges that enabled them forged a sense of identity rooted in the school and centered on their status as students.

Fiallos Gil's vision of community also looked outward, and he stressed the university's obligation to society. In a 1957–1958 report, the university's secretary general, Carlos Tünnermann wrote:

> In accordance with the modern tenets of the university, the National University tried to convert itself into a true organ of cultural diffusion, sponsoring a series of activities destined to foster contact between the University and the public, as universities cannot enclose themselves within their own cloisters but rather, breaking barriers, they must take the results of their research, studies and teachings to the people.[26]

The university administration thus initiated a series of public literary and artistic contests that showcased local artists, poets, and writers. It also organized several talks from national intellectuals on issues ranging from agrarian reform to the oeuvre of Rubén Darío.[27] In addition, individual faculties offered special lectures to further professional development and to reach out to the general public. For example, the law school organized talks on legal issues for practicing lawyers, as well as a series of courses for workers that focused on legal rights, the structure of the government, labor laws, and hygiene.[28] Seeking to put the students' budding professional skills at the service of the community, the dentistry school even opened a public clinic.[29] These outreach efforts exemplified the university's growing commitment to the nation and its people. If such programming did not necessarily break down class borders, it certainly helped connect students, and their alma mater, to various sectors of society.

At the center of Fiallos Gil's vision for a humanist university was the active and engaged *universitario*—a citizen of the university, whether they be faculty, student, or staff. Universitarios had a duty to engage with the day-to-day life of their institution as well as to make that life relevant to the wider society that, in the rector's view, depended on them. Writing in his 1958 letter to the students, Fiallos Gil declared, "The health of all, the nation's prosperity, the agricultural and industrial businesses, the public administration, the future of our children, the orientation of our thought depends on the university."[30] Nicaragua, he felt, was underdeveloped precisely because its university was not producing the number and quality of professionals the country required. Now that the university finally had received its autonomy, he urged students to keep in mind that they were an "elite and for that reason with many more responsibilities than rights, more obligated ... more necessary to the nation than any other group ... because we are UNIVERSITARIOS and in us rests the honor, the pride and prestige of the nation."[31] This call to arms instilled in students a sense of duty to the nation, to each other, and to their alma mater.

The university's growing population also boosted students' understanding of their national importance. Their numbers more than doubled during Mariano Fiallos Gil's seven-year tenure. In 1957, when he became rector, 919 students were enrolled in the Universidad Nacional de Nicaragua; by the time of his death in 1964, there would be 1,913 youths studying at the Universidad Nacional Autónoma de Nicaragua (UNAN) at its two campuses in León and Managua.[32] This population growth was directly related to Fiallos Gil's efforts to modernize the institution. His administration expanded the university and its course offerings. When he took office, students could earn degrees in five fields: law, engineering, medicine, pharmacy, and dentistry. At the time of his death, they had many more options—including

Table 4.1. Enrollment at the UNAN, 1956–1965

School Year	Total Number of Students	Male	Female
1956–1957	970	864	106
1957–1958	919	813	106
1958–1959	946	811	135
1959–1960	1199	1020	179
1960–1961	1267	1037	230
1961–1962	1379	1121	276
1962–1963	1496	1175	321
1963–1964	1621	1255	366
1964–1965	1913	1455	458

Source: UNAN, Oficina de Registro y Estadística, *Composición de la población estudiantil por facultades, escuelas, años de estudio y sexo en la matrícula inicial, 1950–1964* (León, Nicaragua, December 1964)

economics, education, and journalism — and they could study on three different campuses: León, Managua, or Jinotepe.[33]

These expanded offerings enabled a more diverse student body to pursue higher education. A university study from the late 1950s found that the majority of students came from families of "small means."[34] According to Fiallos Gil, many of those studying at the National University were the "children of school teachers, washerwomen, artisans, small business owners and workers." Consequently, many relied on financial assistance from the university, while others had to work to afford room, board, and books.[35] A significant sector of students thus had known economic hardship, whether it occurred while they were growing up or while they were studying in the university. To be clear, the students attending the National University in the late 1950s were still a privileged sector: just 0.004 percent of their age group made it that far in 1955.[36] However, more youth were coming from lower middle-class and working-class families. This slow diversification would continue in the decades to come.

Although men constituted a clear majority of students in this period, the percentage of women grew steadily. For the 1958–1959 school year, 135 of the 946 students were women (14 percent). In Vilma Núñez's entering law school class of 113, only twelve were women.[37] In the traditionally male-dominated space of the university, these women experienced varying degrees of discrimination. Núñez's status as one of the best students in her class gave her access to administrators and decision-making bodies: she was chosen to represent students on the law school faculty board, and she enjoyed an excellent working relationship with Fiallos Gil and other administrators who taught some of the law classes in which she excelled.[38]

Other women, especially those who were married or became pregnant, had very different experiences. For example, one married student, Socorro Jerez de Connolly, asked the president of the CUUN to intervene because her pharmacy professor would not excuse the days she needed to take off to have her baby, and she would thus be unable to take her exams. Frustrated, she wrote, "Only when they declare laws that prohibit married women from studying will I accept [the professor's] decision because it is impossible to demand a woman in such a delicate state attend class."[39] The letter reveals some of the difficulties that married women faced in the university: inflexible professors and rigid attendance policies. Because the university only offered year-long courses, Jerez de Connolly could not take off a month to have the baby and recover because then she would exceed the allowed number of absences and be forced to repeat the entire year of coursework.

The student government's response to Jerez de Connolly suggests they were sensitive to such challenges. A day after discussing her case at one of their meetings, and in the midst of preparing for a momentous protest on July 23, 1959, the student government shot off a letter to the university board asking that it grant her thirty days leave and gently rebuking the body for not addressing her situation in its past two meetings.[40] The threads of the case end there, but their support for Jerez de Connolly indicates that students in the late 1950s were open to the presence of women in their university and tried to help them succeed.

That is not to say that female students did not endure sexism. Núñez recalled, for example, one male student who frequently pinched her. She also recounted a moment when faculty prevented her from joining a student demonstration that was occupying the campus. Although she believed that, at the time, the rector was trying to protect her from both physical harm and negative gossip, the incident, combined with the unwanted touching and the case of Jerez de Connolly, suggests a campus that could be a difficult place for women to navigate.[41]

Under the leadership of Fiallos Gil, the National University underwent unprecedented institutional changes, including the growth of the student population and the expansion of its programs and buildings. The rector's policies and rhetoric empowered students and faculty—urging them to engage with both the university and their country. These changes fostered a greater sense of community, not only inside the institution but also with the society around it, and students would use their newfound privileges to further those ties.

Testing the Bounds of University Autonomy

New students entering the National University for the first time in June 1957 were welcomed with an exhortation scrawled in red on the wall of a central courtyard: "Let us free Tomás Borge."[42] A politically active law student, Borge had been arrested after Somoza's assassination, and the message was a fitting welcome to a university regrouping under a new, empowering administrator and a student body readying to fight the regime.

If students had limited their activism in the early 1950s to issues that were strictly institutional, Fiallos Gil's tenure and the autonomy decree allowed them to expand their focus at the end of the decade. Thus, even though this period was marked by increasing political tension, caused by both the repression following Somoza's death and a rising number of insurgent attempts, students enjoyed an unprecedented level of liberty within the university. Autonomy meant a friendly administration and the freedom to act without fear of political retaliation—at least at school. In this context, students tested the limits of their institution's newfound independence and sought to forge connections with their peers at schools around the country. To free Borge, activists in the university constructed a nation-wide student movement.

Once the dust settled after the dictator's assassination, students began organizing anew. In the course of the "investigation," the regime had arrested more than twenty students, tortured and exiled others, ransacked the offices of the CUUN, destroyed their furniture, and confiscated their papers.[43] Now that a semblance of normalcy had returned, the student government focused on freeing those members of their community still detained, including Borge. The courts had sentenced him to jail time for his role in the conspiracy to kill Somoza. Although the evidence was dubious at best, he languished in prison with two university professors.

The student government initiated a multi-pronged campaign to win their freedom. Young activists formed the Committee for the Liberation of Tomás Borge in 1957. Working closely with the CUUN, the committee worked hard to keep the issue in the limelight. At school events, they virulently condemned their companions' imprisonment. The queen of the student carnival that year petitioned the government to free the universitarios who were still in detention "for the happiness of all of her subjects."[44] After winning university autonomy in March 1958, students took more direct measures. They wrote to Luis Somoza, arguing that the universitarios' continued incarceration contradicted his proposed "democratic transition" and created discord both in the university and in the wider society.[45]

When letters did not work, they went to the president himself. In early October, students heard that a prison administrator was threatening the lives of the three universitarios. In response, they organized an emergency assembly—newspapers reported that two thousand individuals attended—and the student government declared a twenty-four-hour strike. Fiallos Gil proffered his support and volunteered to set up a meeting with the president.[46] Vilma Núñez, who was part of the committee that met with Somoza, recalled that after they asked for their companions' freedom, the president

> became furious. He said that was a lack of respect ... how was it possible that we had come to ask for the freedom of his father's murderers? So then I immediately jumped up right then, and I told him, we did not come here to ask anything from the son, we came here to speak with the president of the republic ... he continued [lecturing us] but you know that reaction made him lower his tone ... it had made him realize that he was the president.[47]

His office notwithstanding, Somoza proceeded to threaten the students: "I'm warning you that I cannot control the soul of a soldier who could very well shoot a student in the head. It would mean little to me to split the heads open of 100 students, arrest 500 and finish with those subversive acts in the way they deserve."[48] For all his democratic posturing, the new president had little regard for the students' free speech and apparently little control over the military.

That was not the biggest bombshell. At one point in the meeting, Somoza seems to have freely acknowledged the use of spies in the university.[49] Students had known this for some time. After Somoza's assassination, several students, members of the Juventud Somocista, had collaborated with the National Guard—some had even turned their peers over to the soldiers.[50] But that was before the university autonomy decree, and students may have felt that now they had the legal grounds to organize more aggressive protests.

Understanding Somoza to be threatening both their civil liberties and university autonomy, they began mobilizing immediately. On October 13, 1958, they declared a forty-eight-hour strike. Eager to avoid any conflict with the military, they announced their intention to hold a peaceful protest, even sending messages to President Somoza and the minister of the interior informing them of their plans.[51] To garner public support, they alerted the media and international student organizations.[52] Tomás Borge's mother publicly called on the nation's mothers to cooperate with and support their striking children.[53] Declarations of solidarity and outrage began pouring in as word spread that spies in the university were betraying their fellow students.[54]

To maximize the effectiveness of their protest, university students needed the support of their peers at other schools. Nearly all of the student body at the National University had struck, but that was still only about a thousand people. The participation of youths at other institutions would significantly enlarge their numbers, but these were students who had been left out of the autonomy decision. For them, protesting would be risky.[55]

Younger teens were just as outraged at Somoza's declaration, however, and they readily joined. Indeed, many believed that his threats underscored the political marginalization of youth more broadly. University student leaders actively promoted this perception. The CUUN sent representatives to organize secondary students around the country. At one assembly in Matagalpa, a college student, Enrique Morazán, explained that their protest "was not political but civic and for the good of students who also have rights." He went on to insist that only by unifying could they force authorities to stop treating them as "social ballast." Another student spoke, saying that they wanted "to be heard as future citizens who will bring honor on the nation."[56]

A manifesto issued by the students of the Escuela Nacional de Agricultura y Ganadería (National School of Agriculture and Animal Husbandry, or ENAG) echoes the words spoken in Matagalpa. Their declaration stated:

> [W]e the students have not been taken into consideration, as if we do not constitute an important part of the popular voice of this nation, . . . [W]e protest the disparagement with which students from throughout the nation have been treated and demand with our voices raised that we have a right to be heard as an integral part of the Nicaraguan pueblo.[57]

The young protestors perceived this struggle to be about their right to participate in national politics without the threat of violence.

The participation of thousands of younger teenagers maximized the protest's disruptive capacity. For two days, hundreds of uniformed students marched through the streets of Managua, holding signs demanding freedom for the universitarios and yelling, "Viva la huelga!" Protesting students shut down traffic as they placed handwritten flyers on cars and asked passersby to join them. At many schools, students stood outside the entries, encouraging their peers to join the strikes, while at others, they stayed on the patios, not attending classes. Vivid images of students marching in the streets alongside their bicycles, of girls gathered in their Catholic school uniforms outside their schools, of enthusiastic boys in button-down shirts and ties pumping their fists in the air as they pose for the camera filled the pages of *La Prensa*.[58]

The threat of violence, however, was never far away, especially as the protests widened beyond the scope of the university. Fearing the Guard's reaction, Fiallos Gil had called President Somoza preemptively to emphasize the protest's peaceful nature. Somoza replied that he was "worried about what would happen but was sure that the matter would turn into a strictly university movement and that the events would be organized only in the university."[59] His statement highlighted the bounds of university autonomy— so long as the mobilization was limited to the campus, students could act.

Youth in secondary schools were not so lucky. In cooperation with local school directors, the regime prevented many from protesting and those who did endured beatings, arrests, and other forms of repression. President Somoza told the press that school authorities had requested Guard intervention and the record shows the military readily complied.[60] In Managua, Jinotepe, León, and elsewhere, soldiers and Somocistas circled secondary schools to prevent students from leaving and agitators from entering.[61] Reports of soldiers beating and threatening students circulated. Administrators locked the doors at a school in the capital. When a group of marching students intensified their protests, the Guard attacked them with rifles and pistols, detaining several and telling passersby to go home.[62] Photos taken that day show police armed with clubs and helmeted soldiers jumping down from jeeps to charge uniformed students.[63]

Secondary students experienced more mundane repression as well. At several schools, administrators threatened to take away funding from scholarship students—a move that constituted a severe blow to a family's finances and possibly the end of their child's education. Elsewhere, youths were suspended for "disrespecting" authorities when the protestors ignored demands to return to class.[64]

The regime's efforts to squash the strike underscored the clear limitations of Luis Somoza's "democratic opening." Even the university students' privileges did not extend beyond campus: the regime prevented students from holding a protest outside the university in León.[65] In Chinandega, soldiers broke up a march of some two hundred students, and then tried to arrest the university youth who had helped organize the demonstration.[66] The state also tried to censor the press, blocking communication from several news outlets and their correspondents. At one point, a soldier even confiscated a photojournalist's camera.[67] Luis Somoza was proving to be just as fearful of collective action as his father and just as willing to repress liberties.

Although Somoza did not free the detained universitarios or remove campus spies, the students did win several tangible victories. For one, the state took measures to improve the prisoners' conditions and, a few weeks after the strike, released Borge and the professors to serve the remainder of their sentences under house arrest.[68] Second, in a short period of time, students had managed to disrupt the nation's educational system. Writing to international student organizations, Carlos Fonseca, then the CUUN secretary of relations, wrote: "The University Center's call to our compañeros for a spirit of solidarity was heard with enthusiasm. We took pride in organizing for the first time in the history of the student movement in Nicaragua a general student strike."[69] Students estimated that ten thousand youths from across the country had participated, and almost three thousand attended the strike's closing assembly in León.[70]

For the student activists, the strike had been a dramatic show of force, a way of proving their organizing power. Writing to Nicaraguan students everywhere, the Centro Universitario explained that the strike had demonstrated to the president that the student movement was a force with which he would have to reckon. More than that, though, university student leaders explained that the protest had "awakened the civic consciousness" of students:

> [T]he precious fruit of the student movement occurred when you risked the scholarship that sustains your studies, when you disregarded the grade that rewards your work, when you confronted your teacher and sacrificed your obedience, when you felt on your body the traitorous blow of the butt of a gun or a rod, when you were taken prisoner by the police; in short when you made any sacrifice for the movement, you joined the ranks of those who have suffered for the country.[71]

The Borge campaign, consciously or not, had been an exercise in base building, and it had worked—a generation of youth had been empowered by their own ability to organize and protest. They had come to understand that they were part of something larger than themselves and that in concert they were working for the betterment of the nation.

Around the country, a new spirit of student *compañerismo*, or fellowship, became visible. University students used the term to describe the community of feeling that existed within the university and that pushed them to campaign for their imprisoned fellows. For example, when the CUUN formally requested that the university administration name the imprisoned teachers honorary professors, they wrote that they trusted in the "spirit of solidarity and *compañerismo* with their unfortunate companions that animates each one of its members."[72] The sense of fellowship extended to youths in other schools. Vocational students at the ENAG announced that "their strike is based in a sentiment of dignity and *compañerismo* and not with political or partisan ends."[73] In deciding to strike, the protestors asserted their membership in a national student body. As the leaders of CUUN wrote to their peers: "When you made the sacrifice of uniting yourself to our ranks, you went on to swell the youthful vanguard that will construct a new Nicaragua."[74] In other words, they were building a movement.

Such beliefs fueled a push for a national student organization. In the aftermath of the strikes, the CUUN sent commissions to all of the schools where secondary students reported harassment to look into the accusations and denounce reprisals.[75] At the meetings between the university delegates and their juniors, participants discussed the need for better organization and decided that each secondary school should form its own student center with democratically elected representatives.[76]

Having witnessed the power of student alliances, the student government at the national university spearheaded the creation of the National Confederation of Students composed of the Federation of Secondary Students and the Federation of University Students. Carlos Fonseca, the CUUN secretary of relations and future founder of the Sandinista National Liberation Front, led the initiative. He had established close links with secondary students when he worked in the library of the Instituto Ramírez Goyena and had been part of the university commission investigating post-strike reprisals.[77] In November 1958, Fonseca and other student government leaders began organizing the first national student assembly.[78]

The meeting agenda reveals the solidification of a national student identity. The topics to be discussed included: the fight to free the jailed universitarios as well as student community relations and the "mission of Latin American students." The planners also hoped the assembly would issue resolutions dealing with the impact of the economic crisis on students, the national educational budget, and the international student movement.[79] Students were beginning to think of themselves as a distinct group linked by common concerns, values, and events, whether it be the abuses of the Somozas or the consequences of the failing cotton crop. Moreover, they were clearly influenced by the international student movement emerging in the middle of the Cold War.

The struggle to free Borge and the two professors illustrated to students both the limits and possibilities of the autonomous university. Now that administrators were not directly beholden to the regime, students were free to protest without fear that the Guard might be called on campus or that they might be suspended by vengeful faculty. This was a significant achievement for the universitarios; yet, because their numbers were relatively small, they needed the participation of that sector of students who did not enjoy those guarantees and who thus faced severe consequences for protesting. Those in the university worked hard to remedy this situation and relied on the university's autonomy to mobilize their juniors. The Borge campaign showcased their power to organize and cause disruption, skills they would continue to develop throughout Luis Somoza's tenure. Indeed, if university autonomy allowed students greater room to protest and organize, then the state would adopt more repressive measures to contain them.

Nicaragua's Cold War

After the success of their campaign to free Tomás Borge, students intensified their anti-Somoza organizing. This surge in militancy was a consequence of the regime's crackdown on student dissidents as well as the revolutionary fervor inspired by developments in Cuba, where a guerrilla movement had toppled the dictator Fulgencio Batista in 1959. As occurred elsewhere, the success of the Cuban Revolution fanned the flame of rebellion, giving Nicaraguans a glimpse of what was possible and inspiring students to join youth groups dedicated to subversive street actions.[80] More threatening to the regime, some even joined the bands of Conservatives, Socialists, and others who embraced guerrilla warfare and staged two separate invasions in the first part of 1959 alone. Nicaragua's Cold War was intensifying, and the subsequent repression unified the student body and helped them mobilize their wider society.

Even before the Cuban revolutionaries had marched into Havana, the Somoza regime had already escalated its persecution of dissidents. Perhaps wary of student demonstrations in the aftermath of the campaign to free Borge, the state increasingly targeted student activists. Carlos Fonseca's experiences, although extreme, illustrate the growing repression of the Cold War era. In 1958, the future Sandinista leader was an overburdened law student. The illegitimate son of an aristocratic Matagalpino landowner and a laundrywoman, Fonseca had spent most his life on the edges of poverty. That background shaped his political consciousness, and by the time he had arrived at the National University, he was already a committed Marxist and member of the Partido Socialista Nicaragüense. He organized the PSN's first student cell, which, although short-lived, connected him to Tomás Borge and Silvio Mayorga, with whom he later founded the FSLN.[81]

Although the regime and its allies in the US embassy regularly denounced communist infiltration in the university, few students actually espoused the ideology. When the National Guard interrogated Fonseca after Somoza's assassination, he told them that Tomás Borge was his only communist friend.[82] Others embraced a simplified version of the doctrine centered on social justice. As Moisés Hassan, a student in this period, recalled: "In a way, my idea of communism was an idea of justice. . . . I saw communism in a very, very, very superficial way. . . . I did not have any serious knowledge [of its tenets]. . . . My sense of social justice was growing, and I began to view communism as a bridge to social justice."[83] For many, Marxism provided a path to ameliorating the vast inequality that existed in Nicaragua at the time. At first, this was not a revolutionary vision, and Fonseca, for one, was committed to the peaceful path to socialism.[84] That changed as the regime made nonviolent protest increasingly difficult.

Fonseca's police record offers a glimpse of the lack of civil liberties under the Somozas. The Guard arrested and held him for almost two months after Somoza's assassination. Months later, upon his return from a communist-organized trip to the USSR, they detained and interrogated him again. In late 1958, the government sent an officer to tail him for several weeks.[85] That November, as he organized the first national student assembly, soldiers arrested him for raising money in the national stadium for the meeting; the Oficina de Seguridad Nacional (Office of National Security, or OSN) also started keeping tabs on his correspondence for the CUUN. The next month, they arrested him again for unknown reasons. Then in March and April 1959, soldiers detained him for painting pro-Sandino signs on walls in Managua and on suspicion of being a communist agitator.[86] By his third year in college, Carlos Fonseca had amassed quite a record for his peaceful, political, and, most often, student-oriented organizing.

As more youths began openly resisting the regime, they too suffered harassment. The OSN also monitored Silvio Mayorga, opening a file on him after he attended a 1956 youth conference in Chicago. He too was detained for scrawling pro-Sandino graffiti in Managua in April 1959.[87] An epidemic of political graffiti kept the Guard very busy: in Rivas and Granada, the National Guard beat and arrested several students after slogans appeared on the walls of each city in April 1959. A month later, two fourteen-year-olds were sentenced to thirty days in jail when they were caught writing "Death to Somoza" on the walls of the cathedral. When journalists asked them what they were doing, the youths replied that they were merely "practicing their handwriting."[88] By the end of the decade, students had become more defiant, and the regime was responding more harshly.

The students' cheeky response was emblematic of a new kind of urban activism inspired by the Cuban Revolution. Throughout Latin America, young people were baldly challenging authoritarian regimes, deploying new and more disruptive tactics.[89] Moisés Hassan recalled that in Nicaragua:

> Small groups of boys began to get together here, groups of boys there. Well, it was something obviously small, but it was important because it was the first time youths began to organize with a clear vision of struggle against the regime and where nobody was afraid of the idea that we needed to take up arms to combat Somoza.

Student and non-student youth in urban barrios began joining anti-Somoza groups like the Juventud Demócrata Nicaragüense (Nicaraguan Democratic Youth, or JDN) and later, the Juventud Patriótica Nicaragüense (Nicaraguan Patriotic Youth, or JPN).[90] Carlos Fonseca's biographer, Matilde Zimmermann, has argued that the JDN and its successors were "important precursors of the FSLN in their emphasis on militant street actions, solidarity with the Cuban revolution, and independence from both the traditional bourgeois parties and the communist party."[91]

Even the university student government adopted a more radical position. In February 1959, on the twenty-fifth anniversary of the death of Sandino, the CUUN issued a manifesto denouncing his "infamous assassination" and praising his struggle to liberate the country from the yoke of the United States. It had been nearly a decade since students had called on the memory of the original anti-Somoza guerrilla leader. Now they paid homage to his struggle and argued that the factors that had led him to take up arms persisted. For the first time, since the 1940s, students issued an economic and social critique, condemning the country's illiteracy and the regime's mishandling of the economic crises. Although the language in the manifesto was vague, it signaled that students once again felt comfortable enough to expand the scope of their activism.[92]

Inspired by the recent success of the Cuban Revolution and their country's own history, the student government demanded political change. Cuba and Fidel Castro, they wrote in their manifesto, "showed the ways that can help our people construct a new era." While they never used the word "revolution," their demands for "a true transformation" and their reference to Cuba made it clear that was the goal. Calling on students to "unite, organize and fight," the student government hoped that next year they would be able to publicly celebrate Sandino "without fear of the dictatorial dynasty's repression."[93]

The regime responded with increased repression, and, in this Cold War context, the few publicly known leftist students were among the first targets. After several arrests and interrogations, Mayorga sought asylum in the Costa Rican embassy.[94] Fonseca's experience was more severe. Soon after his arrest for painting "Viva Sandino" graffiti in April 1959, the law student was jolted awake in the middle of the night and placed on a plane to Guatemala. The national security officer escorting him left him at the Nicaraguan embassy after falsely warning the ambassador that he had been trained in Moscow. The embassy proceeded to drop the student off in the center of Guatemala City with nothing but the clothes on his back.[95]

The repression at home inspired some to turn their revolutionary rhetoric into reality, and a small number of students joined the guerrilla groups training in the mountains. Carlos Fonseca was one. While in exile, he linked up with a Cuban-sponsored guerrilla group training in Honduras.[96] The nearly ninety-man force, made up of veterans from the Cuban Revolution, students, dissident liberals, and socialists, invaded Nicaragua in late June 1959. The expedition was an unmitigated disaster. Honduran and Nicaraguan authorities had been aware of their activities from the start, and soldiers from both militaries ambushed the group in El Chaparral, Honduras, on June 24. Six guerrillas died in battle, fifteen were wounded, and soldiers executed three more in what became known as the El Chaparral Massacre.[97]

After the Borge campaign and the success of the Cuban Revolution, the anti-Somoza student movement became increasingly militant. They were boldly confronting the Somozas, but not in any way that seriously threatened the regime's hold on power. Instead, students were floating the idea of revolution, testing the waters with their manifestos and graffiti. While some like Fonseca took up arms, most did not. The state's violent response to those who did would radicalize still more.

The July 23rd Massacre

The El Chaparral Massacre occurred just as students were returning to León for the 1959–1960 school year, and the news that Carlos Fonseca and another former student, Aníbal Sanchez, had been killed, electrified the student body.[98] Other insurgencies had been similarly crushed, but this time a well-known student activist and member of the student government was reported among the dead. Alejandro Serrano Caldera, a student at the time, noted that the massacre at El Chaparral especially affected students

> [b]ecause of the fact ... that Carlos Fonseca was among the gravely wounded. He had been a university student [and] had shared the university struggle. Actually, that fact ... raised tensions and radicalized positions and even forced those who if they were not in agreement with the Somoza dictatorship [and] were not very belligerent about it, to join the movement against the dictatorship.[99]

The attack made the repression personal. Although students would later learn that Fonseca was not dead, the brutality with which the guerrilla movement had been squashed was a reminder of the regime's moral bankruptcy and convinced students more extreme action was necessary. The regime would respond with deadly force—a move that further radicalized the students at the National University and compelled their society to action.

The shift is apparent in one of the first manifestos the students issued after the massacre. Writing in July 1959 that "university students have taken up the banner waved by Carlos Fonseca and Aníbal Sanchez and the other fallen," they declare themselves "absolutely ready to fight for our country, to defend democratic principles and to work for the victorious consolidation of our revolution."[100] The killing of their own had radicalized their politics, and students doubled down on their revolutionary rhetoric.

Such declarations were risky given that the country had been under martial law since an earlier invasion in May 1959, and the military mobilized to block public demonstrations. Soldiers broke up a protest in Chinandega, wounding several students who had traveled with the CUUN to attend a memorial service for the El Chaparral dead.[101] Vilma Núñez remembered that the student government organized a march from the university in León to the Iglesia el Calvario five blocks away. They planned to hold a mass in honor of the dead, but the military was waiting for them. Despite the bravery of several young women who stood up to the soldiers, the students were not allowed to enter. Undeterred, they found other ways to protest. Núñez recalled that "every day there were meetings, every day there were small marches, reunions and this and that."[102]

In this heady climate, the student government planned their response. The annual freshman parade was rapidly approaching. During this yearly hazing ritual, upperclassmen shaved the heads of the male students and then paraded them through town in costumes. In 1959, though, such a raucous event seemed indecent. As Joaquín Solís Piura, the recently elected student president, remembered: "We decided that there was no reason to make the Parade of the Bald festive because we were mourning the dead of Chaparral and the indignities Carlos Fonseca suffered."[103] Instead, the council decided to "honor our martyrs" with a display of grief: male students would don black ties with a black band around the arm and female students would dress in mourning.[104] With permission from the local National Guard commander, they scheduled the parade for July 23, 1959.

In a massive repudiation of the regime, three thousand people turned out for the demonstration. After a long day of protests, a contingent of soldiers prevented the students from passing by the National Guard headquarters in León's main plaza. To obtain permission for the march, the students had promised not to come near the military headquarters, but in their enthusiasm, they had entered the plaza. There, they found soldiers ready for war. Núñez, who was marching at the front of the demonstration with several other female students, recalled the scene: "The soldiers were in three rows, that I remember ... those in front were lying on their stomachs, those in the second row were on their knees, and those behind were standing."[105] After a lengthy showdown, in which the mass of students, taking up two city blocks, retreated and then attempted to return to the plaza several times, the commander ordered the soldiers to shoot tear gas into the crowd. As the students began to disperse, the soldiers opened fire, wounding almost forty people and killing four students: José Rubí Somarriba, Sergio Saldaña, Mauricio Martínez, and Erick Ramírez.[106]

The university community mourned the dead like a grieving family. Fiallos Gil and other professors organized a vigil in the auditorium of the university. The rector and his colleagues led a silent procession that carried the young men's bodies on park benches to the hall, where the following morning, thousands of grieving students and citizens processed past them. The historian Francisco Barbosa argued that holding the vigil in the university both "drew attention to their membership in a small but privileged group" and allowed the bodies to become public.[107] Indeed, the on-campus vigil underscored the alternative family that the school had engendered. One student recalled in his memoir of the massacre that "whoever saw Mariano Fiallos Gil that night contemplating the cadavers of 'his boys' as he called them, would have realized the love the rector had for the universitarios. He could not stop the tears that rolled down his cheeks."[108]

Students blamed the massacre on the Somozas. In one of the first communiques they issued after the killings, they compared Luis's "ghoulish" behavior to that of a "vicious animal," attributed Anastasio's actions to the "criminal thoughts of a demented person," and accused the Guard of being "a military caste that eats the entrails of the public budget." Such evocative language was meant to insult and incite. They urged the pueblo to get organized to prove that the "fount of power lies with the people and to end the dictatorship ... the time for sacrifice has arrived, and we, the universitarios are ready to offer our blood so that our nation ... on some upcoming morning can break the chains that bind her."[109] The massacre had marked a clear breaking point, and students demanded retribution.

The city responded. Mourning the dead and wounded as their own, Leoneses mobilized to provide support. Núñez remembered:

> All of León, everybody was wanting to give blood. You know the impression that I have of the solidarity and identification of León, of the people of León, with the students, it still moves me. You know I felt then that those dead they were not our dead, they were the university's dead, they were everybody's dead, of all of León.[110]

Leoneses from all sectors of society donated money, blood, and even the use of their personal vehicles to help with the medical response. City businesses closed on July 24 for the funerals; local businessmen provided the coffins, paid for the religious services, and donated money. One radio station raised almost 1,500 córdobas to help defray the costs of medicine, hospital stays, and Sergio Saldaña's funeral.[111] Thousands of people attended the vigil and the funeral procession that followed.[112] Sergio Ramírez described the solemn marchers as a "large family that was burying four of its members. In front of the cathedral, the pained family raised their fists before the [GN] departmental command, with its machine guns ... stationed on the roofs."[113] The students' murder had shaken the city and forced its engagement with the regime.

But that engagement was not necessarily spontaneous—students, specifically young women, had risked further violence to mobilize the community. As the number of female students in the university had grown, so too had their role in the student government—so much so that CUUN had recently created a secretary of women's issues position on their board.[114] Many of these young women felt protected by traditional notions of chivalry, and they often walked at the head of processions and marches.[115] The July 23 march proved them wrong: Natasha Mena, the new Women's Representative on the CUUN was among the injured that day.[116] Nevertheless, female students continued to take great risks to drum up public support, and they crisscrossed the city distributing manifestos and bulletins, some of which they had stayed up all night writing.[117]

To further mobilize the population, the CUUN sent commissions to various communities to raise funds and organize demonstrations and even masses for their martyrs.[118] In this way, they reached out to all sectors of society, from those who would join an angry demonstration to those who might be willing to stage a more silent protest by attending a memorial mass. For example, after student leaders determined to "paralyze León" in retaliation for the massacre, Vilma Núñez was tasked with persuading the city's market sellers to close.

> Imagine what it is to close a market, to convince the women vendors of a market who have all of their goods ready to feed the entire pueblo, because the whole world went ... every day to shop in the market. Well, it was impressive how the market closed. Everybody left their things and everybody went to the funeral.[119]

Through their communiqués and organizing efforts, students both spread information and provided the community with concrete ways to protest the regime.

The funeral march for the students killed in the July 23, 1959, massacre.
Sergio Ramírez Papers, Firestone Library, Princeton University.

Women leading a procession after the July 23, 1959, massacre. Sergio Ramírez Papers, Firestone Library, Princeton University.

As Núñez's memory suggests, the city's women constituted a vital role in the post-massacre opposition. They led a silent candlelit march a few days after the killings that ended with the arson of the local Guard commander's home. Núñez remembered watching as the protestors set fire to the home of Anastasio "Tacho" Ortiz, who had led the troops the day of the massacre. Fleeing from the Guard, she took shelter in the university with several other women, while outside a crowd of more than three hundred people prevented firefighters from extinguishing the blaze.[120] The demonstrators' actions underscored the ways in which the students' murder had galvanized the city and the key role women, whether they were students or community members, played in channeling that anger into action.

The July 23rd Massacre radicalized students and shone a light on the solidarity that had formed between the city and the university. Leóneses risked their safety and sacrificed their financial security when they took to the streets to protest the massacre, but they did so anyway. Their mobilization was a testament to both the students' organizing capacity and the sense of community that had sprung up in the wake of the autonomy decision.

Protecting the Small Great Republic

After burying their friends, students returned to class in early September irrevocably altered. Youthful illusions of invincibility had vanished, both for students and their families.[121] Alejandro Serrano Caldera recalled how the day after the massacre, his mother rushed from Masaya to León, where she refused to leave his side during the funeral service. "I would ask her, Mother, please move aside ... no, she went alongside me and all of the student council ... because she was afraid, afraid for me, not for her, and I was afraid for her."[122] In the midst of such pervasive fear, students prioritized the defense of their university. Shoring up the school's autonomy was one way to exert control and demand justice.

Indeed, the regime was already blaming the victims for the killings. For example, Guillermo Sevilla Sacasa, the Nicaraguan ambassador to the United States, excused the Guard's actions in León as a necessary response to a provocative and subversive protest. The students, he declared, were "communist-led," throwing stones at the Guard and threatening them in other ways. Given this context, he explained, the soldiers "could not remain standing there with their arms crossed" and "there was little else the Guardia Nacional could do under the circumstances."[123]

Such excuses made the students unwilling to cooperate with the military commission that Somoza appointed to investigate the massacre. According to Joaquín Solís Piura, then the president of the CUUN, they suspected the commission would be unduly biased and would "absolve everybody like they always do."[124] Understanding that the regime needed them as the primary witnesses to legitimize the investigation, students demanded certain concessions in exchange for their participation, including the unedited publication of their testimony, the removal of the soldiers surrounding the university, the release of those imprisoned during the national protests after the massacre, and the termination of the reprisals that secondary students were suffering for their solidarity demonstrations.[125] When the regime declined, the student government closed ranks, refusing to assist in the investigation and forbidding their peers to speak with state investigators or even have contact with civil functionaries and military bureaucrats.[126]

In the aftermath of the massacre, the student government decided that the time had come to shore up the borders of their small great republic and expel government interlopers. Drawing a line in the sand, the student government declared they would no longer tolerate Somoza employees in the university. In the wake of the massacre, several students had quit their jobs with the state in protest, and the CUUN issued a manifesto asking all universitarios to follow suit. They warned that anybody who did not do so or who took one of the now empty positions "should not set foot in the university."[127] Faculty even complied, and several professors quit their positions with the government.[128]

The student government had adopted a Manichean attitude toward Somocismo and punished those who did not fall into line. For example, days after the massacre, the pharmacy representative on the CUUN, Carlos Calvo Aguilar, offered his resignation because other members of the student government had charged that he had not participated in the center's initial response to the massacre out of cowardice.[129] Guillermo Soto González wrote to the CUUN to dispute charges that he had consorted with regime officials. He explained that while he had been in contact with Somocistas by happenstance, he never spoke on behalf of the students.[130] Apparently, several students had been giving declarations to the military commission, and the student assembly rebuked their companions who had corroborated the regime's story.[131] Such incidents underscored the hetereogenity that continued to exist in the university with ardent Somocistas on campus.

The student movement saved most of its ire for the soldiers who studied among them. A small number had been pursuing their degrees at the UNAN, but in the aftermath of the massacre, students found it jarring to sit beside some of the very men who served in the battalion that had shot at them. Some had even tried to block rescue efforts. For example, Gastón Cajina, a law student and lieutenant, had threatened a local radio station soon after the massacre, demanding broadcasters stop issuing news flashes and asking people to donate blood.[132] Consequently, in an effort to shore up the sanctity of their campus and extract a measure of retaliation, a student general assembly requested the expulsions of Cajina and three other soldiers studying in the university for being "disloyal and traitors to the pain of the universitarios."[133] On September 2, the student assembly decided to strike, demanding "the cancellation of the registrations of the soldiers, hospital corps and proven spies."[134]

The university board instead called for the soldiers' temporary suspension while a committee investigated their role in the events of July 23, and the strike dragged on.[135] By the beginning of October, the situation had reached a boiling point. The student body met again on October 8 and set a deadline for the soldiers' expulsion.[136] Somoza declared that he would gut the school's budget if they expelled the soldiers. Under that pressure, the board refused to give in.[137] The CUUN now widened their demands to include the board's resignation, and five members of the student council declared a hunger strike.[138]

Students protesting the presence of spies in the UNAN. Sergio Ramírez Papers, Firestone Library, Princeton University.

With no resolution in sight, the situation escalated and the National Guard entered the fray. On October 15, six hundred students, more than half of the student population, attended a general assembly where they voted to occupy the university until the board expelled the soldiers. The rector prohibited women from staying, so after they and those who wanted to leave had been ushered out, approximately one-third of the student body remained holed up on campus. Leoneses stepped in to help, passing provisions to the students through windows. In response, the Guard sent one of its most elite battalions to surround the university and cut off supplies from the outside.[139] Female students barred from occupying their university found other ways to help. Vilma Núñez recalled that the priests at La Merced Church, which shared a wall with the university, allowed them to enter and pass messages and supplies to the demonstrators in the school.[140]

Under siege, the students inside worked hard to keep morale up. Some sang songs and one even played the accordion to drown out the threats blared by the soldiers, warning of an impending attack. Others busied themselves issuing communiqués. Their fear was palpable. After a Guard patrol broke into La Merced Church, cutting off the last remaining supply channel, the students began running out of food and feared a raid was imminent. One bulletin ends with the request: "Citizen, don't leave [the students] alone."[141]

Young women confronting the National Guard. Sergio Ramírez Papers, Firestone Library, Princeton University.

The intervention of a Somoza finally ended the conflict. Anastasio Somoza Debayle, who commanded the army, sent the soldiers to study in Spain, then under the control of the fascist Francisco Franco regime.[142] As word spread, the students abandoned the university in triumph, and the crowd that had gathered outside the main building carried the weakened hunger strikers on their shoulders.[143] It was a stunning victory. Somoza's decision to concede suggests the real power that students were flexing: their protest had become such a quagmire that they had forced the military to stand down. It was also a victory for university autonomy—at any time, the state might have sent in soldiers to dislodge the students or eviscerated the school's budget, but it did not. After the July 23rd Massacre, the regime seems to have understood its limits and shied away from provoking a more severe backlash.

Why had students risked so much to expel four soldiers? For one, they really did fear attending class alongside soldiers whose capacity for violence had been proven. Recalling an incident where he had to intervene to prevent a fight between soldiers and the law students, Alejandro Serrano Caldera wrote in his memoir of the university: "How could it be possible to coexist with the soldiers without confrontations that could lead to new and worse violence?"[144] Only when the soldiers, and the threat of violence they represented, were gone would the students feel safe and secure enough to attend class. Second, they could not forgive the soldiers' complicity in the massacre. Several of their letters and communiqués refer to the four young men as "accomplices to the murders."[145]

Critically, many students saw the soldiers as a stand-in for the Somoza regime and their expulsion was a small measure of justice in an unjust system. For the students, according to Sergio Ramírez:

> The suspension of the soldiers had become a matter of honor, the only possible recourse in their hands to charge in some way the blood of their dead, when the military justice had issued an ambiguous judgment without determining who was responsible and hid the facts instead of making them clear; when no court of the city had initiated criminal proceedings . . . and when the entire attitude of the government was to protect the guilty.[146]

Joaquín Solís Piura similarly explained that they wanted the four men ousted as a "type of sanction," the only kind they could apply to the regime: "to not educate its members."[147] The soldiers' expulsion was a way to exact some small form of retribution for their dead.

Their commitment to obtaining a semblance of justice for their fallen compañeros was tied to notions of student pride. The Committee for Student Dignity had organized the campaign to expel the soldiers, and similar language filled the students' correspondence. One letter requested students and professors join the campaign and "maintain the dignity of our institution."[148] A small group of students, declaring their decision to go on a hunger strike until the soldiers were expelled, explained that they did so because "we believe that killing students is not like killing dogs in the streets and the blood of our martyrs from the bitter bottom of their tombs *still* awaits justice." They added that they struck so that "tomorrow we can raise our heads high, with the dignity of one who has accomplished his duty and has responded to the call of the nation."[149]

Very traditional understandings of gender, age, and honor were embedded within these discussions. In one of their first declarations after the massacre, students wrote that the "deaths of our brothers have raised us up and made us more manly than before and more determined."[150] When the administration refused to expel the soldiers, a student communique accused them of "sabotaging the virile attitude of men that we have adopted to defend our university dignity."[151] Years later, Ramírez recalled that the massacre had "turned us into men, had placed us on the other side of adolescence."[152] Violence had marked their passage to adulthood and the students' defense of their dignity constituted a public announcement of their political maturity.[153]

In adopting the language of masculinity to justify their political engagement, students erased the participation of young women, who had taken great risks to organize wider support for the student demonstrations after the massacre. This form of political engagement, however, was not as visible or newsworthy as occupying their campus—an activity that women had been prohibited from joining. Yet, their work was just as important for turning a student protest into a community-wide one.

Although the July 23rd Massacre had made students acutely aware of the regime's capacity for violence, they grew more confrontational, not less. They responded to the attack by publicly demanding revolution while working to bolster the autonomy of their small great republic. From now on, the students' anti-Somocismo would be marked by a rage heretofore unknown in their movement, but that did not necessarily translate to a willingness to take up arms. In early September 1959, as the administration debated holding the annual Independence Day vacations, members of the CUUN wrote to discourage them for fear that the holiday would give "many students the opportunity to join the ranks of the revolution, at a great danger to their lives."[154] The revolutionary option was gaining favor, but as early as 1959, student leaders understood the dangers, and their opposition to the school holiday suggests that their commitment to armed rebellion had not fully coalesced.

Conclusion

When Fiallos Gil wrote his "Letter to the Students," inviting them to enter and take possession of their newly autonomous university, he had no idea how prescient his words would prove. By the end of the decade, these youths would literally take possession of their school, occupying the main campus building for several days as they fought for the sanctity of their alma mater. They did so out of a firm belief that the university was theirs, and they, as individuals, were part of something larger than themselves, an intellectual community with rights and privileges and an essential role in the future of the nation. Fiallos Gil and his reforms had done much to empower them.

In the 1950s, thanks to Somoza's political decisions, Fiallos Gil's vision, and the students' active participation, a modern independent university emerged in Nicaragua. The school's autonomy gave students both the space and the support to connect with other sectors. The institution developed alongside a closely knit community of students, professors, and, as the aftermath of the massacre confirmed, the general public. Because of the students' ability to marshal all of these members plus their counterparts in secondary schools, the regime learned that the university was a force with which it would have to reckon.

Women were especially critical for mobilizing wider community support. In the 1950s, their numbers were still small, but they became increasingly visible members of the university and the student government. At times, notions of chivalry enabled their activities—as when they, incorrectly, believed that as women, they would be safe at the head of the July 23 march. At other times, it limited their participation—as when the rector refused to let Vilma Núñez occupy the school during the struggle to expel the soldiers from the university. Such contradictions were par for the course in the 1950s and would hinder young women's activism in the years to come.

With the awarding of university autonomy, students were adopting new and more confrontational tactics in the struggle against the regime, which was itself experimenting with more oppressive strategies for containing the opposition. The Somoza brothers had readily embraced violence and greater surveillance after their father's assassination. The Cold War legitimized their growing authoritarianism and heavy-handed tactics—a phenomenon that would spread throughout Latin America in the 1960s.[155] It was precisely that escalation of repression that spurred young Nicaraguans in the 1950s to protest and organize. Yet, it should be noted that students remained divided between Somocistas and anti-Somocistas, between militant activists and those less so.

CHAPTER 5

Reform vs. Revolution, 1960–1968

In a 1968 letter, Carlos Fonseca, the former student activist and co-founder of the Frente Sandinista de Liberación Nacional, scolded Nicaraguan students for their lack of political consciousness and effective activism. Extolling those who had sacrificed their lives for a new Nicaragua, he criticized the "revolutionary students [who] have essentially stayed in the classroom with their arms crossed." These youths had contented themselves with issuing declarations when the regime murdered their peers. In lieu of mass demonstrations, Fonseca charged, they focused their energies on student elections. Instead of demanding the government increase education spending, they organized fundraisers and literacy campaigns — efforts that could never rectify long-standing educational inequities.[1]

Fonseca's portrayal of ineffectual college students is at odds with popular and scholarly understandings of the sixties. The literature on the era's student movements in Latin America has focused heavily on the mass mobilizations that rocked the larger and wealthier nations of Brazil, Mexico, and Argentina. Understanding the sixties to be a historical moment not bounded by the span of a decade, these works have illuminated the complex origins of the aggressive protest movements and the violent state reactions that rocked this era.[2]

Yet, in smaller Latin American countries like Nicaragua, the decade was not marked by significant disruption.[3] Nicaragua did not see any mass student protests in the late 1960s. While there were certainly radicals, more students avoided revolutionary activism in favor of the middle road promised by the increasingly popular, more moderate Christian Democracy, and most stayed out of politics altogether.

This was a dramatic shift from the militant student movement that emerged in the immediate aftermath of the July 23, 1959, massacre. The revolutionary consensus that propelled student activism at the end of the 1950s began to splinter as the Cold War ramped up. Not only did revolution prove hard to forge, but students also increasingly found themselves torn between several political ideologies. This was a process occurring throughout Latin America, as the Cuban Revolution set off fierce debates over how to create change. As Jaime Pensado found to be the case among Mexican students, the vast majority of Nicaraguan students shied away from taking up arms and instead promoted more moderate politics.[4] While in many places, student political demands found expression in the new counterculture that emerged in this era, in Nicaragua, that movement appears to have been small and subordinate to a prevailing interest in university and national politics.[5] This reality complicates notions of the sixties that have focused on the era's revolutionary fervor and the generational challenge to traditional social mores.

Other aspects associated with the sixties, however, did shape student politics in Nicaragua. As was occurring in many places throughout the world, more and more sectors began recognizing the power of youth.[6] From the Soviets to the North Americans, powerful new entities competed for the hearts and minds of students. Their efforts reinforced student exceptionalism but also deepened the political divisions that had always been present among youth.

In this context, the student movement at the National University changed focus. Although the numbers of young people involved in student government and the student associations declined, the competition between political groups grew increasingly heated, and those who did participate stayed busy forging alliances, strategizing against their opposition, and planning campus events. This was a very different type of activism than the revolutionary kind Fonseca envisioned. Indeed, students in the 1960s participated in a variety of activities to a variety of ends. They became enmeshed in global student organizations that enabled them to participate in international advocacy. Those networks, combined with the hemispheric Cold War, inspired a fierce anti-imperialism, and some students participated in demonstrations against the United States. Others concerned themselves with partisan and campus politics, strategizing how best to win control over the student government. Few, however, engaged in the kind of community organizing that past generations had adopted and that Fonseca believed necessary for the success of the revolution. In fact, the early 1960s was a particularly active period for campesino movements, which mobilized repeatedly in Chinandega and León for access to land.[7] Yet, such struggles did not reverberate within the halls of the university.

For many students, the revolutionary project had lost its urgency. In this period, Nicaragua was experiencing a narrow democratic aperture. In 1963, Luis Somoza stepped down from the presidency in favor of his chosen successor, René Schick. That someone outside the Somoza family was to assume the nation's highest office constituted a promising sign that the country had embarked on the path to democracy, but the truth was messier. While Schick was not quite the puppet that history has judged him to be, the Somozas' continued presence limited his power to effect change. Consequently, Nicaragua's democratic aperture of the 1960s never widened to the extent that observers, including students, had hoped.

Still, the democratic opening did have significant consequences. First, both Somoza's and Schick's public promises to protect free speech and, sometimes half-hearted, efforts to guarantee other civil liberties led to the proliferation of dissident political groups in the nation at large and, more specifically, in the university. Second, both administrations' erratic handling of protest increased public criticism of the regime. Third, the promise of democracy, as embodied by the Schick presidency, managed briefly to quiet political protest, even as more militant groups were organizing.

In the 1960s, university students enjoyed greater freedoms and privileges than ever before, but the political climate tempered their militancy and narrowed their focus. As Cold War policies deepened inequality in their own country, students immersed themselves in revitalized middle-class and elite political organizations. They largely abandoned their efforts to build a nationwide student movement and instead focused on forging connections with university students around the world. Instead of seeking alliances with the working class, the CUUN now deepened its connection with political parties. These alliances might amplify their voices, but they would do little to produce the kind of political disruption young people had successfully caused in the past.

The Expansion of the University in the 1960s

A growing student population helped turn youth into a potent force in this era. From 1957 to 1970, student enrollment at the National University nearly tripled, from 930 to 2,731. The percentage of female students grew as well: from 18.2 percent in 1960 to almost a third in 1967.[8] Moreover, the UNAN now competed with the private Universidad Centroamericana (UCA) for students, funding, and international recognition. The growing numbers of students and the expansion of higher education was a global phenomenon, and in Nicaragua, a country that desperately needed professionals, it meant the university took on a more visible role in the nation at large.[9]

In fact, students emerging from the university in the 1960s had a bright future. A researcher who studied student demographics in this period found that "given the high demand in Managua for higher education the difference between *egresados* [students who left without a degree] and graduates was minimal."[10] In other words, students were not facing a particularly difficult job market. To the contrary, Nicaragua had long suffered from a severe shortage of professionals. In his 1958 letter to students, Mariano Fiallos Gil bemoaned the lack of Nicaraguan scientists and researchers and regretted that "businessmen have to send for technicians from the exterior to run their plants, that the government also turns to the foreigners to run the trains, plan services, to balance the currency."[11] Contemporaneous studies corroborated Fiallos Gil's observations. A 1963–1964 yearbook, produced by a team of student researchers associated with the International Student Conference, noted that all of the country's chemical engineers were foreigners and that there was a shortage of sanitation engineers and agricultural technicians.[12] These sources suggest a country badly in need of university-trained professionals.[13]

Consequently, the university and its students were primed to take on a more significant role in their society. Their numbers were growing and their presence throughout the country expanding along with it. Similar changes were occurring around the world, and a rising international student movement further increased the global visibility of youth.

The Networks behind the Global Sixties

During the Long Sixties, students around the world took to the streets to protest authoritarian governments and destructive foreign policies. Historians interested in understanding this phenomenon have pointed to the demographic, technological, and cultural changes that united young people around the world.[14] While the literature on how Latin American students were influenced by global cultural trends that they reshaped to suit their purposes is fairly extensive, less is known about how young people acted on the international stage, engaging with their peers and elders around the world.[15] Such encounters internationalized local movements and helped account for the era's global texture. For young Nicaraguans, these exchanges occurred at international student conferences where they were empowered to think of themselves as global actors and where they developed a sense of solidarity with other students from Latin America and the Third World more broadly.

Membership in international student organizations enabled the National University of Nicaragua to send delegates to conferences as far away as Sri Lanka, Nigeria, and Iraq. Each year, a lucky handful of students, chosen by the student government through a university-wide application process, attended international meetings.[16] Much of the travel occurred under the auspices of the two leading international student organizations: the International Union of Students (IUS) and the International Student Conference (ISC). The former had long been financed (and controlled) by the Soviet Union, while the latter had been covertly funded by the CIA since the early 1950s. Both the USSR and the United States had hoped to tap into these international networks in order to promote their own geopolitical agenda. Their money helped fund conferences, publications, and other activities that brought students together to exchange information and ideas.[17]

The conferences constituted effective forums for consciousness-raising. For some, like Carlos Fonseca, the opportunity to observe other societies helped them rethink what was possible at home. In 1957, Fonseca traveled to Moscow for the Sixth World Festival of Youth and Students for Peace and Friendship, which had been organized by the IUS and the World Federation of Democratic Youth. Funds from the International Solidarity Fund for Youth helped pay some of the costs of his three-month trip. From late July to early November, Fonseca traveled around Eastern Europe and the Soviet Union, where he marveled at the state-provided health care, public transportation, generous education system, and beautiful parks. These experiences deepened his nascent commitment to socialism and hardened his opposition to the Somozas. His travels also shaped the consciousness of students throughout Nicaragua and the region who read about his experiences in his memoir. A student newspaper from Guatemala even sent a correspondent to write a story about him and his visit to the USSR.[18]

The scope of Fonseca's trip was unusual; most students traveled for a much shorter period of time to attend conferences where they mainly engaged with other students. The annual meetings of the ISC, for example, offered break-out sessions for students from a specific region to discuss common problems, as well as open assemblies, which gave delegations the chance to speak to the wider audience about the issues facing their country or to denounce situations occurring elsewhere. Most of the conference was dedicated to plenary sessions that drafted resolutions, as well as to assemblies where the research committee announced the findings of the year's investigative reports.[19] This structure empowered students to think of themselves as international actors with the authority to analyze complex economic and political situations around the world.

It was at these conferences more than anywhere else that the Nicaraguan student movement became internationalized. Students learned about the struggles affecting their peers and brainstormed about how to respond. For example, Algeria was one of the most pressing topics at the conferences in the late 1950s and early 1960s, and several conference resolutions condemned the French government and supported the students fighting it. The Nicaraguan delegates were very interested in their struggle, and in a letter to the president of the Algerian student union in 1961, they wrote, "The Nicaraguan students admire the heroic struggle the Algerian people are waging for their liberation." The letter explains that they are particularly interested in the Muslim student fight, "which in some ways resembles our own." Such flashes of recognition led to concrete action. Nicaraguan students wrote to the French ambassador to Nicaragua, the French president, and the director of the Red Cross, declaring their support for the liberation struggle and pleading for the prevention of the pending execution of an Algerian student leader. They even organized a fundraiser at one conference on behalf of the Algerian student union.[20] These encounters made students aware of their membership in what would later be called the Third World. While they did not use that term, the recognition that they had something in common with Algerian students testifies to the emergence of a kind of Third World consciousness.[21]

Hearing from peers engaged in anti-colonial and anti-imperial struggles around the world fostered a sense of common student identity and purpose. In a speech they made announcing their fundraiser for the Algerian students at a 1959 ISC conference, the Nicaraguan delegation declared:

> There is nobody more than us who can understand the primordial role university students play throughout the world in the struggle for national liberation, they are and will always be the vertical axis, the base, and the vertebral column of those struggles. They fight for education, they fight for the economy, they fight for the vindication of the worker, of the peasant . . . in sum, they fight for liberties.[22]

The students' understanding of their role in society was in many ways a product of these conferences, where delegates privileged discussions of the ways in which students were fighting for social justice.[23]

The international network's publications reinforced notions of student exceptionalism. For example, the ISC's *The Student* offered, in addition to cultural features and student-authored fiction, articles on the most pressing issues facing member countries. Students wrote short pieces highlighting their role in the Cold War battles for a different society. For example, in a 1960 essay, Joaquín Solís Piura, the president of the CUUN, described the harsh censorship that plagued newspapers, denounced the mainstream press for its subservience to the regime, and proclaimed the existence of only two "really independent and free" papers: that of the students and that of the workers. That might have been an overstatement—regime repression meant that the students were only able to publish two issues of their paper that year—but it does show how students were shaping their identity for international audiences. Other articles highlight the key role students played in the emerging guerrilla movement and the arrests of student leaders.[24] Students thus read about how their counterparts seemingly everywhere were taking on a vanguard role in domestic resistance movements.

Like the conferences that sponsored them, these periodicals played a critical role in circulating information. Joining the global student networks gave national student organizations access to an international audience. Through the publications and bulletins sent out periodically from the coordinating bodies of the international student groups, student activists could quickly spread the word about repression at home. In the growing violence of the Cold War era, the network shamed and pressured repressive regimes, including that of the Somozas. In the immediate aftermath of the July 23, 1959, massacre, the student government fired off a letter to their counterparts throughout Central America asking them to please "denounce before the world the mass murder perpetrated against students and the public in general."[25] By August 10, the International Student Conference had already issued a circular to all of its unions publicizing the attack.[26]

International pressure might have been particularly effective during Luis Somoza's tenure when he was determined to rehabilitate Nicaragua's image. On at least one occasion, he actually responded to the petitions from the international student organizations. In June 1960, the National Guard arrested Joaquín Solís Piura, the president of the CUUN, after he returned from a visit to Cuba. The University Student Federation of Cuba immediately notified the ISC, requesting they cable Somoza to demand Solís's freedom. Surprisingly, the president responded promptly, saying that Solís was already at liberty and that they had been "duped by biased propaganda." The next day, however, the Nicaraguan student government cabled the ISC to inform them that Solís was still in jail.[27] It is, nonetheless, surprising that Somoza bothered to respond (and lie) to an international student group. Clearly, he cared enough about his image abroad to correspond with them.

International organizations thus provided a vital service: tracking the repression student groups endured and drawing on their extensive networks to put pressure on regimes.

Moreover, the Nicaraguan student movement built on the connections made through the international student organizations to forge their own informal regional support networks. When Carlos Fonseca found himself wandering the streets of Guatemala City after the Office of National Security deported him in the early hours of April 8, 1959, he immediately sought out contact with other students. Relating the "surprise and solitude" he felt after his exile in a letter to his father, Fonseca explained his next steps: "I could not possibly lose my tranquility. I looked for the student organization, 'Association of University Students,' and they have given me a place to stay and have found work for me . . . which is helping me to start organizing my life here."[28] The Guatemalan students notified the ISC, which issued a circular to all its member unions throughout the world, describing Fonseca's plight and asking for assistance.[29] In fact, the Nicaraguan student union learned of Fonseca's whereabouts through this report, and they in turn wrote to the Guatemalan association to thank their "university brothers" for their support.[30] Years later, in 1965, when Fonseca was again exiled to Guatemala, a new generation of concerned students wrote to the Guatemalan University Student Association to check on him.[31]

Fonseca's experiences were not unique. The informal network of Latin American student organizations helped support the growing number of Cold War exiles and sometimes even incorporate them into their own organizations. When repression forced the young Nicaraguan activist Alfredo Prado Balladares to flee to Caracas, the National University student government wrote to the student federation there asking them to "receive and support him in accordance with student solidarity."[32] Other unions wrote to the CUUN for similar support. For example, in the late 1950s, the Guatemalan student organization grew concerned when they failed to hear from Rodolfo Romero Gómez, a politically active Nicaraguan student who had studied in Guatemala before being deported. They feared he was in prison in Nicaragua and wrote to the National University student government requesting that they lobby Somoza for his freedom. The Nicaraguans complied, taking his story to *La Prensa*. By the following day, Romero Gómez had been released. He later joined the militant anti-Somoza organization, Nicaraguan Democratic Youth.[33]

These connections fostered a powerful sense of student identity that united youth around the world. Even though only one or two students could attend conferences abroad, the Nicaraguan student government strove to keep their peers informed. Once home, delegates reported back to general assemblies, reprinted conference resolutions in local papers, and disseminated urgent bulletins.[34] In this way, young Nicaraguans learned about the struggles of their counterparts around the world and drew connections between the different student movements. These links fortified a Cold War student consciousness in which university youth came to see themselves as a vanguard force in nationalist struggles. Anti-imperialism specifically united the Nicaraguan student movement with its peers around the world, even as it divided young activists at home.

Confronting the Yankees

Considering the historically close relations between US diplomats and the Somozas, it is remarkable that until the late 1950s, students rarely criticized the United States. However, as the Cold War intensified, students increasingly condemned the US alliance with the Somozas, their efforts to destabilize Cuba, and imperialist activities in Latin America. Their antipathy to the global superpower was symptomatic of a larger problem for the United States as their embassies reported an increased number of attacks between 1960 and 1965.[35]

Realizing that they were losing the support of large numbers of youths, the US embassy in Nicaragua sought to improve its image with mixed results. The embassy's active intervention in Nicaraguan affairs, from military aid to student government issues, further politicized youth and illustrated the way in which a Cold War calculus permeated even the most quotidian of decisions in the 1960s. Those calculations divided the student movement and alienated them from their allies.

Student opposition to the United States can be traced to the latter's close alliance with the Somozas. This was a generation of students that had grown up witnessing firsthand the violence of the Somoza regime and its friendly relationship with US Ambassador Thomas Whelan (1951–1961). Telegrams and memos from the US embassy in this period indicate Whelan served as an informal advisor to Anastasio Somoza and then to his son Luis. While the students may not have known the specifics of US support for the regime, they knew well the embassy's refusal to denounce Somocista excesses. They were particularly aggrieved by its actions in the aftermath of the 1959 student massacre. The student government reported that soon after the killings, the United States sent Nicaragua a shipment of arms, part of which Somoza directed to León "with the objective of punishing the university

Secondary students burning a homemade US flag at a 1967 FER-organized demonstration in Managua commemorating the student massacre of July 23, 1959. United States National Archives and Records Administration.

protest."[36] That was not the first time they had tied Somoza to his North American suppliers. In their first memo after the massacre, the student government noted that the soldiers used "automatic guns manufactured in North America."[37] They were thus keenly aware of the military assistance the United States provided the regime. As those weapons became increasingly trained on them and other citizens, their critiques grew louder.

Young Nicaraguans did not just resent US intervention in their home country. They also fiercely criticized its ambitions throughout the region. Students were especially protective of the Cuban Revolution and their international connections came in handy as they sought to defend the island. In early June 1960, a young Nicaraguan broke the story of a pending US coordinated attack against the revolutionary government. Citing evidence provided by the student federations of Cuba and Honduras, Joaquín Solís Piura, the president of the CUUN, publicly accused the Somozas of training a mercenary army to invade Cuba with the consent and aid of the US Department of State and, specifically, Ambassador Thomas Whelan.[38] A year later, Sergio Ramírez and Alejandro Serrano Caldera, the Nicaraguan representatives to the Second Congress of Central American Students held in May 1961, fought hard to get the other representatives to approve a declaration denouncing the US-organized Bay of Pigs invasion.[39]

Other youth organizations also vociferously defended the Cuban Revolution. In August 1960, the militant youth group, Juventud Patriótica Nicaragüense (Nicaraguan Patriotic Youth, or JPN) issued a declaration condemning any OAS effort to denounce the Cuban Revolution as nothing more than a "reflection of the oligarchies and imperialism and not the opinion of the pueblos." They argued that Cuba's enemies "are the owners of the mediums of diffusion, owners of the *latifundios* and investors who have done nothing more than rob us of the riches of the Latin American soil and subsoil and through puppet governments disrespect the human rights of our peoples and . . . trample our sovereignty through onerous treaties and scandalous military interventions."[40]

Cuba was catalyzing a sense of Latin American solidarity, and students saw themselves fighting in a hemispheric struggle against US imperialism. Diane Sorensen has illuminated the ways in which Cuban cultural institutions and revolutionary writings inspired a continental consciousness and sense of "Latin Americanism." The fierce reaction of Nicaraguan students to US intervention in Cuba suggests that US imperialism and its threat to the revolution also helped construct a regional sense of identity.[41]

Although the JPN declaration never mentions the United States, the young authors were clearly referring to the superpower's history of military and economic interventions. They did so knowing that in the Cold War, enemies of the United States were labeled communists. As Salvador Pérez Arévalo, the general secretary of the JPN, explained to an assembly held in honor of the Cuban Revolution, "This act is held in total identification with [the revolution]. We do not care if they call us communists."[42] "They" included both the Somoza government and US diplomats in Nicaragua. Both parties often dismissed opponents as members of the red tide. This is most obvious in US State Department documents, where embassy officials refer to all students who oppose Somoza as "communists" and criticized administrators, like Fiallos Gil, for being "left-leaning."[43] These Cold War biases meant that the embassy was overtly hostile to any student organizing in the early 1960s, and their actions did little to improve the image of the United States in the eyes of many students.

A controversy over the creation of a journalism school at the UNAN highlights the US biases that politicized even the most mundane student activities. In 1961, the US Information Services (USIS) helped create a school of journalism at the National University.[44] Classes started on June 1, and they apparently got off to a good start. That is, until the journalism students tried to organize a student association. Such organizations were the basic building blocks of the student government and were enshrined in the university autonomy law.[45] The journalism students thus did not expect any problems when they held an assembly in early July to elect a directory board. To their surprise, Stuart Ayers, the US embassy's cultural attaché, burst in on the meeting and, grabbing the microphone, forbade them to organize. He argued that the Binational Center, which was part of the US government public diplomacy efforts and thus was funding the school, prohibited student organizations. Angered, the students asked the CUUN to intervene. When their representatives visited Ayers to explain that the journalism school had to comply with the autonomy law, the attaché kicked them out of his office.[46]

Ayers's refusal to speak with the delegates and respect Nicaraguan law illustrated the embassy's dismissive attitude toward the students and their organization. In a memo describing the incident, Ambassador Whelan explained that the embassy opposed the student association because it would be under "the communist controlled university student center."[47] Similar accusations pervade the State Department records, but Whelan and the other staff members never provided evidence to support their allegations. While certainly some student leaders, including Joaquín Solís Piura, the president of the CUUN, had embraced socialism, most were merely firm defenders of Cuba's right to self-determination. However, in the dichotomous Cold War climate of either for or against the US government, the students had chosen a side, and the embassy withdrew their financial support.

The student government viewed the attaché's actions as another example of US imperialism. At that year's inauguration ceremony on July 11, the incoming president of the CUUN explained that this was a clear-cut case of US officials' disregard for the laws that governed the university.[48] On July 13, students marched down a major thoroughfare, holding signs denouncing the embassy's intervention and carrying a small coffin and decapitated doll, which, they told reporters, represented the journalism school. The National Guard violently broke up the demonstration, beating protestors, arresting the student carrying the coffin, and confiscating their signs.[49]

As had now become predictable, state violence triggered still larger student protests. The next afternoon, hundreds of students met at the university, and, amid chants of "Yankees, no; Nicaragua, yes," they burned an effigy of Ambassador Whelan wrapped in a US flag. After speeches denouncing US imperialism, students dragged the figure of Whelan through the streets, spitting on it and lighting a firecracker they had placed inside. In

La manifestación estudiantil del miércoles por la tarde, cua ndo desfilaba por la Avenida Roosevelt, procediendo a enterrar en forma simbólica la Escuela de Periodismo, reciente mente clausurada por la Universidad Nacional. Los estudiantes, como puede verse, portaban cartelones protestan do por lo que ellos consideran ayuda condicionada de los funcionarios nor teamericanos. — (Foto Rivitas).

Students protesting the closure of the journalism school held a symbolic funeral for their department. Their signs read: "The School of Journalism Died in Combat"; "We Don't Want Yankee Help with Conditions. Out!"; and "We are Worthy Journalists at the Service of the Pueblo or We are Nothing." *La Prensa*, July 15, 1960.

contrast to the battered US flag, the students proudly waved a red and black banner. Conscious of their critics, the protestors preemptively explained that it was not a communist symbol, although "it was alleged to be communist. It is the flag of Fidel Castro, the flag of the Latin American Revolution, the flag of Sandino."[50] The demonstration and the speeches that day suggest that for young protestors, the Cold War had little to do with the conflict between global superpowers or between communism and capitalism and was instead about the hemispheric battle for sovereignty. Such nuance was lost in the response to the students' protest.

The incident set off a firestorm of controversy. The press denounced the students' demonstration, but Somoza blamed the university authorities' permissiveness for the student protest. For their part, the administration issued a statement expressing regret over the incident but also noting that the students' actions reflected the "irreflexive attitudes of the moment," a fairly subtle rebuke of the US embassy. The diplomatic staff was not pleased and believed the administration's statement confirmed "the deliberate nature of a communist inspired insult to the United States government and the rector's responsibility for allowing it to stand."[51] Mistaking criticism for communism, the US embassy refused to actually analyze the students' claims.

The conflict exacerbated the already tense relations between the embassy and the university. From then on, both the rector and the students would face a diplomatic corps that actively worked against their institution. When Ambassador Whelan was finally recalled in 1961, many in the National University hoped a new era was dawning. But by the time Aaron Brown, a Kennedy appointee, arrived in Nicaragua, he had already embraced many of his predecessors' biases. Commenting on the students' desire to meet with him, Brown noted that they were leaders of the "communist-dominated" CUUN.[52] Later, when the university reelected Mariano Fiallos Gil to the rectorship, the embassy unhappily noted, "Mariano Fiallos Gil is apparently popular within his own University, but his reelection prolongs in office for another term a man who is, if not pro-communist, certainly no friend of the United States."[53]

Having dismissed the National University as a seedbed for radicalism, the US embassy aggressively championed the Universidad Centroamericana (Central American University, or UCA), the new Catholic university that opened in June 1961. In early October of that year, the Ford Foundation donated $200,000 to the UNAN for a science building—much to the chagrin of the embassy, which protested to the State Department. Brown wrote:

> The embassy has more than once expressed grave doubts over the advisability of channeling most or all US governmental aid for Nicaraguan higher education ... to the National University. We hold these doubts ... because aid given in this manner excludes Nicaragua's other university, the Central American University, which many of us consider also worthy of US assistance, and which some of us in fact believe *more* worthy of assistance than the national university.[54]

Not surprisingly, Brown would have no qualms about offering large and expedited loans to the UCA and none to the UNAN. Months later, the ambassador denounced an International Development Bank loan to the national universities of Central America and instead proposed a funding package for the UCA, "an institution which is slowly but so far surely being developed on sound academic and political lines."[55] These memos and others reveal how the embassy politicized the distribution of educational aid.

The embassy's biases were common knowledge. Mariano Fiallos Gil understood that his university faced an uncooperative US embassy precisely because of the UNAN's commitment to free expression and its refusal to automatically support US policies. Even *La Prensa* reported that "the National University's failure to issue a declaration of support for the naval blockade against Cuba had been a determining factor in the break of relations [with the US embassy]."[56] In contrast, the rector of the UCA had proven to be particularly supportive. After the Cuban Missile Crisis, Father León Pallais wrote a congratulatory telegram to the US ambassador and took the opportunity to complain about the Ford Foundation snub. It was a savvy move. As Ambassador Brown noted:

> By associating these two subjects in the same message, Father Pallais was making the point that the Catholic University, which is friendly toward the US, is being ignored, while the National University, whose rector would never dream of congratulating the American ambassador for US policy is being helped financially by US private sources. There is indeed irony in this circumstance.[57]

Apparently, the ambassador expected universities to take a public position in the Cold War conflict. If they did not fall in line with the regional hegemon, there would be consequences.

Many Nicaraguan students resented these expectations, and the US embassy began to realize that when it came to youth, they had developed a serious public image problem. University and secondary students involved with the Juventud Socialista Nicaragüense (Nicaraguan Socialist Youth, or JSN) and JPN actively denounced the anti-Castro policies of the United States and praised Cuba's revolution, and their actions ranged from leafleting to arson. In August 1961, the embassy was dismayed that students at the Escuela Normal de Varones in Managua did not respond well to their propaganda video, "Castro and Cuba." A group of students greeted each clip of Castro with raucous applause, and when the movie ended, they made their displeasure known by throwing stones at the organizer's car.[58]

Other protests illustrated a growing sense of rage, and US embassy property became the target of several acts of vandalism. At least four cars belonging to embassy employees were set on fire in the first half of 1961. The perpetrators also scratched anti-Yankee slogans on other vehicles.[59] The National Guard detained several youths in connection with these crimes, many of whom apparently admitted their connection with the JPN and other dissident groups.[60] As was happening elsewhere in Latin America, the Cuban Revolution and specifically, the threat to its survival, had led some youth to take up more extreme tactics.[61]

Nicaraguan students were not the only young people frustrated with US intervention. On January 9, 1964, Panama City teenagers, angered that a high school in the Canal Zone was not flying the Panamanian flag, clashed with the school's American students and four days of violent rioting ensued. In the final tally, two dozen lay dead. The incident spurred a diplomatic crisis that culminated in the renegotiation of the Canal treaties.[62] Almost immediately after the initial protest, the CUUN issued a statement condemning the United States for its role in the riots. Proclaiming the Panamanians to be vanguard heroes in a battle for vindication against the North Americans, the students wrote, "We know that the sacrifices of the Panamanian students and people is an example of the heroic struggle waged by our pueblos to win their full independence." At a series of demonstrations, Nicaraguan students condemned the cruelty of the "Yankee occupation forces," calling for their removal and demanding that the "US government respect all people's sovereignty and self-determination."[63]

The inter-American quality of student rage in this period is particularly noteworthy, and the United States went on the defensive. The State Department instructed embassies in the region to assess their country's "youth problems" and take "the offensive on the problem of Latin American youth" in 1962.[64] Even President John F. Kennedy came to consider reaching out to youth worldwide a "priority activity." In a memo signed two days before his assassination, Kennedy wrote, "It is essential to the successful conduct of our foreign affairs that we reach young people abroad to obtain their understanding and support."[65]

In Nicaragua, the US embassy response was hindered by its unwillingness to fully study the context behind student unrest. The report they prepared for the State Department actually failed to discuss any of the real problems facing Nicaraguan youth. Instead of seeking to understand student politics, the country team focused on the dilemma the diplomatic staff believed themselves to be in. Pro-communists and their youth contingent blamed the United States for keeping the Somozas in power, while the non-communist opposition also critiqued the United States for not helping to rid them of the Somozas. Meanwhile, the pro-Somoza forces were on alert for any indication that the State Department had changed its "inclination" and was withdrawing support. In this context, the embassy worried that these sectors would interpret any effort to address youth as a signal of US political intentions, as stated in this dispatch:

> If any US Government agency, for example, should launch a new youth project or youth organization in Nicaragua, it would be regarded with suspicion as to our motives, and we in turn would have tremendous difficulties

controlling it so as to keep it out of politics. However harmlessly we might try to guide it toward making democracy more popular among youth, its "pro-democratic" orientation would be suspected—and probably rightly so, in view of its likely membership—of cloaking a new opposition activity. Yet if such a new activity should have, or even appear to have, close ties with the Nicaraguan Government, many Nicaraguans would shun it as a Somocista activity and perhaps would interpret our connection with it as an indication of confirmed American support of the Somozas.[66]

These musings reveal the hypocrisy that characterized US Cold War policy. In its propaganda battle against the Soviet Union, the United States loudly proclaimed its democratic values. On the ground in Latin America, however, it refused to take any action that might jeopardize its relations with authoritarian allies who were severely circumscribing civil liberties and attacking human rights.[67] This meant that any real effort to promote democracy would be severely restricted.

In this situation, the US embassy opted for a public relations campaign that remained startlingly out of touch with the context behind student unrest. The authors of the report recognized that for young Nicaraguans the continuation of the Somozas in power was the primary source of their discontent, but they remained committed (in Nicaragua, at least) to a policy of "impartiality." The embassy staff determined to focus its efforts on convincing youth that "American democracy is a wonderful thing."[68] Such an emphasis, however, could do little to stem young people's growing frustration with US support for the regime and intervention elsewhere. Despite their repeated avowals to neutrality, the US embassy was not neutral. It pumped millions in military aid to the Somozas despite the family's human rights abuses and blamed dissidents for the regime's repression. Moreover, its active intervention elsewhere betrayed any claim to impartiality.[69]

Unwilling to recognize how its own policy contributed to student unrest, the US embassy focused on showcasing the wonders of "American democracy." To do this, they suggested more scholarships for study in the United States. To increase contact between US officials and students, they recommended turning the country's two Binational Centers into social centers. Finally, they proposed using baseball to reach young people. The report noted that the ambassador and his wife "have often deplored the lack of interscholastic and inter-collegiate sports in countries like Nicaragua, in the presumably well-founded belief that teenagers or undergrads healthfully working off their youthful zeal in athletics would have less enthusiasm for semi-professional—and usually misdirected politicking." They proposed creating a baseball league for teenagers centered at the American School that would reach youngsters "before unhealthy interest in politics becomes too firm an addiction."[70]

The embassy's plan seemed more like an effort to distract students from their country's political problems. For the ambassador, students were misplacing their energy into politics when it could be better exerted through sports and studying. Their perception of youthful political passion as a symptom of pent-up energy suggests how out of touch the embassy was when it came to the actual "problems of Latin American youth," and exemplified their government's larger ignorance of the realities on the ground in Cold War Latin America. Moreover, their solution was hardly systematic. Instead, it was based on targeting small groups of individuals: the lucky handful who won a scholarship abroad, the dozens of young men who formed the baseball teams, and the select group of students who socialized at the US-sponsored gatherings. Despite these limitations, the embassy continued to suggest scholarships and cultural events as ways to reach out to local youth throughout the decade.[71]

Emblematic of this policy agenda were the lunch parties Ambassador Brown began organizing in July 1961. Hoping to get to know students, Brown periodically invited fifteen young men and women to his house for an afternoon of swimming, dining, and dancing. A fairly self-selecting group gathered for these events. Mostly they were students who, if not exactly friendly to the United States, were pre-disposed to interact on amicable terms with its officials.[72]

A September 1962 exposé threatened the continuation of the pool parties and reveals some of the nuance of Cold War student politics. In late August, the president of the National University's student union, Juan José Ordoñez, obtained an invitation to one of the lunches. Immediately after the party, Ordoñez sent a scathing communiqué to local media, denouncing the gathering as a blatant attempt to indoctrinate students with the pleasures money provides. Ordoñez alleged that the ambassador and his staff were attempting to "destroy student unity and moderate their patriotic and anti-imperialist sentiments" through the distribution of "dollars: thousands for the 'big ones' and some pesos plus whisky for cheap snitches."

Tellingly, Ordoñez spent just as much time denouncing the United States as he did his peers, who, he argued, were playing into North American machinations. Mentioning several students by name, he criticized these "servile pilgrims" for their opportunistic attendance at these "binges."[73] In response, two of the students publicly denounced Ordoñez, and one threatened to sue for slander. Eventually, even the secretary general of the student government publicly distanced the body from Ordoñez. These responses highlight the divisions within the student body and suggest that the revolutionary fervor that had emerged after the 1959 student massacre was beginning to dissipate—in fact, the more moderate Christian Democrats would take over the student government two years later.[74]

The embassy, however, chose to view the incident through the Manichean lens of the Cold War. Diplomatic staff issued a statement reaffirming their commitment to intellectual exchange and accused Ordoñez of being part of a larger attempt to "destroy the solidarity among the free nations."[75] The ambassador concluded that Ordoñez was a "student stooge" doing the bidding of his communist masters who perhaps had become wary of a "counter infiltration of the student body as represented by our association with the young people."[76] Such an interpretation was perhaps convenient for the embassy—it lent credence to its suspicions of the student government at the UNAN and inflated the threat posed by Nicaragua's Communist Party.[77] As such, it may have helped the ambassador legitimize his support for the regime, but it did not reflect Nicaragua's increasingly complicated political reality.

The incident underscores the growing competition for the loyalties of the young that characterized the era. US actions in the hemisphere politicized and radicalized students who took to the streets to protest attacks on national sovereignty throughout Latin America. Resenting student opposition and fearing the demise of US hegemony, diplomats sought to improve their country's public image. Pool parties and baseball games became avenues for spreading US propaganda and enacting policy objectives. In the US Cold War calculus, the only variables were communists and democrats, allies or enemies. But such calculations could not keep up with changes on the ground. As the conflict between Ordoñez and the other students suggests, student politics were much more diverse. Young people were increasingly divided not just on the question of communism, but also on the issue of US imperialism, and revolution versus reform. Many were growing weary of the tense political climate, and the Schick presidency would provide them with a brief respite.

The Schick Opening: 1963–1966

In 1963, Nicaraguans witnessed the ascension of their first president unrelated to the Somozas in twenty-six years, and his election tempered the student movement's revolutionary fervor. While Luis Somoza's decision to hand the reins of power over to his chosen successor, René Schick, could hardly be called a transition to democracy, it did constitute a sea change. None of the students then attending university would have been able to recall Nicaragua without a Somoza in charge, and for them and their parents, the political situation must have looked promising. Schick's tenure, cut short by his death in 1966, constituted a fleeting political opening.[78] Schick quietly attempted to stand up to both the Somozas and the US embassy, with limited success.

When Schick took office in May 1963, Nicaraguans had reason to be hopeful. Despite the suspiciously high voter turnout (79 percent) and landslide results (Schick won 90 percent of the votes), the election was uneventful and many accepted its legitimacy even if they questioned its accuracy.[79] Moreover, the economy was growing rapidly, the result of record export rates and increasing foreign and domestic investment.[80] Additionally, there were signs that Schick, a longtime Liberal, intended to be a more transparent and accessible leader. He instituted live press conferences and held public audiences, in which he received hundreds of people and entertained their requests for personal assistance.[81]

On occasion, the new president even defied the Somoza family. Privately, he took steps to rein in General Anastasio Somoza Debayle's political activities. Soon after Schick's inauguration, the general had begun campaigning for the 1967 presidential election and his activities were generating negative publicity, public suspicion, and even revolutionary stirrings.[82] President Schick demanded Somoza limit these appearances, even going so far as to offer his resignation should the general ever decide he wanted to be president immediately.[83] Publicly, Schick maintained a firm stance, telling journalists that he had spoken with Somoza and the latter had agreed to stop such activities.[84]

Not all Somocistas had transferred their loyalties to Schick. In fact, disgruntled government officials were organizing the fetes for General Somoza and encouraging him to take power.[85] They likely resented the president's efforts to stem corruption. Schick was especially interested in ending the rampant graft and tax evasion. Perhaps more threatening for the Somozas' cronies in the military was Schick's plan to close the gambling houses that had provided an important, if illegal, source of income for military officers.[86] Furthermore, Somoza-owned newspapers harshly criticized his administration—so much so that he established a working relationship with Pedro Joaquín Chamorro at the historically anti-Somocista *La Prensa*.[87]

Schick also took measures to guarantee some level of civil liberties. From the beginning, he was relatively lenient with the regime's opponents and allowed many to return from exile.[88] He also vocally opposed suggestions that he limit freedom of speech. In August 1964, for example, *La Prensa* accused him of harboring communist sympathizers in the Ministry of Education and exhorted him to take drastic measures. Schick replied that he "was not going to violate public liberties on the pretext of combating communism" and "would never tolerate any threat to freedom of thought in schoolrooms."[89] The members of *La Prensa* editorial board were not Schick's only critics. The US embassy was particularly frustrated with the president's relative tolerance toward the suspected communists in the government. Criticizing Schick's commitment to civil liberties, the embassy claimed he had "confused the suppression of a serious totalitarian menace with the prevention of freedom of expression."[90] For Schick and his supporters, their tolerance of political dissidents reflected their liberal roots, but for Chamorro and the embassy, it was a sign of "fuzzy" logic and misplaced priorities.

Despite these hopeful signs, repression remained commonplace and the administration was riddled with contradictions. For one, Schick's government still went after leftists in the labor movement. In June 1963, the government used the threat of communist subversion to justify sending troops to repress a strike among customs house employees.[91] Furthermore, despite Schick's professed desires to protect civil liberties, he maintained strict control of public demonstrations. The National Guard, for example, prevented students protesting the detention of Carlos Fonseca from completing a march from León to Managua in July 1964.[92] During a 1965 student protest of US intervention in the Dominican Republic, Schick privately told the US embassy staff that "license to assemble did not include license to demonstrate and that the police were to be firm in the latter eventuality."[93] Such measures suggest that Schick, like the Somozas before him, recognized the potential instability that mass demonstrations could generate and sought to prevent them.

In addition, economic inequality continued unabated. The long-promised land reform provided just 5 percent of landless families with acreage, and most still lacked access to credit and other services that would have made farming a viable option.[94] Moreover, the benefits of the decade's economic growth were still very unevenly distributed. Cotton generated much of this prosperity, but each year, it drove more and more peasants off the land and into marginalized urban barrios.[95]

Finally, the Somozas did not stay out of the picture. Anastasio Somoza Debayle remained commander of the National Guard, using his position to further his presidential ambitions. Squashing labor unrest and pursuing the Sandinistas, he stayed in the limelight, biding his time until the 1967 elections. Opting for a lower profile, his brother Luis traveled for much of

Schick's first year. When he was in the country, he exerted some control over his younger brother, helping to convince him to quit his early campaigning. However, Luis also remained in positions of power as an active member of both the Nicaraguan Agrarian Institute, which was administering land reform, and the Liberal Party.[96]

These factors fueled a small but dedicated revolutionary movement. A group of erstwhile students, including Carlos Fonseca and Silvio Mayorga, had founded several anti-Somoza groups in the early 1960s, each incarnation more broad-based and radical than the last. The Sandinista National Liberation Front emerged from these organizations in 1963. The Sandinistas advocated for the overthrow of the Somozas and the creation of a socialist state. Inspired by Che Guevara's foco theory, the FSLN initially sought to build a revolutionary movement in the Nicaraguan mountains, with disastrous results. An early effort in the region where the Coco and Bocay Rivers met floundered on their inability to forge a connection with the local populace that could sustain the movement, and the National Guard managed to kill many of the guerrillas in 1963. As Fonseca's biographer Matilde Zimmermann observed, "The Sandinistas engaged in guerrilla operations off and on for seventeen years without bringing down a single enemy soldier."[97] For much of this period, their numbers were simply too small and the Guard too powerful to pose any real threat to the status quo.

In terms of their revolutionary sentiments, the Sandinistas were an exception, and for many, Schick's presidency suggested that peaceful electoral change was possible.[98] This belief propelled the rise of the Social Christian Party, which advocated for a middle ground between capitalism and communism and became especially popular in the university. The conflict between these moderates and a small but vocal sector allied with the FSLN would consume student politics for the rest of the decade.

A Divided Student Movement

The era's small democratic opening combined with the promise and, to some, threat of the Cuban Revolution resulted in the emergence of various new organizations. During this time, Nicaraguans experimented with new political ideologies and tactics. Even the Sandinistas briefly embraced electoral politics, and its cadres worked with the leftist coalition, Republican Mobilization.[99] This flourishing of political engagement was occurring throughout Latin America, and scholars of the Long Sixties in Mexico, Uruguay, and elsewhere have illuminated the debates and divisions that marked a revitalized left in the wake of Cuba's success.[100] In Nicaragua, the historian Matilde Zimmermann found that support for the revolutionary left actually declined in this era, and the contests for student government at Nicaragua's National University reflected its diminished status.[101] More and more young people embraced a middle-class vision of democratization that focused on working through existing institutions to reform the state and promote social justice.

Several new organizations offered students at the National University a wide range of political options, from the revolutionary to the apolitical, and the most active students focused their energies on campus and electoral politics. The era's political diversity splintered what had once been a fairly unified anti-Somoza student movement at the same time that it energized student political competition.[102] Student government elections grew increasingly heated as various sectors vied for control of the university's resources. Under the political opening of the 1960s, youth in the university reasserted their faith in the institution's ability to lead their society, but they no longer agreed on the end goals.

Although globally the decade is associated with a rise in revolutionary fervor, the appeal of radical student politics declined quickly in the early 1960s in Nicaragua. The early history of the Revolutionary Student Front illustrates this surprising development. In early December 1962, the JSN and the JPN organized the First Revolutionary Congress of Democratic Students. More than one hundred university and secondary students attended the symposium, where they founded the Frente Estudiantil Revolucionario (Revolutionary Student Front, or FER), which "constitutes the revolutionary organization of the country's democratic and progressive students."[103] Embracing Marxism, anti-imperialism, and revolution, the FER was the most aggressive student group of the Somoza era, and it became a staunch advocate for and critical ally of the nascent FSLN. Many of the FER's founding members also participated in the student government at the National University, and they were able to coordinate and influence the CUUN toward a more radical direction, at least until 1964.

In the Cold War context, the FER's revolutionary politics drew the ire of government and university officials. Like its predecessor, the JPN, the FER made a name for itself organizing militant street demonstrations that celebrated the memory of Sandino and condemned the regime.[104] They held annual homages and distributed pamphlets and posters that promoted Sandino's legacy. Not surprisingly, many of these actions also included a vehement denunciation of US imperialism. Within months of its organization, the group was already in trouble with state authorities and UNAN administrators for its militant tactics, which included vandalizing a US AID office and boycotting the visit of the Costa Rican president to the university because they regarded him to be a "submissive lackey of American imperialism."[105] Such overt hostility toward the United States drove a wedge between revolutionary students and their allies. After the FER and the student government of the National University protested the Costa Rican president's visit, the university rector publicly excoriated their "disrespect and discourtesy," and the media judged them to be "spoiled brats."[106] This new emphasis on respectable protest marginalized young radicals.

Another factor that may have limited the FER's popularity was the Schick government's relative tolerance. When the Sandinista Silvio Mayorga, a former student at the National University, was arrested in 1964, his peers mobilized on his behalf and the government soon released him.[107] When Carlos Fonseca was arrested in 1964 and charged with "crimes against the constitution," the FER-controlled student government organized a series of demonstrations, even occupying their campus. The protests lasted two days before Schick agreed to meet with the students. He promised that the guerrilla leader would not be mistreated and allowed the students to visit him in prison.[108] The government's relative responsiveness curtailed student demonstrations in this period and limited public displays of dissent.

The FER remained quite small for many of its early years. Michele Najlis, who joined the FER when she arrived at the UNAN-Managua in 1965, recalled, "We were a handful of people. I don't know how we were able to achieve all the commotion we did."[109] Santiago Sequiera, who enrolled at the UNAN-León in 1964, recalled that the FER lacked clear organization. He remembered that it was directly linked to the FSLN leadership, which in this period was reeling from the loss suffered in the action at the Coco and Bocay Rivers.[110] In addition, its members' militancy put off many would-be allies. For example, Hugo Mejía Briceño, who entered the university in the mid-1960s, remembered the FER as a tiny, hostile group. "We saw them as people who were not very friendly. They were ... always fighting." Mejía was particularly put off by the fact that they did not seem to welcome Catholics. "The people in the FER believed that those who were Catholics didn't belong with them." He explained that the revolutionary students thought their Catholic peers were not interested in actually fighting for change but only in the religious aspect of social justice.[111] Their suspicion was likely rooted in their conflict with the Social Christians, who were slowly gaining control of the student government.

The growing popularity of Christian Democracy illustrates the diversity of student politics in the 1960s. In the 1940s, the writings of Jacques

Maritain, Emmanuel Mounier, and other French thinkers inspired a generation of young Catholics around the world to organize Christian Democratic movements. Reinaldo Antonio Téfel, who had played a leading role in the student protests of the 1940s, helped promote the ideology in Nicaragua—first, through the National Union of Popular Action, then within the ranks of the Conservative Party, and finally, through the creation of the Nicaraguan Social Christian Party in 1963. Perhaps recalling his own time as an activist in the university, Téfel encouraged student participation in the movement and advised the party's youth wing. Many of the party leaders—young professionals and often recent university graduates—hailed from the middle class.[112] The rapid growth of Nicaragua's Christian Democratic Party, like its counterparts throughout Latin America, occurred in the 1960s—in part, as a negative reaction to the Cuban Revolution.[113]

Rooted in the idea that Christians had a moral imperative to address inequality, the doctrine advocated communitarianism, a middle way between communism and capitalism. The national Christian Democratic Party promoted social welfare, labor protections, planned economic growth, fiscal reform, and corporate representation. The party's autonomous student wing, the Frente Demócrata Cristiano (Christian Democrat Front, or FDC), thus rejected armed struggle, advocated for reform via existing institutions, and promoted the theory of the two imperalisms. Danilo Aguirre, a student at this time, recalled that this was one of the biggest differences between the FER and the FDC. "The Social Christians said that just as there was North American imperialism there was Soviet imperialism. The others never spoke of that. They said that Soviet imperialism did not exist." Aguirre believed that the Social Christians were young men and women who "felt the necessity of confronting the dictatorship but didn't subscribe to the extreme ideas of the FER nor did they want to risk their life to confront the Guard."[114] Jesús Miguel "Chuno" Blandon likewise remembered that the movement gained popularity in the 1960s:

> Because the Cuban Revolution provoked a reaction at the national level and in addition there was a campaign against communism, against Marxism, against the Sandinista Front. Then, the Christian Democrat Youth presented themselves as an alternative with the same ideals of social justice, but Catholic.[115]

Christian Democracy thus constituted a safer option during a time when revolutionary struggles were proving to be much harder than many had anticipated. Moreover, anti-communism continued to be a strong current in

Nicaraguan society, and various public intellectuals regularly denounced the doctrine.

The religious dimension was also critical to the group's rapid growth. Thomas Walker, who studied Christian Democracy in the 1960s, found that the movement flourished in this time because several priests started to offer short workshops on "Nicaraguan social problems" that helped push students toward the FDC.[116] Moreover, in a Catholic country, like Nicaragua, practicing Catholics felt some pressure to join the organization. Hugo Mejía Briceño recalled, "Our Social Christian friends demanded to know why we, being Catholics, didn't join the Social Christians."[117]

Connections with adult allies both facilitated and hindered the FDC's organizing efforts in the university. Because the Social Christian movement was then taking off throughout Latin America, the FDC enjoyed access to an international network that funded student travel to Chile, Venezuela, and even Europe.[118] At the national level, Moisés Hassan recalled that the student group was very well organized because of its close association with the official party.[119] These ties, however, were also a liability. Hugo Mejía distrusted the organization for precisely that reason: "During that time, there was much suspicion within the student movement toward the political parties. At the same time, these compañeros, these Social Christians, were also [members of] the party, and we didn't think that was correct."[120] Some students clearly continued to regard any political party with suspicion, and Mejía's critique speaks to widely held fears of student susceptibility to adult manipulation. The Social Christian students' close relationship with the US embassy did not help much in that regard. The embassy had closely monitored the growth of the party and its student movement, eager to see the rise of a vocally anti-communist organization.[121] Leaders of the FDC visited with Ambassador Brown and his staff to talk about student elections and once even asked them to intervene.[122]

The FER and the FDC were not the only groups vying for student loyalty. Several other organizations were mobilizing around very different ideas about the role of the state and the university in society. Somocista youth groups had always had a presence in the National University, and, in the 1960s, they too increased their organizing efforts. By June 1966, Somocistas had won control of the Law Student Association—apparently by not disclosing their politics.[123] Rumors of secret Somocista proclivities appear to have been common. That year, Juan Doña, the frontrunner for student body president, lost his lead amid charges that he was a secret Somocista.[124]

Taking a different tack, several new groups advocated for an apolitical student government. The Student Democratic Front and its counterpart in León, the Frente Reivindicador Estudiantil (Student Defense Front), wanted students to stay out of national politics.[125] Although some suspected these organizations were Somocista fronts, a growing segment of the student population *was* pushing for a politically neutral student government. Even secondary students found themselves under internal pressure to stay out of politics. In June 1966, a bitter contest was ensuing for the student government at the prestigious Ramírez Goyena Institute. In the midst of the election season, a popular philosophy teacher, the FER activist Michele Najlis, was fired for being a communist and lacking her diploma and replaced with a well-connected Somocista. Her students took her side, but the school's student government wrote a letter to the local press enjoining them to leave politics aside. The young writers argued that "the school is not a political field and for that reason the [student government] should remain in the hands of those students who only have one priority: the well-being of the institute."[126]

Influenced by all these tendencies, the Christian Democrats, who controlled the student government at the National University from 1965 to 1969, changed gears, moving away from the disruptive tactics of past generations and toward a more conventional form of political activism. Instead of trying to mobilize against the state, students in the 1960s sought to reinforce and bolster the institutions that underwrote it. The FDC-led CUUN organized forums on democracy, educational reform, and national politics that helped create public spaces where people across the ideological spectrum could debate ideas.[127]

For many students, interactions with workers and campesinos were limited to the university's extension program, which some youth helped organize, and other social uplift projects. The Association of Students from the Atlantic Coast, for example, sent a dozen volunteers to work with communities in Bluefields and Puerto Cabezas in 1965. In addition to offering hygiene and development courses, they scouted out potential leaders who could collaborate with the Alliance for Progress program in the United States.[128] These were activities that did not threaten existing structures or even address the impending return of the Somozas to power. Instead, they embraced conservative institutions, like the Catholic Church and the US embassy. Reflecting the Christian Democrats' class roots, this was a distinctly middle-class political agenda. Students, as future young professionals, sought to reform a political economic system they were readying to join.[129]

To be sure, the FER continued organizing defiant protests, but their activities were severely hampered by an escalating tide of anti-communism. Although their rallies drew hundreds of students, the audiences were smaller than they had been in the past and received much more negative coverage in the media.[130] In fact, by the time Michele Najlis ran for president of the CUUN in 1966, her open Marxism had become a liability. At a forum for the presidential candidates that year, a student questioned her political loyalties: "You have said that you have no connections to foreign doctrines. If that is true, why did you play a recording of the third Communist Internationale" during a recent protest? *La Prensa* reported that Najlis was unable to give an effective answer.[131]

With fewer numbers, the radical students saw their efforts to ally with other sectors severely limited. The FER at the National University seems to have concentrated more on campus politics than on community organizing. A survey of their newspaper, *El Estudiante*, rarely mentions any kind of community organizing in this period, and Michele Najlis's 1966 platform mentioned workers once—in a promise to defend their rights.[132] Secondary students were more active. In Jinotega, they spearheaded an alliance with workers and peasants.[133] Jacinto Suárez recalled that the students associated with the FER and the FSLN at the Ramírez Goyena Institute did teach literacy in the barrios, but that effort seems to have been small and relatively short-lived.[134]

The political diversity of the 1960s underscores the political agency of youth: they were making active choices about which party to join, if any. They were not knee-jerk revolutionaries persuaded by a single "language of dissent," but rather thoughtful activists picking and choosing from a variety of political ideologies and languages.[135] For the small number of students who embraced revolutionary politics, those sentiments emerged from a deep-rooted discontent with the country's inequality, authoritarianism, and client relationship with the United States. Those who chose the moderate Christian Democratic path acted out of an optimistic belief in the power of the country's institutions and its alliance with the United States. During the brief period of time when the Somozas, at least publicly, had stepped down from power, students were having lively debates about what Nicaragua could look like without the dictatorship. The family's return to the public eye would once again unite students of very different political persuasions and jolt them back into the kind of community organizing they had abandoned.

Conclusion

The democratic interlude Luis Somoza set in motion when he took office had contradictory effects on the students at the National University. University autonomy, combined with a small political aperture, fostered a plurality of political opinions that in turn led to a growth in student organizations. The openness of the Schick period allowed for greater and more aggressive expressions of dissent, but it was not inevitable that students would embrace political militancy. Indeed, just as Schick was loosening the state's grip on civil liberties, the Cuban Revolution was deterring some students from adopting more radical activism. For these youths, it was precisely the promise of change embodied by Schick's presidency that tempered their politics and led many toward the more moderate Social Christian organization.

When Carlos Fonseca critiqued the revolutionary students' lack of militancy, he was speaking to trends that had begun in the early 1960s. Radical youth, consumed with anti-imperialist rage and international solidarity, distanced themselves from the concerns of the masses and alienated some of their peers and allies. Meanwhile, moderates promoting a middle road to change won control of the student government. They used that position to promote a middle-class vision of democratization that was centered on institutional reforms and social uplift. Unlike their predecessors, the Christian Democrats were not as inclined to organize public protests, and the student movement's visibility declined.

The kinds of activism that prevailed in the university in this period reinforced student isolation from the lower classes, and the university student movement lacked a concrete social consciousness. Neither the volunteer opportunities organized by the Christian Democrats or the radical rhetoric of the FER were grounded in the everyday reality of the poor and working class. That would change under the administration of Anastasio Somoza Debayle.

CHAPTER 6

Radicalizing Youth, 1966–1972

On April 21, 1971, Melvin Rivas, president of the CUUN, and César Aróstegui, secretary general of the UCA student government, issued a letter from the notorious prison, La Aviación. The two had been arrested along with dozens of their peers and their parents on April 20 for occupying the UCA campus. The origins of that protest were complex: months earlier, students seized the school to demand the dismissal of their authoritarian rector, Father León Pallais. In retaliation, the administration expelled sixty-five student activists. Such a severe response catalyzed further protest. Students again seized the private university, and young people occupied Catholic churches, including the National Cathedral in Managua, in solidarity.

Now from their jail cell, the two officers expanded their demands to include the plight of Nicaragua's political prisoners. Most were Sandinistas who had completed their sentence long ago, but the regime had refused to release them. Rivas and Aróstegui pledged to remain in their cells until their "prison compañeros" were freed. They called for continued demonstrations, and their peers answered. By April 26, secondary students at private and public schools were striking and occupying churches. Nuns and priests, parents and parishioners all rallied to support the students and, by extension, the Sandinistas. Teenagers in the public schools protested until the military and paramilitary forced them out with tear gas. In Masaya, students fought the retired Guardsmen, attacking their school and, with help from the community, managed to repel them. The protests forced Somoza to intervene: the regime began releasing some political prisoners, and the rector of the private university was given a government job at the Nicaraguan embassy in Washington, DC.[1]

These protests were remarkable for several reasons. For one, students from across the country and social spectrum were moved to defend the rights of a small handful of their peers at the private university as well as the rights of the Sandinista militants working to overthrow the government. Second, parents, clergy members, and ordinary parishioners all participated in the protests and helped extend them. Third, this alliance ultimately compelled the regime to respond. The protests of 1971 were especially significant given the status of the anti-Somoza student movement for much of the 1960s, when the student body at both universities had largely rejected armed struggle and Marxist politics. Now they were risking their lives to support Sandinista political prisoners and compelling their families and friends to do the same. What had happened?

Under the regime of Anastasio Somoza Debayle, a new militant and aggressive student consciousness began to gradually emerge. The regime's repression and corruption disillusioned youth who had previously hoped that reform was possible. The rise of Catholic liberation theology in Latin America persuaded students of the immorality of inequality, and many began organizing youth groups where they could discuss what to do about the country's problems. Meanwhile, the Sandinistas, reeling from several debilitating losses in the 1960s, realized the need for mass organizing and encouraged students to help lead the way. Finally, the emergence of new movements demanding social justice provided students with an avenue for activism. All these factors politicized young people, jolting them out of the political lethargy that had characterized much of the previous decade.

The radicalization of students in Nicaragua mirrored trends occurring around the world and especially in Latin America. Historians of Brazil, Mexico, Uruguay, and the United States have all illuminated the "dialectics of repression" that marked the late sixties: protest was met with state violence, which in turn resulted in more aggressive widespread protest and still more state violence. Repression, these historians conclude, catalyzed still greater grassroots organizing. In many places, the cycle that began in the 1960s ended with the overpowering violence of the state and the splintering of protest movements.[2]

Nicaragua had been experiencing such "cycles of protest" since at least the 1940s.[3] What makes this period different, however, is that this cycle effectively continued for a decade and culminated in revolution. Under Anastasio Somoza Debayle, a new cycle of protest and repression began, but this time, it escalated to the point that young people were organizing barrio-based commando units and the National Guard was bombing neighborhoods. In the late 1960s, students began helping to build a broad-based movement that would sustain the revolutionary struggle for the decade to come.

Young women were especially active in this process and several took on leadership roles in student organizations, like the Revolutionary Student Front and the Christian Democrat Front.[4] They were part of a long tradition of women's activism in Nicaragua, where women had been visible members of both the national government as well as the urban workforce during the Somoza regime.[5] Women's rights were not a primary or even stated goal for the young Nicaraguans who took up the fight against the dictatorship. Nevertheless, women's activism still challenged gender norms and helped break down some of the traditional hierarchies that characterized Nicaraguan society.[6]

Students turned universities into vibrant centers of dissent. This was possible because the National University's autonomy and the struggle for student rights that preceded the attainment of that autonomy had helped cement notions of student exceptionalism in the public sphere. The idea that university students required liberties denied other sectors meant that when students were punished for expressing a political opinion, various sectors rallied to their defense. It meant that when students faced the regime's brutality, communities intervened to defend them. Now students would increasingly intervene to defend the barrios. Indeed, their protected status enabled student political activism under the repressive regime of Anastasio Somoza Debayle to flourish, and young people moved beyond campus-based organizing. The connections students forged across their society forced the dictator to make concessions and began to illustrate the power of broad-based movements.

Students against Somoza

Perhaps the single greatest radicalizing factor for young Nicaraguans was the Somoza regime itself. Anastasio Somoza Debayle had made his designs on the presidency clear from the earliest days of the Schick administration, but it was only when he began campaigning in earnest in 1966 that students began mobilizing against him. The divisions within the ranks of the student movement in the 1960s, however, limited the efficacy of their efforts. Students pursued various strategies, from the electoral to the insurrectionary, to keep him out of office with little success, and once in power, the regime's repression and corruption persuaded many to abandon their hopes for peaceful reform.

Somoza's campaign electrified campus politics at the UNAN where, remarkably for the era, two young women were vying for control of the student government. Representing the left, Michele Najlis was a highly visible leader of the FER, editing their newspaper and delivering speeches throughout campus. The FDC, which was particularly popular among female students, nominated a little-known engineering student, Brenda Ortega, to run against Najlis.[7] Young female activists were taking on more visible and riskier roles across the continent in this era, but they continued to face pressure from the media and even their male counterparts to conform to traditional gender-based norms that restricted women's public activism. In Nicaragua, the weakness of the student movement in the 1960s may have mediated such gender discrimination: low rates of participation in student organizations meant that skilled activists, male or female, quickly rose through the ranks because of an urgent need for human resources.[8]

The 1966 student government election at the National University was especially important for students. Both the revolutionary students and the Christian Democrats hoped to use the resources of the CUUN to influence the national election, while a popular "independent" candidate, Juan Doña, vowed to take the student center out of national politics altogether. After rumors that Doña was actually a Somocista ended his candidacy, the contest came down to the FER and the FDC candidates. In the largest voter turnout in the university's history, Ortega won by seven votes: 756 to 749.[9]

Once the elections were over, both groups needed the other's cooperation to effectively oppose Somoza, and they intermittently banded together. In October 1966, they staged a daring protest at the first baseball game of the season. Before an audience of twenty-five thousand, which included Somoza and the US ambassador, several students joined the parade of players marching into the stadium and unfurled a banner reading, "No More Somozas." The crowd went wild. Police chased the protestors off the field while people in the stands reached out their hands to pull them up into the bleachers. The Guard followed the students out of sight of the crowd, then brutally attacked them. Photos in *La Prensa* show soldiers clubbing the protestors and hitting them with their pistols. Two were later hospitalized with critical injuries sustained during the beatings.[10]

Bystanders rushed to protect the embattled students. A journalist, for example, tried to intervene when he saw the Guard dragging one student, María Teresa García, by the hair, and the soldiers beat him up as well. He was jailed along with at least a dozen protestors.[11] Najlis recalled how a police officer's sympathy helped her escape her peers' fate. As the students ran away from the field, the Guard followed them. When Najlis reached the outside of the stadium, a police officer recognized her and told her to run "because if they catch you they'll kill you." He stopped a taxi, pushed her and her companion in, and told the driver to get them away from there.[12]

The democratic aperture of the decade was closing, and ordinary Nicaraguans understood that politically active youth would require protection in an increasingly hostile climate.

Najlis escaped harm that day, but many did not. As the crowds flooded out of the stadium at the end of the game, those seated in one section found their exit blocked. A scream rose up, and the crowd stampeded. By the time it was over, twelve were dead and more than a hundred wounded.[13] The incident threw the capital into a state of turmoil, and hundreds turned out for the funerals of the dead. In the aftermath, rumors spread to explain what happened. While an official investigation found that the exit had been blocked by an ice cream truck and that the screams came from a confrontation between a woman and a drunk sports fan, the opposition circulated more menacing explanations. Some radio stations reported that the Guard had locked the gates to search the fans, who panicked because they were afraid of the soldiers. *La Prensa* reported that the Guard had blocked the exits so they could look for students hiding in the crowd. For their part, the students were certain that the Guard, wanting to conceal their misdeeds, had closed the exit to confiscate the cameras of journalists. Somoza blamed communist agitation for the panic. These varied theories suggest how tense and fearful society had become, and Somoza had not even been elected yet.[14]

Galvanized by the repression and the tragedy that ensued, university students mobilized anew. They organized a strike to free their imprisoned companions and painted graffiti on the walls of Somoza's party offices. A bomb even went off in a León theater, wounding two. The protests, however, were short-lived. The Social Christian leadership of the CUUN was deeply disturbed by the Guard's violent reaction at the stadium, and many feared what the next few years would bring.[15]

Still hopeful that reform was possible, young moderates remained committed to working through traditional political channels. They now focused on electoral activism. During November, young Social Christians organized the Comités Ciudadanos de Vigilancia Electoral y Defensa del Sufragio (Citizen Committees for Electoral Vigilance and the Defense of Suffrage, or CIVES), which promoted Somoza's opponent, the Conservative Fernando Agüero. CIVES also monitored voter registration and worked to prevent electoral fraud. Branches of the committee formed throughout the country, but its members were reluctant to work with leftist students, who were much more confrontational.[16]

The FER itself was torn between those who wanted to campaign for Agüero and those who rejected electoral politics. This divide reflected a tension in the FSLN, which for much of Schick's presidency had experimented with political organizing via the leftist opposition coalition Movilización Republicana. By November 1966, however, the Sandinista leadership had decided to reject the "electoral farce" in favor of advancing revolution.[17] The FER newspaper, *El Estudiante*, took a similar stance. In September 1966, it published an article condemning the idea of an opposition block. Calling Agüero a "potential dictator," they argued that the upcoming elections would result either in Somoza's fraudulent victory or "we will have a government headed by the representative of the most nefarious oligarchy," the Conservatives. For them, it was no choice at all, and change would only come from "a truly popular struggle."[18]

Despite such rhetoric, some of the revolutionary students still supported Agüero's campaign. FER leaders attended a January 22, 1967, opposition rally in which Agüero called for the National Guard to revolt. Convinced the elections would be fraudulent, the Conservative candidate called on the people to march through the streets while they awaited the military's decision. Thousands followed him up Roosevelt Avenue, including some 250 students led by the FER leader Michele Najlis. The protestors soon found themselves face to face with the National Guard and their bayonets. The soldiers fired into the crowd, killing scores of demonstrators. The massacre was a harbinger of the brutality to come. A few days later, under a cloud of repression and voting irregularities, Nicaraguans went to the polls and elected Anastasio Somoza Debayle to the presidency.[19]

The regime's continued violence, particularly against students, prompted more protests. The Christian Democrats remained in charge of the student governments at both universities, but they grew more militant. While their connections to the broader society continued to be filtered through party politics and social uplift programs, they increasingly, if intermittently, took to the streets to protest attacks on members of their own community. For example, there do not seem to have been any protests after the National Guard killed Casimiro Sotelo, the former president of the student government at the UCA and leader of the FER, in early November 1967. However, a strike ensued later that month when the Guard arrested two youths studying at the UNAN, Romeo López and Lesbia Carrasquilla. The demonstrations forced the regime to remand the two students for trial.[20] There were also protests after students learned of the April 1968 arrest and torture of two brothers, René and David Tejada, former soldiers turned Sandinista student activists. After David died from his wounds, his torturer, Major Oscar Morales, a close ally of the dictator, ordered his body thrown in a volcano. The government had reached new depths of depravity, and the outcry was so great that the regime brought Morales to trial.[21]

The Guard's growing violence politicized a new generation. The Sandinistas were most often the targets—the news of their torture and abuse in the nation's prisons outraged students—but Somoza also relied on the military to punish dissenters of all stripes. During a teacher's strike in 1968, the Guard brutally beat secondary students who were marching peacefully in solidarity with their instructors.[22] Many who joined the FER, and eventually the FSLN, recalled that such violence was a turning point. Irving Larios traced his political consciousness to an early encounter with a soldier: "I was about thirteen years old when a soldier on a bicycle ran into me. Instead of stopping to help me, he took out his gun and began pistol-whipping me. That marked me."[23] César Aróstegui decided to join the Sandinistas after the National Guard arrested and beat him for participating in a student protest in 1970.[24] These early experiences with the Guard's cruelty persuaded youth of the regime's brutality.

Somoza's machinations to stay in power also disillusioned many. To circumvent the constitution's prohibition against reelection, Somoza, like his father, proposed a power-sharing agreement. The deal with the Conservatives would dissolve the government in 1971 and allow him to run again as a civilian in 1974. Persuaded by the promise that the Organization of American States would supervise elections, his former opponent, Fernando Agüero, agreed to the pact, called Kupia Kumi. The stage was set for Somoza's reelection.[25]

In this context, moderate students began losing elections. Moisés Hassan, an UNAN professor at the time, recalled that the Social Christian Party declined as more and more people "saw that the process was going to repeat itself," that Somoza would manipulate the structures of government in the same way that his father had.[26] Those Christians who had been drawn to the doctrine for its emphasis on social justice grew frustrated with the party. Mónica Baltodano explained that "because Christian Democracy continued promoting electoral struggle, at a time when we believed that the electoral route was not the way, other movements began to emerge" that advocated more militant strategies.[27] The Christian Democratic Party and its youth front continued operating during the seventies, but many of its leading members eventually embraced revolution and joined the Sandinistas.[28]

Trust in state institutions broke down rapidly in the early years of Anastasio Somoza Debayle's rule. The violence that marked his campaign, the fraud that characterized his election, and the regime's continued brutality weakened the state's legitimacy, especially in the eyes of young people. Many have observed that the younger Somoza son lacked the political finesse of his brother and father, and from his earliest years in office, that distinction was readily apparent. While Anastasio Somoza García and Luis Somoza had been just as ruthless, corrupt, and violent, both had paired these offenses with strategic concessions that mollified or divided the opposition. The father had made deals with workers and built schools for students; Luis had granted the university autonomy and made gestures toward democracy.[29] When Somoza made a deal with Agüero, he was trying to follow in their footsteps, but he neglected two powerful sectors of the opposition, workers and students.

A Radicalizing Church

The emergence of liberation theology also had a radicalizing influence on the generations of young people coming of age in the late 1960s and 1970s. Most famously, it drove priests and nuns across the continent to leave their convents and rectories to live and work among the poorest of their parishioners. But it also dramatically affected the politics of the young men and women who studied with them in private Catholic schools or worshipped in their parishes.[30] Compelled by the stark inequality that surrounded them and encouraged by the more progressive nuns and priests, these youths formed dozens of Christian groups, which eventually merged into the Revolutionary Christian Movement in 1973. Through these organizations, students participated in study circles, and youth groups visited impoverished urban and rural barrios. In these settings, young men and women worked side by side, teaching literacy, leading Bible groups, analyzing Marx, and organizing with workers. These experiences radicalized young Christians from various class backgrounds, and many eventually joined the Sandinistas.

Although the origins of liberation theology are often traced to Vatican II, the papal conference actually institutionalized changes that already had been occurring in many places in Latin America. Inspired by Catholic social thought, which criticized the destructive effects of capitalism and advocated for reform, priests, nuns, and laypeople in Brazil, El Salvador, and elsewhere had a long history of working with the poor. In the 1950s and 1960s, they began experimenting with ways to promote the political engagement of their parishioners. Some, like students and workers, were already politically organized via the Catholic Action movement, which sought to organize Catholics and promote their participation in both the Church and their wider society.[31] Catholic Action organizations, like Juventud Obrera Católica (JOC) and Juventud Universitaria Católica (JUC), practiced the "see, judge, act" method that called on participants to observe their surroundings, make judgements, and take action to improve the contemporary world. This strategy, known as "Revision of Life," led many lay Catholics to embrace a social justice-oriented vision of their religion. To serve more remote areas, clergy experimented with lay-led pastoral work. For example, in Brazil, the Movement for Base Education employed the methods of Paulo Freire to teach literacy and raise the consciousness of the poor.[32]

Vatican II embraced these developments. Out of that conference, which lasted from 1962 to 1965, came a push to break down the hierarchy that had traditionally characterized the church. Mass would now be said in vernacular languages, instead of Latin, as had been the case for centuries; the priest would face parishioners during services; and clergy would encourage ordinary Catholics to interpret the Bible for themselves. It also gave priests and nuns greater autonomy to figure out how to serve the needs of their parishes and missions. In 1968, Latin American bishops met in Medellín, Colombia, to determine just how to do that. At this gathering, the bishops drew on Catholic Action's Revision of Life strategy: the attendees observed the region's poverty, determined that such dramatic inequality was a sin, and concluded that the Gospel required Catholics to work for social justice on earth.[33] As these ideas, which formed the basis of liberation theology, spread and took root in Latin America, clergy members would use its tenets to galvanize young people in their Catholic schools and parishes.

In Nicaragua, priests like Fernando Cardenal and nuns like Luz Beatriz Arellano brought their commitment to social justice to the Catholic schools where they taught the children of the middle class and elite. They began initiating conversations with their students about the morality of poverty and the dictatorship. The work was not easy. While many of their students had been exposed to the country's pervasive inequality, often through school-organized charity work, they were not necessarily predisposed to question it. There remained a wide gulf between their experiences and those of the vast majority of Nicaraguans who lived in poverty. Sr. Luz Beatriz recalled to an interviewer that getting their wealthy charges to care about their neighbors was a difficult process: "The kids ... had absolutely no interest in their religious formation. We were knocking ourselves out trying to teach these kids who couldn't care less, while the mass of the population became poorer, more miserable, and more humiliated."[34]

To raise student consciousness, clergy members offered special seminars, workshops, and lectures by guest speakers who linked the message of the Gospel to Nicaragua's contemporary situation. Fr. Fernando Cardenal, for example, remembered joining thirty to thirty-five students on retreats where for several days they would reflect on the political implications of their faith. At events like this, he often gave a talk in which he compared Nicaraguan society to a triangle. He would ask the audience where they were located in the triangle, saying "I would gesture to the apex, the five percent of people with the most money in Nicaragua." Then he would show the slightly larger portion below the tip of the triangle that symbolized the middle 15 percent, finally pointing to the 80 percent of the very poor that formed the base of the triangle and describing the conditions they endured. He explained that the triangle was a way of helping students understand the vast level of inequality that characterized the country and to move them to action. "Then, they who were people of good will, it made them sad to see how they were enjoying everything and the people at the bottom had nothing. They were embarrassed and sad. They felt a desire to be in solidarity, to do something for them."[35] These conversations helped participants who had grown up in relative comfort realize the injustice of inequality, but they were not yet questioning its structural origins. Still, many participants recalled these seminars and courses as formative experiences.[36]

Young people continued these conversations in one of the many Christian youth groups springing up in neighborhoods and schools. A small team of nuns and priests were key to organizing and maintaining these organizations. Clergy members like Sr. Luz Beatriz or Fr. José María Sacedón formed groups at private schools and offered community classes, where they scouted potential members.[37] In eastern Managua, Fr. Félix Jiménez and Sr. Catalina Mulligan set up youth groups in several neighborhoods that made up the parish of San Pablo Apóstal.[38] Groups like these brought young men and women together regularly to discuss the Bible and its relevance to their lives.[39]

At these meetings, participants discussed the role that they as young people should take in ameliorating the country's political and economic situation. For example, Dharmalila Carrasquilla recalled them asking, "What were our objectives? To evangelize? Raise awareness? Organize youth for a just Nicaragua?"[40] Vidaluz Meneses participated in a Christian group for young married couples in the early 1970s and remembers that they "analyzed the social reality and saw that the dictatorship was anti-Christian. Without talking about socialism or communism, but in fact we were moving toward [supporting] a change in structures and not just government."[41] Through these dialogues, participants came to fully believe they could and, in fact, must effect change on a societal level.

For the young people growing up in Nicaragua's marginalized barrios, Christian youth groups provided a social, religious, and political space where they could both relax and organize. At their weekly meetings, members of the Movimiento Juvenil Cristiano in Reparto Schick, a barrio in east Managua, discussed their experiences as young people and how to serve their communities. They planned fundraisers to build a new church, spearheaded a neighborhood literacy campaign, and organized to demand potable water and then later electricity for their barrio. They also sang songs and recited poetry, debated ideas, and just spent time together.[42] This combination of activities empowered young people, some of whom were students and some of whom were working full-time. Rafael Escorcia, one of the group's members, recalled that "in the youth movement, I gained the knowledge and experience of how to be a leader. In practice, I learned how to organize protest marches, strikes, and unions. I learned how to not be afraid to speak before diverse audiences."[43] It was in these groups that some young people began to envision a different world. Decades later, Óscar Quijano, an early member of the youth group, wrote that "the youth movement opened a new stage of dreams and hopes." He went on to join the FSLN in the late seventies.[44]

Middle-class and wealthy students also began working and organizing in poor barrios—an experience that deepened their commitment to ameliorating the country's poverty. As part of these groups, elite young men and women visited people in their homes to teach literacy, to discuss the Bible and current events, and to sing songs and play with the children. Several students even chose to leave the comforts of their family homes to live in the capital's poorest neighborhoods. In the early 1970s, a group of young men from Nicaragua's most prominent families, including the Carrións and Cuadras, approached Fr. Uriel Molina about setting up a Christian community in his parish in El Riguero, a poverty-stricken barrio in Managua, where they could live communally and in solidarity with the poor. The University Community, as it was called, lasted for some time. Its members attended school during the day and then at night returned to the barrio, where they supported themselves and their work by selling bread. For many of these young men, such work was a way of affirming their commitment to social justice.[45]

A similar women's community is much less known, perhaps in part because it was relatively short-lived, but its existence highlights both the key role women played in the Catholic student movement and the ways in which their participation challenged traditional gender norms. Indeed, young women filled the ranks of the Catholic youth groups springing up in the 1960s. Flor de María Monterrey recalls a meeting with several young women: "We asked ourselves what can we do as women? And we went to live in the barrios." Like the young men in El Riguero, the fifteen women went to work, teaching residents how to read and supporting themselves through odd jobs, like tutoring and offering music classes, all while still attending classes at the university. At first, they lived in the homes of some of the residents, and then eventually they rented their own house "that was like theirs or worse." Monterrey remembers that "it was beautiful. We lived like the people . . . it was a way of committing yourself."[46]

To be sure, Monterrey and the other middle-class and elite young men and women were not living exactly like the people: they had the help of their parents and well-connected family members to fall back on. Still, their move to the barrio highlights their commitment to solidarity with the poor, as well as the distance that they had come from their privileged class background. They had gone from sleeping in their beds in familial homes to living with a group of young people, sleeping on floors, and working to make ends meet. For them, the decision to leave those comforts behind was a way of living their faith.

It was also a radical act that attacked the patriarchal nature of the family. Both the young men and women who participated in these communities acknowledged that part of the impetus for creating them was to get away from the strict oversight of their parents. Young women especially, like their politically active counterparts throughout the region, faced a tremendous amount of pressure from their parents, who tried to restrict their movements. For Monterrey, leaving home to live in community with women "was like a liberation, liberating us from the family."[47] The young men who lived in El Riguero cited similar reasons for their decision. One participant, Joaquín Cuadra, explained:

> We had all been living at home with our parents and that put limits on our freedom of movement. There were always family commitments to meet, you were always subject to a certain social influence. And also the criticisms. For example, our families didn't like it if we went around on motorcycles or on the bus instead of cars. We started to discuss our way of life. The problem for us was that we had new ideas but still lived in a traditional manner. So during the holidays we finally decided to go and live outside the influence of our families for a time.[48]

Cuadra alludes to the conflict between the young men's class background and their new ideals, but it is also clear that their desire for independence played a factor in the decision to leave home. These varied reasons for leaving home underscore the students' youthfulness as well as the changing mores that marked the era.[49]

The breakdown of hierarchy that liberation theology initiated had unintended consequences for Nicaraguan society. Not only did it mean that clergy members and their young parishioners became active in struggles for social justice, it also spurred a weakening of traditional family structures, especially among the elite and middle class. Young adults, driven by their commitment to social justice, began questioning not just the way society was organized but also the way their families were organized. When young women like Flor de María Monterrey and young men like Joaquín Cuadra left home to get away from parental oversight, they defied traditional patriarchal values and began envisioning a different way of life for themselves— one that would be different from that of their families.

The Sandinistas and the Student Movement

At the very moment that the hierarchical order that had historically characterized conservative institutions like the state, the Catholic Church, and the family was beginning to weaken, the Sandinistas were promoting a revolutionary option as a way to rectify long-standing inequality and corruption. Hoping to build its support base, the guerrilla organization turned to university students, whose efforts would help drum up wider support for the revolutionary movement. The focus on finding allies in the student movement was both a necessary and strategic decision. By the end of the 1960s, the FSLN was reeling from several debilitating losses.

After repudiating the electoral route in 1966, the Sandinistas intensified their revolutionary activities, robbing banks and bombing political targets.[50] These dramatic actions gave the FSLN more visibility, but they hid a discouraging reality: the organization was now smaller than it had been when it was founded.[51] Nonetheless, its leadership was determined to move forward with a revolutionary strategy. In May 1967, forty guerrillas in three columns made their way to the northern region of Pancasán to win recruits and engage the military. In August, a pitched battle with the Guard decimated one entire column and forced the guerrillas to retreat.[52] It was a crushing defeat—key leaders, including Silvio Mayorga, had been killed—and the Sandinistas were forced to rethink their strategy.

The regime's victory at Pancasán did not end the repression. With $1.6 million in US military aid, the National Guard turned its attention to rooting out the Sandinistas in both rural and urban communities. *La Prensa* carried stories of disappeared and murdered campesinos as the military sought to "eliminat[e] *campesino* groups which supported and collaborated with" Sandinistas in the north.[53] In urban areas, meanwhile, the Guard orchestrated raids that killed or arrested skilled Sandinista organizers. By 1968, these measures had taken their toll, and the FSLN had fewer than one hundred members.[54]

In response to these setbacks, the Sandinistas focused on building their base. In April 1968, Carlos Fonseca wrote his "Message to Revolutionary Students," which excoriated youth in the university for their political inefficacy. The goal of the letter was to jump-start the revolutionary student movement. Specifically, Fonseca wanted young leftists to move past the electoral activism and volunteerism that had characterized the student movement in the 1960s and focus on building a revolutionary student organization that was capable of "lead[ing] the popular struggle" against the dictatorship, capitalism, and US imperialism. He was not necessarily calling them to arms—that could come later. For now, when Fonseca talked about the students' revolutionary role, he primarily envisioned them building a mass movement—forging connections across student populations and with communities, workers, and campesinos.[55]

Fonseca optimistically believed that the FER had reserves of untapped support in the university, but the reality was less promising. At the UNAN, the revolutionary student organization was quite small. René Núñez remembered that in 1969, "the FER was weak; Pancasán had just happened," and many of the Sandinistas who helped with urban organizing had died in the uprising, been arrested, or gone underground. In León, both the FER and the FSLN shared a small handful of organizers. Consequently, new members, like Omar Cabezas and Bayardo Arce, rose to positions of leadership quickly.[56]

Tasked with revitalizing the student movement, FER activists organized high-profile protests to rally the student body. In the month after Fonseca's letter came out, they organized a strike to demand David Tejada's body and held a memorial for Casimiro Sotelo.[57] They continued staging demonstrations in favor of the FSLN and against US imperialism, and slowly their standing improved. In the 1968 UNAN student government elections, they gained an important new ally. Hugo Mejía Briceño had won the presidency of the CUUN as an independent, beating out the FER candidate. Mejía was part of a small Catholic Action youth organization, Juventud Universitaria Católica (Catholic University Youth, or JUC), which embraced a social justice-oriented vision of the church. Several important Sandinista leaders—for example, Mónica Baltodano, Edgar Munguía, and Bayardo Arce—came out of JUC and a similar organization, Juventud Estudiantil Católica (Catholic Student Youth, or JEC). In the late sixties, some members of these groups were already part of the FSLN/FER.[58] Mejía was not one of them, but he shared some of their beliefs—specifically, a total dis-illusionment with the country's political system. Thus, although the Social Christians helped get him elected, Mejía soon joined the FSLN and coordi-nated some protests with the FER. He even formed a student government committee to fight for the rights of political prisoners. Despite these devel-opments, the attendance at these events continued to be fairly small—some two hundred showed up to protest a visit by Nelson Rockefeller in May 1969, and only a handful interrupted a US State Department organized con-cert at the National University in León.[59] Still, the president of the CUUN helped boost the FER's legitimacy.

The regime's violence, meanwhile, had a contradictory effect on the FSLN: while it decimated their urban cadres, it also galvanized students across the country. In June, Mejía rallied the UNAN to strike for a week after the Guard arrested several young Chinandegans suspected of work-ing with the Sandinistas.[60] The Guard's disproportionate use of force also rallied dissidents. In one particularly well-publicized action on July 15, 1969, one hundred soldiers, some safely ensconced in a Sherman tank and others in helicopters, aimed automatic weapons and tear gas at a Sandinista safe house in Managua. After several hours, two soldiers and five Sandinistas lay dead. Only seven people had occupied the house.[61] Students at both the UCA and the UNAN protested the deadly show of force. When teenagers in Estelí staged an impromptu funeral procession, the National Guard opened fire, killing two students and arresting four more.[62] Blaming youth for the disorder, Somoza threatened the National University's autonomy, and the UCA closed for several days.[63] Such attacks boosted the moral authority of both the FSLN and the FER, and by the November 1969 student elections at the National University, FER ranks had grown to nearly one hundred.[64]

Desiring the resources that the National University student government had at their disposal, the FER poured all of its energy into winning the 1969 election. This time, their candidates for the presidency and vice presidency, Edgar Munguía and Bayardo Arce, openly discussed their Marxist politics and revolutionary beliefs.[65] A handsome and charismatic biology student, Munguía had been a member of JUC before becoming an FER leader in the late 1960s.[66] His political trajectory thus followed that of a cohort of students whose religious values were motivating their radicalization. In this new context, in which various students had lost faith in the political system, the FER's militancy attracted new adherents, and Munguía and Arce won the election.

Once in power, the FER used their position to build support for the Sandinistas and to better organize the student body. Most of the leaders of the FER—including Omar Cabezas, Edgar Munguía, and Bayardo Arce—were already Sandinista militants, and they freely used the resources of the student center on behalf of the FSLN. Cabezas recalled that they even gave portions of the center's funds to the Sandinistas. Beyond supporting the guerrilla movement, FER leaders organized recruitment drives to grow the ranks of the various student associations that made up the CUUN. Organizing these youths meant that when the student government called for specific actions, large numbers would be ready to join them. According to Cabezas, it also meant that more and more students were sympathetic to the FER.[67]

The revolutionary students also took advantage of the legitimacy of the student government to begin organizing outside the university. With a directive from their FSLN *responsable*, or contact, Edgar Munguía and Bayardo Arce began redirecting the interests of the FER away from its traditional focus on the university. Then a journalism student, Arce remembered:

> The FER organized congresses and the FER elected an executive committee ... when I entered they told us: "Okay, that is finished now." We have to create a clandestine FER, a FER that works through the CUUN and whose members don't present themselves as members of the FER and we are going to organize compartmentally.[68]

Part of this work involved community organizing, and students used their affiliation with the university as a cover. Sometime in 1970 or 1971, Omar Cabezas began collaborating with Magnus Bervis in Subtiava. This indigenous community outside León had a long history of collective organizing in defense of communal land and autonomy.[69] Cabezas proposed forming a study group with local residents and asked Bervis "to get some people together to study—not mentioning the Frente, but saying it was university students, coming into the barrio to do consciousness raising." They discussed the *Communist Manifesto*, as well as indigenous and Nicaraguan history. Working with Subtiavans who lived in other parts of León, their group grew quickly, and Cabezas recalled that "FER was beginning to have a real presence in the barrios."[70] At the very same time that young Catholics were beginning to work in urban neighborhoods, so too were students reaching out to these sectors. In both instances, their identity as students or Christians paved the way for these early forays into community organizing.

That identity also offered young Sandinistas some protection. In fact, that was how Edgar Munguía had become the FER candidate for the presidency of the National University student government in 1969. According to Arce, Munguía "had been living in [the Sandinista] Julio Buitrago's house" when the National Guard killed Buitrago. "So, as a way to offer him a certain form of protection, he is nominated as a candidate for President of the CUUN, so that he can move around in the university environment."[71] When René Núñez, a Sandinista student, was captured in early 1970, he managed to convince the Office of National Security that he was part of FER, and as a result received a shorter prison sentence.[72] The FER's efforts to organize the student body at the UNAN also gave activists greater protection. When María Haydée Sequiera saw the National Guard brutally beating fellow student Orlando Castillo and then arresting him, she headed straight for the FER and the student government. "I went to Omar Cabezas, and all of the student movement went to the house of compañero Carlos Tünnermann [the rector]. They had put a hood on [Castillo]; they were interrogating him and we gave them 24 hours to free him, otherwise, the students would rise up . . . and he was freed."[73] Even under the newest Somoza, students continued to hold an exceptional status—they were still guaranteed a measure of leniency. That was beginning to change, but at least in the first few years of Anastasio Somoza Debayle's rule, students continued to enjoy some protection.

Those protections, unique to students, proved incredibly valuable in the early years of Anastasio Somoza Debayle's regime. It allowed youth affiliated with the university to organize openly and move freely within the city. Now in control of the student government, members of the FER used those privileges to organize demonstrations that reasserted student political power on the national stage. They were organizing themselves, forming connections with other sectors, and making demands on the state. Their status as students and specifically their ties to the university made this possible. Somoza would threaten the National University's autonomy, and his regime would violate it at several points, but for the most part, the campuses functioned as safe spaces for dissent and dialogue.

"An Island of Liberty in the Midst of the Dictatorship," 1967–1972

Since winning its autonomy in 1958, the National University had fiercely defended its right to freedom of expression not only for students, but for the faculty and staff as well. In the 1970s, that privilege, which the regime denied the rest of society, increasingly marked the National University campus as a relatively democratic and open space where students could debate Marxism, print socialist pamphlets, protest the regime, and even oppose the university's administration. Carlos Tünnermann, who fought for autonomy in the 1950s and later became the rector of the National University, recalled that the school functioned as an "island of liberty in the midst of the dictatorship."[74] The democratic nature of the institution was by no means perfect: there were conflicts between faculty and students, little student representation on institutional boards, and societal backlash. For the most part, however, citizens of the National University enjoyed the right to express ideas and opinions that outside the school gates would have landed them in prison, or worse. As such, the UNAN became an important consciousness-raising site, where an expanding student population learned about the most pressing issues facing the country and debated what to do about it.

The rapidly increasing number of students made youth a growing political force in this period. In 1967, 2,731 students enrolled at the UNAN.[75] A decade later, 14,889 students registered for the 1977–1978 school year.[76] By then, the National University had spread over three campuses: León, Managua, and Jinotepe. The school's budget, however, did not grow proportionally with the student body. Between 1967 and 1977, as the university population ballooned, the amount of money the state spent on each student actually decreased, from about 3,300 to 2,530 córdobas per person.[77] Many observers believed the regime was purposely depriving the university in retaliation for the students' anti-Somocismo.[78] A campaign for more funds from the state rallied youth from both the university and the secondary schools throughout the decade, but with few results.

The rapid growth of the university student population was a global phenomenon. In Europe and the United States, this increase could be traced to the postwar baby boom. In Latin America, it was the result of better health care that had reduced infant mortality. The inability (or refusal) of government to expand the resources needed to adequately educate these new generations was repeated around the world. As the historian Jeremi Suri has observed, "extensive student interaction within the framework of crowded, usually urban, educational institutions provided the infrastructure for dissent within many societies."[79] In Mexico, Uruguay, and elsewhere in Latin America, inadequately funded schools spurred students to organize mass protests, which were met with mass repression in the Long Sixties.[80] Grossly underfunded schools had been the norm in Nicaragua for much of the Somoza regime, but the problem became more acute as enrollments rose.

Despite the school's poverty, the influx of students and professors in the late 1960s and 1970s made the university a vibrant place to be. For one, the rectors of the university enjoyed great freedom to hire teachers and advisers.[81] This meant that several former student leaders, including leftists, would return to teach at their alma maters. For example, in the late

1960s, Rector Carlos Tünnermann, who had participated in the university's struggle for autonomy, hired former FER student leader Michele Najlis to teach at the UNAN. He also placed the poet Fernando Gordillo, an outspoken anti-Somocista student activist who once edited the FER magazine *El Estudiante*, in charge of freshman orientation.[82] In this way, former student dissidents continued to exert influence on new cohorts of young activists.

Other prominent leftists also found work at the university. Félix Contreras, a member of the Nicaraguan Socialist Party, recalled that upon returning from his studies in Czechoslovakia in 1973, he had trouble finding work, but some friends in the university helped him get a job teaching economics at the UNAN. The presence of a Soviet-trained economics professor at the National University underscores the level of autonomy the university enjoyed, and Contreras recalled a welcoming community of progressive professors, several of whom were outspoken leftists and supporters of the Sandinistas.[83] Throughout the 1960s and 1970s, there would be professors of all ideological persuasions, even Somocistas.[84]

These hires opened Tünnermann up to criticism from all sides, but the rector argued that freedom of thought was essential to the functioning of the university. *Novedades*, the unofficial organ of the regime, blared headlines like, "The University under Extremist Control," while Social Christian students bitterly complained that Tünnermann had "filled his administration with communist sympathizers and ex-FER members."[85] The rector faced these charges throughout his tenure, which lasted from 1964 to 1974, but he held fast to the belief that exposing students to a diversity of thought was key to the university's mission and the intellectual development of its students.[86]

Further, considering the administration's ardent protection of the freedom of thought, it is not surprising that ideological debate flourished on campus. Groups of all political persuasions—from Trotskyites to Maoists, from Christian Democrats to Somocista Liberals—formed and fell apart in the 1960s and 1970s.[87] Mónica Baltodano recalled the heated debates over revolutionary theory that occurred in the early 1970s.[88] Omar Cabezas remembered hearing Leónel Rugama, a Sandinista student who died in an encounter with the Guard in 1970, exhort one of the discussion groups that were springing up in the university "to be like Che" Guevara.[89] Such topics were verboten outside campus, but inside, students were free to celebrate Che's example and debate the merits of armed insurrection.

These conversations meant that the university had become an important consciousness-raising site for students and members of the surrounding communities. Many former participants recalled that the annual student congresses fostered heated intellectual exchanges, as youth crafted the student government's agenda and debated how to solve the nation's problems.[90] School events also provided non-student speakers with a safe forum where they could spread information about the regime and the revolutionary option. Recently released political prisoners especially found a welcoming and receptive audience. For example, Ricardo Morales Avilés, a former professor at the university who became a Sandinista militant, spoke at the fifth student congress in León in 1973, just after his release from prison for his role in the Sandinista robbery of the Bank of America in 1968.[91] The attendance of community members at university events allowed speakers to amplify their message even further. René Núñez recalled that "at least 50% of the population" of León gathered at a student assembly in 1969 to demand justice for Doris Tijerino, a Sandinista who had been tortured and sexually assaulted while in prison.[92] The National University thus provided a safe space where Sandinistas and their student allies could seek wider support.

The protection from Guard intervention also meant that the UNAN became a gold mine for literature on such forbidden topics as Marxism and Sandinismo. Often students' introduction to such works occurred at the university.[93] Félix Contreras explained that because of the scarcity of books on Marxism and socialism in Nicaragua, students would photocopy them and then distribute individual chapters, sometimes selling them to raise funds for a particular organization. One student, a nun, came to him and asked if he could find her a copy of the *Communist Manifesto.* While such texts "were prohibited, you couldn't publish or sell publicly," Contreras remembered, "there in the university anybody could find any pamphlets on historical materialism, on dialectical materialism, all of *Capital*."[94] Reproducing entire books was a time-intensive endeavor in the era of mimeograph machines, so the widespread circulation of so many different texts speaks to a vibrant culture of dissent. In this climate, students were able to read and discuss the works of Marx and Engels, as well as those of Ho Chi Minh and Mao Tse-tung. They also paid close attention to theories of revolution and social change coming out of Latin America, and they read work by Fidel Castro, Che Guevara, Paulo Freire, and Eduardo Galeano.[95]

While the school itself was relatively immune from National Guard incursion, there were no such guarantees off campus. Although the administration and faculty worked hard to keep them safe, students were arrested, beaten, and sometimes killed. Michele Najlis recalled the rector going to the jails to try to free imprisoned students. Even Somocista faculty attempted to protect students. In the lead-up to the 1967 presidential election, Najlis was organizing a protest when a journalism professor, notorious for being a spy for the regime, warned her that "the Guardia has orders to kill." He suggested that the protestors occupy the journalism school and he even gave her the keys to do so.[96] Tünnermann remembered once intervening during a tense showdown between students and a National Guard battalion, led by General José Somoza, who had arrived with a tank to put down a protest. "That's how it was . . . I started [the day] with an academic agenda, and I finished [it] in the streets or taking prisoners out of the [GN] command."[97]

The faculty's concern for students did not mean that relations were always harmonious. Students resented their minimal representation on the university board and other bodies, and this tension led to several conflicts. The autonomy law called for student participation in the decision-making process, but there was only one student representative on the National University board. In June 1968, for example, the Social Christian-led CUUN demanded the administration give one-third of the seats on the university board to students. When that effort failed, the student representative to the board, Cairo Manuel López, used a university ceremony to demand greater student representation and received rousing applause from the audience. On stage, Rector Tünnermann turned his back to the young speaker.[98] Students would only win additional seats after a month-long protest in October 1971.[99] Even if students never attained the full level of representation they demanded, they still exercised quite a significant amount of freedom and power in the university, which they were fast turning into a center of anti-regime organizing.

Indeed, students in this period used their privileges to create safe spaces for non-student dissenters, of which there were many. The early years of Anastasio Somoza Debayle's tenure were a particularly effervescent time for organized labor: construction workers, teachers, service workers, and campesinos all held strikes in the late 1960s and early 1970s.[100] Teachers in the Federación Sindical de Maestros de Nicaragua (Nicaraguan Federation of Teachers' Unions, or FSMN) were especially active, and they staged massive strikes in this period as part of a years-long campaign, "The Movement to Restore Dignity to the Nation's Teachers." Among other things, the teachers demanded better wages and benefits and reforms to the retirement system.[101]

Years later, several teachers still recalled the important logistical aid the CUUN provided throughout these struggles. In August 1969, Somocista teachers working with the National Guard attacked the headquarters of the teacher's union in Managua. Fearing for their safety, the union leadership took refuge in the headquarters of the UNAN student government.

According to Bruno Gallardo, one of the strike organizers, "the University Center became our central quarters" for one week. When, a year later, in October 1970, the teacher's demands had still not been met, the union organized a massive march that paralyzed the capital and which, in another sign of the students' key support role, began at the National University's student center. After the protest, the leaders returned to the student center. This time, however, the university's autonomy did not protect the educators, and the Guard attacked the offices of the student government, forcing the labor activists to flee.[102] The shocking violation threw the students' privileges into relief—the army had not attacked a National University building since the assassination of the elder Somoza in 1956. Although the students were ultimately unable to provide the teacher's union with a truly safe space, their efforts highlighted the way in which they were allying with other sectors to protest the regime's injustices.

Not all students enjoyed the freedoms of the National University youth. At the Central American University in Managua, students risked expulsion when they protested the regime or even the school administration. The student government at the National University would become a key ally in those struggles too, joining their protests and staging solidarity strikes. The UNAN would even take in students and faculty expelled from the private school for political reasons. That openness was just one of the many reasons why so many former student leaders and faculty members described the National University as an island of democracy during the dictatorship.[103] It was by no means a completely free space—conflict between students and faculty was common and the threat of Guard intervention always loomed. Still, the administration respected academic freedom and the free exchange of ideas. The rector and many professors had themselves once been student activists and now they protected a new generation's right to participate in politics.

Politics and Protest at the Universidad Centroamericana

From its inception, the Jesuit-run Central American University was closely linked to the Somozas. The family had donated the land for the school, and Fr. León Pallais, a cousin of the dictator, was appointed its rector.[104] Under his leadership, the university became a microcosm of the larger society: an authoritarian administrator held power and opposition of any kind was not tolerated. The threat of punishment, however, did not stop UCA students from protesting. Even without the liberties that their peers at the autonomous National University enjoyed, they too managed to turn their campus into a hub of dissent, and their alliances with various sectors destabilized society and forced the regime to make concessions.

Father Pallais ran the university much like his cousins ran Nicaragua. Guadalupe Salinas Valle, who attended the UCA under Pallais, remembered that "he considered himself the owner of the university."[105] César Aróstegui arrived at the school in 1969, and he recalled that the authorities were "very tolerant of cultural activities, of sporting activities, of any kind of activity that did not question the university establishment."[106] For those who did dare to question the administration, the consequences could be severe. When Casimiro Sotelo headed the Centro Estudiantil Universitario de la Universidad Centroamericana (University Student Center of the Central American University, or CEUUCA), the administration had refused to allow the students to organize a commemoration of the July 23 Massacre. The CEUUCA did so anyway, but off campus. In response, Pallais, apparently unilaterally, expelled Sotelo.[107]

While the rector's administrative style aligned with the Catholic Church's traditional hierarchical structure, looming change was making it increasingly anachronistic. Vatican II had called for greater parishioner participation in the church, and priests and nuns, inspired by liberation theology, were breaking down traditional hierarchies. Moreover, the massive student protests worldwide were demonstrating the power of organized youth. Such sea changes inspired students, with the support of younger priests and some faculty, to begin demanding a greater role in the institution's administration.[108] Pallais and some of the other faculty, however, refused to budge.

The conflict came to a head in 1970. In the middle of the year, three faculty members resigned, citing Pallais's authoritarianism, and students seized the opportunity to demand the democratization of the university. Specifically, they wanted the removal of the rector and three unpopular professors, as well as other reforms, and they occupied the campus for six days in late August. The demonstration ended only after Somoza intervened for fear that UNAN students and teachers who were then striking might merge their causes. Under pressure from the regime, Pallais agreed to create a commission to look into the students' grievances, and the protest ended.[109]

Emboldened and organized, the students soon found another reason to mobilize. In late September 1970, the police arrested dozens of suspected Sandinistas, including two UCA students. The state refused to release any information about their whereabouts. The regime's strategy, a ploy to increase the time they could keep them for questioning, was part of a larger trend in which the regime held suspected Sandinistas for weeks and months without remanding them for trial. Sometimes, the state continued holding them even after they finished their sentences. Rumors of abuse and torture drove the UCA students to action.[110] At a student congress held that month, the conversation turned to the country's political situation. Cèsar Aróstegui recalled that the students were convinced:

> The only way to save the lives of those compañeros was to denounce their capture .... How were we going to do this protest? What should we do? Somoza does not care if we are yelling in the streets. It will end with him sending the Guard and we will go running. What can we do to be effective? ... Somebody says, "Let's seize the cathedral."[111]

It was a clever strategy. Cathedrals have historically been identified as places of sanctuary, and the move would generate considerable publicity, especially since Managua's National Cathedral was located next to the National Palace. Moreover, for a generation of students inspired by liberation theology, the church might have seemed an ideal place to launch a critique of the regime's disregard for human dignity.[112]

Wide support was essential to the protest's success. On September 26, forty students attended the early morning mass. When it finished, the occupation began. The students locked the doors and unfurled a banner from the top of the Cathedral that read "Freedom for the Political Prisoners." Within hours, the National Guard had arrived, but so did the local population.[113] They came together to protect the students and stand up to the state.

Students immediately received an outpouring of support. Within twenty-four hours, the protest spread to other churches in Managua, Granada, Masaya, and León, where students, likely organized by the FER and Christian youth groups, rose up in solidarity.[114] Parents also joined the protest. Rector Tünnermann sent his colleague at the UCA a message of support and urged the Catholic hierarchy to protest the regime's human rights abuses.[115] Many priests were already doing so: three had joined the students in the occupation, and twenty-two others had signed a letter demanding respect for the rights of the detained. The archbishop, Miguel Obando y Bravo, also supported the cause, asking the government to permit a human rights committee to check on the prisoners. Clergy members, students, and four members of the FSMN, the teachers' union, even went on a hunger strike.[116]

Under pressure from so many sectors, Somoza relented. On September 28, he met with the archbishop and agreed to allow a commission of students and priests to visit the prisoners, and he began releasing some of the detained. Satisfied, the students ended the occupation. Although the Guard later arrested several of the participants for disturbing public order, the students' action was a significant success.[117] They had staged a daring protest by taking over the National Cathedral, and their actions had motivated various other powerful groups to join them. This combined pressure forced the regime to respond. It was an early lesson in the power of broad-based protest.

In the meantime, the status quo ruled at the UCA. Little had come of the commission created after the August 1970 strikes, and the frustrated student council began protesting again in January 1971. Taking a hard line, the administration closed the university until the school year began again in April. Protestors responded by taking over the main building and the school library, but the military removed them the next day. A few weeks later, sixty-five students received notices in the mail that they had been summarily expelled. The incident resembled the struggles at the National University in its pre-autonomy days. Middle-class and elite students won the support of various influential sectors: parents formed a committee to negotiate with the administration, the opposition press protested the mass expulsion, and a supportive law professor and several students even met with Jesuit leaders in Rome to discuss the case.[118] Once again, a struggle against authoritarian administrators had come to stand for a struggle against an authoritarian state.

Perhaps for that reason, the protests expanded rapidly. When the UCA reopened in April 1971, twenty youths, accompanied by their parents, several progressive priests, and students from the National University, barricaded themselves inside the administration building. Again, the UCA called in the Guard, and soldiers carted the students and their supporters off to jail.[119] The military's ready participation highlighted the university's alliance with the regime, and it underscored the very real dangers that protestors faced as they fought for greater freedoms under the Somoza regime.

Indicative of the students' support and organization, the arrests set off a chain of solidarity protests. Apparently, the families of imprisoned Sandinistas approached the students at the UCA to join causes, and on the day of the arrests, Sandinista mothers, working with student protestors and priests, took over the National Cathedral.[120] From their jail cells, student leaders from the National University and the UCA jointly declared solidarity "with our compañeros in prison who are 'political prisoners' and who are . . . demanding . . . the freedom of those who (long ago) have completed their sentence or who have been absolved by the court of public opinion." They now called on their supporters to demand the freedom of Sandinista prisoners. The university student governments sent circulars to schools throughout the country, and secondary students answered their call.[121] Supportive priests, nuns, and Christian youth groups helped spread the protests to the Catholic secondary schools, where students took over their campuses. Youth at the public schools followed suit. By April 26, the nation's secondary school system was at a standstill. Youth in Managua and León took over churches. As the strike threatened to spiral out of control, the government and the UCA administration capitulated. The state began releasing prisoners, and the university announced the appointment of a new rector who would reassess the expulsion orders.[122]

The protest's success was another testament to the power of a student-centered mass movement. The UCA students' connections to so many disparate sectors—priests, parents, students in public schools, Christian youth groups, Catholic parishes—enabled them to rally a large swath of society. The rapid mobilization of Catholic youth in particular showcased their growing organization. That such disparate sectors supported the UCA students reveals the widely held belief that students deserved special privileges and spaces that were open to freedom of thought, but it also underscored the population's growing dissatisfaction with the Somoza regime. It is striking that the protests spread so quickly after the students announced their solidarity with Sandinista prisoners, which suggests both the growing popularity of the guerrilla movement as well as the role of students in making that support visible.

Conclusion

During Anastasio Somoza Debayle's first term in office, universities in Nicaragua became powerful sites of opposition to the regime. At the UNAN, the privileges that came with university autonomy protected student protest and enabled their activism. Students at the UCA demanded similar liberties, and the precedent set by the National University meant they found widespread support. The different conditions at the public and private university shaped the forms of opposition. The students at the National University turned their school into a center for the distribution of literature and propaganda that were forbidden off campus. They used school resources to help sustain the Sandinista guerrilla movement and began mobilizing the student body and their community against the regime. Much more restricted, students at the UCA managed to stage dramatic protests that attracted the participation of powerful sectors. The school's authoritarian response to their relatively peaceful protests only triggered more unrest—a pattern that repeated throughout Latin America and that would continue in Nicaragua for the next decade.

In this period, students grew increasingly critical of conservative institutions like the Catholic Church and its university, the family, and the state. These institutions upheld the status quo of the regime, which arrested, tortured, and even murdered those who dreamed of a different Nicaragua. In the wake of the corruption and violence, students were looking for change. Progressive clergy and the Sandinistas offered a vision of a more just society and a way to achieve it. Both inspired students, who became key proselytizers for the two movements. Indeed, student activism in this period was vital for the FSLN, which was once again in the midst of rebuilding its organization in the face of severe repression. Not only did students win the liberty of imprisoned Sandinistas, but also, according to René Núñez, the 1970 Cathedral takeover led to the creation of a mass "movement supportive of Sandinista activities."[123] Students were moving beyond the principally middle-class and elite arena of the university and forging connections with the wider society.

The freedoms of the university and the privileges associated with being students allowed youth the space to begin building a culture of insurrection. Their protests and actions in this period helped build their own organization in the university as well as their links to powerful institutions, like the Catholic church, and to those who were denied a similar margin of protection, such as secondary students and teachers. These growing connections meant that university students were primed to take on a larger role in the anti-Somoza opposition.

CHAPTER 7

Un Trabajo de Hormiga, 1970–1979

In 1948, when a National Guardsman killed the student activist, Uriel Soto-mayor Ramírez, the outcry was so great that it compelled a young Anastasio Somoza Debayle to reflect on the dangers of state violence. In a letter to a US embassy staff member, the then-colonel acknowledged that the military's growing reputation for violence weakened his father's hold on power. However, he seemed to recognize that the greatest danger to the regime was not mass opposition, but mass organization: only a society that was "fighting mad," he wrote, could truly threaten his father's dictatorship.[1]

Thirty years later, Somoza's words came back to haunt him. By 1978, Nicaraguan society was fighting mad, and his family's decades-long rule was on the verge of collapse. The younger Somoza apparently had forgotten the lesson he drew from the democratic effervescence of the 1940s. Under his tenure, state violence and mismanagement earned his regime mass opposition. But it was not inevitable that ordinary people would become fighting mad. The sociologists Francis Fox Piven and Richard A. Cloward have argued that "the emergence of a protest movement entails a transformation both of consciousness and of behavior."[2] To understand why Nicaraguans became willing to take up arms against the regime, it is first necessary to understand how their political perceptions of the world and their role in it changed.

Victor Tirado López, a Sandinista *comandante* who fought alongside Carlos Fonseca, has articulated one compelling theory for why the Nicaraguan Revolution succeeded. "The armed struggle here," he argued, "is a political cultural movement. Here, there is a culture different than there was before." According to Tirado, "the armed movement created a culture" that embraced revolution as a path to social and structural change. To support his thesis, he pointed to the musical aspect of the revolutionary struggle, such as the songs of Carlos Mejía Godoy, and the historical dimension, exemplified by Fonseca's writing on Sandino.[3] In his chronicle of the Sandinista Revolution, George Black similarly argues that the emergence of "a culture of resistance" that parallels that of the power holders is a requirement for revolution. This parallel culture diffuses news about the armed resistance and raises people's consciousness through alternative channels, including radio, theater, and music.[4] But these two critical observations, still leave behind an unanswered question: How does an insurrectionary culture reach a critical level of mass diffusion and acceptance?

Scholars have not fully explored the role of students in revolutionary movements. Historians of Nicaragua's revolution have focused more on peasants and workers and the work of the Sandinistas and their allies in the middle and upper classes in fomenting armed rebellion.[5] All of these groups were critical to the success of the revolution, but students, in particular, played an essential role in spreading information and providing avenues of engagement that made the revolutionary option more palatable to large sectors of society. In other words, students, both in the university and secondary schools, helped transform their nation's consciousness and behavior, creating cross-class alliances that mobilized in favor of the Sandinistas and against the regime.[6]

Young women, of course, played an active role in the student movement and the larger revolutionary struggle. Strikingly, they participated in a wide variety of activities—from acting in street theater performances to attacking soldiers. As Margaret Randall, Karen Kampwirth, and others have shown, young women's activism moved beyond the so-called support roles to which so many women in Cold War revolutionary organizations were relegated.[7] Although the exact number of women who participated in the student movement and the FSLN cannot be stated with certainty, it is clear that they participated in nearly all forms of revolutionary activism.

In the 1970s, university students increasingly left the security of their campuses to organize other sectors in secondary schools and marginalized barrios, with teachers and with workers. If in previous eras, these efforts had been marked by paternalism and condescension, youth in the seventies built alliances based on mutual respect and assistance. Drawing on strategies associated with such diverse sources as liberation theology and the countercultural movement, they devised creative ways to spread information and drum up opposition to the regime. Through these activities, they helped recover and spread a rebellious national history that encouraged citizens to believe revolution was a national legacy, one in which students played a key part. In the end, they helped create a culture of insurrection through painstaking organizing and compelling political protests. As in the past, the repression they endured for these actions galvanized their society, but the connections they had forged with the country's diverse sectors ensured that a wide cross-section of Nicaraguans were moved to act.

The Silent Accumulation of Forces

The very impetus that pushed the FSLN to take seriously the student movement in the late 1960s also compelled them to adopt a new strategy. By 1970, so many Sandinistas had been arrested or killed, the organization had effectively lost much of its urban network of collaborators. Reeling from these losses, leaders like Carlos Fonseca came to believe that the FSLN's weakness lay in the lack of broad support for the guerrilla movement.[8] To remedy this situation, urban organizers adopted a new tactic they called the "Silent Accumulation of Forces."[9] Because of the protection afforded by their status as students, the members of the FER had largely escaped the repression, and the Sandinistas relied on these youths to rebuild their urban support networks.

Sandinista leaders realized early on that regime repression, which had escalated after the guerrillas' defeat at Pancasán, would hinder any effort to openly organize a mass movement. As Bayardo Arce recalled, "Obviously, our legal organizers could not go [to the teachers' union] and say they are Sandinista militants tasked with organizing teachers within a revolutionary project."[10] In the context of the regime's violence and the FSLN's numerical weakness, Arce explained, "The best thing we could do was make the dictatorship and the office of National Security believe that the Sandinista Front had been wiped out."[11] They would have to organize discreetly. The Sandinistas' few remaining urban organizers—Oscar Turcios, Ricardo Morales Avilés, Pedro Aráuz, and Arce—began seeking out existing groups that could function as intermediary organizations—that is, organizations that supported the Sandinistas and took direction from them, but appeared to operate independently.[12] By the end of the 1970s, they had amassed various associations, and those centered around students were among the oldest and most extensive.

The students' existing organization made them ready targets for recruitment. Some of the Sandinistas' key urban militants had close connections with the UNAN: Arce and Aráuz had been politicized as students, and Morales Avilés had been a professor. These ties likely inspired them to begin recruiting on campus. Arce recalled that starting with "CUUN and FER, we began to organize a series of social formations with the objective of linking ourselves to the pueblo and identifying progressive sectors."[13] This was, as Arce called it, "the work of the ant," the subtle but laborious base building that would slowly organize their society, and students were to be key players. Arce remembered that because the Managua network had been decimated, León became the epicenter of this new organizing effort, and Sandinistas began reaching out to new sectors via the CUUN and FER.[14]

Students were especially able organizers because their membership in various networks meant they enjoyed "weak ties," or passing relationships, with people from different sectors, and thus could widely transmit information.[15] Nicaraguan students moved in many different spheres: for example, the school, the neighborhood, the church, their families, and their workplaces. These versatile identities meant they were versatile organizers—they already had in-roads into various existing institutions and organizations. The Sandinistas capitalized on these connections. Arce encouraged new recruits "to continue in the social movement from which we had recruited them or if we hadn't identified them via one we would send them to create one." In this way, he explained, the FSLN "linked itself with the people and could detect who were the progressive elements so that they could talk to them about the FSLN and recruit them."[16]

The FER's push to organize the student body constituted one manifestation of this strategy. Now in control of the student government at the National University, the FER focused on fortifying student associations and boosting the ranks of their own organization. A member of the FER in the mid-1970s, Patricia Orozco recalled that "we would set goals for how many students we were going to speak to about the reality of the country, about the significance of the dictatorship."[17] The structure of the FER was also expansive enough to include several different levels. Students could participate as activists, pre-militants, or militants, with the last requiring the most commitment as well as strict adherence to the FER's political line.[18]

The FER's focus extended beyond the universities. The organization had long-established ties to many of the nation's largest secondary schools and now it sought to expand on them.[19] In the 1970s, the FER sent university students like Irving Dávila, Patricia Orozco, and Humberto Román to work with teenagers across the country. In fact, Orozco remembers that several university students acted as advisers to a youth club that she joined in the early 1970s as a high school student and organized social justice actions. Later, in 1977, she did similar work at secondary schools, organizing talks, workshops, and other activities.[20] These university students would help coordinate the dramatic actions that characterized the secondary student movement in the 1970s.

As an intermediary organization, the FER operated under the direction of the FSLN and the leadership of the two organizations often overlapped. Arce, for example, helped lead the Sandinistas' urban resistance while also serving as vice president of the student government at the National University.[21] By design, the FER and the FSLN's shared membership meant that it was not always clear where one ended and the other began. This overlap afforded Sandinistas the protections associated with being a student. To this end, the FER operated both overtly and clandestinely. As the organization spread, a national executive committee and regional committees formed to oversee the many cells emerging in schools across the country.[22]

The students inspired by liberation theology were also appealing allies for the Sandinistas. Joaquín Cuadra, who lived in the university student community in El Riguero, recalled that the Sandinistas

> had heard that some Christians living in the barrio were doing mass organizing. This was tempting to the FSLN. Our class background meant that we'd have access to material resources: houses, cars, farms to use as training centres, etc. And we had dozens of people organized into circles from which cadres might be recruited. We had developed a kind of political structure throughout the neighborhood.[23]

In addition to the neighborhood groups Cuadra describes, young Christians had organized a second political structure. In early 1972, they formed the Christian Movement, an umbrella organization that linked the various Christian young people who participated in the Catholic youth groups and volunteered in the country's marginalized barrios.[24] This double level of organization meant that if they could recruit young Christian activists, the Sandinistas would have access to a wide and diverse network of potential sympathizers.

To build their base, the Sandinistas were willing to be ideologically flexible. Recruits did not have to adopt all of the guerrilla organization's tenets, and some Christians joined the FSLN although they personally believed in non-violence.[25] Still, Sandinistas worked hard to persuade recruits of their line of thinking, providing them with pamphlets that introduced them to Marx and Sandino.[26] Ricardo Morales Avilés was especially committed to engaging Christian students. He spoke at their retreats where he explained the legitimacy of the revolutionary option.[27] These efforts paid off as more and more members of the Christian Movement began working with the FSLN, eventually forming the Movimiento Cristiano Revolucionario (Revolutionary Christian Movement, or MCR).[28]

For the Silent Accumulation of Forces strategy to work, it was critical that youth continued organizing publicly as students or Christians. Mónica Baltodano remembered that "when we joined, we thought our work would change, but it didn't. The FSLN told us to keep being leaders in the Christian movement, to go to masses, everything. They were interested in linking the work that we were already doing with the FSLN."[29] That identity permitted them to move safely within the city. According to Baltodano, as Christians, "we were less subject to repression. We could go into a barrio, talk politics and still be protected by the mantle of Christianity."[30] These protections made them especially adroit organizers.

The situation may have looked bleak for the FSLN in the late sixties, yet the organization managed to thrive in the first half of the seventies. This was possible because key leaders dedicated significant energy to developing covert relationships with activists who could move about freely, many of them students. Although the Silent Accumulation of Forces strategy ended in 1974, the young people recruited during that phase would continue to use their privileges to build mass support for the FSLN. In the process, they helped develop the collective power of long-marginalized sectors of society.

The Work of the Ant

Whether they were inspired by the Sandinistas' revolutionary project or by liberation theology's directive to fight injustice, students in the 1970s increasingly took action off-campus, crisscrossing Nicaragua's urban landscapes and forging connections among disparate sectors. Moving beyond unidirectional volunteer work, they started cooperating with and learning from the people they sought to organize. Their work in marginalized communities, secondary schools, youth groups, and even among friends and family politicized ordinary Nicaraguans and promoted their active engagement with and later rebellion against the state. This was the "work of the ant," to use the Spanish idiom—the slow and steady, diligent labor that can create change. By organizing barrios and providing logistical support to the FSLN, students constructed a powerful pro-Sandinista movement.

In a 1973 talk with youth from the Revolutionary Christian Movement, Ricardo Morales Avilés explained that in order to organize the masses, militants had to do two things: offer people political guidance *and* opportunities to act against the state.[31] In essence, they had to build the consciousness of their wider society. This would not be an easy task—opposing the regime posed severe risks, as the experience of the Sandinistas, labor unions, and others had shown. Consequently, students would have to organize in ways that did not overtly threaten Somoza, and they centered their efforts on issues that, at least on the surface, were unconnected to the dictator and that instead highlighted the government's inadequacies. Demands for public utilities or better schools were not revolutionary, but they underscored the decay that four decades of Somoza rule had wrought and provided compelling reasons for communities to work collectively.

Students had long offered their services as pre-professionals to the urban poor, and under the guidance of the FSLN and the FER, they now expanded on these efforts. Working in a barrio of León in the early 1970s, the medical student, Agustín Lara, proposed that the community organize a pharmacy that would be run by his fellow med students at the UNAN. To stock the shelves, the young volunteers solicited donations or simply took supplies from the hospital where they were training. "Rain or shine, we were there attending to the needs of the people. In that way, we won their hearts, sympathy and confidence and then we would identify their main leaders and recruit them."[32] By offering concrete services, students developed the community's trust and began building cross-class alliances among themselves, the Sandinistas, and the residents of marginalized barrios.

Not all approved of these tactics. Other radical groups critiqued the FER for volunteerism. According to Arce, students engaged in a wide variety of service activities:

> building latrines, teaching literacy in the barrios, medical students serving very poor populations. . . . I remember the communists of the Socialist party in the university . . . would say that instead of confronting capitalism, we were softening it; that instead of raising the working class, we were mitigating their problems with the things we were doing.[33]

But as Agustín Lara's experience shows, they were not just offering charity, they were also actively looking for potential recruits. The goal, according to Arce, was for the Sandinistas to one day be able to "move through [these neighborhoods] like fish in water, able to detect people, be able to recruit people and safe houses there."[34] Students thus helped provide the entry way into communities. Once there, they served as the FSLN's eyes on the ground, looking for sympathizers and would-be collaborators.

Beyond identifying potential recruits, students also organized communities to make demands on the state. Their identity as students proved especially useful for these endeavors. For example, for her community health course as a medical student in León, Dora María Téllez visited the barrio

San Carlos. As she recalled, she carried "a list of houses and I went house by house seeing what the children had and what the women had and I would take them vaccines or medicines for the problems that the kids had or I would try to establish what kind of illnesses they had." Later, she would revisit those homes, "under the same pretext," to do work with her Sandinista cell, composed of three students who were trying to organize the neighborhood into committees that campaigned for water and other necessities.[35]

Young activists also used the challenges posed by current events to promote collective action. In 1971 and 1972, the price of milk and gasoline rose dramatically. According to Irving Dávila, "they would raise the cost of milk by five cents and we would be out in the streets. [They would raise the cost] of gasoline by one peso and we were in the streets. Five cents [increase] for the bus and we would head for the streets."[36] According to Doris Tijerino, a Sandinista militant who had just arrived at the university after a harrowing experience in prison, "the student movement detailed all the activist teams to work in the marginal neighbourhoods, organizing them to struggle against the dairies and the gasoline processors, and against the government, which, through taxes on these products, allows the dairies and service stations to raise the prices." This effort, she recalled, helped organize several neighborhoods, which, with the aid of the Sandinistas, went on to demand more services from the state.[37] These quality-of-life issues provided citizens with a compelling reason to protest, and in so doing, they began envisioning (and demanding) a different kind of state government.

Perhaps because of their age, students were especially adept at organizing neighborhood youth programs. Patricia Orozco recalled how university students helped direct a social justice-oriented youth club when she was growing up in Ocotal in the early 1970s. The group raised money for a poverty-stricken barrio in the town and then, at the suggestion of their advisers, began agitating around the city's water problems. They held a community meeting in the town plaza where they burned an effigy of the town's corrupt mayor. Orozco remembered, "In the town, there weren't other organizations and it didn't appear the mayor had any interest in resolving the problem. So then, the Guard came out and shot in the air to break up the gathering and the next day they arrested the group . . . that's where the youth club finished." These groups introduced young people to collective organizing, and the state's repressive response helped radicalize them.[38]

Christian students were particularly dedicated community organizers. In the early 1970s, still inspired by liberation theology, they shifted their focus from charity work to consciousness-raising and community organizing. The university community in El Riguero illustrates this transformation. One of the founding members, Álvaro Baltodano had built houses and taught literacy in poor neighborhoods in Managua as a secondary student. He recalled, "We went to 'help.' We wanted to show that being Christian involved more than just going to church on Sundays. . . . We soon began to realize that the work was somewhat paternalistic and lost some of our original enthusiasm."[39] As they confronted the limits of volunteerism, a small group of elite young Catholics wanted a deeper commitment and decided to live in El Riguero in 1972.[40]

In so doing, these youths acknowledged that they had much to learn from the very people they were trying to organize. Luis Carrión remembered, "Our mission [with the base communities] was to try to raise people's consciousness, that is, to represent a new revolutionary vision of Christianity for social change. At the same time, we realized we too would be educated, that we would learn from the work and contact with people."[41] The conversations young people had inside this base community and others like it helped both students and community members realize that a different world was possible. According to Álvaro Baltodano, they "would read the Bible and talk about the need to liberate people. We'd agree that a Christian was not simply someone who just goes to mass, but rather someone who participates in the community for the good of the neighborhood."[42]

Young Christians were engaged in similar work around the country. The groups associated with the MCR, for example, taught literacy in various urban neighborhoods using the pedagogy of Paulo Freire, which emphasizes dialogue and reciprocity between teacher and student.[43] As their use of Freire's pedagogy of liberation suggests, these activities had moved beyond charity. Now young people were helping to raise people's consciousness about the reasons for the country's vast inequality and what could be done about it.

This new active definition of Christianity empowered Nicaraguans to take action. David Chavarría Rocha, who lived in El Riguero when he was young, remembered that while there certainly had been political discussions before the university community was established, afterward "we began to take up more concrete tasks: support for strikes against the rise in milk prices and bus fares, and participation in the movement for release of political prisoners. . . . We did become clearer about the need to act."[44] Chavarría's memory of the change that took place with the students' arrival highlights the fact that Nicaragua's working classes were not political blank slates—they acutely understood the nature of inequality and its consequences. What had changed was a new impetus for action—a consequence of liberation theology's emphasis on building a kingdom of heaven in the present day.

The 1972 earthquake that razed parts of the capital intensified the Christian Movement's organizing efforts. In the early morning of December 23, a massive earthquake struck Managua, killing more than ten thousand people and leaving hundreds of thousands without homes. The regime reached new heights of corruption in the wake of the crisis. The National Guard virtually dissolved as soldiers participated in looting downtown businesses. Somoza eventually regained control of the military, but they soon embarked on the more lucrative practice of selling the food and medicine donated to the relief effort. As the city rebuilt, Somoza and his allies meanwhile began speculating on land and got into the construction business.[45]

In the context of the regime's gross mismanagement, the Christian Movement rushed to aid the city's devastated residents. According to Mónica Baltodano, "young Christians dispersed in other departments of the country organically organized shelters where they served thousands of affected people and that was also an opportunity to do political work and organizing."[46] A college student at the time, Baltodano helped set up a shelter at the private school, LaSalle, in León.[47] By that point, Baltodano and several other young Catholics had already embraced the FSLN, and even more would do so as a result of these experiences.[48]

With its members increasingly aligned with the Sandinistas, the Christian Movement continued to be a vital tool for organizing communities. According to Baltodano:

> Inside the barrios, we would do work around health and from health we would question the system that did not offer us health, or through literacy, we would question the system that did not offer us education and from there we would bring the people to reflect on those things and the organization to fight for the solution to those problems.[49]

These conversations, which exemplified the discussions liberation theology inspired, reframed inequality as a structural problem that could be remedied and empowered residents to think of themselves as agents with the power to create change.

Students also reached out to sectors of society that were already organized. Their support for the labor struggles of the 1970s promoted a sense of good will between urban workers and the FSLN, which had neglected the labor movement in its commitment to creating a guerrilla *foco* in the mountains.[50] When managers at the Sacos de Centroamérica factory in Carazo fired ninety-nine people for demanding better pay and better working conditions in late 1974, three hundred workers struck. Arlen Siu, a student in the Christian Movement who became a Sandinista militant, visited the workers. Gonzalo Navarro Marín, then a socialist labor organizer, remembered that Siu "came two nights to accompany us, preach, and encourage the *compañeros*."[51]

Beyond moral support, university students offered workers logistical aid that helped sustain their strikes and link them to the Sandinistas. As noted, students were more than willing to share their campus and the protection it offered with organized labor. After the 1972 earthquake, conditions for construction workers deteriorated. When they struck, they turned to the university for help, and the campus became the strikers' headquarters. Doris Tijerino recalled that the workers asked students to help print and distribute a document explaining the reasons for the stoppage and asking others to join their strike. "We organized a few teams to take charge of distributing this material, as it was difficult for the workers to move from one center to another because they could be more easily detected by the police."[52] Once again, students' privileged status facilitated their activism, this time in co-operation with construction workers. According to Bayardo Arce, by then a professor at the university, "we organized 500 workers in worker-student brigades and we went out to stop all the worksites. We created a national strike: the whole country stopped." The strike lasted nearly two months, and by the end, several dozens of workers had joined Sandinista study circles.[53]

The students' revolutionary activism often drew in their friends and families, and these personal connections were essential for the survival of the FSLN and especially for the work of the urban underground. Because students were so deeply embedded within the family and their friend groups, their activities often compelled the involvement of their loved ones.[54] When they needed to find a safe house or arrange transportation, they drew on these close relationships. As Mónica Baltodano has pointed out, parents often cooperated willingly, but at great risk. She recalled that a Sandinista militant, Helen Hall, "would say that her house was a safe house, but in reality, it was her parents who were collaborating because that house was theirs. Moreover, they were risking everything: their business, their home, their lives, their other kids, even those who did not participate."[55] This kind of logistical support was so critical that former Sandinistas like Baltodano and Humberto Román have acknowledged that students were the backbone of the urban organizing effort.[56]

Students also drew their families into more overtly oppositional activities. The country's widespread educational deficiencies proved to be a lightning rod for secondary students and their parents in the 1970s. In 1976, these teenagers, with the help of some college youth, organized a wave of protests around institutional conflicts.[57] Between May and September, there were at least eight school occupations and dozens more solidarity strikes. Most of the takeovers occurred at National Institutes, the large regional public secondary schools that taught thousands of middle- and working-class teenagers. During that year, these youths organized to remove dictatorial, corrupt, or ineffective faculty and improve school facilities. In the walkouts that rocked the Escuela de Comercio in Granada, for example, students alleged that the director, Virgilio Morales, knew the social science teacher, Adolfo Rosales, had slept with a student who became pregnant, but Morales had done nothing about it.[58] Students also protested financial corruption: in Jinotega, protestors demanded a five-year audit of their school's accounts as well as a study of its inventory in order to understand what had happened to funds raised for school improvement.[59] In making these demands, students highlighted the state's mismanagement and widespread corruption.

These protests compelled the wider organization of students and their families. The Asociación de Estudiantes de Secundaria (Association of Secondary Students, or AES) emerged from one of the 1976 protests. In June 1976, students at the Instituto Nacional Eliseo Picado (Eliseo Picado National Institute, or INEP) in Matagalpa occupied the school to demand the removal of four professors. Students founded the AES after the Guard violently removed them from the campus.[60] In the following months, the organization spread to other schools as youth and their families united to demand a better education.

Parental support made secondary student activism particularly powerful. During the June strike at the INEP, parents took food and blankets to their children holed up in the institution and prevented soldiers from forcibly removing the strikers during the early days of the protest.[61] Some were even staying in the school alongside their children and were dislodged with them on June 7. After the Guard removed the protestors, parents sent angry missives to the Ministry of Education, demanding to know who had called in the Guard and why the families had not been consulted.[62] Parents hastily organized themselves, forming groups to support their children and negotiate on their behalf. In Matagalpa, a delegation made up of forty-four parents and fifteen students traveled to the capital to meet with the minister of education within a week of the takeover. Some of the parents in the delegation did not even have children at the National Institute—their children attended one of the city's other schools. However, the solidarity strikes also affected them, and they wanted the problem solved.[63] Student activism had paved the way for adult mobilization.

Remarkably, the school strikes of 1976 were fairly successful. The protests were resolved relatively democratically: the ministry sent investigators, negotiated with students, and often ceded their demands. After all, their grievances shone a light on enduring problems within the educational system and the sheer number of students impacted put considerable pressure on the government to respond. As such, secondary school strikes were particularly effective because they mobilized both students and their families around issues that were at once nonpartisan — or, at least on the surface, had nothing to do with Somoza — and deeply political in that they were making demands on the state and claiming for themselves the power to remove corrupt officials.[64]

The protestors' status as students, however, did not protect them from the regime's brutality for long. By April 1977, the most militant secondary schools were under constant supervision. Brigadas Especiales Contra Actividades Terroristas (Special Antiterrorist Activity Brigades, or BECATS) monitored them regularly. On other campuses, armed guards stood watch inside the schools. The directors of some institutes cooperated with the Guard, denouncing their own students and turning them over.[65] When the military violently ejected striking students at INEP in Matagalpa, students charged that the soldiers "pawed immorally at the compañeras and squeezed the private parts of the compañeros, making them yell in pain." Further, they stated, "it also must be added that the compañeros they regarded as 'special cases' were brutally tortured and later labeled subversive elements, so that then 34 compañeros who had occupied the institute were expelled from their respective schools."[66] The dictatorship's attack on young teenagers was a sign of the violence to come.

Oral histories with former students and Sandinistas suggest that the early 1970s were marked by a flurry of community organizing. In major cities, students were reaching out to marginalized sectors of society and encouraging ordinary citizens to engage the state and demand better services. They provided neighbors, families, friends, and strangers with a variety of ways to become politically active — from lending a car to marching in a protest, from writing a letter to meeting with government officials. Once again, parents and communities acted to defend the young, but the escalating violence now required a degree of courage that previous eras had not. This array of activities drew in diverse sectors of society and even led some people to join the FSLN. In this way, student efforts at the grassroots level helped the FSLN gain numerical strength and wider sympathy.

Creating a Culture of Insurrection

Student organizing in schools and communities promoted wider civic engagement, but such actions would not in themselves lead to revolution. As Ricardo Morales Avilés had told Christian youth organizers in 1973, ideological orientation was also necessary. To build a culture of insurrection, the Sandinistas needed to delegitimize the dictatorship and legitimize armed struggle. They would have to push back against Cold War narratives of communist subversion and promote a unifying vision of their revolutionary project.[67] Sandinista leaders, like Carlos Fonseca, worked hard to explain themselves to the public via their writings and through interviews, but logistically, they needed help to spread this message. Intermediary organizations were key and so were young people.[68] Students drew on their resources and their privileges to create and disseminate propaganda in a variety of ways, and in so doing, they helped shape popular understandings of the Sandinista struggle.

Young people turned their campuses into prolific centers of propaganda. Using their school mimeograph machines, and sometimes even stealing them, young militants churned out communiqués and reports that denounced regime abuses, criticized economic conditions, and promoted the Sandinista ideology. At a time when censorship was so great that journalists resorted to reading the news at churches, it is entirely likely that the circulars coming out of the country's universities and secondary schools were the most aggressive and perhaps informative sources of anti-regime information.[69]

To be sure, the Sandinistas enjoyed relatively friendly coverage in the mainstream media in this era. The country's major newspaper, *La Prensa*, had opposed the regime almost since its inception. Under the direction of Pedro Joaquín Chamorro, the paper did the best it could within the bounds of censorship to publicize the dictatorship's corruption and abuse. At the same time, its coverage of the Sandinistas and their supporters in the 1970s, if not always favorable, did not discredit the rebels or paint them, as it had in the 1960s, as dangerous threats to society. This did not mean that the paper supported the FSLN—Chamorro had a contentious relationship with Carlos Fonseca—but the paper's neutrality prevented the demonization of the guerrillas that occurred in other countries.[70] As we have seen, *La Prensa's* coverage of student protest was often sympathetic.[71] However, in a country with high rates of illiteracy and severe censorship, neutral or even favorable media attention was not enough to reach a broad audience.

Students at all levels were not bound by censorship laws, and they used that freedom to churn out documents that attacked the legitimacy of the regime. Student communiqués focused on two lines of attack: the government's indiscriminate repression and the endemic poverty caused by misgovernment. Student flyers publicized regime atrocities. For example, in December 1977, the FER issued a *comunicado* denouncing several human rights abuses, including the treatment of a Sandinista prisoner who wrote to inform them that the Guard was making the prisoners "work like slaves in the most subhuman conditions a person can survive" and to name the GN officers who were terrorizing campesinos in northern Nicaragua.[72] They distributed information about the arrests of guerrillas or political dissidents and demanded to know their whereabouts.[73] Finally, they repeatedly linked the country's poverty to the dictatorship. One communiqué explained that so many were poor because a few were rich and denounced the "minority of people who follow Somoza who live a pleasurable and happy life as a result of the exploitation of Nicaraguan workers and campesinos."[74] Such documents show how students helped perpetuate a narrative that pitted Somocista exploiters against the exploited masses. They fiercely condemned the regime for both structural and physical forms of violence and, in so doing, promoted an idea of shared persecution: the Sandinistas were being repressed because they were trying to secure social justice.[75]

To further promote a shared oppositional identity, young activists frequently employed the language of family. The imprisoned Sandinistas or those killed in the struggle were the country's "best children." The FER initiated a campaign called "Pueblo: Claim your Jailed Children" and printed flyers that explained that "among the prisoners we find Nicaraguan brothers from" across the country and representing a variety of sectors.[76] Other documents refer to Sandinistas as "our brothers" and many flyers greet the reader as their brother.[77] Such language established a revolutionary family. The struggle bound ordinary Nicaraguans together in opposition to the dictatorship.

Students traced the origins of that revolutionary national family to Sandino, and their flyers helped spread the notion that Nicaragua had a national revolutionary history of which they should be proud. Although Sandino had amassed an international following that included the likes of Fidel Castro, his political legacy was still open to debate in Nicaragua, where widely disparate sectors venerated him. Carlos Fonseca was determined to recover Sandino's memory for the FSLN's revolutionary struggle. He wrote prolifically on the guerrilla leader, and students made sure his view of Sandino entered into the public consciousness.[78] Many of their flyers reference or narrate Sandino's history and stress his struggle against US imperialism and the regime it supported in Nicaragua. These communiqués trace Sandino's struggle forward to contemporary revolutionary efforts — the martyrs of the 1970s are the "children of Sandino's pueblo."[79] In describing how Sandino's guerrillas brought the US Marines to their knees, these short narratives drew a parallel between the movement in the 1930s and the current iteration of Sandinismo and its battle with the US-backed Somoza.[80] These narratives essentially paraphrased Fonseca's interpretation of Sandino, which students often reproduced and distributed.[81]

Student propaganda also spread information about the Sandinista's revolutionary project. Students reproduced FSLN documents and interviews with key leaders.[82] In general, however, they limited their use of Marxist language to discussions of class conflict and bourgeoisie corruption, which they often deployed to explain the state of the nation and legitimize the Sandinista struggle. Indeed, very few documents mention explicit policy goals. Students were focused instead on furthering the contemporary fight against the regime (as opposed to the construction of a future society), and many communiqués concluded with a call for the readers to organize themselves and join with one of the mass organizations in the process of forming.[83] Thus, they played a critical role in raising the consciousness of their wider society: not only did they circulate information, they also suggested concrete ways the population could take action.

As was the case elsewhere in Latin America, young activists dutifully recorded their own accomplishments and sacrifices in an effort to galvanize others. They printed leaflets memorializing the students who died on July 23, 1959; they disseminated "Posthumous Homages" dedicated to the regime's victims; and they celebrated their successes.[84] Documents meticulously record the anniversary of the deaths of student militants like Casimiro Sotelo and Leónel Rugama and exhort the reader to honor their memory by mobilizing as they had done.[85] Historians of Cold War–era student movements have long emphasized the mobilizing effects of martyrdom and memory. In Guatemala, for example, the historian Heather Vrana has argued that the violent repression of youth created a "politics of death," in which students and their communities mobilized around the memory of the fallen — not just to protest the single act of violence but also to make larger demands on the state.[86] Commemorating acts of repression thus helped craft a "shared identity of resistance" — a reminder of students' "role as both martyrs and militants."[87] In Nicaragua, student communiqués served a similar function: they sought at once to preserve their history and to provide tactical inspiration to new audiences. A 1977 *comunicado* that FER issued to students and the general public argued that the struggles to protect political prisoners in 1970 and 1971 were successful actions because they mobilized diverse sectors of the population, and FER promised to continue this kind of organizing.[88] In this way, they enshrined their own place in the revolution and shared successful strategies.

Students worked hard to get their circulars out into the communities, and they came up with resourceful ways to combat the problems presented by illiteracy and state repression. Perhaps realizing that their *comunicados* would have little effect in a country with a 50 percent illiteracy rate, students boarded buses and read their declarations to the passengers.[89] A student newspaper described how they managed to distribute their flyers: "We have to perform a practically heroic operation, watching the BECATs watching the spies, etc."[90] Humberto Román remembers waiting until just the right time, usually midday, to shove the flyers under people's doors as fast as possible.[91]

They also staged impromptu consciousness-raising events on street corners in barrios. Román remembers the spontaneous protests they called "Focos de Resistencia." "We would meet up on one corner, gather the people. We would make a barricade of stones. Then, there we would make a bonfire. We would burn tires and we started to do the work of convincing the population." He recalled that they read FSLN communiqués aloud.[92] These activities were surprisingly effective in that passersby could easily stop to listen. Israel Sánchez Salinas, a worker who lived near the National University campus in Carazo, regularly observed the students giving speeches and lighting bonfires on the streets until one day he joined one of their events. A month later, he was participating in the city's student movement, distributing flyers, painting graffiti, and organizing bonfires.[93] As the decade wore on, such activities became increasingly dangerous. The Guard would immediately arrive whenever they saw one of the bonfires or any kind of large gathering.[94]

Like their peers throughout Latin America, young people also drew on theater, music, and literature to spread revolutionary ideas. As elsewhere, culture constituted another "arena of struggle." Young Nicaraguans deployed cultural forms primarily to garner support for the popular struggle against the regime.[95] The tools they used may have been associated with the countercultural movement of the Long Sixties, but, for the most part, young musicians and actors in Nicaragua did not articulate a revolt against traditional values.[96] Instead, they attempted to link the origins of revolution to precisely those norms. Of course, such a project inherently challenged traditional sources of authority, like the state, but students located that challenge within an historic tradition of struggle. Through art, students thus sought to make revolution mainstream and tie socialism to Nicaraguan values.

Street theater was a powerful tool for spreading information and delegitimizing the regime. Students built on a long tradition of subversive popular theater, best exemplified by the widely performed colonial-era play *El Güegüense*, in which indigenous characters subvert colonial hierarchies as they satirize Spanish authorities.[97] In the 1970s, young people staged plays that mocked Somocista officials. Sandra López remembers that the secondary students in Matagalpa would stage plays "to show what we wanted the people of the barrios to understand. I remember that the Minister of Education [María Helena de] Porras . . . had gotten rid of a ton of teachers and students. So, I would dress like the Señora Minister in the barrios. I would put on big heels, my sisters' skirts, and I would do all of Minister Porras' facial expressions. It was the comic theatre of the street."[98] The performers often encouraged audience participation. Irving Dávila who participated in a theater troupe recalled: "We would go to the barrios, to the workers' centers, to the community of Subtiava in León, and we performed a play and then we would discuss with the population the theme of the play, of the sketch we presented, and we would talk with the people. We raised people's consciousness and called them to mobilize."[99] Other youth groups performed didactic plays that introduced communities to revolutionary figures, like the guerrillero priest Camilo Torres, and to their thinking.[100]

Music was another tool that students employed to provide ideological instruction and build support for the FSLN. Like other Latin American youth, Nicaraguan students were particularly drawn to the new protest music emerging in the late sixties and early seventies.[101] At the UNAN, students organized public concerts by rising young musicians like Carlos Mejía Godoy, whose music had a clear political line. Elsewhere students performed protest music in musical showcases and festivals.[102] Félix Contreras remembers that after the 1972 earthquake, students constantly visited the barrios: "Many were singers, and they would go to the barrios to play."[103] At first, they played songs coming from South America's Nueva Canción movement, but over time, they began creating their own music rooted in the conditions that ordinary Nicaraguans faced. Pancho Cedeño, who cofounded the group Pancasán when he was a student at the UCA, remembered that the CUUN president, Francisco Meza, encouraged this shift: "He would insist: rehearse, make songs; it's fine that you play Chilean songs, but it would be great if you could make Nicaraguan songs that reflect our reality, that call people to the struggle, that insist that youth join and commit themselves."[104] Young musicians started writing songs that valorized Sandino and the Sandinista struggle, portrayed the repression, and paid homage to the ordinary Nicaraguans fighting for survival.[105] In this way, they emphasized Nicaragua's revolutionary tradition.

Protestors marching with the image of the student Sandinista Arlen Siu in
Jinotepe, circa 1978 or 1979. Photo by Susan Meiselas, Magnum Photos.

Meza and other students recognized that music could be a powerful organizing tool. Student songwriters perceived their music to be one more
weapon to wield against the hegemony imposed by the United States. A
1977 student advertisement for a music festival, for example, claimed that
in contrast to the music of North America, which was part of a "premedi-
tated plan of alienation and ideological domination," "revolutionary protest
canto" could do the opposite: compel people to get organized. Maribel Duriez's experience bears this out. Duriez vividly recalled Arlen Siu's visits
to her home in the mid-1970s. Duriez was nine when the student Sandinista would "do political work with us, education, discussions, consciousness
raising. She also played the guitar, and we would sing. I loved her, she was
wonderful and she won me over completely." When the Guard killed Siu in
1975, Duriez took the news hard. "My papa told me that we have to follow Arlen's example, and that was the beginning of my integration into the
revolutionary movement."[106]

As Duriez's memory reveals, the students were forging personal connections with people who came from very different backgrounds. These ties
turned passive supporters into active ones, and many former student activists
recalled how the communities they worked in helped them when the Guard
came after them.[107] In León, families sheltered students running from the

Guard after protests. Humberto Román remembers how they would let him cross over the walls in their patios to get to another house.[108] Sandra López similarly recalls that during one of her performances mocking the minister of education in Matagalpa, the Guard began to shoot at them. Forced to flee, she took shelter with a friend's family who lived nearby.[109] The affective bonds between students and community members offered them some protection while also facilitating wider engagement in the Sandinista struggle. Each time they sheltered a young activist, adult allies took a grave risk. That they did so anyway is a testament to the connections between students and communities and the growing support for the revolutionary struggle.

Students' sheer dedication to producing and disseminating propaganda helped create a culture of insurrection. Through their flyers, plays, and songs, young people helped the Sandinistas build a hegemonic narrative that condemned the regime's violence and celebrated the nation's revolutionary history and the tenacity of its people. To be sure, this was the narrative that key Sandinista leaders, like Carlos Fonseca, had constructed, but students helped move those stories into the public imagination.

Students and Insurrection (1977–1979)

Between 1977 and 1979, a wave of uprisings rocked Nicaragua. Some had been planned by the Frente Sandinista, but others were spontaneous. In this insurrectionary period, a growing number of youths joined the guerrilla movement in the mountains while others stayed behind to continue organizing in the cities, where they took on increasingly dangerous supportive actions. They organized strikes, took over churches, and even attacked the National Guard. They learned how to build bombs and threw them at military vehicles. In this way, they destabilized their society, mobilized their communities, and created the conditions in which the revolution could succeed. The aggressive activism of youth made them targets for arrest and assassination, but that repression only further legitimized the revolutionary option.

The years between 1977 and 1979 were the most violent of the Somoza era. The military was waging a brutal rural campaign against the Sandinistas, and, in 1976, they killed Carlos Fonseca. The following year, only eleven *guerrilleros* remained in the mountains. The urban insurgents faced their own share of repression, and several key leaders, like Pedro Aráuz, were also killed. Despite these setbacks, the FSLN ranks continued to grow, especially in urban areas. New recruits joined a divided organization: by this time, the Frente had split into three tendencies or subgroups: the Guerra Popular Prolongada (Prolonged People's War, or GPP), the Proletariats, and the Terceristas. The Proletariats, believing mass organization in urban areas was key to revolution, placed their energies accordingly. The GPP embraced Mao's emphasis on rural guerrilla tactics, and the Terceristas prioritized creating alliances over strict adherence to Marxist ideology.[110] For example, with the encouragement of the Terceristas, prominent businessmen, professors, and priests formed the Group of Twelve in 1977 to denounce the regime. Both the GPP and the Terceristas staged several dramatic attacks in late 1977.

The following year, ordinary Nicaraguans rose up spontaneously against the regime. When *La Prensa* editor Pedro Joaquín Chamorro was assassinated in January 1978, the country erupted—fifty thousand people demonstrated and riots broke out in the capital. The next month, the indigenous community of Monimbó, a barrio of Masaya, took over their neighborhood after the Guard had attacked a peaceful ceremony in honor of the slain journalist. The military bombed the barrio and eventually regained control. Other cities soon followed and each was brutally repressed.[111] These uprisings initiated the period of insurrection when spontaneous actions destabilized the regime and revealed the population's willingness to take up arms.

Students contributed to the instability by staging massive nationwide demonstrations that revealed the depth of the disillusionment with the regime. In April 1978, a wave of student strikes paralyzed the nation's educational system. The strikes originated in three distinct episodes. The first occurred at the National School of Agriculture and Animal Husbandry when students protested the dismissal of eighteen professors and demanded their reinstatement in late March.[112] Around the same time, a series of protests over the treatment of political prisoners erupted. Albertina Serrano Jaen, the mother of the imprisoned Sandinista, Marcio Jaen, joined several other women and students on a hunger strike to protest the solitary confinement of her son and Tomás Borge.[113] For the first few days of April, the students of the UNAN-León protested the treatment of political prisoners, and on the third of the month, secondary students left their classes in solidarity.[114] The third key moment occurred early in the morning on April 5, when a group of thirty students seized the National Institute of Masaya to protest the presence of spies on campus. The youth alleged that soldiers were operating undercover, posing as students, professors, and janitors. Later, more than forty-five hundred young people from private and public secondary schools throughout the city joined.[115] Although distinct motives prompted each protest, all three signaled students' unwillingness to tolerate the regime's growing repression.

The strikes quickly spread to secondary schools throughout the country as students merged the three causes and declared twenty-four hour strikes in solidarity with their protesting peers and the Sandinista prisoners. The students also denounced the lack of free expression, demanded the right to organize, and called for an investigation into Chamorro's murder. To spread the word on their campuses, youth went from classroom to classroom asking for support. After taking over a building, they hung banners from the balconies or propped up protest signs and stopped traffic in front of the schools to ask for support. At the Colegio Teresiano, an all-girls Catholic school, striking students spent the day praying and meditating.[116] Soon, young people began occupying churches. Even primary students participated.[117] As Mario López, a university student who helped organize the protest recalled, "Never had there been a pro-Sandinista political demonstration like this."[118]

To delegitimize the protests, the minister of education claimed that outside forces directed the students.[119] She was not entirely wrong. Humberto Román, one of the FER university students tasked with organizing in secondary schools, recalled working in Masaya, where he helped extend the protest beyond the National Institute to the other private schools like the Teresiano and the Salesiano.[120] Other FER activists did the same in cities across the country. According to Victor Hugo Tinoco, university students coordinated all the strikes: "We organized them with the secondary students, and they were directed by us inside the university."[121] Román recalled that the Sandinistas hoped to use these protests to increase people's political activity and that the issue that started the Masaya conflict was a pretext. The students did want to get rid of the director, but the primary goal was to draw attention to the plight of prisoners. Román remembered that this decision came from the very top of the Sandinista hierarchy.[122]

The leadership of the university students does not minimize the younger peers' political agency. As was the case elsewhere in Latin America, secondary students had a long history of political militancy. Historians have traced their record for political radicalism to the weakness of institutional student organizations (such as a national secondary student union) and the diversity that often marks secondary schools and their surrounding environs. Public secondary schools, in particular, have historically attracted students from across class and regional backgrounds as well as non-student youth — a mixture that at times has had a radicalizing effect on young people.[123] This certainly seems to be the case in Nicaragua, where national student organizations were controlled by the FER, which sent both student and non-student organizers to work with high school youth.

Secondary students, it should be stressed, were autonomous and diverse political actors. The strikes were possible because students clearly had grievances that the Sandinistas were able to build on. Of course, not all students supported the April 1978 demonstration—violence broke out at the Colegio Andrés Bello in Managua between protestors and a small group of students opposed to joining the strike.[124] But, as was true at Andrés Bello, a majority of students were in favor of protesting, and the level of participation in the strikes was astonishing. The walkouts ultimately extended to almost fifty secondary schools and affected more than ninety thousand secondary students.[125] Although university student activists helped spark the unrest, the younger teenagers proved to be ready kindling. Their willingness to protest and support the Sandinista prisoners suggests a high level of politicization—after all, the FER had been operating in secondary schools since the 1960s. The earlier 1976 strikes, while more atomized, had illustrated these youths' unique ability to act quickly, en masse, and garner popular support.

As in the earlier strikes, parents stepped in to support young protestors. *La Prensa* reported that on the first day of the Masaya strike, housewives ferried food to their children. That night, students at the various secondary schools in Masaya organized a meeting for their parents to explain their actions, and parents throughout the country quickly expressed their unconditional support for their children.[126] Within a week of the strikes, parents had formed their own committees, and some even participated in the negotiations.[127] In Managua, on April 16, the parents' associations of ten schools held an assembly where they requested the removal of the minister of education, María Helena de Porras, who, in response to the strike, had closed the nation's schools indefinitely.[128]

Once again, the student protest had catalyzed the organization of their elders.[129] In an editorial in *La Prensa*, Raúl Orozco observed that while in the past, parents instilled in their children ideas about civic duty, "today the children help their parents to recapture that consciousness."[130] Student protests provided parents a legitimate and almost unassailable reason to protest the Somoza regime: they had to secure the safety of their children. As such, they could act as parents, mothers, and fathers—positions of moral authority that were hard to discount.

Communities also united behind their young residents. In Jinotepe, nuns tried to intervene on behalf of students, and in San Marcos, worshipers prevented soldiers from forcibly ejecting a group of youths who were seizing the church.[131] At times, whole towns rallied behind the students. The people of Estelí took food to the protestors.[132] When the GN detained several students in Jinotepe, the pueblo demanded and won their freedom.[133] Each of these acts constituted its own form of resistance—an acknowledgment not only of the regime's capacity for violence but also a recognition of the students' right to protest.

In a Cold War climate where dissent was equated with subversion, protest was dangerous. At one point, a teacher shot at protesting students, wounding two.[134] There were a few incidents where students were poisoned with donated food.[135] The National Guard appeared at the occupied schools almost instantly, and the military's specialized counterinsurgency units, BECATs, patrolled the streets around campuses. An Air Force helicopter hovered above the protestors at the National Institute of Somoto.[136] Images from *La Prensa* show soldiers armed in full military gear, with helmets and rifles, patrolling the streets as unarmed students in the white blouses and dark pants of their school uniforms look on. These pictures are particularly compelling because the students hold only books and binders as they are confronted with the menacing postures of the military.[137]

The photos are testament to the Guard's use of disproportionate force. Soldiers indiscriminately deployed tear gas and fired at peaceful protesters.[138] They even violated the sanctity of the church, shooting at students who were ringing the bells in the Iglesia Santiago in Jinotepe.[139] The violence intensified as soldiers dislodged students from the schools. In Masaya, the National Guard attacked one of the secondary schools at three in the morning, beating students and shooting indiscriminately. *La Prensa* described the evocative scene of soldiers at one school washing the blood off the floor.[140] Facing the regime's violent intransigence, the students began evacuating their schools in early May.[141]

The students won virtually none of their demands, but they had demonstrated considerable political muscle. Their protest paralyzed the national educational system and motivated their parents to denounce the regime. It thus revealed the organizing potential of the population. The protests, Román believed, had been "a way of showing that there was already a strong student movement, not just in the university, but also in secondary, and it was united to the population."[142] In this regard, the action was a resounding success. A wide array of society rose up to defend its children, and in so doing, stood up to the regime.

As their leadership in the April demonstrations suggests, university students continued to be key organizers in this period. Under the leadership (1974–1984) of the rector Mariano Fiallos Oyanguren, the campuses of the National University became a haven for activists of all stripes.[143] According to Mónica Baltodano, who helped lead the FER in the late 1970s, the University Club at the UNAN campus in Carazo "was a center for anti-dictatorial conspiracy, a meeting place for secondary students and even a refuge for those who could no longer live in their homes because of the repression."[144] However, as the state's violence escalated, the university's historic autonomy was no longer enough to keep the school and its citizens entirely safe. In August 1978, the National Guard occupied the University Club in Carazo and used it to launch several attacks on the community.[145] The regime's willingness to defy university autonomy suggested a more extreme commitment to ferreting out dissent.

That attitude was likely a response to the FSLN's mounting threat to dictatorship. In August, the Sandinistas attacked the National Palace, holding the entire congress hostage for nearly three days. The two thousand hostages included several high-level Somocistas, and the dictator was forced to negotiate, ultimately freeing dozens of imprisoned Sandinistas and giving the guerrillas $500,000, among other concessions.[146] The attack underscored the regime's vulnerability and encouraged others to mobilize. A reformist coalition led by wealthy business owners and political elites, the Frente Amplio Opositor (Broad Opposition Front), which had formed in May, organized a general strike. They were joined by the Movimiento de Pueblo Unido (United People's Movement, or MPU), which Sandinista intermediary organizations had formed in July. The FSLN, meanwhile, continued preparing for armed insurrection, and university and secondary school students were ready to join them.[147]

The Sandinistas had begun training urban activists for the insurrection in 1977, and young allies embraced the opportunity for more aggressive action. Members of the Association of Secondary Students, the Movement of Secondary Students, and even neighborhood gangs, like Managua's Black Sheep Movement, began attacking soldiers who entered their neighborhoods.[148] Many also joined the pre-combat units that the three Sandinista tendencies were organizing. Members of the GPP joined the Committee for Popular Action (CAP), the Popular Brigades were associated with the Proletariats, and the Popular Militias were the Tercerista's urban organization. According to Mónica Baltodano, these barrio-based groups were geared toward youth, and their goal was to "exhaust the enemy, reinforce the military struggle and prepare us for the coming insurrections."[149] Those who wanted more training could join one of the combat units the tendencies were forming: Revolutionary Commandos (Proletariats), Combat Units (GPP), and Combat Tactical Units (Terceristas). Members of these units attended a military training camp, where Sandinistas taught them how to use a variety of weapons and prepared them for the psychological rigors of warfare. There was considerable overlap between the pre-combat units and the commandos, and both operated at the neighborhood level in the larger cities like Managua, León, and Jinotepe.[150]

Working with these groups, students brought the guerrilla struggle into the cities. Besides painting pro-Sandinista messages on walls and organizing nightly bonfires, young people in the pre-combat units learned how to make contact bombs, which they used throughout 1978 and 1979. Alma Nubia Baltodano lost both her arms making one of these improvised weapons. "We didn't just throw them at the BECAT jeeps," she said, "but also at the Somocista thugs or simply threw them in the streets. It was a way of saying we are here."[151] The Sandinistas gave the combat units more aggressive operations. For example, América Libertad Vidaurre, a secondary student in the Revolutionary Commando in Managua, was tasked with burning down a radio station, kidnapping visiting members of the Organization of American States, and executing neighborhood spies.[152] Most often though, they attacked the soldiers patrolling their neighborhood. Vidaurre remembered, "We would make like 50 contact bombs. We'd go out into the street, attack the BECAT jeeps, roll it over and then take their weapons." Sometimes, the units killed the soldiers they found inside.[153] By embracing violence against a regime that terrorized and murdered its citizens, youth were able to exact a measure of autonomy for their neighborhoods. Mónica Baltodano remembered that they were so effective that the "Guards [were] afraid every time they entered the barrios."[154]

With the exception of contact bombs, these groups were virtually unarmed. The Sandinistas had a very difficult time acquiring enough weapons for themselves, much less for the urban support squads. When Rodolfo Porras attended combat training clinics, his teacher gave them "brooms, clubs, mop handles to simulate weapons, because we didn't have any."[155] Consequently, when youth attacked the heavily armed soldiers, they knew they were risking everything. As Mauricio Valenzuela said, the CAPs were made up of "young kids who were now actively, not passively, ready to give their lives" to the cause.[156]

At times, their youthfulness offered them some protection. At Managua's Modesto Armijo Institute, students took over a classroom and used it as an improvised safe house, where they stored guns and fabricated contact bombs. According to Vidaurre, "Nobody could enter and we would stand guard to protect what we had [there]."[157] The students must have enjoyed a high level of administrative support to be able to requisition part of their school. When Eva María Samqui Chan was organizing students in Jinotepe in 1977, she recalled how the community supported its young people's revolutionary activities. When the director of the Permanent Human Rights

Commission in Jinotepe would find out that "a group of youth were going out to throw contact bombs, he would grab the organization's flag and run behind them to protect the kids. Later, the Red Cross would do the same. Everybody in some way was recruited, but not organically, instead it was to defend the kids."[158] Such protection became increasingly necessary as the regime intensified the repression.

This was the period when it became "a crime to be young in Nicaragua." That phrase, adopted by dissidents and the media, only hints at the everyday violence that marked the lives of Nicaraguans. By February 1979, notices of the missing and detained began appearing in newspapers nearly every day. Some of them were students, and some were workers; some were arrested at home by plainclothesmen, and others were arrested in the streets by heavily armed soldiers. Nearly all were young. Ana Xiomara Morales Bermúdez, age sixteen and a student at the Instituto Ramírez Goyena, was one of sixteen people arrested in the early morning hours of February 8. Fourteen of the detained were under twenty-one and the youngest was fourteen.[159] It seemed that bodies with gunshot wounds to the head were turning up in the city daily, with no evidence as to the killers. In the countryside, the violence was worse. On February 1, Santos Castillo Montenegro (age nineteen), Eleuterio Dolmus Martínez (age eighteen), Octavio Carrión Barrera (age twenty-one), Domingo Osorio Carrillo (age seventeen), Mario Avilés Amador (age sixteen), and Juan Ríos set out for a day of fishing near El Sauce in northwestern Nicaragua. Only Avilés Amador returned. Ríos disappeared, but the badly beaten bodies of the other four youths were found in a field, their hands tied behind their backs. The Guard had assumed they were Sandinista *guerrilleros* and beaten them to death.[160]

Campesinos were perhaps the most victimized sector, but their deaths received less media scrutiny than the killing of students. *La Prensa*, for example, reported that on January 16, 1979, the National Guard arrested everybody in the village of El Carrizo in Estelí. The following day, they killed Don Marvos Rayo and his son Gregorio, and a woman, María Elsa Ramírez Laguna, was raped and murdered. The paper, however, did not follow up on what happened to the rest of the villagers detained in El Carrizo.[161] At other points, the newspaper was even more vague. On February 4, it reported the arrest of a twenty-three-year-old campesino, Audilio Rivera Peralta, in the department of Estelí. The article mentions that "in that zone, many campesinos have been found dead after having been captured by GN patrols," but offers no more detail.[162] In part, this might be because the information often came from the Permanent Human Rights Commission, which likely did not have the human resources to investigate the many reports of violence, but it might also reflect the biases of an urban-based newspaper that catered to a small elite and middle-class readership.

The situation in Nicaragua by early 1979 had become untenable. The regime's violence had seriously destabilized the country. Unemployment was rising rapidly. With the Guard focused on ferreting out subversives, crime rates escalated. Schools reported lower enrollments as parents kept their children home or, if they could afford it, sent them abroad.[163] Strikes became more common, and Somoza seemed to care little about negotiating. In mid-January 1979, eighteen hospital workers had gone on a hunger strike to protest the sudden dismissal of two thousand workers. A month later, the regime still refused to budge, and the protestors were perilously ill. One of the striking nurses, Silvia Ferrufino, ultimately died.[164] The protest garnered the support of multiple sectors of society, and journalists, doctors, and even entire Catholic parishes issued declarations of solidarity and donated money to the health workers' union, FETSALUD.[165]

The regime's intransigence, combined with its escalating violence, meant that protest continued to be dangerous, so the Sandinistas and their supporters opted for an unmistakably peaceful demonstration: occupying Catholic churches. In solidarity with the FETSALUD hunger strikers, youth from the CAPs and the MPU occupied all the churches in León on February 15, 1979. Church takeovers had become a popular protest tool. Sergio Lira, a Sandinista leader in León, recalled that at root takeovers were a community protest "because behind every church takeover there was a barrio: the people would pass them food, drinks and encourage them to keep at it. In light of their inability to do anything, because there was no other way and especially with the censorship of the press, at that time, the kids would take over a church as a protest."[166] Church occupations thus constituted a last-resort public statement—a historically safe way to demonstrate dissent in a violent climate. Moreover, its communal aspect meant that any attempt to repress a church occupation would occur before the eyes of the entire community.

At 7:30 in the morning on February 15, five youths entered León's El Calvario Church. Mauricio Díaz Müller, Julio César Ayerdis, Frank Rubí, Oswaldo Lanzas, and Benito Jirón Herrera informed the priest that they were planning to occupy the building for twelve hours in solidarity with FETSALUD. After promising not to damage the church, they climbed to the bell tower, where they hung a protest banner. Similar occupations were occurring throughout the country, but this one would be very different. The National Guard arrived soon after the protest began. Optimistically, the young men shouted for the soldiers' solidarity. The latter shot at them in reply. Reinforcements soon arrived, and the Guard entered the church. A crowd outside heard the young men plead for mercy and then the sounds of shots firing. By 10:15 a.m., the soldiers had carted away the bodies of the five youths.[167]

The violation of such a sacrosanct space electrified the country. Barrio residents across the city rushed to warn the young people occupying other churches to get out.[168] The military meanwhile issued a statement declaring that the young men "had weapons and had attacked" the soldiers.[169] Unconvinced, ordinary Nicaraguans reacted with an outpouring of grief and rage. The day of the massacre radio stations played funeral music.[170] Students at the UNAN declared a strike, while their peers at the UCA resorted to burning tires in front of their campus.[171] The Catholic hierarchy denounced the violence, with Archbishop Miguel Obando y Bravo telling reporters: "Apparently our unfortunate country is in the hands of Cains."[172] Adult allies occupied churches in protest: Reinaldo Antonio Téfel, Socrates Flores, and Moisés Hassan, former student activists and now leaders of the National Patriotic Front (a pro-FSLN coalition of various parties and organizations), took over a church in Managua.[173] Faculty, staff, and students from the UNAN occupied the archbishop's curia, and seventeen organizations—including unions, professional societies, and political parties—sent representatives to occupy El Calvario Church a week after the massacre.[174] When a group from the Movimiento de Mujeres Militantes en La Lucha Popular (Movement of Militant Women in the Popular Struggle) occupied the Church of September the 14th, they preemptively declared that they did not have arms in order to forestall any regime accusations.[175] In adopting the murdered youths' strategy, adult allies acknowledged the legitimacy of their protest and whipped up further opposition.

The Sandinistas renewed their calls for Nicaraguans to organize and intensified their assaults on the regime. Daniela Lanzas, whose fourteen-year-old brother, Oswaldo, had been murdered at El Calvario, remembered that the attack galvanized many who had been hesitant to act. "In the houses where the mothers or brothers did not join [the struggle], they started joining precisely because everything that was happening—these abuses were intolerable. In each house where somebody had died, the whole family joined." As the military's violence escalated, more and more families experienced firsthand the regime's brutality and opted to fight it. Lanzas concluded, "That is really what led to Somoza's overthrow—the addition of all of us who could not bear it anymore."[176]

Passive supporters had plenty of opportunities now to act. A week after the massacre, Sandinistas and their urban allies staged simultaneous uprisings in cities throughout the country to mark the forty-fifth anniversary of Sandino's death. In Managua, young people effectively blocked the streets to prevent the military from entering neighborhoods. It took half an hour for the soldiers to remove the obstacles they had placed in the roads, and in that time, they held rallies, threw dozens of contact bombs, and painted the walls of their barrios with pro-FSLN slogans.[177] This dramatic show of force revealed the opposition's growing organization and ability to stymie the National Guard.

The uprisings of February 1979 foreshadowed the role youth would play in the final offensive that toppled the regime. In fact, much of the revolution's success can be attributed not to the Sandinista militants in the mountains but to the sympathizers in the city who rose up of their own accord.[178] The indigenous community of Monimbó had been the first to rebel in February 1978, and for two weeks, they managed to repel the National Guard, with the assistance of only one Sandinista, Camilo Ortega Saavedra. Similar uprisings and repression occurred in Diriamba and Subtiava.[179]

The anti-Somoza student movements were key participants in other spontaneous uprisings. In August 1978, young Matagalpinos led an uprising that almost forced the GN to negotiate. This was the "Insurrección de los Niños," the Children's Insurrection. Isabel Castillo, who fought in it, recalled, "They called it that because we were there in the barricades, boys and girls of fourteen or fifteen years, of course, with all of the population's support." Castillo remembered that the Guard's murder of a secondary student activist on August 28 kicked off the insurrection:

> The morning they found his body . . . I went to go see what happened, and I saw a ton of people with the compañero in their arms and the people were furious, nothing could stop them, and they began making barricades. Many of us then joined them. . . . The effervescence exploded there—all of that rage that had been contained.[180]

Marcos Largaespada remembered that students and workers began building barricades and collecting weapons. The death of a child had compelled their communities to rise up, and young activists followed their lead. For nearly five days, the rebel residents held the city.[181] Eventually, Guard reinforcements arrived and pushed back the insurgents, by then running low on ammunition, with a wave of aerial bombings, sniper attacks, and indiscriminate repression.

Similar uprisings occurred in the cities throughout the country, as young people rose up in rebellion, only to be crushed as the military bombed their neighborhoods.[182] The repression was brutal—an estimated three thousand

civilians were killed and thousands displaced as the military took back rebellious neighborhoods. The uprisings had once again revealed the regime's
weakness, and the Guard's violence had underscored its moral bankruptcy.[183]

Nicaraguan youth played a critical role in the final months of the revolution. Unbidden, they staged uprisings and assaults and joined the Sandinistas in ever-increasing numbers. In fact, many of the combatants in those
final months were secondary and university students. In one study, a sociologist found that out of a random sample of 640 Sandinistas who died
during the revolution, 75 percent were under age twenty-four and almost
one-third were students.[184] These figures suggest that participation of large
numbers of non-student youth was critical to the success of the revolution
and highlights the broad cross-class coalition that had emerged to support
the FSLN. The struggle and sacrifice of the young inspired their families and
communities to join the rebellion and unite behind the Sandinistas and their
promise of structural change.

Whether or not they were students, young people filled the ranks of the
FSLN and provided critical support during the final offensive. In June, the
Sandinistas staged a coordinated attack that quickly overran the cities of
the north, while another wing moved up from the south. As the political
scientist John Booth notes, "In almost every battle in a populated center,
the Front found its numbers multiplied severalfold by volunteers."[185] The
National Guard again responded by bombing entire neighborhoods, killing
thousands. That show of force proved to be the regime's last gasp. By the
beginning of July, the National Guard held control only in Managua, and
Somoza had declared his intention to resign. The Sandinistas were closing
in on the capital, and on July 17, 1979, Anastasio Somoza Debayle left the
country.[186]

The revolution had come to pass. The regime's violence combined with
the organizing efforts of the Sandinistas and their young allies had finally
made ordinary Nicaraguans "fighting mad." They acted not as individuals
but as part of communities that rose up to defend their children, their lives,
and their human rights. Working together to barricade neighborhoods and
attack the National Guard, Nicaraguans of all ages had demonstrated their
collective power and defeated the dictator and his army.

Conclusion

Throughout the 1970s, Nicaragua experienced a second democratic effervescence, but this time the organizing effort was much more extensive and

the result much more dramatic. Unlike in the 1940s, students approached workers and other sectors as equal partners and built reciprocal relationships. In so doing, they forged cross-class alliances that meant students rose up when workers were threatened, and the residents of marginalized barrios took in youths hunted by the military. Students were key to the success of the revolution, but so were the many other sectors that rebelled against the regime: women, campesinos, business owners, and many others. Together they created the revolutionary coalition that had not materialized over the long course of the Somoza regime.

Students had created a culture of insurrection the painstaking way: door-to-door organizing, long conversations, churning out propaganda, and staging dramatic and risky actions. These efforts helped raise the political consciousness of their society. Ordinary Nicaraguans came to blame the regime for the violence of everyday life and then, crucially, they chose to do something about it. With help from university, secondary, and even primary students, parents and communities got organized and demanded change.

Examining student organizing in the 1970s complicates our understanding of how revolutions are made. Building barricades in the cities and provoking skirmishes with the military in the mountains may be the most newsworthy tactics, but there are many other activities that help persuade ordinary people to overthrow the state. Analyzing student activism sheds light on the quotidian tasks that make revolutions viable. It forces us to rethink the revolutionary division of labor that privileges direct combat (often the realm of men) over "support tasks" (frequently assigned to women).[187] All too often the jobs scholars have labeled as the latter—"message carriers, providing safe house, providing food and medicines, hiding and moving arms"—actually constituted the work of the urban underground, which students, both male and female, helped perform and which, as this chapter argues, was vital to the success of the revolution.[188]

Moreover, that divide between "support" tasks and direct combat elides the critical work of consciousness-raising that is essential for revolution to occur and that students helped accomplish. To be very clear, these young people were not alone responsible for raising the consciousness of their society—base communities, labor unions, and other groups were just as critical. However, scholars have explored the contributions of those sectors, while the role of students in revolutionary projects has been largely neglected in the historical literature. Yet, studying student organizing moves us away from a view of revolution as an explosive event and toward an understanding of the long and uneven process through which a society comes to accept the legitimacy of armed uprising.

Conclusion

When Somoza fled the country in July 1979, he left behind a devastated nation. Nearly fifty thousand people had been killed and 20 percent of the population had been displaced. The country was $1.5 billion in debt, and to make matters worse, Somoza and his cronies had fled with a significant portion of the national treasury.[1] Facing the monumental task of rebuilding the nation, the Sandinistas chose to organize a literacy campaign as one of their first social projects. On March 24, 1980, the crusade began and fifty-five thousand literacy workers, the vast majority high school students, set out for the countryside.[2]

Considering the nation's many pressing problems, the decision to focus on literacy might have seemed an odd choice, but it served the larger project of nation building. Robert Arnove in his study of the campaign explained that the Sandinistas believed literacy was key to citizenship and moving the country past the "feudal system of the Somoza dynasty."[3] Moreover, it presented an unparalleled nation-building opportunity and a way to show the beneficial power of the state. Indeed, the crusade would require a massive mobilization, as the Ministry of Education would have to train the volunteers, organize room and board for those who would be working in rural areas, and outfit the literacy workers with pedagogical materials and supplies.[4]

It was not going to be an easy task, yet it was one made plausible by the level of student mobilization that already existed. Given the history of student activism in 1970s Nicaragua, it is not a coincidence that the Sandinistas prioritized an educational project that would largely rely on student labor. This population had revealed itself to be easily mobilized, well organized, and committed to the idea of a new Nicaragua. Students in the 1970s had proven their capacity for large-scale cooperation and the strength of their numbers. If students were involved, so were their families and their communities. In this way, the National Literacy Campaign could continue operating through the networks that had sprung up in the 1970s, using them now to rebuild the state.[5] The FSLN leadership, many of whom had either been student activists or advisors, understood well the power of youth and their capacity for organized political action.

This book has shown that students in the secondary schools and universities were central players in the revolutionary struggles of the 1970s. To do that, it first traced the emergence of student exceptionalism in the 1940s, as students spearheaded the struggle against the regime. It then examined the student movement itself, its politics and strategies and how they changed over time. In so doing, this study revealed students' unique capacity to mobilize their society.

Throughout the Somoza era, Nicaraguan students fought hard against the regime and won significant concessions. Slowly, through their defiant protests, they carved out a space for dissent unlike any other in the nation. They demanded and won autonomy for the university and then used that extraordinary independence from the state to promote wider political engagement. University autonomy was possible because students had long waged a campaign to persuade the nation of their exceptional status—the idea that these young people, as the nation's future leaders, required the basic civil rights the regime denied to most everybody. That notion was essential to the students' capacity to challenge the regime. It won them a spectrum of potential allies who were ready to support their claims for greater freedoms. It gave them the breathing room to defy the regime in bold and impertinent ways in the 1940s and 1950s. However, it did not make them invulnerable. As we have seen, the state still cracked down on student dissenters, imprisoning and even murdering them.

Such violence against students, however, mobilized their society throughout the Somoza era. This phenomenon was not true everywhere. In larger countries, with larger student populations, authoritarian regimes managed to demonize and delegitimize student activism.[6] That did not happen in Nicaragua, where the student population remained disproportionately small and the major opposition newspaper, controlled by a former student activist, remained staunchly supportive of the anti-Somoza student movement.

In fact, Nicaragua was such a small country that former student leaders often remained in touch with the movement, providing new generations with guidance and support. No doubt remembering his own days as an activist in the generation of 1944, Pedro Joaquín Chamorro often provided friendly coverage of student protests in his newspaper, *La Prensa*. At several junctures, he collaborated with young people, suggesting strategies, seeking their opinions, and offering positive publicity in his papers. In the 1960s, Carlos Fonseca urged youth in the university to adopt the very strategies of movement building that he had attempted in the late 1950s. In the 1970s, several former student activists turned Sandinistas began teaching in the National University, a position from which they advised new cohorts. This continuity meant students learned from the mistakes of previous generations and applied them to the ongoing struggle against the regime.

Tracing these generational connections does not minimize student political agency. As we have seen, student politics was rooted in intensely local and often quite personal grievances. They opposed Somoza in the 1940s because his regime restricted their civil rights and threatened their class privileges. In the early 1950s, they protested the mismanagement of the university and its authoritarian administration. By the end of the decade, however, they had broadened their agenda and were publicly criticizing the regime's brutality, which they had experienced firsthand. In the 1960s, the democratic opening tamed their militancy, but US imperialism, the country's inequality, and the Somozas' continued political presence still concerned students who experimented with relatively new ideologies, like Christian Democracy, and embraced older ones, like Marxism. Under Anastasio Somoza Debayle, the regime's growing violence, corruption, and disregard for the poor radicalized young people. Apart from the reality of US imperialism, these concerns had very little to do with the global conflict between the United States and the USSR, but they were part of the Cold War debates over what the state should look like and what were the fundamental rights of its citizens.

There were no easy answers, but, in general, most students agreed that the state should not look like the Somozas. For nearly forty years, students had suffered repression and censorship, albeit not to the degree that campesinos and workers endured. Nonetheless, decade after decade witnessed violent clashes between heavily armed soldiers and unarmed students. The dictatorship had a long history of repressing its opposition, and students, despite their exceptional status, often found themselves in the crosshairs. To be sure, such violence was infrequent, but it remained a fact of life—a threat that shaped student politics and strategies.

This long history of state violence, corruption, and mismanagement prompted generations of student unrest. It is not a coincidence that perhaps the quietest decade in the student movement, the 1960s, coincided with a brief democratic aperture, and the brief ascension of a non-Somoza to the presidency. But with the exception of that small window, most of the Somoza era, and, by extension, of Nicaragua's cold war, was marked by student protest. The dissent of young people in the university and in secondary schools was not the product of some knee-jerk rebellion but was instead rooted in their experiences, first with the regime's repression and then later with the country's deep inequality. This history forces us to think of young people as political agents, driven by their own understandings of power and who should wield it.

Indeed, opposition to the family's long tenure forced students to seek out allies across the political spectrum.[7] As early as 1939, when students staged a play that declared war on the Axis powers and critiqued Somoza, conservative and liberal youth readily worked together against the regime. In the 1960s, Christian Democrat students allied with their more radical peers to protest Anastasio Somoza Debayle's bid for the presidency, and, a decade later, students from all ideological stripes—socialists, communists, and undecided—joined together in dramatic actions against the regime. Such collaboration, which was mirrored in the larger society in the 1970s, spoke to the level of antipathy that the Somozas had historically generated among youth.

It also reveals their understanding of the regime's strength. From the beginning, it was obvious that Somoza had force on his side: both in terms of the National Guard and the unspoken but often demonstrable support of the United States. The working class position toward the regime was less clear-cut. The historian Jeffrey Gould has argued that "Somoza's strength resided primarily in the social and political distance between campesino and union militants, and the opposition."[8] It would take young activists a long time to understand how to bridge that gulf, but even as early as the 1940s, they understood that any effort to remove the Somozas would require the participation of workers and campesinos. Each decade, a new generation sought to collaborate with these sectors, with varied success. Often, their own biases, class and gendered, got in the way of forming sustainable alliances, but they kept trying.

Young women were especially critical in this endeavor. They had been participating in the student movement for much of the Somoza era. As early as the 1940s, Joaquina Vega, student speaker at the opening ceremonies, was celebrating the inauguration of the Free University as a space where women could exercise their political rights. In the 1950s, they marched at the head of processions and met with the president to demand the freedom of their peers. Besides these highly visible roles, they also worked behind the scenes, circulating communiqués and reaching out to the local populace. Their position in the movement would grow in the following two decades, as women took on greater responsibility in student organizations. By the 1970s, they were attending co-ed religious retreats, visiting striking workers, and leading commandos. Focused on national liberation, their activism defied traditional gendered notions, and they constituted a critical part of the revolutionary struggle against the regime.

Many young men and women, like Arlen Siu, would enter into the pantheon of Sandinista heroes who died fighting to overthrow the regime. Their memory compelled still wider activism. Indeed, the violence that student activists endured inspired their families to get involved. As we have seen, Nicaraguan parents had long been involved in their children's political struggles, ferrying food to the prisons where they were being held and lobbying for their release. Parental involvement grew in the 1970s as their children became fodder in the regime's battle against the Sandinista guerrillas and as the National Guard began cracking down indiscriminately on dissenters. As the final chapters demonstrated, student strikes in their universities and secondary schools provided parents with a channel for activism and an unassailable reason for engaging with the state.

But students were not only martyrs, they were also militant activists and organizers. Their deeply held political beliefs led many to sacrifice their lives in the struggle against Somoza. As the sociologist Carlos Vilas's statistics show, students were a significant percentage of combatants, and many died for their beliefs.[9] They also lived for them. In the 1970s, many youth left their studies behind as they prioritized activist work. Moisés Hassan, a professor at the UNAN in that era, laughed at the memory of his students' dismally low grades in the 1970s.[10] Irving Dávila and Patricia Orozco remembered how classes fell by the wayside as their involvement in the student movement grew.[11] For them and countless others, a degree was not their priority. They risked arrest, beatings, torture, and even the safety of their loved ones to organize in barrios and schools and drum up resistance to the regime. In so doing, they helped create a culture of insurrection and the conditions necessary for revolution to occur.

Along the way, they revealed the sheer power of an organized student movement. Students from schools across the country cooperated and coordinated strikes and other actions against the regime. Throughout the Somoza era, students were among the regime's most vocal opponents, and their identity as students, the support of their families and teachers, and their access to information about political theories and current events facilitated their ability to act spontaneously and effectively in coordination. The nation's secondary schools and universities constituted a ready network for transmitting information and ideas quickly not just among students but also to their families and communities.

Much of the work of revolution happens behind the scenes—in conversations that do not make it into newspapers or the historical record. It happens in one-on-one encounters, in group discussions, in favors requested of friends. This was the task students took on during the Somoza era. They did not always prioritize it and they did not always do it effectively, but it was ultimately vital to the success of the 1979 revolution. More often, they focused on other more disruptive actions: protests, strikes, and school occupations. These forms of direct action garnered considerable publicity and persistently shone a light on the regime's brutality and mismanagement. But it was their efforts to engage with others—whether they be neighbors, workers, other students, or their families—that helped spread revolutionary ideas and persuade ordinary Nicaraguans that it was possible to overthrow the regime. That process took years and required considerable organization.

None of this history was lost on the Sandinista leadership as they set about remaking the country and implementing the National Literacy Campaign. They relied on schools and student groups to attract volunteers, shore up support, and even provide technical assistance.[12] It was a tremendous success. Arnove reported that in the campaign's first five months, the level of illiteracy among people over ten fell from around 50 percent to an estimated 23 percent. Some 55,000 volunteers had taught 406,056 of their fellow citizens to read.[13] It was a testament to both the Sandinistas' revolutionary commitment to a more just society and the organizing potential of youth. Once again, a generation of students had cooperated and collaborated for a larger cause, and, in the process, they transformed their nation and its citizens. It was not the first time.

Notes

List of Source Acronyms

AGN	Archivo General de la Nación
BLAC	Benson Latin American Collection
CC	Colección CUUN
CDF	Central Decimal Files
CFPF	Central Foreign Policy Files
CME	Colección Movimiento Estudiantil
CUSDPR 1930–1945	Confidential US Diplomatic Post Records: Central America and the Caribbean, 1930–1945, Nicaragua, 1930–1945 [microform]
F	Folleto
FGC	Fondo Fernando Gordillo Cervantes
FSD	Foreign service dispatch
IHNCA	Instituto de Historia de Nicaragua y Centroamerica
ISC-RIC	International Student Conference, Research and Information Commission
NARA	United States National Archives and Records Administration at College Park, Maryland
OSN	Oficina de Seguridad
RDS-RIAN, 1930–1944	Records of the Department of State, Relating to Internal Affairs of Nicaragua, 1930–1944
RG 59	Record Group 59
SDCF 1945–1949	Confidential US State Department Central Files
SMC	Salvador Mendieta C.
SNF 1970–1973	Subject Numerical Files, 1970–1973
UNAN-León	Universidad Nacional Autónoma de Nicaragua-León

Introduction

1. César Aróstegui, author's interview, June 10, 2011.

2. "Catedral tomada, protesta y campanas a rebato," *La Prensa*, September 27, 1970.

3. Ibid.; "22 jesuitas se suman a la protesta," *La Prensa*, September 27, 1970; "Arzobispo con estudiantes a la seguridad," *La Prensa*, September 27, 1970; "Iglesias cierran; Misas en la calle," *La Prensa*, September 28, 1970; "Militar preso por estar con estudiantes," *La Prensa*, September 28, 1970.

4. "Mujeres piden agua y lamentos por doquier," *La Prensa*, September 28, 1970. César Aróstegui, author's interview, June 10, 2011.

5. Telegram from the US Embassy, Managua, to Secretary of State, Subject: Cathedral Seizure, September 29, 1970; POL 23 NIC, Political and Defense, Box 2503, Subject Numerical Files, 1970–1973 (hereafter, SNF 1970–1973), Record Group 59 (hereafter, RG 59), United States National Archives and Records Administration at College Park, Maryland (hereafter, NARA); "Tomados templos de León y Granada," *La Prensa*, September 28, 1970.

6. "La protesta de las campanas," *La Prensa*, September 28, 1970.

7. This language comes from an article written by an official who worked at American embassies in Cuba and Venezuela. Francis Donahue, "Students in Latin-American Politics," *Antioch Review* 26, no. 1 (Spring 1966): 91–106.

8. To be sure, the 1960s were marked by more than just student protest. It was a period of tremendous labor upheaval and social unrest in many countries. Nicaragua likewise experienced a period of labor effervescence in this decade, as the work of Jeffrey Gould has illuminated. Yet, this movement was not linked to broader movements of the sort students joined in Mexico, Brazil, Uruguay, and elsewhere in this era. See Jeffrey Gould, *To Lead as Equals: Rural Protest and Political Consciousness in Chinandega, Nicaragua, 1912–1979* (Chapel Hill: University of North Carolina Press, 1990); Jeffrey Gould, "Solidarity under Siege: The Latin American Left, 1968," *American Historical Review* 114, no. 2 (2009): 348–375.

9. On the Long Sixties in Latin America, see Jaime Pensado, *Rebel Mexico: Student Unrest and Authoritarian Political Culture During the Long Sixties* (Stanford, CA: Stanford University Press, 2013); Victoria Langland, *Speaking of Flowers: Student Movements and the Making and Remembering of 1968 in Brazil* (Durham, NC: Duke University Press, 2013); Vania Markarian, *Uruguay, 1968: Student Activism from Global Counterculture to Molotov Cocktails* (Oakland: University of California Press, 2017).

10. Pensado traces the origins of student unrest in the Long Sixties to the dark side of Mexico's economic miracle. Jeremi Suri locates the origins of the global 1968 unrest in the postwar modernization efforts that sought to create an educated technocratic citizenry. Jeremi Suri, *Power and Protest: Global Revolution and the Rise of Détente* (Cambridge, MA: Harvard University Press, 2003), 89.

11. Recent scholarship suggests the same might hold true for student movements in Guatemala—a country that also experienced dictatorship in the 1930s and 1940s and whose experiment with democratization was violently cut short in 1954. Heather Vrana, *The City Belongs to You: A History of Student Activism in Guatemala, 1944–1996* (Oakland: University of California Press, 2017).

12. Gilbert M. Joseph, "Latin America's Long Cold War: A Century of Revolutionary Process and US Power," in *A Century of Revolution, Insurgent and Counterinsur-*

gent Violence During Latin America's Long Cold War, ed. Greg Grandin and Gilbert M. Joseph (Durham: Duke University Press, 2010), 402.

13. The historian Jeffrey Gould has argued that Anastasio Somoza García's rise was predicated on his challenge to existing social hierarchies. Specifically, he reached out to workers and campesinos and offered them concrete concessions. Such efforts helped sustain the dictatorship in moments of crisis and, in the end, were part of a reactionary effort to forestall a democratic movement in the 1940s. Gould, *To Lead*.

14. Knut Walter, *The Regime of Anastasio Somoza, 1936–1956* (Chapel Hill: University of North Carolina Press, 1993), 26–65; Paul Coe Clark, *The United States and Somoza, 1933–1956: A Revisionist Look* (Westport, CT: Praeger, 1992), 4–34; Matilde Zimmermann, *Sandinista: Carlos Fonseca and the Nicaraguan Revolution* (Durham, NC: Duke University Press, 2000).

15. For a broad overview of the success of the Sandinistas, see John A. Booth, *The End and the Beginning: The Nicaraguan Revolution* (Boulder, CO: Westview Press, 1985), and George Black, *Triumph of the People: The Sandinista Revolution in Nicaragua* (London: Zed Press, 1981). See also Zimmermann, *Sandinista*.

16. Jesús Miguel [Chuno] Blandón, *Entre Sandino y Fonseca: La Lucha de los Pueblos de Nicaragua, Centroamérica y el Caribe Contra las Dictaduras y las Intervenciones USA, 1934–1961*, 3rd ed. (Managua: Segovia Ediciones Latinoamericanas, 2010).

17. Zimmermann, *Sandinista*.

18. Gould, *To Lead*.

19. Francisco Barbosa Miranda, *Historia Militar de Nicaragua: Antes del Siglo XVI al XXI* (Managua: Hispamer, 2010). See also Richard Millett, *Guardians of the Dynasty* (Maryknoll, NY: Orbis Books, 1977).

20. On Somocista hegemony and its unraveling, see Amalia Chamorro, "Estado y Hegemonía durante el Somocismo," in *Economía y Sociedad en la Construcción del Estado en Nicaragua*, ed. Alberto Lanuza, et al. (San José: Instituto Centroamericano de Administración Pública, 1983), 241–272.

21. In the Nicaraguan historiography, there have been two articles on the student movement. Francisco Barbosa analyzes in detail the July 23 student massacre in 1959 and its legacy. Francisco Barbosa, "July 23, 1959: Student Protest and State Violence as Myth and Memory in León, Nicaragua," *Hispanic American Historical Review* 85, no. 2 (May 2005): 187–222. Barbosa's article derives from his doctoral dissertation, which provides a cultural history of the student movement from 1959 to 1979. Francisco J. Barbosa, "Insurgent Youth: Culture and Memory in the Sandinista Student Movement" (PhD diss., Indiana University, 2006). Marcia Traña Galeano published a brief chronicle of the student movement from independence to the mid-twentieth century. Marcia Traña Galeano, "Algunas Notas Sobre el Movimiento Estudiantil Nicaragüense en la Primera Etapa del Siglo XX," *Revista De Historia* 1, no. 1 (Enero–Junio 1990): 97–110. Traña Galeano's article is based on thesis research at the UNAN. Marcia Traña Galeano, Xiomara Avendaño Rojas, and Roger Norori Gutiérrez, "Historia del Movimiento Estudiantil Universitario (1939–1979)" (Undergraduate thesis, UNAN, 1985). Also Darling Ochoa and Yessenia Vergara, "El Movimiento Estudiantil Como Agente de Cambio (1914–1969)" (Undergraduate thesis, UNAN, 2002).

22. Among many others, see Carlos Tünnermann Bernheim, *Noventa Años de la Reforma Universitaria de Córdoba (1918–2008)* (Buenos Aires: Consejo Latinoamericano de Ciencias Sociales [CLACSO], 2008); Juan Manuel Gamarra Romero, *La Reforma Universitaria: El Movimiento Estudiantil de los Años Veinte en el Perú* (Lima,

Perú: OKURA, 1987); Luis Marco del Pont, *Historia del Movimiento Estudiantil Reformista* (Córdoba: Universitas, Editorial Científica Universitaria de Córdoba, 2005). See also Renate Marsiske and Lourdes Alvarado, eds., *Movimientos Estudiantiles en la Historia de América Latina*, 3 vols. (México: Centro de Estudios Sobre la Universidad, Universidad Nacional Autónoma de México: Plaza y Valdés Editores, 1999); Jaime R. Ríos Burga, *La Universidad en el Perú: Historia, Presente y Futuro: La Universidad en la Primera Mitad del Siglo XX* (Surco [Perú]: Asamblea Nacional de Rectores, 2009); Jeffrey L. Klaiber, "The Popular Universities and the Origin of Aprismo, 1921-1924," *Hispanic American Historical Review* 55, no. 4 (November 1, 1975): 693-715; Mark J. van Aken, "The Radicalization of the Uruguayan Student Movement," *The Americas* 33, no. 1 (July 1976): 109-129; Natalia Milanesio, "Gender and Generation: The University Reform Movement in Argentina, 1918," *Journal of Social History* 39, no. 2 (Winter 2005): 505-529; Julio V. González, ed., *La Revolución Universitaria, 1918-2008, Su Legado: Compilación de la Fundación, 5 de Octubre 1954* (Buenos Aires: Librería Histórica, 2008).

23. For a brief overview of student activism in this period, see Arthur Liebman, Kenneth N. Walker, and Myron Glazer, *Latin American University Students: A Six Nation Study* (Cambridge, MA: Harvard University Press, 1972), 24-29; Juan Sebastián Califa, "La Militancia Estudiantil en la Universidad de Buenos Aires Entre Golpe y Golpe, 1943-1955," in *Apuntes Sobre la Formación del Movimiento Estudiantil Argentino (1943-1973)*, ed. Pablo Buchbinder, Juan Sebastián Califa, and Mariano Millán (Buenos Aires: Final Abierto, 2010): 31-81; Marcel Caruso, "La Amante Esquiva: Comunismo y Reformismo Universitario en Argentina (1918-1966)," in *Movimientos Estudiantiles en la Historia de América Latina*, vol. 2, ed. Renate Marsiske (México: Centro de Estudios sobre la Universidad, Universidad Nacional Autónoma de México: Plaza y Valdés Editores, 1999), 123-162. See also Richard J. Walter, *Student Politics in Argentina: The University Reform and Its Effects, 1918-1964* (New York: Basic Books, 1968); Jaime Suchlicki, *University Students and Revolution in Cuba, 1920-1968* (Coral Gables, FL: University of Miami Press, 1969); Justo Carrillo, *Cuba 1933: Students, Yankees, and Soldiers* (New Brunswick, NJ: Transaction Publishers, 1994).

24. Among many others, see Barbosa, "Insurgent Youth"; Eric Zolov, *Refried Elvis: The Rise of the Mexican Counterculture* (Berkeley: University of California Press, 1999); Pensado, *Rebel Mexico*; and Langland, *Speaking of Flowers*. On gender and the student movements in this period, see Elaine Carey, *Plaza of Sacrifices: Gender, Power and Terror in 1968 Mexico* (Albuquerque: University of New Mexico Press, 2005), and Lessie Jo Frazier and Deborah Cohen, *Gender and Sexuality in 1968: Transformative Politics in the Cultural Imagination* (New York: Palgrave Macmillan, 2009).

25. See the essays in Elizabeth Jelin and Diego Sempol, eds., *El Pasado en el Futuro: Los Movimientos Juveniles* (Buenos Aires: Siglo XXI, 2006). See also Valeria Manzano, *The Age of Youth in Argentina: Culture, Politics and Sexuality from Perón to Videla* (Chapel Hill: University of North Carolina Press, 2014).

26. Vrana, *The City*; Langland, *Speaking of Flowers*.

27. Pensado, *Rebel Mexico*; Markarian, *Uruguay, 1968*.

28. On student relations with other sectors during the Long Sixties, see Gould, "Solidarity Under Siege."

29. See Manzano, *Age of Youth*; Pensado, *Rebel Mexico*; Deborah Levenson, *Adios Niño: The Gangs of Guatemala City and the Politics of Death* (Durham, NC: Duke University Press, 2013); Vrana, *The City*.

30. Margaret Randall, *Sandino's Daughters: Testimonies of Nicaraguan Women in Struggle* (New Brunswick: Rutgers University Press, 1995).

31. Langland, *Speaking of Flowers*; Carey, *Plaza of Sacrifices*.

32. On women's political activism under Somoza, see Victoria González-Rivera, *Before the Revolution: Women's Rights and Right-Wing Politics in Nicaragua, 1821–1979* (University Park: Pennsylvania State University Press, 2011).

33. See among others Blandón, *Entre Sandino*; Gould, *To Lead*; Zimmermann, *Sandinista*; Booth, *The End*; Black, *Triumph of the People*. For firsthand accounts, see Omar Cabezas, *Fire from the Mountain: The Making of a Sandinista* (New York: Crown, 1985); Gioconda Belli, *The Country under My Skin: A Memoir of Love and War* (New York: Knopf, 2002); Tomás Borge, *The Patient Impatience: From Boyhood to Guerrilla: A Personal Narrative of Nicaragua's Struggle for Liberation* (Willimantic, CT: Curbstone Press, 1992); Humberto Ortega Saavedra, *La Epopeya de la Insurrección* (Managua: Lea Grupo Editorial, 2004). The sociologist Orlando Núñez Soto briefly discusses the role of students and youth more broadly in the Sandinista Revolution in his short article, "The Third Social Force in National Liberation Movements," *Latin American Perspectives* 8, no. 2 (1981): 5–21.

34. Joaquín M. Chávez, *Poets and Prophets of the Resistance: Intellectuals and the Origins of El Salvador's Civil War* (New York: Oxford University Press, 2017).

35. Timothy P. Wickham-Crowley, *Guerrillas and Revolution in Latin America: A Comparative Study of Insurgents and Regimes Since 1956* (Princeton, NJ: Princeton University Press, 1992), 33–35, 42–43.

36. On studies of civil society in Latin America, see among others, Lillian Guerra, "'To Condemn the Revolution Is to Condemn Christ': Radicalization, Moral Redemption, and the Sacrifice of Civil Society in Cuba, 1960," *Hispanic American Historical Review* 89, no. 1 (2009): 73–109; John Booth and Patricia Bayer Richard, "Civil Society, Political Capital, and Democratization in Central America," *Journal of Politics* 60, no. 3 (1998): 780–800. Tracy Fitzsimmons and Mark Anner, "Civil Society in a Postwar Period: Labor in the Salvadoran Democratic Transition," *Latin American Research Review* 34, no. 3 (1999): 103–128. For a broader discussion, see Michael W. Foley and Bob Edwards, "The Paradox of Civil Society," *Journal of Democracy* 7: no. 3 (1996): 38–52.

37. Mark Schuller, "Haiti's 200-Year Ménage-a-Trois: Globalization, the State, and Civil Society," *Caribbean Studies* 35, no. 1 (January–June 2007): 141–179.

38. Aziz Choudray, *Learning Activism: The Intellectual Life of Contemporary Social Movements* (New York: University of Toronto Press, 2015), 33–34. For a concise overview of Marx's theory of consciousness, see Sara Carpenter and Shahrzad Mojab, "Adult Education and the 'Matter' of Consciousness in Marxist Feminism," in *Marxism and Education: Renewing the Dialogue, Pedagogy, and Culture*, ed. Peter E. Jones (New York: Palgrave Macmillan, 2011): 117–140.

39. This understanding of student identity can be found in other contemporaneous movements. Vrana explains in the case of Guatemalan student activists that the impetus to act was part of what she has termed "student nationalism." She argues insightfully that between 1944 and 1996, Guatemalan students "forged a loose consensus around faith in the principles of liberalism, especially belief in equal liberty, the constitutional republic, political rights and the responsibility of university students to lead the nation." Vrana, *The City*, 2.

40. For examples of a similar process elsewhere in Latin America, see Langland, *Speaking of Flowers* and Vrana, *The City*.

41. Núñez Soto observes that at times youth can serve "as the burning torch that mobilizes all the social forces against the capitalist order." Núñez Soto, "The Third Social Force," 20. *Students of Revolution* examines why and under what circumstances students are able to do just that.

42. Mariano Fiallos Gil, "El Dinero que Necesita la Universidad," *A la Libertad por la Universidad y Otros Ensayos* (Managua, Nicaragua: Editorial Nueva Nicaragua, 1994), 127.

43. For a thoughtful analysis of student class background, see Karen Kampwirth, *Women and Guerrilla Movements: Nicaragua, El Salvador, Chiapas, Cuba* (University Park: Pennsylvania State University Press, 2002), 138–145.

44. Pensado, *Rebel Mexico*, 201–234.

45. James C. Scott, *Weapons of the Weak: Everyday Forms of Peasant Resistance* (New Haven: Yale University Press, 1985) 29, 33. See also Frances Fox Piven and Richard A. Cloward, *Poor People's Movements: Why They Succeed, How They Fail* (New York: Vintage, 1979).

46. Víctor Tirado López, a Sandinista *comandante*, introduced me to the term "culture of insurrection," which I explain in more detail in chapter 6. George Black elaborates on the concept, which he calls a "culture of resistance," in his overview of the Sandinista Revolution. He writes that for revolution to occur, the rebels must develop an "authentic parallel culture," in which alternate sources of information—whether radio, music, or theater—erode the hegemony of the ruling power, spread awareness about the revolutionary option, and demonstrate support for the struggle. Víctor Tirado López, author's interview, June 17, 2011. See Black, *Triumph of the People*, 169–170.

47. These documents are part of the Colección CUUN and Colección Movimientos Estudiantiles held at Instituto de Historia de Nicaragua y Centroamerica (hereafter, IHNCA) at the Universidad Centroamericana. (Note: in 2012, the archivists informed me that they had decided to merge and completely reorganize these collections. Consequently, the citations here may no longer correspond with the new system.)

48. I was unable to gain access to the Centro de Historia Militar.

49. Michel Gobat, *Confronting the American Dream: Nicaragua under US Imperial Rule* (Durham, NC: Duke University Press, 2005).

50. See Greg Grandin, *The Last Colonial Massacre: Latin America in the Cold War* (Chicago: University of Chicago Press, 2004), 17. See also Gilbert M. Joseph, "What We Now Know and Should Know: Bringing Latin America More Meaningfully into Cold War Studies," in *In from the Cold: Latin America's New Encounter with the Cold War*, ed. Gilbert M. Joseph and Daniela Spencer (Durham, NC: Duke University Press, 2008), 4.

Chapter 1. The Origins of Student Anti-Somoza Consciousness, 1937–1944

1. David S. Parker, "Introduction: The Making and Endless Remaking of the Middle Class," in *Latin America's Middle Class: Unsettled Debates and New Histories*, ed. David S. Parker and Louise Walker (Lanham, MD: Lexington Books, 2013), 12.

2. Booth, *The End*, 11–13.

3. Cameron D. Ebaugh, *Education in Nicaragua*, Bulletin 1947, no. 6 (Washington, DC: US Government Printing Office, 1947), 43.

4. Miguel de Castillo, *Educación y Lucha de Clases en Nicaragua* (Managua, Nicaragua: Departamento de Filosofía, Universidad Centroamericana, 1980), 82–83.

5. Walter, *The Regime*, 8–9; Booth, *The End*, 22–25.

6. Booth, *The End*, 30–31; Walter, *The Regime*, 9–10.

7. Walter, *The Regime*, 10–14. Gobat, *Confronting the American Dream*, 125–175.

8. Gobat, *Confronting the American Dream*, 205–231.

9. Sergio Ramírez, *Mariano Fiallos: Biografía* (León: Universidad Nacional Autónoma de Nicaragua, 1971), 28–29. Traña Galeano, "Algunas Notas," 98–100.

10. Walter, *The Regime*, 18, 30–31; Booth, *The End*, 41–46. On elite relations with Sandino, see Gobat, *Confronting the American Dream*, 232–266.

11. Gobat argues that many Nicaraguan elites simultaneously respected US political institutions and resented US intervention. Gobat, *Confronting the American Dream*.

12. Ibid., 205–231, 279. On the creation of the National Guard, see Andrew Crawley, *Somoza and Roosevelt: Good Neighbour Diplomacy in Nicaragua, 1933–1945* (Oxford: Oxford University Press, 2007), 17–20; Millett, *Guardians*, 41–83; Walter, *The Regime*, 18.

13. Walter, *The Regime*, 17–19, 29–33. On the Good Neighbor policy in Nicaragua, see Crawley, *Somoza and Roosevelt*.

14. Crawley, *Somoza and Roosevelt*, 31, 45–46; Walter, *The Regime*, 29–31.

15. Walter, *The Regime*, 44–47; Crawley, *Somoza and Roosevelt*, 109–110; Gould, *To Lead*, 39.

16. Walter, *The Regime*, 50–63; Crawley, *Somoza and Roosevelt*, 64–65, 112–119.

17. Walter, *The Regime*, 80–90, 91–94.

18. Ibid., 67–70, 91–94, 100–105. On Somoza's relations with labor, see Gould, *To Lead*, 46–82. Letter from Boaz Long to Secretary of State, Subject: Tendency of Guardia Nacional to Assume Control in Nicaragua, September 3, 1936; Confidential letter from Boaz Long to Secretary of State, Subject: Political Situation of Nicaragua after Six Months of the Administration, July 19, 1937; NARA, Records of the Department of State, Relating to Internal Affairs of Nicaragua, 1930-1944, (hereafter, RDS-RIAN, 1930-1944), Decimal File 817, Reel 9. Confidential letter to Secretary of State from Laverne Baldwin, Subject: Nicaraguan Political Situation as Influenced by Accumulated Errors of the President; Condition of the Guardia, December 2, 1939; NARA, RDS-RIAN, 1930-1944, Decimal File 817, Reel 9.

19. Traña Galeano, Avendaño Rojas, and Norori Gutiérrez, "Historia del Movimiento Estudiantil," 18.

20. Ibid., 12–18. Langland observed a similar process in 1940s Brazil. See Langland, *Speaking of Flowers*.

21. Traña Galeano, Avendaño Rojas, and Norori Gutiérrez, "Historia del Movimiento Estudiantil," 20–21.

22. "300 universitarios en manifestación de protesta por las calles de León," *La Prensa*, August 24, 1939. See also, Traña Galeano, Avendaño Rojas, and Norori Gutiérrez, "Historia del Movimiento Estudiantil," 20–21.

23. "Ayer fueron puestos en libertad los estudiantes detenidos por atacar al jefe del gobierno alemán," *La Noticia*, November 1, 1939. Confidential letter from Laverne Baldwin to Secretary of State, Subject: Arrest of Nicaraguan students for alleged vio-

lation of Nicaraguan neutrality, November 2, 1939; Benson Latin American Collection (hereafter, BLAC), Confidential US Diplomatic Post Records: Central America and the Caribbean, 1930-1945, Nicaragua, 1930-1945 [microform] (hereafter, CUSDPR 1930-1945), Reel 18. Confidential letter from Laverne Baldwin to Secretary of State, Subject: Further material concerning arrest of Nicaraguan students for alleged violation of neutrality, November 3, 1939; BLAC, CUSDPR 1930-1945, Reel 18.

24. "Ayer fueron puestos en libertad los estudiantes detenidos por atacar al jefe del gobierno alemán," *La Noticia*, November 1, 1939. Confidential letter from Laverne Baldwin to Secretary of State, Subject: Arrest of Nicaraguan students for alleged violation of Nicaraguan neutrality, November 2, 1939; BLAC, CUSDPR 1930-1945, Reel 18.

25. "Ayer fueron puestos en libertad los estudiantes detenidos por atacar al jefe del gobierno alemán," *La Noticia*, November 1, 1939.

26. Blandón, *Entre Sandino*, 141.

27. Walter, *The Regime*, 111.

28. See Klaiber, "The Popular Universities," 693-715. Jaime Suchlicki, "Stirrings of Cuban Nationalism: The Student Generation of 1930," *Journal of Inter-American Studies* 10, no. 3 (July 1968): 350-368. Frank Bonilla, "The Student Federation of Chile: 50 years of Political Action," *Journal of Inter-American Studies*, 2, no. 3 (July 1960): 311-334.

29. Luis Alberto Sánchez, "La Universidad en Latinoamerica," in *La Universidad en el Perú: Historia Presente y Futuro*, vol. 4: *La Universidad en la Primera Mitad del Siglo XX* (Surco, Perú: Asamblea Nacional de Rectores, 2009): 43-46.

30. Traña Galeano, "Algunas Notas," 102. See also Jorge Eduardo Arellano, *Brevísima Historia de la Educación en Nicaragua* (Managua: Instituto Nicaragüense de Cultura Hispánica, 1997), 99.

31. Universidad Central de Nicaragua, "Memoria de su Fundación," 15; IHNCA.

32. Ibid., 10.

33. Ibid., 89.

34. Ibid.

35. Joseph, "What We Now Know," 21.

36. Strictly confidential correspondence from James B. Stewart to Secretary of State, Subject: Some Important Political Developments in the Somoza Administration (1937-1943) and an Evaluation of the President's Position Today, October 13, 1943; NARA, RDS-RIAN, 1930-1944, Reel 42.

37. Letter from James B. Stewart to Secretary of State, Subject: Report on Institutions of Higher Learning in Nicaragua, June 18, 1942; BLAC, CUSDPR, 1930-1945, Reel 26. International Student Conference, Research and Information Commission (hereafter, ISC-RIC), *RIC Yearbook, Reports on Higher Education in Algeria, Cuba, Cyprus, Hungary and Nicaragua, 1956-57* (Leiden, Netherlands: ISC Research and Information Commission, 1964), 131. Miguel de Castilla Urbina, *Educación para la Modernización*, (Buenos Aires, Argentina: Editorial Paidos, 1972), 88. Ebaugh, *Education*, 23. On higher education in Nicaragua, see Ebaugh, *Education*, 43-54.

38. Walter, *The Regime*, 79-80. Strictly confidential correspondence from James B. Stewart to Secretary of State, Subject: Some Important Political Developments in the Somoza Administration (1937-1943) and an Evaluation of the President's Position Today, October 13, 1943; NARA, RDS-RIAN, 1930-1944, Reel 42.

39. Intelligence report from the Office of the Assistant to the Naval Attaché in

Managua, Nicaragua, Subject: Nicaragua, Political Forces Stability of Party in Power, January 19, 1942; BLAC, RDS-RIAN, 1930–1944, Reel 44. Memorandum from a Confidential Source within the Government, Enclosure from Secretary of State to American Minister, Managua; BLAC, RDS-RIAN, 1930–1944, Reel 44.

40. Strictly confidential correspondence from James B. Stewart to Secretary of State, Subject: Some Important Political Developments in the Somoza Administration (1937–1943) and an Evaluation of the President's Position Today, October 13, 1943; NARA, RDS-RIAN, 1930–1944, Reel 42.

41. Strictly confidential letter from James B. Stewart to Secretary of State, Subject: Political Situation in Nicaragua Ends in Closing of Most Important Daily Newspaper, June 9, 1943; NARA, RDS-RIAN, 1930–1944, Reel 42.

42. Memorandum from J. Edgar Hoover to Adolf A. Berle Jr., Subject: Nicaraguan Political Situation, June 13, 1943; NARA, RDS-RIAN, 1930–1944, Reel 42.

43. Strictly confidential letter to the Secretary of State from James B. Stewart, Subject: Political Conditions; Text of Proposed Constitutional Reform, June 19, 1943; BLAC, RDS-RIAN, 1930–1944, Reel 44.

44. Francisco Morán, *Las Jornadas Cívicas de Abril y Mayo de 1944* (San Salvador: Editorial Universitaria, 1979); Patricia Parkman, *Nonviolent Insurrection in El Salvador: The Fall of Maximiliano Hernandez Martinez* (Phoenix: University of Arizona Press, 1988); Pierro Glijeses, *Shattered Hope* (Princeton: Princeton University Press, 1992), 23–25; Secret letter from James B. Stewart, US Embassy, Managua, to Secretary of State, Subject: "Political Disturbances in Nicaragua," July 3, 1944; BLAC, RDS-RIAN, 1930–1944), Reel 43.

45. "Efervescente espectación por los centenares de jóvenes presos en las cárceles del hormiguero," *La Prensa*, June 29, 1944. Secret letter from James B. Stewart, US Embassy, Managua, to Secretary of State, Subject: "Political Disturbances in Nicaragua," July 3, 1944; BLAC, RDS-RIAN, 1930–1944, Reel 43.

46. Secret letter from James B. Stewart, US Embassy, Managua, to Secretary of State, Subject: "Political Disturbances in Nicaragua," July 3, 1944; BLAC, RDS-RIAN, 1930–1944, Reel 43. Memorandum included in correspondence from John Edgar Hoover to Adolf A. Berle, Subject: Possible Revolution in Nicaragua, August, 29, 1944; BLAC, RDS-RIAN, 1930–1944, Reel 43.

47. On the implication of Roosevelt's war-time rhetoric, see M. Glenn Johnson, "The Contributions of Eleanor and Franklin Roosevelt to the Development of International Protection for Human Rights," *Human Rights Quarterly* 9, no. 1 (February 1987): 19–48. Elizabeth Borgwardt, "FDR's Four Freedoms as a Human Rights Instrument," *OAH Magazine of History* 22, no. 2 (April 2008): 8–13.

48. "Queremos vivir libre de temor fue la frase cumbre en la manifestación estudiantil," *La Nueva Prensa*, June 28, 1944.

49. Ibid.

50. "Efervescente espectación por los centenares de jóvenes presos en las cárceles del hormiguero," *La Prensa*, June 29, 1944. Secret letter from James B. Stewart, US Embassy, Managua, to Secretary of State, Subject: "Political Disturbances in Nicaragua," July 3, 1944; BLAC, RDS-RIAN, 1930–1944, Reel 43.

51. "Los manifestantes del martes pasado serán juzgados por los tribunales comunes," *La Prensa*, July 1, 1944.

52. "Exposición" (undated), Archivo General de la Nación (Managua, Nicaragua), Archivo Particular de Anastasio Somoza García, Caja 9, exp. 226.

53. "Efervescente espectación por los centenares de jóvenes presos en las cárceles del hormiguero," *La Prensa*, June 29, 1944.

54. "Al cerrar la edición," *La Prensa*, June 29, 1944.

55. "Ayer comenzaron a salir de la cárcel algunos de los detenidos en la manifestación del martes," *La Prensa*, July 2, 1944.

56. "Algunos manifestantes salen con 12 pesos de multa," *La Prensa*, June 29, 1944.

57. Gould examines the language of *obrerismo* that Somoza employed to win over labor. See Gould, *To Lead*.

58. "El panorama político de ayer," *La Prensa*, July 6, 1944.

59. "Tópicos de las manifestaciones políticas en la ciudad de León," *La Prensa*, July 11, 1944.

60. "Vetada la ley que permite la reelección," La *Prensa*, July 6, 1944.

61. "El panorama político de ayer," *La Prensa*, July 6, 1944.

62. "Ayer se había iniciado en esta capital una verdadera persecución publica," *La Prensa*, July 7, 1944.

63. Confidential letter from James B. Stewart to Secretary of State, Subject: Nicaraguan Government "Liquidates" the Opposition, July 14, 1944; BLAC, CUSDPR 1930–1945, Reel 36.

64. "Dentro de pocos días será reabierta la Universidad Central de Nicaragua," *La Nueva Prensa*, July 19, 1944; "Habrá una manifestación en Guatemala de solidaridad con el estudiantado nicaragüense," *La Prensa*, July 16, 1944.

65. Memorandum included in correspondence from John Edgar Hoover to Adolf A. Berle, Subject: Possible Revolution in Nicaragua, August, 29, 1944; BLAC, RDS-RIAN, 1930–1944, Reel 43.

66. "Estudiante Costarricense expulsado del país," *La Prensa*, July 19, 1944. "Los estudiantes Granadinos en huelga piden la renuncia de los dres. Manuel Escobar H. y Ernesto Ramírez Valdés," *La Prensa*, July 22, 1944.

67. As quoted in "Libertad Universitaria," *La Nueva Prensa*, July 28, 1944.

68. Ibid.

69. See Walter, *The Regime*, 140–141.

70. "Universidad técnica o universidad política?" *Novedades*, July 29, 1944.

71. Edguardo Buitrago, "Persecución contra los estudiantes universitarios," *La Prensa*, July 30, 1944.

72. "Declaración de la juventud de Granada ante los recientes acontecimientos estudiantiles y sociales del país," *La Prensa*, July 12, 1944.

73. Edguardo Buitrago, "Persecución contra los estudiantes universitarios en León," *La Prensa*, July 30, 1944.

74. Ismael Reyes Icabalceta, "La juventud actual acusa como criminal el continuar inculcando al pueblo nicaragüense," *La Nueva Prensa*, July 26, 1944.

75. "Los estudiantes de León piden la universidad autónoma," *La Prensa*, July 30, 1944. "Los Estudiantes fijan condiciones," *La Prensa*, August 1, 1944.

Chapter 2. Protest and Repression during the "Democratic Effervescence," 1944–1948

1. Correspondence from John Edgar Hoover to Adolf A. Berle Jr., Subject: "Conference of Youth for Victory" Francisco Frixione Saravia; Alfredo Vales Rodriguez

Nicaragua Communist Activities, July 23, 1944; BLAC, RDS-RIAN, 1930–1944, Reel 43. Secret letter from James B. Stewart to Secretary of State, Subject: The Political Situation in Nicaragua, October 17, 1944; BLAC, RDS-RIAN, 1930–1944, Reel 43.

2. Secret letter from James B. Stewart to Secretary of State, Subject: The Political Situation in Nicaragua, October 17, 1944; BLAC, RDS-RIAN, 1930–1944, Reel 43. Secret letter from James B. Stewart to Secretary of State, Subject: Political Situation in Nicaragua, October 27, 1944; BLAC, RDS-RIAN, 1930–1944, Reel 43.

3. Joseph, "What We Now Know," 19–22; Grandin, *Last Colonial Massacre*, 5–10; Leslie Bethell and Ian Roxborough, eds., *Latin America Between the Second World War and the Cold War* (New York: Cambridge University Press, 1992).

4. Secret letter and enclosures from A. M. Warren to Secretary of State, Subject: Incidents Involving Nicaragua Revolutionaries and Relations Between Nicaragua, Costa Rica and Panamá, October 5, 1944; BLAC, RDS-RIAN, 1930–1944, Reel 43.

5. Rafael Córdova Rivas, *Contribución a la Revolución* (Managua: Centro de Publicaciones de Avanzada, 1983), 177.

6. See Walter, *The Regime*, 133–144. On labor organizing in this period, see Gould, *To Lead*, 48–49. Memorandum included in correspondence from John Edgar Hoover to Adolf A. Berle, Subject: Possible Revolution in Nicaragua, August 29, 1944; BLAC, RDS-RIAN, 1930–1944, Reel 43.

7. Confidential correspondence from Fletcher Warren to Secretary of State, Subject: *Novedades* Editorial Sheds Light on General Somoza's Intentions Regarding a Further Term in the Presidency, July 20, 1945; Confidential US State Department Central Files, Nicaragua, 1945–1949 [microform]: internal affairs and foreign affairs (hereafter, SDCF 1945–1949), Reel 1.

8. Confidential correspondence from Fletcher Warren to Secretary of State, Subject: Immediate Reaction in the Nicaraguan Press to *Novedades* Editorial Supporting the Thesis that President Somoza Was not Elected in 1938 and that the Constitution Therefore Does not Prohibit his Election in 1947, July 20, 1945; BLAC, SDCF 1945–1949, Reel 1. Secret telegram from Fletcher Warren to Secretary of State, July 21, 1945; BLAC, SDCF 1945–1949, Reel 1.

9. Telegram from Fletcher Warren to Secretary of State, July 23, 1945; BLAC, SDCF 1945–1949, Reel 1. Secret correspondence from Fletcher Warren to Secretary of State, Subject: The Nicaraguan Electoral Campaign Gets Under Way, July 26, 1945; BLAC, SDCF 1945–1949, Reel 1.

10. Secret airgram from Fletcher Warren to Secretary of State, August 20, 1945; BLAC, SDCF 1945–1949, Reel 1.

11. Airgram from Fletcher Warren to Secretary of State, September 26, 1945; BLAC, SDCF 1945–1949, Reel 1.

12. Telegram from Fletcher Warren to Secretary of State, December 6, 1945; BLAC, SDCF 1945–1949, Reel 1.

13. Telegram from Fletcher Warren to Secretary of State, October 11, 1945; BLAC, SDCF 1945–1949, Reel 1. Secret airgram from Fletcher Warren to the Secretary of State, August 20, 1945; BLAC, SDCF 1945–1949, Reel 1.

14. Telegram from Benson to Secretary of State, October 17, 1945; BLAC, SDCF 1945–1949, Reel 1.

15. Confidential correspondence and enclosures from Fletcher Warren to Secre-

tary of State, Subject: Conversation with Dr. Gerónimo Ramírez Brown, October 24, 1945; BLAC, SDCF 1945–1949, Reel 1. Telegram from Fletcher Warren to Secretary of State, October 22, 1945; BLAC, SDCF 1945–1949, Reel 1. Telegram from Fletcher Warren to Secretary of State, October 24, 1945; BLAC, SDCF 1945–1949, Reel 1.

16. Telegram from Fletcher Warren to Secretary of State, October 22, 1945; BLAC, SDCF 1945–1949, Reel 1.

17. Telegram from Fletcher Warren to Secretary of State, October 25, 1945; BLAC, SDCF 1945–1949, Reel 1.

18. For statistics on education from this time, see Ebaugh, *Education*. ISC-RIC, *RIC Yearbook*, 131.

19. Telegram from Fletcher Warren to Secretary of State, October 26, 1945; BLAC, SDCF 1945–1949, Reel 1.

20. Telegram from Fletcher Warren to Secretary of State, October 24, 1945; BLAC, SDCF 1945–1949, Reel 1. Telegram from Fletcher Warren to Secretary of State, October 25, 1945; BLAC, SDCF 1945–1949, Reel 1. Telegram from Fletcher Warren to Secretary of State, November 5, 1945; BLAC, SDCF 1945–1949, Reel 1. Correspondence and enclosures from Fletcher Warren to Secretary of State, Subject: The "Estado de Sitio" in Nicaragua, November 10, 1945; BLAC, SDCF 1945–1949, Reel 1. "Protesta de la federación universitaria por atropellos en estudiantes de Granada," *La Noticia*, November 6, 1945.

21. Correspondence from Frank T. Hines to Secretary of State, Subject: Arrival of Nicaraguan Political Refugees at Panama, November 24, 1945; BLAC, SDCF 1945–1949, Reel 1.

22. Confidential correspondence and enclosures from Fletcher Warren to Secretary of State, Subject: Conversation with Dr. Gerónimo Ramírez Brown, October 24, 1945; BLAC, SDCF 1945–1949, Reel 1.

23. Walter, *The Regime*, 145–147.

24. Telegram from Fletcher Warren to Secretary of State, November 9, 1945; BLAC, SDCF 1945–1949, Reel 1. Telegram from Fletcher Warren to Secretary of State, November 12, 1945; BLAC, SDCF 1945–1949, Reel 1.

25. Telegram from Fletcher Warren to Secretary of State, November 12, 1945; BLAC, SDCF 1945–1949, Reel 1.

26. Telegram from Fletcher Warren to Secretary of State, November 30, 1945; BLAC, SDCF 1945–1949, Reel 1.

27. Eduardo Pérez Valle, "Fichero de El Universitario, 1945–1947," *El Nuevo Diario*, December 21, 1982.

28. Eduardo Pérez Valle, "Fichero de El Universitario, 1945–1947," *El Nuevo Diario*, December 19, 1982. For reprints from *El Universitario*, see the issue of *Ahora*, January 20, 1946. See also dispatch from Fletcher Warren to Secretary of State, Managua, "Subject: Transmitting Article Describing Guardia Nacional Brutality during the Student Demonstration of June 27th," August, 2, 1946; BLAC, SDCF 1945–1949, Reel 2; "El Centro Universitario de Managua y el caso del estudiante Octavio Caldera," *La Prensa*, December 15, 1946.

29. See, for example, *El Universitario*, December 27, 1945.

30. See, for example, *El Universitario*, fourth week in February, 1946, and *El Universitario*, January 31, 1947.

31. "Editorial: Hacia el estado de sitio?" *Ahora*, February 10, 1946.

32. Restricted correspondence from Fletcher Warren to Secretary of State, Subject: Civil Liberties in Nicaragua Since Lifting of State of Siege on November 29, 1945; BLAC, SDCF 1945–1949, Reel 2.

33. "La Prensa protesta por estos procedimientos violitarios de la ley," *La Prensa*, February 23, 1947.

34. See Grandin, *Last Colonial Massacre*; Joseph, "What We Now Know," 20–21; and Bethell and Roxborough, *Latin America*.

35. "Respaldo de los obreros organizados y sectores progresistas de Nicaragua," *Ahora*, January 27, 1946; "Importante Manifiesto de los Universitarios," *Ahora*, January 27, 1946.

36. "Sobre universitarios y trabajdores organizados," *Ahora*, January 20, 1946.

37. "Llamado a la organización universitaria hace un estudiante de medicina," *La Verdad*, August 9, 1942.

38. As quoted in *La Nueva Prensa*, January 30, 1946, which the US embassy reprinted in restricted correspondence from Fletcher Warren to Secretary of State, Subject: Anti-Somoza Demonstration of January 27th, January 30, 1946; BLAC, SDCF 1945–1949, Reel 2.

39. Excerpt from *Noticia*, January 29, 1946, reprinted in restricted correspondence from Fletcher Warren to Secretary of State, Subject: Anti-Somoza Demonstration of January 27, January 30, 1946; BLAC, SDCF 1945–1949, Reel 2.

40. "Exitosamente ese desarrollo," *Ahora*, May 19, 1946.

41. "Mirado político de la semana," *Ahora*, June 16, 1946.

42. "Importante manifiesto de los universitarios," *Ahora*, January 27, 1946. On the bipartisan opposition to labor protections in this period, see Jeffrey Gould, "Nicaragua," in *Latin America Between the Second World War and the Cold War*, ed. Leslie Bethell and Ian Roxborough (Cambridge, UK: Cambridge University Press, 1992), 248–254.

43. Gould makes a similar observation, "Nicaragua," 262.

44. David Sánchez Sánchez, "El estudiantado come fuerza política," *El Universitario*, December 27, 1945.

45. Juan F. Gutiérrez, "Hagamos patria," *El Universitario*, first week in March, 1946.

46. David Sánchez Sánchez, "El estudiantado come fuerza política" *El Universitario*, December 27, 1945.

47. Vrana observes a similar exclusionary logic in the Guatemalan university student movement in the 1940s. See Vrana, *The City*, 27–61.

48. Confidential correspondence, Subject: Formation of Autonomous Universities in Nicaragua, July 26, 1946; BLAC, SDCF 1945–1949, Reel 2.

49. Restricted correspondence from Fletcher Warren to Secretary of State, Subject: Opposition Demonstrations at Juigalpa (March 24) and Masaya (March 31), April 5, 1946; BLAC, SDCF 1945–1949, Reel 2.

50. "El mitin estudiantil de León fue suspendido por la GN," *La Prensa*, June 28, 1946.

51. Correspondence from John Edgar Hoover to Frederick B. Lyon, Subject: Revolutionary Activities in Nicaragua, July 3, 1946; BLAC, SDCF 1945–1949, Reel 2. "Sangre de estudiantes corrió ayer en Managua," *La Prensa*, June 28, 1946.

52. "Sangre de estudiantes corrió ayer en Managua," *La Prensa*, June 28, 1946.

53. Ibid.

54. Ibid; Telegram from Fletcher Warren to Secretary of State, June 27, 1946; BLAC, SDCF 1945–1949, Reel 2.

55. "Sangre de estudiantes corrió ayer en Managua," *La Prensa*, June 28, 1946.

56. Unsigned telegram from Managua to Secretary of State, June 29, 1946; BLAC, SDCF 1945–1949, Reel 2. Correspondence from John Edgar Hoover to Frederick B. Lyon, Subject: Revolutionary Activities in Nicaragua, July 3, 1946; BLAC, SDCF 1945–1949, Reel 2. Correspondence from John Edgar Hoover to Frederick B. Lyon, Subject: Revolutionary Activities in Nicaragua, July 10, 1946; BLAC, SDCF 1945–1949, Reel 2. Secret correspondence from Fletcher Warren to Spruille Braden, July 1, 1946; BLAC, SDCF 1945–1949, Reel 2. Confidential correspondence, Subject: Formation of Autonomous Universities in Nicaragua, July 26, 1946; BLAC, SDCF 1945–1949, Reel 2. Confidential communication and enclosures from John Edgar Hoover to Frederick B. Lyon, Subject: Political Activities in Nicaragua, August 29, 1946; BLAC, SDCF 1945–1949, Reel 2.

57. "La incalificable agresión del jueves," *La Prensa*, June 29, 1946. See also "Sangre de estudiantes corrió ayer en Managua," *La Prensa*, June 28, 1946.

58. "Clausurada la universidad central," *La Prensa*, June 28, 1946.

59. "En la cámara de diputados protestan por los desmanes del 27 de Junio," *La Prensa*, July 3, 1946. "El problema fundamental es el conflicto entre el ejército y la ciudadanía—Cuadra Pasos," *La Prensa*, July 4, 1946.

60. "Cartillas del director: El presidente no puede suprimir la Universidad," *La Prensa*, July 6, 1946.

61. "Los estudiantes universitarios exigen la renuncia del rector de la Universidad," *La Prensa*, June 29, 1946.

62. Correspondence from John Edgar Hoover to Frederick B. Lyon, Subject: Revolutionary Activities in Nicaragua, July 10, 1946; BLAC, SDCF 1945–1949, Reel 2. "Solidaridad estudiantil," *La Prensa*, June 30, 1946. "Manifiesto de los estudiantes de Granada," *La Prensa*, July 3, 1946.

63. Correspondence from Fletcher Warren to Secretary of State, July 30, 1946; BLAC, SDCF 1945–1949, Reel 2. Gould, "Nicaragua," 264.

64. "Siguen los atropellos contra estudiantes," *La Prensa*, June 30, 1946.

65. Telegram from Fletcher Warren to Secretary of State, July 3, 1946; BLAC, SDCF 1945–1949, Reel 2.

66. "Estalla la huelga en colegios de Jinotepe", *La Prensa*, July 5, 1946.

67. "Notas Editoriales: Día del universitario," *Ahora*, June 30, 1946.

68. Gould, "Nicaragua," 263, cf. 260–264.

69. Confidential communication and enclosures from John Edgar Hoover to Frederick B. Lyon, Subject: Political Activities in Nicaragua, August 29, 1946; BLAC, SDCF 1945–1949, Reel 2. Also Gould, "Nicaragua," 264; "Los estudiantes de ingeniería vuelven a sus clases," *La Prensa*, July 7, 1946.

70. "Fracaso la doctrina del tercer frente," *La Prensa*, July 5, 1946.

71. On the divide between Conservatives and Socialists and the divisions within the student movement, see Gould, "Nicaragua," 249.

72. "La juventud conservadora toma su puesto de lucha y vanguardia," *La Prensa*, July 11, 1946.

73. Petition sent to Gustavo Manzanares, Secretary of the Supreme Directorate of the Conservative Party of Nicaragua, from Jorge Solís et al., September 13, 1946,

Managua, reprinted in "Universitarios Conservadores piden candidatos a diputado," *La Prensa*, September 14, 1946.

74. "Después de borrascosa sesión fueron electos los diputados por Managua de liberalismo independiente," *La Prensa*, October 3, 1946.

75. "Cuartillas del director: estudiantes legisladores," *La Prensa*, September 14, 1946. Such language is commonly used to discredit youth politics. See Hava Rachel Gordon, *We Fight to Win: Inequality and the Politics of Youth Activism* (New Brunswick, NJ: Rutgers University Press, 2009) and Jessica K. Taft, *Rebel Girls: Youth Activism and Social Change Across the Americas* (New York: New York University Press, 2011).

76. Confidential correspondence, Subject: Formation of Autonomous Universities in Nicaragua, July 26, 1946; BLAC, SDCF 1945–1949, Reel 2. Also letter from Carlos Santos Berroteran to Salvador Mendieta, July 12, 1946, reprinted in *Inauguración de la Universidad Libre* (Managua, 1946), 35.

77. Confidential correspondence, Subject: Formation of Autonomous Universities in Nicaragua, July 26, 1946; BLAC, SDCF 1945–1949, Reel 2.

78. "Acta de la reunión general de catedráticos, estudiantes y autoridades universitarias," September 27, 1946; IHNCA Fondo Salvador Mendieta C. (hereafter, SMC) D36 G2 0157–17.

79. Letter from Salvador Mendieta to David Stadthagen, VP de la junta directive de la S.A, July 30, 1946; IHNCA SMC D37 G4 0415.

80. "Acta de la reunión general de catedráticos estudiantes y autoridades universitarias," September 27, 1946; IHNCA SMC D36 G2 0157–17. Unclassified communication from US Embassy, Managua, Subject: Information about the Universidad Libre, February 10, 1947; BLAC, SDCF 1945–1949, Reel 9.

81. "Discurso de Gerónimo Ramírez Brown," *Inauguración*, 19.

82. "Discurso de la Senorita Joaquina Vega, en Representación del Estudiantado Universitario Femenino," *Inauguración*, 20–21.

83. "Discurso del Bachiller Rafael Córdova Rivas," *Inauguración*, 23.

84. "Discurso de la Senorita Joaquina Vega," *Inauguración*, 21.

85. A list of students under twenty-one in the Universidad Libre for the year 1947–1948; IHNCA SMC D36 G1 0145. Letter from Salvador Mendieta to Reynaldo Téfel, September 3, 1947; IHNCA SMC 0157–16.

86. *Inauguración*, 28.

87. "Estatuos del Centro Universitario de Managua, 1946," IHNCA SMC D36 G1 0145.

88. "Discurso del Rector de la Universidad Libre de Nicaragua, Dr. Salvador Mendieta," *Inauguración*, 18.

89. Notice advertising a talk by Nela Martinez, November 7, 1947; IHNCA SMC D36 G1 0145.

90. "Clausura del ciclo de actos culturales de la universidad libre"; IHNCA SMC D36 G2 0157–17.

91. "Actividades de la Universidad Libre"; IHNCA SMC D36 G1 0145.

92. "Extensión universitaria," December 27, 1946; IHNCA SMC D36 G2 0157–17.

93. Meeting minutes (incomplete), undated; IHNCA SMC D36 G 0157–05.

94. On women's support for Somoza, see González-Rivera, *Before the Revolution*.

95. "Plan general para el ciclo de conferencias que dictarán los universitarios de la universidad libre de Nicaragua en los barrios de Managua"; IHNCA SMC D36 G1 0157–12.

96. See Gould, *To Lead*, 46–82.

97. Jeffrey L. Gould, "'For an Organized Nicaragua': Somoza and the Labour Movement, 1944–1948," *Journal of Latin American Studies* 19, no. 2 (1987), 364–365. See also Gould, "Nicaragua," 256–258.

98. See Walter, *The Regime*, 136–139; Gould, "Nicaragua," 248–251.

99. Unclassified communication, Subject: Information about the Universidad Libre, February 10, 1947; BLAC, SDCF 1945–1949, Reel 9.

100. Meeting minutes (incomplete), undated; IHNCA SMC D36 G 0157-05.

101. Walter, *The Regime*, 153–155.

102. "Hoy sale *El Universitario*," *La Prensa*, January 4, 1947.

103. "Mas de mil personas concurrieron al mitin universitario leones," *La Prensa*, February 2, 1947.

104. Walter, *The Regime*, 155–156.

105. "Sentencia contra Reinaldo A. Téfel y R. E. Fiallos," *La Prensa*, February 23, 1947.

106. "Contra los editores del extinto 'Universitario' presentaron acusación," *La Nueva Prensa*, February 26, 1947. Airgram from Fletcher Warren to Secretary of State, February 26, 1947; BLAC, SDCF 1945–1949, Reel 3. Restricted correspondence from Fletcher Warren to Secretary of State, Subject: Further Developments in the Government Suppression of El Universitario, March 13, 1947; BLAC, SDCF 1945–1949, Reel 3.

107. Restricted correspondence from Fletcher Warren to Secretary of State, Subject: Further Developments in the Government Suppression of El Universitario, March 13, 1947; BLAC, SDCF 1945–1949, Reel 3.

108. "Acusación contra Avanzada presentó ayer Ortiz Núñez," *La Prensa*, March 14, 1947.

109. Walter, *The Regime*, 153–160; Gould, "Nicaragua," 272.

110. Gould, "Nicaragua," 273–274.

111. "Sigue el movimiento de presos y exiliados en la república," *La Prensa*, May 30, 1947.

112. Confidential correspondence from Maurice Bernbaum to Secretary of State, Subject: Anti-Government Meeting Forcibly Dissolved by Troops; Government Restricting Political Liberties, June 23, 1947; BLAC, SDCF 1945–1949, Reel 4.

113. "Consecuencias del atraso político," *Avanzada*, June 24, 1947. "El pueblo tiene que lanzarse al ataque en guerra a muerte," *Avanzada*, June 24, 1947.

114. Eduardo Pérez Valle, "Fichero de *El Universitario*," *El Nuevo Diario*, December 22, 1982. Airgram from Maurice Bernbaum to Secretary of State, June 25, 1947; BLAC, SDCF 1945–1949, Reel 4.

115. Confidential correspondence from Maurice Bernbaum to Secretary of State, Subject: Events Leading to Coup d'etat of May 25–26, May 26, 1947; Box 5177, Central Decimal Files (hereafter, CDF) 1945–49, RG 59, NARA. Airgram from Maurice Bernbaum to Secretary of State, May 27, 1947; Box 5177, CDF 1945–49, RG 59, NARA.

116. Airgram from Maurice Bernbaum to Secretary of State, June 9, 1947; BLAC, SDCF 1945–1949, Reel 4. Telegram from Maurice Bernbaum to Secretary of State, June 26, 1947; BLAC, SDCF 1945–1949, Reel 4. Confidential correspondence from Maurice Bernbaum to Secretary of State, Subject: Anti-Government Meeting Forcibly Dissolved by Troops; Government Restricting Political Liberties, June 23, 1947; BLAC, SDCF 1945–1949, Reel 4.

117. Airgram from Maurice Bernbaum to Secretary of State, June 27, 1947; BLAC, SDCF 1945–1949, Reel 4. Telegram from Managua to Secretary of State, June 28, 1947; BLAC, SDCF 1945–1949, Reel 4.

118. Correspondence from Maurice Bernbaum to Secretary of State, Subject: De Facto Government's Attempts to Pin Communist Label on Argüello, July 1, 1947; BLAC, SDCF 1945–1949, Reel 4.

119. Correspondence from Maurice Bernbaum to Secretary of State, Subject: Internal Political Situation in Nicaragua; Question of Political Prisoners. July 31, 1947; BLAC, SDCF 1945–1949, Reel 4.

120. Correspondence from Maurice Bernbaum to Secretary of State, Subject: Further Governmental Restrictions on Political Liberties, July 1, 1947; BLAC, SDCF 1945–1949, Reel 4. Also quoted in Gould, *To Lead*, 61, n57.

121. Ebaugh, *Education*, 54. "El universitariado de León pedirá al gobierno la terminación de la U. Nacional," *La Prensa*, May 22, 1948.

122. "Gestor amigable entre los Universitarios Managuas y Excelmo. Sr. Presidente y el Ministro de la Guerra," *La Prensa*, August 13, 1948.

123. "Indignación y protesta por la muerte del preso Br. Uriel Sotomayor," *La Prensa*, December 21, 1948. "Continuo ayer en la ciudad de León el consejo de guerra contra el raso Braulio Meneses," *La Prensa*, March 31, 1949. Airgram from Geo. P. Shaw to Secretary of State, December 21, 1948; BLAC, SDCF 1945–1949, Reel 5.

124. Airgram from Geo. P. Shaw to Secretary of State, December 21, 1948; BLAC, SDCF 1945–1949, Reel 5.

125. "Indignación y protesta por la muerte del preso Br. Uriel Sotomayor," *La Prensa*, December 21, 1948.

126. Partido Liberal Independiente, *Memoria* (León, Nicaragua: Partido Liberal Independiente 1969).

127. Restricted correspondence from Phillip P. Williams to Secretary of State, Subject: "Escape" of Murderer of Uriel Sotomayor, June 22, 1949; BLAC, SDCF 1945–1949, Reel 6. "Asesino del bachiller Uriel Sotomayor se fuga," *Flecha*, June 17, 1949.

128. Airgram from Geo. P. Shaw to Secretary of State, December 21, 1948; BLAC, SDCF 1945–1949, Reel 5.

129. Airgram from Phillip P. Williams to Secretary of State, March 11, 1949; BLAC, SDCF 1945–1949, Reel 5. See "Cadáver que se secaba al sol en mañana de ayer," *Flecha*, March 8, 1949, and "No era sangre de herida la del 'pañuelo' que encontraron cerca del cadáver del bachiller Ernesto Flores García," *Flecha*, March 19, 1949.

Chapter 3. Defending Student Dignity, 1950–1956

1. "El Br. César Carter Cantarero se va para Guatemala," *La Prensa*, August 9, 1947.

2. Airgram from Geo. P. Shaw to Secretary of State, December 21, 1948; BLAC, SDCF 1945–1949, Reel 5.

3. Traña Galeano, Avendaño Rojas, and Norori Gutiérrez similarly argue that, after the regime shuttered the universities in Granada and Managua, students focused on finding a way to protect their institution from the regime's intervention and to participate in the functioning of the university. Traña Galeano, Avendaño Rojas, and Norori Gutiérrez, "Historia del Movimiento Estudiantil," 34.

4. Scott, *Weapons of the Weak*, 33.

5. Ibid., 31.

6. Air pouch from Managua to Department of State, Subject: Political Campaigning in Nicaragua Takes Shape, April 24, 1950; BLAC, SDCF, 1950–1954, Reel 1.

7. Air pouch from Managua to Department of State, Subject: Nicaraguan Elections of May 21, 1950, May 22, 1950; BLAC, SDCF, 1950–1954, Reel 1.

8. Air pouch from Managua to Department of State, Subject: Results of Nicaragua Election, May 21, 1950, June 2, 1950; BLAC, SDCF, 1950–1954, Reel 1.

9. Walter, *The Regime*, 178–181, 187–195.

10. Foreign service dispatch (hereafter, FSD) from US Embassy, Managua, to the Department of State, Subject: Summary Comment on Nicaraguan Politics, March 11, 1953; BLAC, SDCF, 1950–1954, Reel 1.

11. Walter, *The Regime*, 182–185.

12. Ibid., 183–195, esp. tables 5.4 and 5.10.

13. FSD from US Embassy, Managua, to the Department of State, Subject: Summary Comment on Nicaraguan Politics, March 11, 1953; BLAC, SDCF, 1950–1954, Reel 1.

14. Walter, *The Regime*, 193.

15. Ibid., 227.

16. FSD from US Embassy, Managua, to the Department of State, Subject: Summary Comment on Nicaraguan Politics, March 11, 1953; BLAC, SDCF, 1950–1954, Reel 1.

17. Gould, *To Lead*, 85–96.

18. Walter, *The Regime*, 168–179.

19. On the opposition during this period, see ibid., 216–233.

20. FSD from US Embassy, Managua, to the Department of State, Subject: Consolidation of Nicaraguan National University, May 25, 1951; BLAC, SDCF, 1950–1954, Reel 9. ISC-RIC, *RIC Yearbook*, 133.

21. Zimmermann, *Sandinista*, 42.

22. ISC-RIC, *RIC Yearbook*, 137–138.

23. For example, the transfer students complained that their professors were deliberately failing them after making them sit for exams that sometimes lasted six hours. "Tensión en la universidad oficial," *La Prensa*, October 24, 1951.

24. Zimmermann, *Sandinista*, 42–43. On the PSN during this period, see Booth, *The End*, 115.

25. ISC-RIC, *RIC Yearbook*, 137–138.

26. Ibid. 132, 134. Traña Galeano, Avendaño Rojas, and Norori Gutiérrez, "Historia del Movimiento Estudiantil," 34.

27. "Educación pública protegerá a los Rompe-Huelgas en la universidad" *La Prensa*, November 3, 1950.

28. "Amenazas de Lacayo nos tienen sin cuidado, dicen estudiantes," *La Prensa*, November 4, 1950.

29. Ibid.

30. "Educación pública protegerá a los Rompe-Huelgas en la universidad," *La Prensa*, November 3, 1950.

31. Ibid.

32. "Amenazas de Lacayo nos tienen sin cuidado, dicen estudiantes," *La Prensa*, November 4, 1950.

33. On university autonomy in Latin America see, Milanesio, "Gender and Gen-

eration"; Carlos Tünnermann Bernheim, *Universidad y Sociedad: Balance Histórico y Perspectivas Desde Latinoamérica* (Caracas: Comisión de Estudios de Postgrado, Facultad de Humanidades y Educación, Universidad Central de Venezuela: Ministerio de Educación, Cultura y Deportes, 2000), 49–88; Andrés Bernasconi, "Is there a Latin American Model of the University?" *Comparative Education Review* 52, no. 1 (February 2008): 27–52.

34. Traña Galeano, Avendaño Rojas, and Norori Gutiérrez, "Historia del Movimiento Estudiantil," 34.

35. "Censuran discursos universitarios para acto público en C. de León," *La Prensa*, June 29, 1951.

36. Ibid. See also *Excelsior*, June 27, 1951.

37. "Cuartillas del director: La universidad autónoma," *La Prensa*, September 7, 1951.

38. "Voz del pueblo: Fracaso universitario," *La Prensa*, September 30, 1951.

39. "Estudiante de León es perseguido por hacer crítica a la Universidad oficial," *La Prensa*, October 4, 1951.

40. "Carta al rector de una universidad," *La Prensa*, October 7, 1951.

41. "Algazara estudiantil en contra de un profesor. 'Sublevación' con 'olotes' provoca una queja," *La Prensa*, July 31, 1953.

42. "Conflicto en Universidad N." *La Prensa*, August 12, 1954. "Estalla huelga en Universidad León," *La Prensa*, August 13, 1954.

43. "Sigue la huelga universitaria," *La Prensa*, August 17, 1954.

44. Ibid.

45. Ibid. The dean of the pharmacy school denied doing so. "No ha amenazado a estudiantes dice Granera Padilla," *La Prensa*, August 19, 1954.

46. "M. educación retiene pensión de parados," *La Prensa*, August 18, 1954. "Educación pública no interviene en huelga," *La Prensa*, August 20, 1954.

47. "Dividida en León la opinión sobre huelga y actitud Dr. Ortega," *La Prensa*, August 18, 1954.

48. "Sigue la huelga universitaria," *La Prensa*, August 17, 1954.

49. "Termina la huelga en c. León," *La Prensa*, August 22, 1954.

50. Ramírez, *Mariano Fiallos*, 87. Carlos Tünnermann, author's interview, April 6, 2011. See also Borge, *The Patient Impatience*, 88.

51. Ramírez, *Mariano Fiallos*, 87. "Continúa la inquietud en la Universidad Nacional," *La Prensa*, November 16, 1952. "Crece la protesta en ciudad León," *La Prensa*, November 18, 1952.

52. "Crece la protesta en ciudad León," *La Prensa*, November 18, 1952.

53. "Sitio pone GN a la Universidad" *La Prensa*, November 19, 1952.

54. "Cordón aisle a más de 100 estudiantes," *La Prensa*, November 19, 1952. "Verdadera cacería se llevó a efecto," *La Prensa*, November 20, 1952. Joaquín Solís Piura, author's interview, June 29, 2011.

55. Robert Scott has observed that after the struggles for university reform in the 1920s, "students discovered, as have so many in a modernizing world, that they need the assistance of, as well as protection from, government." Robert E. Scott, "Student Political Activism in Latin America," *Daedalus* 97, no. 1 (Winter 1968): 77.

56. "Crece la protesta en ciudad León," *La Prensa*, November 18, 1952. "Suprimen Universidad de Granada," *La Prensa*, May 25, 1951.

57. "Crece la protesta en ciudad León," *La Prensa*, November 18, 1952.

58. "Maestros emplazan a junta," *La Prensa*, November 21, 1952.

59. "Toda la prensa del país . . . de acuerdo," *La Prensa*, November 21, 1952.

60. Pedro Joaquín Chamorro, "Ciudadanos privados del derecho a opinar," *La Prensa*, November 19, 1952.

61. "Protesta y adhesión de UNAP en el asunto universitario," *La Prensa*, November 19, 1952. On UNAP, see Gould, "Nicaragua," 276–277.

62. "Culpa de la junta," *La Prensa*, November 20, 1952.

63. "Reina calma ya en aquella metrópolis," *La Prensa*, November 21, 1952. "Nada de política repite estudiantes," *La Prensa*, November 21, 1952.

64. "Nada de política repite estudiantes," *La Prensa*, November 21, 1952.

65. "Burla oficial a los universitarios," *La Prensa*, November 23, 1952.

66. "Dos estudiantes universitarios fueron puestos presos en ciudad de Diriamba," *La Prensa*, November 27, 1952.

67. "Incipiente persecución," and "Llaman la atención," *La Prensa*, November 21, 1952.

68. As quoted in "Toda la prensa del país . . . de acuerdo," *La Prensa*, November 21, 1952.

69. Carlos Tünnermann, author's interview, April 6, 2011.

70. FSD from US Embassy, Managua, to Department of State, Subject: Buenos Aires Radio Station Reports Shooting Incident in Nicaragua, December 16, 1952; BLAC, SDCF, 1950–1954, Reel 1.

71. "Estudiantes anuncian que sigue la huelga," *La Prensa*, November 29, 1952.

72. Carlos Tünnermann, author's interview, April 6, 2011.

73. "Estudiantes anuncian que sigue la huelga," *La Prensa*, November 29, 1952.

74. Ibid.; FSD from US Embassy, Managua, to Department of State, Subject: Buenos Aires Radio Station Reports Shooting Incident in Nicaragua, December 16, 1952; BLAC, SDCF, 1950–1954, Reel 1.

75. "Somoza llega a quitar su medallón," *La Prensa*, November 28, 1952.

76. "A pesar de las declaraciones del pdte. niegan regreso para los expulsados," and "Segura remoción del Rector. Va a ser el Dr. Luis A. Martínez," *La Prensa*, December 3, 1952.

77. "Arreglo en León," *La Prensa*, December 4, 1952; "Cnel. Delgadillo toma posesión como comandante en León," *La Prensa*, December 6, 1952.

78. This discussion is inspired by Scott's observation that elites "wish to maximize the discretionary character of the benefits at their disposal, because it is precisely this aspect of their power that yields the greatest social control and hence conformity." Scott, *Weapons of the Weak*, 194.

79. Ibid., 283. Scott observed that when the peasants he studied in Malaysia "chose not to burn their bridges . . . their prudence preserves a surface decorum that serves the symbolic interests of the wealthy."

80. Pedro Joaquín Chamorro, "Más vale tarde que nunca," *La Prensa*, November 28, 1952.

81. Vilma Núñez, author's interview, August 2, 2012.

82. Alejandro Serrano Caldera, author's interview, April 26, 2011.

83. Carlos Tünnermann, author's interview, April 6, 2011.

84. On university autonomy in Latin America, see Bernasconi, "Is There a Latin

American Model of the University?"; Milanesio, "Gender and Generation"; Tünnermann, *Noventa Años*; Walter, *Student Politics in Argentina*; Marsiske and Alvarado,
eds., *Movimientos Estudiantiles*; Gabriel del Mazo, *Estudiantes y Gobierno Universitario*
(Buenos Aires: El Ateneo, 1956).

85. Ramírez, *Mariano Fiallos*, 88–89.

86. Ibid., Carlos Tünnermann, author's interview, April 6, 2011. Carlos Tünnermann Bernheim, *Breve Reseña de la Conquista de la Autonomía Universitaria de Nicaragua* (León, Nicaragua: Editorial Universitaria, UNAN-León, 2008), 5, 30.

87. Tünnermann, *Breve Reseña*, 7–10, 13.

88. Ibid., 11–15.

89. Ibid. The Nicaraguan autonomy bill closely followed the agenda of the Córdoba
movement of 1918. See also Billy F. Cowart, "The Development of the Idea of University Autonomy," *History of Education Quarterly* 2, no. 4 (December 1962): 261; John P.
Harrison, "The Confrontation with the Political University," *Annals of the American
Academy of Political and Social Science* 334 (March 1961) 74–83.

90. See Tünnermann, *Breve Reseña*, 30–54.

91. FSD from US Embassy, Managua, to the Department of State, Subject: A Review—President Somoza—Internal Political Situation—the Forthcoming Elections,
February 3, 1956; BLAC, SDCF 1955–1959, Reel 1.

92. "Bloque estudiantil anti-reeleccionista," *La Prensa*, August 7, 1955. "Universitarios del PLI," *La Prensa*, August 26, 1955.

93. "Bloque estudiantil anti-reeleccionista," *La Prensa*, August 7, 1955. "Bella Reina
que no se re-elige," *La Prensa*, August 13, 1955.

94. "'Acepto cualquier sacrificio'—Anastasio Somoza," *La Prensa*, February 14,
1956.

95. For an account of the conspiracy, see Blandón, *Entre Sandino*, 279–350.

96. FSD from US Embassy, Managua, to Department of State, Subject Joint
Weeka No. 39, Part 1, September 28, 1956; BLAC, SDCF 1955–1959, Reel 2. FSD
from US Embassy, Managua, to Department of State, Subject: Joint Weeka No. 40,
Part 1, October 5, 1956; BLAC, SDCF 1955–1959, Reel 2.

97. FSD from US Embassy, Managua, to Department of State, Subject: Joint
Weeka No. 39, Part 1, September 28, 1956; BLAC, SDCF 1955–1959, Reel 2. To the
contrary, Rigoberto López Pérez was an Independent Liberal. Zimmermann, *Sandinista*, 43; Blandón, *Entre Sandino*, 279–310.

98. FSD from US Embassy, Managua, to Department of State, Subject: Joint
Weeka No. 39, Part 1, September 28, 1956; BLAC, SDCF, 1955–1959, Reel 2.

99. Walter, *The Regime*, 235; Booth, *The End*, 71; Zimmermann, *Sandinista*, 44.

100. Clemente Guido, *Noches de Torturas (Consejo de Guerra de 1956)* (Managua:
Editorial Artes Gráficas, 1965), 76.

101. Pedro Joaquín Chamorro, *Estirpe Sangrienta: Los Somoza* (Buenos Aires: Editorial Triángulo, 1959), 74–75, 85–87.

102. Universidad Nacional de Nicaragua (UNAN), *Memoria: Presentada por el Rector a la Junta Universitaria* (León: Universidad Nacional de Nicaragua, 1957/58).

103. ISC-RIC, *RIC Yearbook*, 140–141.

104. "Universitarios del PLI, lanzan un manifiesto," *La Prensa*, August 26, 1955.

105. The student paper was printed at the press of Edwin Castro, the alleged leader
of the plot. Borge, *The Patient Impatience*, 89–91.

106. Telegram from Managua to Secretary of State, January 30, 1957; BLAC, SDCF, 1955–1959, Reel 1.

107. Office memorandum from MID Park F. Wollam to the Files, Subject: Nicaragua: Comments on Situation by Ambassador Whelan, February 15, 1957; BLAC, SDCF, 1955–1959, Reel 1.

Chapter 4. "La Pequeña Gran República," 1956–1959

1. Vilma Núñez, author's interview, August 2, 2012.

2. Ibid.

3. On Latin American women's activism in the sixties, see Carey, *Plaza of Sacrifices*; Langland, *Speaking of Flowers*.

4. Confidential office memorandum from Park F. Wollam to Mr. Neal and Mr. Sowash, Subject: Nicaragua Possible Trouble Spots, October 10, 1956; BLAC, SDCF 1955–1959 Reel 1. FSD from US Embassy, Managua, to the Department of State, Subject: Evaluation of Administration of President Luis Somoza, After Approximately One Month, October 29, 1956; BLAC, SDCF, 1955–1959, Reel 1. On these guerrilla movements, see Blandón, *Entre Sandino*.

5. FSD from US Embassy, Tegucigalpa, to Department of State, Subject: OAS Investigative Commission in Honduras, June 19, 1959; BLAC, SDCF 1955–1959, Reel 8. Blandón, *Entre Sandino*, 445–494. On the insurgencies of the late fifties, see Blandón, *Entre Sandino*, 351–388, 409–532.

6. On the military after Somoza's assassination, see Booth, *The End*, 91–93.

7. Ibid., 66; Gould, *To Lead*, 98–99.

8. FSD from US Embassy, Managua, to Department of State, Subject: Politics in Nicaragua—January 1957, January 8, 1957; BLAC, SDCF, 1955–1959, Reel 1.

9. Office memorandum from MID-Park F. Wollam to The Files, Subject: Nicaragua Comments on Situation by Ambassador Whelan, February 15, 1957; BLAC, SDCF, 1955–1959, Reel 1.

10. Ramírez, *Mariano Fiallos*, 1–94. Carlos Tünnermann, author's interview, April 6, 2011.

11. Carlos Tünnermann, author's interview, April 6, 2011.

12. On Fiallos Gil's tenure under Somoza García, see Ramírez, *Mariano Fiallos*, 49–59.

13. Ibid., 104–105.

14. Ibid., 187–191.

15. Mariano Fiallos Gil, "Carta del Rector a los Estudiantes," in Universidad Nacional de Nicaragua, *Memoria Anual Presentada por el Rector 1958–59* (León, Nicaragua: Editorial Hospicio, 1960), 14.

16. Ramírez, *Mariano Fiallos*, 100–101. Universidad Nacional de Nicaragua, *Memoria 1957–58*, 2, 7, 62–106.

17. Ramírez, *Mariano Fiallos*, 100.

18. ISC-RIC, *RIC Yearbook*, 132. Research and Information Commission, *Nicaragua 1963–64* (Leiden, Netherlands: International Student Conference), 17.

19. Ramírez, *Mariano Fiallos*, 101.

20. UNAN, *Memoria Anual 1958–59*, 55.

21. UNAN, *Memoria* 1957–58, 5–6.

22. ISC-RIC, *RIC Yearbook*, 134; Research and Information Commission, *Nicaragua 1963–64*, 16; UNAN, *Memoria Anual 1958–59*, 158.

23. Ramírez, *Mariano Fiallos*, 102.

24. *Memoria Anual 1958–59*, 157; Ramírez, *Mariano Fiallos*, 102.

25. Ramírez, *Mariano Fiallos*, 101–102. UNAN, *Memoria Anual 1958–59*, 285. UNAN, *Memoria* 1957–58, 4, 6–7.

26. UNAN, *Memoria* 1957–58, 3.

27. Ibid., 3–5.

28. UNAN, *Memoria Anual 1958–59*, 61.

29. Ramírez, *Mariano Fiallos*, 101–102. Barbosa suggests that student visibility within León helped create a sense of community with the university's neighbors. I would argue that it was a much more active and conscious effort on the part of both the students and the administration. Barbosa, "Insurgent Youth," 76.

30. Fiallos Gil, "Carta del rector a los estudiantes," reprinted in UNAN, *Memoria Anual 1958–59*, 13.

31. Ibid., 16.

32. UNAN, Oficina de Registro y Estadistica, *Composcion de la Población Estudiantil por Facultades, Escuelas, Años de Estudio y Sexo en la Matrícula Inicial, 1950–1964* (León, Nicaragua, Diciembre de 1964). Ronald Jay Fundis, *Población Estudiantil, 1960–1967: Evolución Histórica de la Matrícula, Eficiencia del Sistema, Aspectos Demográfico, Proyecciones* (Managua, Nicaragua: Universidad Nacional Autónoma de Nicaragua, 1967), grafica 1. The *RIC Yearbook* for 1963 lists enrollment at 1,619 students. Research and Information Commission, *Nicaragua*, 14.

33. Fundis, *Poblacíon Estudiantil*, 13, cuadra 11–1. UNAN, *Composición de la Población Estudiantil*.

34. UNAN, *Memoria Anual 1958–59*, 47.

35. Mariano Fiallos Gil, "El Dinero," 127.

36. This statistic comes from Ramírez, *Mariano Fiallos*, 83.

37. UNAN, *Composición de la Población Estudiantil*, 17.

38. Vilma Núñez, author's interview, August 2, 2012.

39. Letter from Socorro Jerez de Connolly to Salvador Guadamuz, president of CUUN, July 8, 1959; IHNCA Colección CUUN (hereafter, CC) Folleto (hereafter, F), no. 3.

40. Letter from Joaquín Solís Piura to Junta Universitaria, July 21, 1959; IHNCA CC F, no. 3.

41. Vilma Núñez, author's interview, August 2, 2012.

42. Alejandro Serrano Caldera, *Desde la Universidad, 1957–1974: Un Enfoque de la Universidad y la Sociedad Nicaragüense* (León, Nicaragua: Editorial Universitaria, UNAN, 2007), 26.

43. UNAN, *Memoria Anual 1958–59*, 50. ISC-RIC, *RIC Yearbook*, 135.

44. UNAN, *Memoria* 1957–58, 51.

45. Form letter organized by the Comité Universitario Pro-Libertad del Universitario to Ing. Luis A. Somoza, September 1958; IHNCA CC F, no. 31, "Comunicaciones CUUN, 1959, 1960, 1962."

46. "Huelga universitaria contra el gobierno," *La Prensa*, October 9, 1958. Letter from Carlos Fonseca Amador, Srio de relaciones del Centro Universitario de la UNAN to Estimado Compañero, November 14, 1958; IHNCA CC F, no. 5.

47. Vilma Núñez, author's interview, August 2, 2012.

48. As quoted in Ortega, *La Epopeya*, 105–106. He cites *El Gran Diario*, October 13, 1958.

49. Ramírez, *Mariano Fiallos*, 110. "Universitarios plantean la huelga general y el problema de los 'orejas,'" *La Prensa*, October 12, 1958.

50. ISC-RIC, *RIC Yearbook*, 137–138, 141.

51. Their replies are preserved in the CUUN Archives. Telegram from Luis Somoza D., Casa Presidencial, to Salvador Guadamuz, October 15, 1958; IHNCA CC F, no. 3. Telegram from Julio Quintana, Palacio Nacional, to Salvador Guadamuz, October 15, 1958; IHNCA CC F, no. 3.

52. "Nuevo paro de 48 horas inician los estudiantes hoy," *La Prensa*, October 14, 1958. Letter from Carlos Fonseca Amador, Srio. de Relaciones del Centro Universitario de la UNAN, to Estimado Compañero, November 14, 1958; IHNCA CC F, no. 5.

53. "Voz del pueblo: Carte de la madre de Tomás Borge a las madres de los estudiantes," *La Prensa*, October 12, 1958.

54. "Universitarios plantean la huelga general y el problema de los 'orejas,'" *La Prensa*, October 12, 1958.

55. Vrana similarly notes the vulnerability of secondary students in Guatemala. Vrana, *The City*, 115–116.

56. "Guardias vigilan reunión estudiantil en Matagalpa," *La Prensa*, October 16, 1958.

57. "Manifiesto de los estudiantes de la ENAG," October 13, 1958; IHNCA CC F, no. 2.

58. "Managua, Granada, Masaya, Jinotepe, Matagalpa y otras ciudades en el paro," *La Prensa*, October 15, 1958; "La huelga en horas de la tarde," *La Prensa*, October 15, 1958; "Otros estudiantes golpeados en el segundo día de huelga," *La Prensa*, October 16, 1958; "3000 personas ven final de la huelga estudiantil" *La Prensa*, October 17, 1958; "Guardias vigilan reunión estudiantil en Matagalpa," *La Prensa*, October 16, 1958; López Lumbí, "Inquietud se mantiene en el Instituto del Norte," *La Prensa*, October 17, 1958.

59. "Completo éxito alcanzó paro universitario," newspaper article reprinted in UNAN, *Memoria Anual 1958–59*, 226–228.

60. "Si cumplen con el decreto 85 las minas paran, dice el presidente," *La Prensa*, October 16, 1958.

61. "Huelga estudiantil en todo el país," *La Prensa*, October 15, 1958.

62. "Otros estudiantes golpeados en el segundo día de huelga," *La Prensa*, October 16, 1958.

63. The edition of *La Prensa*, October 16, 1958.

64. "Profesor da otra razón en expulsión de alumno," *La Prensa*, October 18, 1958.

65. "Dr. Armijo dice que dejen a jovenes obrar en libertad," *La Prensa*, October 15, 1958.

66. "Otros estudiantes goleados en el segundo día de huelga," *La Prensa*, October 16, 1958.

67. "La huelga en horas de la tarde," and "Estudiantes sitiados en todo el país," *La Prensa*, October 15, 1958.

68. "Voz Público: Los presos están bien tratados dice, T. Borge," *La Prensa*, October 22, 1958. Borge, *The Patient Impatience*, 105–106.

69. Letter from Carlos Fonseca Amador, Srio. de Relaciones del Centro Universitario de la UNAN to Estimado Compañero, November 14, 1958; IHNCA CC F, no. 5.

70. "3000 personas ven final de la huelga estudiantil," *La Prensa*, October 17, 1958. "Managua, Granada, Masaya, Jinotepe, Matagalpa y otras ciudades en el paro," *La Prensa*, October 15, 1958.

71. CUUN, "Carta a los estudiantes nicaragüenses," *La Prensa*, October 21, 1958.

72. The students' letter is quoted in an unaddressed letter on UNN Sria. Gral. letterhead from Carlos Tünnermann, October 30, 1958; CC F, no. 44 "Correspondencia Secretaria General UNAN."

73. "Manifiesto de los estudiantes de la ENAG," October 13, 1958; IHNCA CC F, no. 2.

74. CUUN, "Carta a los estudiantes nicaragüenses," *La Prensa*, October 21, 1958.

75. "Comisión Universitaria denuncia 24 expulsiones en Instituto de Masatepe," *La Prensa*, October 21, 1958.

76. Letter from Carlos Fonseca Amador to Compañeros Estudiantes, November 18, 1958; IHNCA CC F, no. 5.

77. Zimmermann, *Sandinista*, 38–41. Credencial from Salvador Guadamuz González, October 18, 1958; IHNCA CC F, no. 3.

78. Letter from Carlos Fonseca Amador to Compañeros Estudiantes, November 18, 1958; IHNCA CC F, no. 5.

79. "Temario de las sesiones de la primera asamblea nacional de estudiantes de Nicaragua," November 24, 1958; IHNCA CC D17 G3 F, no. 41.

80. For the consequences of the Cuban Revolution in Mexico, see Pensado, *Rebel Mexico*, 147–180.

81. Zimmermann, *Sandinista*, 12–17, 43.

82. Oficina de Seguridad, Guardia Nacional, "27 de septiembre de 1956"; Managua, Nicaragua. IHNCA Fondo de la Oficina de Seguridad (hereafter, OSN), exp. CFA Interrogatorios.

83. Moisés Hassan, author's interview, June 21, 2011.

84. Zimmermann, *Sandinista*, 43.

85. See the records of the Guard's surveillance in IHNCA OSN files.

86. See the reports in IHNCA Fondo OSN, exp. Carlos Fonseca Historial. "Amador y otros tres presos interrogados por seguridad," *La Prensa*, April 6, 1959.

87. See the file in IHNCA OSN, File: Silvio Mayorga.

88. "Jóvenes guardaron prisión por competir en caligrafía," *La Prensa*, May 11, 1959.

89. Pensado, *Rebel Mexico*, 179.

90. Moisés Hassan, author's interview, June 21, 2011.

91. Zimmermann, *Sandinista*, 71.

92. "Manifiesto del Centro Universitario de la Universidad Nacional de Nicaragua," February 21, 1959; IHNCA CC F, no. 25.

93. Ibid.

94. "Estudiante Silvio Mayorga refugiado en embajada tica," *La Prensa*, April 9, 1959.

95. Letter from Carlos Fonseca Amador to his father, Guatemala City, April 22, 1959; IHNCA Fondo OSN, exp. CFA Manuscritos.

96. Zimmermann, *Sandinista*, 56.

97. Blandón, *Entre Sandino*, 139; Booth, *The End*, 471–496; Zimmermann, *Sandinista*, 54–59.

98. Zimmermann, *Sandinista*, 57.

99. Alejandro Serrano Caldera, author's interview, April 26, 2011.

100. "Primer día de lucha colectiva," July 2, 1959; IHNCA CC F, no. 25.

101. Untitled report from the directory board of the CUUN, undated, c. 1960; IHNCA, Colección Movimiento Estudiantil (hereafter, CME) D9 G4, no. 7.

102. Vilma Núñez, author's interview, August 2, 2012. "Primer día de lucha colectiva, July 2, 1959; IHNCA CC F, no. 25.

103. Joaquín Solís Piura, author's interview, June 29, 2011.

104. Untitled report from the directory board of the CUUN, undated c. 1960; IHNCA CME D9 G4 F, no. 7. Vilma Núñez, author's interview, August 2, 2012.

105. Vilma Núñez, author's interview, August 2, 2012.

106. The majority of victims were shot in the back. "Heridos," document listing the nature of the wounds on the victims, Archivo General de la Nación (hereafter, AGN), Fondo Guradia Nacional, Seccion OSN, Caja 9, exp. 70. On the massacre, see Rolando Avendaña Sandino, *Masacre Estudiantil: 23 de Julio de 1959* (León, Nicaragua: Tipografico America, 1960); Fernando Gordillo Cervantes, "La Tarde del 23," in *Obra* (Managua: Editorial Nueva Nicaragua, 1989), 289–306; Barbosa, "Insurgent Youth"; and Barbosa, "July 23, 1959." See also, Traña Galeano, Avendaño Rojas, and Norori Gutiérrez, "Historia del Movimiento Estudiantil," 42–46; Ochoa and Vergara, "El Movimiento Estudiantil," 92–103; Ramírez, *Mariano Fiallos*, 120–137; Serrano Caldera, *Desde la Universidad*, 36–44; and Zimmermann, *Sandinista*, 57–58.

107. Barbosa, "July 23, 1959," 201.

108. Avendaña, *Masacre Estudiantil*, 96.

109. "Boletín mensaje de los estudiantes al pueblo de Nicaragua," July 26, 1959; IHNCA CME D9 G4 exp. 1.

110. Vilma Núñez, author's interview, August 2, 2012.

111. Undated document on Radio Atenas letterhead; IHNCA CC F, no. 7. Avendaña, *Masacre Estudiantil*, 94–97, 110.

112. Avendaña cited two thousand. Avendaña, *Masacre Estudiantil*, 106. US embassy reported twelve hundred to two thousand attended. Telegram from Managua to Secretary of State, July 24, 1959; BLAC, SDCF, 1955–1959, Reel 2.

113. Ramírez, *Mariano Fiallos*, 135; Avendaña, *Masacre Estudiantil*, 106–107.

114. Undated report from the directory board of the University Student Center; IHNCA CC D17 G3 F, no 18.

115. Vilma Núñez, author's interview, August 2, 2012.

116. Avendaña, *Masacre Estudiantil*, 86–87.

117. Untitled report from the Junta Directiva on the 1959–1960 academic year; IHNCA CME D9 G4, exp. 7.

118. Ibid.

119. Vilma Núñez, author's interview, August 2, 2012.

120. Ibid.; Ramírez, *Mariano Fiallos*, 135–136.

121. Ramírez, *Mariano Fiallos*, 137. Barbosa, "July 23, 1959," 213–214.

122. Alejandro Serrano Caldera, author's interview, April 26, 2011.

123. Office memorandum from H. L. Taylor to ARA/Mr. Rubottom, Subject: Telephone Conversation with Ambassador Sevilla Sacasa, July 24, 1959; BLAC, SDCF 1955–1959, Reel 8. Barbosa calls this response "the myth of subversion." Barbosa, "July 23, 1959," 207.

124. Joaquín Solís Piura, author's interview, June 29, 2011.

125. Letter from Joaquín Solís Piura and Humberto Obregón A. to the Junta Universitaria, August 7, 1959; IHNCA CC F, no 31. Letter from students wounded in the July 23rd Massacre to the Centro Universitario, August 7, 1959; IHNCA CC F, no. 31.

126. Comunicado from CUUN, September 2, 1959; IHNCA CC F, no. 31.

127. Manifesto, July 30, 1959; IHNCA CC F, no 31.

128. Comunicado, September 1, 1959; IHNCA CC F, no. 100.

129. Document on CUUN letterhead signed by Carlos Calvo Aguilar, August 4, 1959; IHNCA CC F, no. 15.

130. Letter from Guillermo Soto González to CUUN, August 31, 1959; IHNCA CC F, no. 7.

131. Comunicado, September 2, 1959; IHNCA CC F, no. 31.

132. Ramírez, *Mariano Fiallos*, 127; Avendaña, *Masacre Estudiantil*, 95.

133. Untitled report from the Junta Directiva on the 1959–1960 academic year; IHNCA CC F, no. 18.

134. Incomplete comunicado from the Asamblea General de Estudiantes, September 2, 1959; IHNCA CC F, no. 31.

135. Ramírez, *Mariano Fiallos*, 139–140.

136. Letter from Manuel Morales Peralta, treasurer of CUUN, to José Montalván, October 9, 1959; IHNCA CC F, no. 27.

137. Joaquín Solís Piura, author's interview, June 29, 2011.

138. "Manifiesto del Centro Universitario al Pueblo de Nicaragua," October 13 1959; IHNCA CC F, no. 25. Letter from Humberto Obregón Aguirre to Compañero, October 13, 1959; IHNCA CC F, no 8.

139. The communiqué suggests five hundred students participated; Ramírez cites two hundred and fifty. Communiqué, "Universidad ocupada por los estudiantes," October 15, 1959; IHNCA CC F, no. 77. Ramírez, *Mariano Fiallos*, 141. Vilma Núñez, author's interview, August 2, 2012.

140. Vilma Núñez, author's interview, August 2, 2012.

141. "Boletín," n.d.; IHNCA CC F, no. 32. Joaquín Solís Piura, author's interview, June 29, 2011. Serrano Caldera, *Desde la Universidad*, 48. Ramírez, *Mariano Fiallos*, 142.

142. Serrano Caldera, *Desde la Universidad*, 47.

143. Ibid., 47–48; Ramírez, *Mariano Fiallos*, 142.

144. Serrano Caldera, *Desde la Universidad*, 46.

145. Comunicado to the Pueblo de Nicaragua, October 13, 1959; IHNCA CC F, no. 77; Letter to Profesor o Amigo, October 9, 1959; IHNCA CC F, no. 101.

146. Ramírez, *Mariano Fiallos*, 140.

147. Joaquín Solís Piura, author's interview, June 29, 2011.

148. Form letter addressed to Profesor o Amigo, October 9, 1959; IHNCA CC F, no. 101.

149. Comunicado to the Pueblo de Nicaragua, October 13, 1959; IHNCA CC F, no. 77. Students in Guatemala also deployed the language of dignity to defend their rights and legitimize their struggle against the government. Vrana, *The City*, 98–127.

150. "Mensaje de los estudiantes al pueblo de Nicaragua" n.d.; IHNCA CC F, no. 31.

151. Comunicado to the Pueblo de Nicaragua, October 13, 1959; IHNCA CC F, no. 77. "Alerta" from Centro Universitario, n.d.; IHNCA CC F, no. 25. Barbosa noted

that during the July 23 protest, students also drew on gendered and class-based insults to attack the soldiers. He argues that "gendered understandings of power and identity were crucial to making those struggles culturally intelligible." Barbosa, "July 23, 1959," 195.

152. Ramírez, *Mariano Fiallos*, 137.

153. Langland has argued that students in Brazil also built their political legitimacy on the suffering they had endured. Langland, *Speaking of Flowers*, 16.

154. Letter from the Centro Universitario to Dr. Jose Montalván, et al., September 9, 1959; IHNCA CC F, no. 55.

155. On the state's changing strategies for dealing with student dissent in Mexico in the sixties, see Pensado, *Rebel Mexico*. For the Southern Cone, see Markarian, *Uruguay, 1968*.

Chapter 5. Reform vs. Revolution, 1960–1968

1. Carlos Fonseca Amador, "Mensaje del Frente Sandinista de Liberación Nacional, FSLN, a los estudiantes revolucionarios," *Obras*, tomo 1 (Managua: Editorial Nueva Nicaragua, 1985) 129–148.

2. See Diane Sorensen, *A Turbulent Decade Remembered: Scenes from the Latin American Sixties* (Stanford: Stanford University Press, 2007); Pensado, *Rebel Mexico*; Langland, *Speaking of Flowers*; Markarian, *Uruguay, 1968*; and Manzano, *Age of Youth*.

3. Vrana, *The City*, 122.

4. Pensado, *Rebel Mexico*, 151.

5. For a contrasting analysis of Nicaragua's counterculture movement, see Barbosa, "Insurgent Youth."

6. Sorenson, *A Turbulent Decade*, 3.

7. Gould, *To Lead*, 133–241.

8. UNAN, *Memoria Anual* 1958–59, 47; Fundis, *Población Estudiantil*, 9, cuadro 1–1, 110.

9. On the expansion of higher education, see Suri, *Power and Protest*, 88–94. On the growing role of university students in domestic and international affairs, see Martin Klimke, *The Other Alliance: Student Protest in West Germany and the United States in the Global Sixties* (Princeton, NJ: Princeton University Press, 2010).

10. Fundis, *Población Estudiantil*, 35.

11. Fiallos Gil, *A la Libertad*, 120.

12. ISC-RIC, *Nicaragua, 1963–1964* (Leiden, Netherlands: ISC Research and Information Commission, 1964), 17.

13. Ibid., 17.

14. See Suri, *Power and Protest*; Klimke, *The Other Alliance*.

15. For the former, see Zolov, *Refried Elvis*; Manzano, *Age of Youth*; Franciso Barbosa, "Insurgent Youth." One of the few studies to do the latter is Klimke, *The Other Alliance*.

16. This process was not without controversy, and students complained that the delegates were unfairly picked from the ranks of the CUUN board. Letter from Fernando Gordillo Cervantes to Salvador Guadamuz González, January 31, 1959; IHNCA CC F, no. 3.

17. On the international student organizations see, Joël Kotek, *Students and the Cold War*, trans. Ralph Blumenau (New York: St. Martin's Press, 1996); Philip G. Altbach, "The International Student Movement," *Journal of Contemporary History* 5, no. 1 (January 1970): 156–174.

18. Lara C. Armengol to Jefe de la Vigilancia GN, "Asunto: Informe de vigilancia," December 30, 1957; IHNCA, Fondo OSN, exp. "CFA Informes de Vigilancia." Declaración completa de Carlos Alberto Fonseca Amador, December 17, 1957; IHNCA Fondo OSN, exp. "CFA Interrogatorios." On his trip to the USSR, see Carlos Fonseca Amador, *Un Nicaragüense En Moscú* (S.l: s.n, 1961); Zimmermann, *Sandinista*, 45–48.

19. For example, "73 national unions join in the creation of new student strength," *The Student* 4, nos. 8–9 (October 1960): 6–17.

20. Letter from Fernando Gordillo Cervantes to Messaoud Ait Challal; IHNCA CC F, no. 8. Letter from Fernando Gordillo Cervantes to Robert Kiley; IHNCA CC F, no. 8. "Moción presentada por la delegación de la unión nacional Nicaragüense en la viii Conferencia Internacional de Estudiantes, celebrada en Lima, Perú, del 15 al 25 de Febrero de 1959"; IHNCA CC F, no. 3.

21. In his study of the emergence of the Third World as a political project, Vijay Prashad notes that in the mid-1950s, attendees at the African-Asian Conference in Bandung were beginning to articulate a notion of "Third World unity" that centered on anti-imperialism and anti-colonialism. Vijay Prashad, *The Darker Nations: A People's History of the Third World* (New York: New Press, 2008), 34. On the notion of the Third World and the student movements of the 1960s, see Quinn Slobodian, *Foreign Front: Third World Politics in Sixties West Germany* (Durham, NC: Duke University Press, 2012), and Manzano, *Age of Youth*, 168–176. For a parallel example in Guatemala, see Vrana, *The City*, 54, 90.

22. "Moción presentada por la delegación de la unión nacional Nicaragüense en la viii Conferencia Internacional de Estudiantes, celebrada en Lima, Perú, del 15 al 25 de Febrero de 1959"; IHNCA CC F, no. 3.

23. See, for example, "A new sense of purpose for the student movement," *The Student* 6, nos. 7–8 (September 1962), 3.

24. Joaquín Solís P. "Suppression of the press in Nicaragua," *The Student* 4, no. 7 (August 1960); Carlos Falck, "Solidarity with brethren in Nicaragua," *The Student* 4, nos. 8–9 (October 1960), 28–29; "Latest news from the student world," *The Student* 7, no. 11 (November 1963).

25. Letter from Humberto Obregón Aguirre. Srio. General to Hermanos Universitarios Centroamericanos, July 30, 1959; IHNCA CC F, no. 8.

26. The circular is mentioned in a letter from Carlos Calvo Aguilar to Eustace Mendis, August 17, 1959; IHNCA CC F, no. 27.

27. Letter from the Secretaria Coordinadora of COSEC, June 17, 1960; IHNCA CC F, no. 26.

28. Letter from Carlos Fonseca Amador to his father, Guatemala City, April 22, 1959; IHNCA OSN exp. CFA Manuscritos.

29. Letter from the Hans Dell, Secretaria Coordinadora, June 11, 1959; IHNCA CC F, no 26.

30. Letter from Somarriba García, CUUN, to Asociación de Estudiantes Universitarios, June 26, 1959; IHNCA CC F, no 10.

31. Letter from Patricio González, Secretario de Relaciones Internacionales, CUUN, to Asociación de Estudiantes Universitarios de Guatemala, January 9, 1965; IHNCA CC F, no 27.

32. Undated credencial, circa 1959, from Joaquín Solís Piura and Humberto Obregón A; IHNCA CC F, no 3.

33. Silvio Mayorga described Romero Gomez's experiences when he was being interrogated by security forces. Interrogation, April 6, 1959; IHNCA OSN File: Silvio Mayorga Delgado. "Estudiante deportado de Guatemala a Nicaragua," *La Prensa*, August 15, 1957. "Fue libertado el estudiante Gómez Romero," *La Prensa*, August 16, 1957. On the Guatemalan students' participation in these networks, see Vrana, *The City*, 121–122.

34. Letter from Carlos Fonseca Amador to Adán Selva, et al., November 22, 1958; IHNCA CC F, no. 5.

35. Alan McPherson, *Yankee No! Anti-Americanism in U.S.-Latin American Relations* (Cambridge, MA: Harvard University Press, 2003) 2.

36. Report from the Junta Directiva del Centro Universitario 1959–1960; IHNCA CME D9 G4 F, no. 7.

37. "Boletín: Mensaje de los Estudiantes al Pueblo de Nicaragua," July 26, 1959; IHNCA CC F, no. 32.

38. FSD from US Embassy to Department of State, Subject: Joint Weeka No. 22, June 3, 1960; 717.00(W)/3-460, Box 1528, CDF 1960–63, RG 59, NARA; Report of the Junta Directiva del Centro Universitario 1959–1960; IHNCA CME D9G4, exp. 7. Blandón writes that the information about the invasion came from the Cuban ambassador to Nicaragua, Quintín Pino Machado, who had formed a close relationship with Solís Piura and other students. See Blandón, *Entre Sandino*, 613.

39. "Informe de la delegación de Nicaragua ante el II Congreso Centroamericano de Estudiantes celebrado en la ciudad de Panama del 15 al 20 de Mayo de 1961"; IHNCA CC F, no. 62.

40. Excerpt of the August 16, 1960, JPN manifesto reprinted in "'Juventud Patriotica Nicaragüense' ante la Conferencia de Cancilleres," *Noticias de Nicaragua: Vocero de la Juventud Nicaraguense en el Exilio*, no. 3, c. 1960 (Caracas, Venezuela); IHNCA CME D9 G4, exp. 8.1 "UNEN 1971."

41. Sorensen, A *Turbulent Decade*, 15–42.

42. As quoted in *Noticias de Nicaragua: Vocero de la Juventud Nicaraguense en el Exilio*, no. 3, c. 1960 (Caracas, Venezuela); IHNCA CME D9 G4, exp. 8.1 "UNEN 1971."

43. Airgram from US Embassy, Managua, to Department of State, Subject: Weeka No. 24, June 12, 1964; POL 2-1 NIC, Political and Defense, Box 2510, Central Foreign Policy Files (hereafter, CFPF) 1964–66, RG 59, NARA.

44. FSD from US Embassy, Managua, to Department of State, Subject: Joint Weeka No. 20, May 19, 1961; 717.00(W)/1-661, Box 1528, CDF 1960–63, RG 59, NARA.

45. The law granting the National University autonomy enshrined the students' right to "form student organizations that are essential for the exercise of their rights." Universidad Nacional Autónoma de Nicaragua, *Guia Organica de la Universidad Nacional de Nicaragua* (León, Nicaragua: 1963), 73.

46. Untitled report from the Junta Directiva del Centro Universitario (1959–1960); IHNCA CME D9 G4, exp. 7.

47. Telegram from Managua to Secretary of State, No: 19, July 15, 1960; 717.00/4–160, Box 1527, CDF 1960–63, RG 59, NARA.

48. "Asumen cargos los directivos estudiantiles," *La Prensa*, July 15, 1960.

49. "Marcha estudiantil disuelta a culatazos," *La Prensa*, July 15, 1960.

50. Telegram from Managua to Secretary of State, July 15, 1960; 717.00/4–160, Box 1527, CDF 1960–63, RG 59, NARA. FSD from US Embassy, Managua, to Department of State, Subject: Joint Weeka No. 28, July 15, 1960; 717.00(W)/3–460, Box 1528, CDF 1960–63, RG 59, NARA. "Demonstraciones anti-americanas en la Universidad," *La Prensa*, July 16, 1960.

51. FSD from US Embassy, Managua, to Department of State, Subject: Joint Weeka No. 29, July 22, 1960; 717.00(W)/3–460, Box 1528, CDF 1960–63, RG 59, NARA. Sergio Ramírez briefly describes this episode in *Mariano Fiallos*, 155–156.

52. FSD from US Embassy, Managua, to Department of State, Subject: Joint Weeka No. 19, May 12, 1961; 717.00(W)/1–661, Box 1528, CDF 1960–63, RG 59, NARA.

53. FSD from US Embassy, Managua, to Department of State, Subject: Joint Weeka No. 3, January 19, 1962; 717.00(W)/10–661, Box 1528, CDF 1960–63, RG 59, NARA.

54. Airgram from US Embassy, Managua, to Department of State, Subject: Joint Weeka No. 41, October 11, 1962; 717.00(W)/9–762, Box 1529, CDF 1960–63, RG 59, NARA.

55. Airgram from US Embassy, Managua, to Department of State, Subject: Regional Approach to Economic Assistance, December 15, 1962; 817.432/6–762, Box 2354, CDF 1960–63, RG 59, NARA.

56. *La Prensa* article is quoted in airgram from US Embassy, Managua, to Department of State, Subject: Weeka No. 2, January, 12, 1963; 717.00(W)/9–762, Box 1529, CDF 1960–63, RG 59, NARA.

57. Airgram from US Embassy, Managua, to Department of State, Subject: Joint Weeka No. 44, November 2, 1962; 717.00(W)/9–762, Box 1529, CDF 1960–63, RG 59, NARA.

58. FSD from USIS-Managua to USIA, Washington, Subject: Pro Castro Sentiment Among Youth Students, August 29, 1961; 817.392/4–3062, Box 2354, CDF 1960–63, RG 59, NARA.

59. FSD from US Embassy, Managua, to Department of State, Subject: Joint Weeka No. 25, June 23, 1961; 717.00(W)/1–661, Box 1528, CDF 1960–63, RG 59, NARA. FSD from US Embassy, Managua, to Department of State, Subject: Joint Weeka No. 2, January 13, 1961; 717.00(W)/1–661, Box 1528, CDF 1960–63, RG 59, NARA. FSD from US Embassy, Managua, to Department of State, Subject: Joint Weeka No. 3, January 20, 1961; 717.00(W)/1–661, Box 1528, CDF 1960–63, RG 59, NARA.

60. FSD from US Embassy, Managua, to Department of State Subject: Joint Weeka No. 3, January 20, 1961; 717.00(W)/1–661, Box 1528, CDF 1960–63, RG 59, NARA.

61. In Guatemala, several young officers, angered about their country's involvement in the Bay of Pigs operation, formed MR-13, a guerrilla group that attempted to overthrow the Guatemalan government. Vrana, *The City*, 112. For the case of Mexico, see Pensado, *Rebel Mexico*, 147–149, 179–180.

62. See Alan McPherson, "From 'Punks' to Geopoliticians: US and Panamanian

Teenagers and the 1964 Canal Zone Riots," *The Americas* 58, no. 3 (January 2002): 395–418.

63. Communiqué to the students and people of Nicaragua from the CUUN, n.d.; IHNCA CC D17 G3, no. 31. Airgram from US Embassy to Department of State, Subject: Nicaraguan Students React against United States over Panama Riots, January 16, 1964; RG 59 US CFPF 1964–66, Box 2513, NARA.

64. FSD from US Embassy to Department of State, Subject: Nicaraguan Youth Problems, March 26, 1962; RG 59 CDF 1960–63, Box 2354. On the US State Department interest in youth in the early 1960s, see Klimke, *The Other Alliance*, 144–150.

65. Confidential memorandum from John F. Kennedy to the Secretary of State, November 20, 1963; "Pol 13–2" Records Relating to Nicaragua 1963–1975, General Records of the Department of State, RG 59, NARA.

66. FSD from US Embassy, Managua, to Department of State, Subject: Nicaraguan Youth Problems, March 26, 1962; 817.432/6-762, Box 2354, CDF 1960–63, RG 59, NARA.

67. On US Cold War public diplomacy, see Laura Belmonte, *Selling the American Way: US Propaganda and the Cold War* (Philadelphia: University of Pennsylvania Press, 2008). For a contrasting example of US cultural diplomacy as geared toward youth, see Klimke, *The Other Alliance*, 143–235.

68. FSD from US Embassy, Managua, to Department of State, Subject: Nicaraguan Youth Problems, March 26, 1962; 817.432/6-762, Box 2354, CDF 1960–63, RG 59, NARA. Throughout the decade, the embassy repeatedly asserted its commitment to being impartial.

69. For example, in the telegram alerting the Secretary of State to the National Guard's massacre of peaceful protestors, the ambassador begins: "Communist-inspired university demonstration at León having antagonized Guardia Nacional, latter opened fire on demonstrators result 35 wounded, of which 4 so far dead." Telegram from Managua to Secretary of State, July 23, 1959; BLAC, SDCF, 1955-1959, Reel 2. On military aid to Somozas, see Walter Lafeber, *Inevitable Revolutions*: The United States in Central America (New York: W. W. Norton, 1993), 108–113.

70. FSD from US Embassy, Managua, to Department of State, Subject: Nicaraguan Youth Problems, March 26, 1962; 817.432/6-762, Box 2354, CDF 1960–63, RG 59, NARA.

71. Airgram from Department of State to US Embassy, Managua, Subject: Youth Program in Nicaragua, November 23, 1965; EDX Educational and Cultural Exchange NIC, Culture and Information, Box 400, CFPF 1964–66, RG 59, NARA.

72. "Statement Released to the Press by the Embassy, September 13, 1962," enclosure to Airgram from US Embassy, Managua, to Department of State, Subject: Embassy Contacts with Youth Draw Communist Fire, September 27, 1962; 817.432/6-762, Box 2354, CDF 1960–63, RG 59, NARA. Airgram from US Embassy, Managua, to Department of State, Subject: Emphasis on Youth: Youth Program in Nicaragua, August 26, 1964; EDX Educational and Cultural Exchange NIC, Culture and Information, Box 400, CFPF 1964–66, RG 59, NARA.

73. Juan José Ordoñez, "Ante el Estudiantado y Pueblo en General," enclosure to airgram from US Embassy to Department of State, Subject: Embassy Contacts with Youth Draw Communist Fire, September 27, 1962; 817.432/6-762, Box 2354, CDF 1960–63, RG 59, NARA.

74. On the complexity of anti-Americanism in Latin America, see McPherson,

Yankee No!, 7. On the long and complex history of anti-American sentiment in Nicaragua, see Gobat, *Confronting the American Dream*.

75. "Statement Released to the Press by the Embassy, September 13, 1962," enclosure to airgram from US Embassy, Managua, to Department of State, Subject: Embassy Contacts with Youth Draw Communist Fire, September 27, 1962; 817.432/6-762, Box 2354, CDF 1960–63, RG 59, NARA.

76. Airgram from US Embassy, Managua, to Department of State, Subject: Embassy Contacts with Youth Draw Communist Fire, September 27, 1962; 817.432/6-762, Box 2354, CDF 1960–63, RG 59, NARA.

77. On the PSN during this time, see Zimmermann, *Sandinista*, 90–95; Gould, *To Lead*, 182–188, 219–220.

78. Gould, *To Lead*, 247. See also Zimmermann, *Sandinista*, 89.

79. Airgram from US Embassy, Managua, to Department of State, Subject: Weeka No. 9, March 2, 1963; POL 2-1 Joint Weekas NIC, Box 3996, CFPF 1963, RG 59, NARA.

80. Airgram from US Embassy, Managua, to Department of State, Subject: Summary of Economic Conditions in Nicaragua, Third Quarter, 1963, November 19, 1963; E Economic Affairs (General) NIC, Box 3390, CFPF 1963, RG 59, NARA. Zimmermann, *Sandinista*, 89–90.

81. Confidential airgram from US Embassy, Managua, to Department of State, Subject: Weeka No. 32, August 10, 1963; POL 2-1 Joint Weekas NIC, Box 3995, CFPF 1963, RG 59, NARA.

82. Confidential airgram from US Embassy, Managua, to Department of State, Subject: Weeka No. 36, September 7, 1963; POL 2-1 Joint Weekas NIC, Box 3995, CFPF 1963, RG 59, NARA.

83. Confidential memorandum of conversation between Aaron S. Brown and René Schick Gutierrez, July 11, 1963; POL 2 General Reports and Statistics, Box 3995, CFPF 1963, RG 59, NARA. See also confidential airgram from US Embassy, Managua, to Department of State, Subject: Political Activities of General Somoza, August 31, 1963; POL 2-1 Joint Weekas NIC, Box 3995, CFPF 1963, RG 59, NARA.

84. Confidential airgram from US Embassy, Managua, to Department of State, Subject: Weeka No. 36, September 7, 1963; POL 2-1 Joint Weekas NIC, Box 3995, CFPF 1963, RG 59, NARA.

85. See also confidential airgram from US Embassy, Managua, to Department of State, Subject: Political Activities of General Somoza, August 31, 1963; POL 2-1 Joint Weekas NIC, Box 3995, CFPF 1963, RG 59, NARA.

86. Confidential memorandum of conversation between Aaron S. Brown and René Schick Gutierrez, July 11, 1963; POL 2 General Reports and Statistics, Box 3995, CFPF 1963, RG 59, NARA. Confidential airgram from US Embassy, Managua, to Department of State, Subject: Political Activities of General Somoza, August 31, 1963; POL 2-1 Joint Weekas NIC, Box 3995, CFPF 1963, RG 59, NARA.

87. Airgram from US Embassy, Managua, to Department of State, Subject: Weeka No. 38, June 29, 1963; POL 2-1 Joint Weekas NIC, Box 3995, CFPF 1963, RG 59, NARA.

88. Airgram from US Embassy, Managua, to Department of State, Subject: Weeka No. 35, September 5, 1964; POL 2-1 Joint Weekas NIC, Political and Defense, Box 2510, CFPF 1964–66, RG 59, NARA.

89. Airgram from US Embassy to Department of State, Subject: Weeka No. 30,

August 8, 1964; POL 2-1 Joint Weekas NIC, Political and Defense, Box 2510, CFPF 1964–66, RG 59, NARA.

90. Ibid.

91. Gould, *To Lead*, 246–247.

92. Airgram from US Embassy, Managua, to Department of State, Subject: Weeka No. 27, July 10, 1964; POL 2-1 Joint Weekas NIC, Political and Defense, Box 2510, CFPF 1964–66, RG 59, NARA.

93. Airgram from US Embassy, Managua, to Department of State, Subject: Weeka No. 19, May 15, 1965; POL 2-1 NIC, Political and Defense, Box 2511, CFPF, 1964–66, RG 59, NARA.

94. Gould, *To Lead*, 248, 260.

95. Zimmermann, *Sandinista*, 89–90.

96. On the Somozas' activities in this time period, see Gould, *To Lead*, 249–250; Borge, *The Patient Impatience*, 171.

97. Zimmermann, *Sandinista*, 72–83.

98. Airgram from US Embassy to Department of State, Subject: Student Center Election at National University, August 31, 1963; Box 3246, CDF 1960–63, RG 59, NARA.

99. Zimmermann, *Sandinista*, 88–95.

100. See, among others, Pensado, *Rebel Mexico*, 147–180, and Markarian, *Uruguay, 1968*, 62–101.

101. Zimmermann, *Sandinista*, 104.

102. Ramírez, *Mariano Fiallos*, 180.

103. Comité Central, "Primer Congreso: Éxito Rotundo, Boletín Informativo," December 5, 1962; IHNCA CC F, no. 11.

104. Airgram from US Embassy, Managua, to Department of State, Subject: Weeka No. 9, March 2, 1963; POL 2-1 Joint Weekas NIC, Box 3996, CFPF 1963, RG 59, NARA.

105. Airgram from US Embassy, Managua, to Secretary of State, Subject: National University Student Organizations Attack Costa Rican President's Visit, Are Reprimanded by University Rector, October 5, 1963; POL 12 Political Parties NIC, Box 3996, CFPF 1963, RG 59, NARA. Airgram from US Embassy, Managua, to Department of State, Subject: Weeka No. 9, March 2, 1963; POL 2-1 Joint Weekas NIC, Box 3996, CFPF 1963, RG 59, NARA.

106. Airgram from US Embassy, Managua, to Secretary of State, Subject: National University Student Organizations Attack Costa Rican President's Visit, Are Reprimanded by University Rector, October 5, 1963; POL 12 Political Parties NIC, Box 3996, CFPF 1963, RG 59, NARA. For more on this incident, see Ramírez, *Mariano Fiallos*, 179–180.

107. Airgram from US Embassy to Department of State, Subject: Weeka No. 38, September 26, 1964; POL 2-1 Joint Weekas NIC, Political and Defense, Box 2510, CFPF 1964–66, RG 59, NARA.

108. Airgram from US Embassy to Department of State, Subject: Weeka No. 27, July 10, 1964; POL 2-1 Joint Weekas NIC, Political and Defense, Box 2510, CFPF 1964–66, RG 59, NARA. Airgram from US Embassy to Department of State, Subject: Weeka No. 29, July 24, 1964; POL 2-1 Joint Weekas NIC, Political and Defense, Box 2510, CFPF 1964–66, RG 59, NARA.

109. Michele Najlis, author's interview, June 9, 2011.

110. Santiago Sequiera, author's interview, June 29, 2011.

111. Hugo Mejía Briceño, author's interview, June 30, 2011.

112. Denis Lynn Daly Heyck, "Reinaldo Antonio Téfel," in *Life Stories of the Nicaragua Revolution*, ed. Denis Lynn Daly Heyck (New York: Routledge, 1990), 22–26. Thomas Walker, *The Christian Democrat Movement in Nicaragua* (Tucson: University of Arizona Press, 1970), 24–30, 46, 50–52.

113. Christian Democratic parties were also strong in Venezuela and Chile at this time. See, Michael Fleet, *The Rise and Fall of Chilean Christian Democracy* (Princeton, NJ: Princeton University Press, 1985). On Christian Democracy in Guatemala and El Salvador, where Christian Democrats ascended to the presidency, see Phillip J. Williams and Guillermina Seri, "The Limits of Reformism: The Rise and Fall of Christian Democracy in El Salvador and Guatemala," in *Christian Democracy in Latin America*, ed. Scott Mainwaring and Timothy R. Scully (Stanford: Stanford University Press, 2003), 301–329.

114. Danilo Aguirre, author's interview, June 21, 2011.

115. Jesús Miguel [Chuno] Blandón, author's interview, April 11, 2011.

116. Walker, *The Christian Democratic Movement*, 47.

117. Hugo Mejía, author's interview, June 30, 2011.

118. Walker, *The Christian Democratic Movement*, 45.

119. Moisés Hassan, author's interview, June 21, 2011.

120. Hugo Mejía Briceño, author's interview, June 30, 2011.

121. Airgram from US Embassy, Managua, to Department of State, Subject: Weeka No. 34, August 27, 1966; POL 2-1 NIC, Political and Defense, Box 2512, CFPF 1964–66, RG 59, NARA.

122. Airgram from US Embassy, Managua, to Department of State, Subject: Weeka No. 41, October 15, 1966; POL 2-1 NIC, Political and Defense, Box 2512, CFPF 1964–66, RG 59, NARA. Airgram from US Embassy, Managua, to Department of State, Subject: Weeka No. 30, July 31, 1965; POL 2-1 Joint Weekas NIC, Political and Defense, Box 2511, CFPF, 1964–66, RG 59, NARA.

123. "Pelean en facultad," *La Prensa*, October 20, 1966. "Somocistas eliminados del CUUN," *La Prensa*, October 26, 1966.

124. Airgram from US Embassy, Managua, to Department of State, Subject: Weeka No. 37, September 17, 1966; POL 2-1 NIC, Political and Defense, Box 2512, CFPF 1964–66, RG 59, NARA.

125. Confidential airgram from US Embassy to Department of State, Subject: Weeka No. 24, June 18, 1966; POL 2-1 NIC, Political and Defense, Box 2511, CFPF 1964–66, RG 59, NARA. Confidential airgram from US Embassy to Department of State, Subject: Weeka No. 20, May 21, 1966; POL 2-1 NIC, Political and Defense, Box 2511, CFPF 1964–66, RG 59, NARA.

126. "Estudiantes rechazan a profesor Somocista," *La Prensa*, June 11, 1966. "Llaman a la apoliticidad a estudiantes," *La Prensa*, June 13, 1966.

127. Confidential airgram from US Embassy to Department of State, Subject: Weeka No. 25, June 19, 1964; POL 2-1 NIC, Political and Defense, Box 2510, CFPF 1964–66, RG 59, NARA.

128. "Estudiantes in Labor Social en Costa Atlántica," *La Prensa*, March 15, 1965. "En Matagalpa Tambien Los Cursos de Verano," *La Prensa*, March 17, 1965.

129. On the class background of Christian Democratic leaders, see Walker, *The Christian Democratic Movement*, 52.

130. Zimmermann observes that, contrary to scholarly belief that the Cuban Revolution radicalized Latin Americans, the 1960s witnessed a lull in revolutionary activism. Zimmermann, *Sandinista*, 104.

131. "Tendencia extremista preocupa en la UNAN," *La Prensa*, October 21, 1966.

132. "Programa revolucionario de Michele," *El Estudiante*, año 2, no. 9, September 1966; Fondo Fernando Gordillo Cervantes (hereafter, FGC) 0062, IHNCA.

133. "Nueva organización revolucionaria," *El Estudiante*, año 2, no. 9, September 1966; FGC 0062, IHNCA.

134. Pilar Arias, *Nicaragua Revolución: Relatos de Combatientes del Frente Sandinista* (Mexico: Siglo XXI, 1980), 35–36. *Y Se Rompio el Silencio* (Managua: Editorial Nueva Nicaragua, 1981), 13.

135. Examining student politics in Mexico, Uruguay, and Brazil in the 1960s, Jeffrey Gould has similarly argued against the assumption by some scholars that the era was marked by political superficiality and "generalized rebelliousness." Gould, "Solidarity Under Siege." On the "language of dissent," see Suri, *Power and Protest*, 88–130.

Chapter 6. Radicalizing Youth, 1966–1972

1. Octavio Rivas G. and César Aróstegui, "CUUN CEUUCA Desde la Cárcel," c. April 1971; IHNCA Colección CUUN F, no. 52. Airgram from US Embassy to Department of State, Subject: Political Developments, April 13–May 3, May 7, 1971; POL 2 NIC, Political and Defense, Box 2502, SNF 1970–1973, RG 59, NARA. Airgram from US Embassy to Department of State, Subject: Political Developments, May 4–May 24, May 30, 1971; POL 2 NIC, Political and Defense, Box 2502, SNF 1970–1973, RG 59, NARA.

2. On the "dialectics of repression," see Edward J. Escobar, "The Dialectics of Repression: The Los Angeles Police Department and the Chicano Movement, 1968–1971," *Journal of American History* 79, no. 4 (1993): 1483–1514. For the concept's application to Brazil, see Langland, *Speaking of Flowers*, 109–110, 131–132. On the "cycle of protest" in Uruguay, see Markarian, *Uruguay, 1968*, 40–61. On this process in Mexico, see Pensado, *Rebel Mexico*, 205–209, 288, n9, and Ariel Rodríguez Kuri, "Los primeros días. Una explicación de los orígenes inmediatos del movimiento estudiantil de 1968," *Historia Mexicana* 53, no. 1 (July–September 2003): 179–228. The end of a cycle of protest and repression does not necessarily mean an end to protest. Many historians note that protest continues but in different ways. Moreover, cycles sometimes ended when the government conceded to the students demands (see chapter four).

3. Gould, "Nicaragua," 249. See also, Claudia Rueda, "Agents of Effervescence: Student Protest and Nicaragua's Post-War Democratic Mobilizations," *Journal of Social History* 52, no. 2 (November 2018), 390–411.

4. In contrast, historians have observed the dearth of female leadership in the student movements of Brazil and Mexico in the 1960s. See Langland, *Speaking of Flowers* and Carey, *Plaza of Sacrifices*.

5. Victoria González-Rivera, "Somocista Women, Right-Wing Politics, and Feminism in Nicaragua, 1936–1979," in *Radical Women in Latin America Left and Right*, ed. Victoria González-Rivera and Karen Kampwirth (University Park: Pennsylvania State University Press, 2001) 41, 57. González-Rivera, *Before the Revolution*.

6. These young activists were part of a larger uptick in women's grassroots organiz-

ing that took place in the 1970s in the midst of a growing global women's movement. On the divisions within that movement, see Jocelyn Olcott, *International Women's Year: The Greatest Consciousness-Raising Event in History* (New York: Oxford University Press, 2017). On women's experiences in student movements, see Carey, *Plaza of Sacrifices*. On women in social justice movements, see Francesca Miller, *Latin American Women and the Search for Social Justice* (Hanover, NH: University Press of New England, 1991).

7. Michele Najlis, author's interview, June 9, 2011; Danilo Aguirre, author's interview, June 21, 2011. Young women's affinity for the FDC might reflect the organization's origins in Catholic Action, which in Latin America had welcomed women's political activism. Ana María Bidegaín, *Participación y Protagonismo de las Mujeres in la Historia del Catolicismo Latinoamericano* (Buenos Aires: San Benito, 2009) 112–113, 120.

8. Carey notes that times of crisis led to greater flexibility regarding women's roles in Mexico's student movement of the sixties. Carey, *Plaza of Sacrifices*, 87–89. See also Langland, *Speaking of Flowers*, 138–139.

9. Airgram from US Embassy, Managua, to Department of State, Subject: Weeka No. 41, October 15, 1966; POL 2-1 NIC, Political and Defense, Box 2512, CFPF 1964–66, RG 59, NARA. Airgram from US Embassy, Managua, to Department of State, Subject: Weeka No. 42, October 22, 1966; POL 2-1 NIC, Political and Defense, Box 2512, CFPF 1964–66, RG 59, NARA.

10. Michele Najlis, author's interview, June 9, 2011. Telegram from US Embassy, Managua, to Secretary of State, Subject: Baseball Game Tragedy, October 29, 1966; SOC Social Conditions, Social, Box 3231, CFPF 1964–66, RG 59, NARA. Telegram from US Embassy, Managua, to Secretary of State, Subject: Baseball Crowd Panic Ends in Tragedy with Possible Political Consequences, October 28, 1966; SOC Social Conditions, Social, Box 3231, CFPF 1964–66, RG 59, NARA.

11. Telegram from US Embassy, Managua to Secretary of State, Subject: Baseball Game Tragedy, October 29, 1966; SOC Social Conditions, Social, Box 3231, CFPF 1964–66, RG 59, NARA. Telegram from US Embassy, Managua, to Secretary of State, Subject: Baseball Crowd Panic Ends in Tragedy with Possible Political Consequences, October 28, 1966; SOC Social Conditions, Social, Box 3231, CFPF 1964–66, RG 59, NARA.

12. Michele Najlis, author's interview, June 9, 2011.

13. Airgram from US Embassy, Managua, to Department of State, Subject: Weeka No. 43, October 29, 1966; POL 2-1 NIC, Political and Defense, Box 2512, CFPF 1964–66, RG 59, NARA.

14. Airgram from US Embassy, Managua, to Department of State, Subject: Weeka No. 44, November 5, 1966; POL 2-1 NIC, Political and Defense, Box 2512, CFPF 1964–66, RG 59, NARA. Airgram from US Embassy, Managua, to Department of State, Subject: Weeka No. 43, October 29, 1966; POL 2-1 NIC, Political and Defense, Box 2512, CFPF 1964–66, RG 59, NARA.

15. Telegram from US Embassy, Managua, to Secretary of State, Subject: Baseball Game Tragedy, October 31, 1966; SOC Social Conditions, Social, Box 3231, CFPF 1964–66, RG 59, NARA.

16. Airgram from US Embassy to Department of State, Subject: Weeka No. 46, November 19, 1966; POL 2-1 NIC, Political and Defense, Box 2512, CFPF 1964–66,

RG 59, NARA. Telegram from US Embassy to Secretary of State, November 29, 1966; POL 23-8, Box 2514, CFPF 1964-66, RG 59, NARA. A 2010 newspaper account of the stadium incident claims that the idea to create CIVES came from Pedro Joaquín Chamorro, but was led by Dionisio Marenco and Brenda Ortega. "Una chispa en el estadio," *El Nuevo Diario*, April 18, 2010.

17. Zimmermann, *Sandinista*, 94–95.

18. "Unión opositora no es solución," *El Estudiante*, año 2, no. 9, September 1966; IHNCA, Fondo FGC, F, no. 0062.

19. The number of deaths is disputed. Millett says forty and Jaime Wheelock cites more than three hundred. Millet, *Guardians*, 229; Jaime Wheelock, *Imperialismo y dictadura: crisis de una formación social* (Mexico City: Siglo Veintiuno Editores, 1980), 130. Telegram from US Embassy to Secretary of State, Subject: Agüero Calls on National Guard to Join Him in Saving Nicaragua, January 22, 1967; POL 14 NIC, Political and Defense, Box 2367, CFPF 1967-69, RG 59, NARA. Confidential telegram from US Embassy, Managua, to Secretary of State, Subject: Significance of Somoza's Election for US, February 10, 1967; POL 14 NIC, Political and Defense, Box 2367, CFPF 1967-69, RG 59, NARA.

20. Telegram from US Embassy to Secretary of State, Subject: GON Counterinsurgency Effort: UNAN Strikes to Protest Arrests, November 28, 1967; EDU NIC, Culture and Information, Box 350, CFPF 1967-69, RG 59, NARA. Telegram from US Embassy to Secretary of State, Subject: GON Counter-insurgency Effort: UNAN Strike Called Off, December 2, 1967; EDU NIC, Culture and Information, Box 350, CFPF 1967-69, RG 59, NARA.

21. Telegram from US Embassy to Secretary of State, Subject: Tejada Case, April 18, 1968; POL 23-8 NIC, Political and Defense, Box 2368, CFPF 1967-69, RG 59, NARA. Telegram US Embassy to Secretary of State, Subject: Tejada Case, April 19, 1968; POL 23-8 NIC, Political and Defense, Box 2368, CFPF 1967-69, RG 59, NARA.

22. Document produced by the Movimiento de Estudiantes de Secundaria, "Analisis de Secundaria y Nuestro Compromiso Historico," April 1978; IHNCA CC F, no. 117, "MES Folletos 1978."

23. Interview with Irving Larios in Mónica Baltodano, *Memorias de la Lucha Sandinista: De la Forja de la Vanguardia a la Montaña*, vol. 1 (Managua: Instituto de Historia de Nicaragua y Centroamerica de la Universidad Centroamericana, 2010), 309.

24. César Aróstegui, author's interview, June 10, 2011.

25. Eduardo Crawley, *Dictators Never Die: Nicaragua and the Somoza Dynasty* (New York: St. Martin's Press, 1979), 146-147. Airgram from US Embassy, Managua, to Department of State, Subject: A *Constituyente*—Will it Happen? October 7, 1970; POL 12 NIC, Political and Defense, Box 2502, SNF, 1970-73, RG 59, NARA. Confidential airgram from US Embassy, Managua, to Department of State, Subject: Kupia Kumi Report Number One, September 26, 1971; POL 12 NIC, Political and Defense, Box 2502, SNF, 1970-73, RG 59, NARA.

26. Moisés Hassan, author's interview, June 21, 2011.

27. Mónica Baltodano, *Memorias de la Lucha Sandinista: El Crisol de las insurreciones: Las Segovias, Managua y León*, vol. 2 (Managua: *Instituto de Historia de Nicaragua y Centroamerica* de la Universidad Centroamericana, 2010), 424.

28. In 1970, several student Christian Democrats refused to join an anti-Somoza

electoral coalition and instead, with the FER and JUC, expressed their desire for revolution. Memorandum of conversation with Pedro Joaquín Chamorro and James E. Briggs, May 6, 1970, *Foreign Relations of the United States, 1969–1976*, vol. E-10, Documents on American Republics, 1969–1972, ed. Douglas Kraft and James Siemeier (Washington: Government Printing Office, 2009), Document 493, https://history .state.gov/historicaldocuments/frus1969–76ve10/d493.

29. On the Somozas' relations with workers see Gould, *To Lead*.

30. Susan Fitzpatrick Behrens, "Knowledge is not Enough: Creating a Culture of Social Justice, Dignity, and Human Rights in Guatemala: Maryknoll Sisters and the Monte María 'Girls,'" *US Catholic Historian* 24, no. 3 (Summer 2006): 111–128.

31. Scott Mainwaring and Timothy R. Scully, "The Diversity of Christian Democracy in Latin America," in *Christian Democracy in Latin America: Electoral Competition and Regime Conflicts*, ed. Scott Mainwaring and Timothy R. Scully (Stanford, CA: Stanford University Press, 2003), 34–35.

32. On Catholic Action in Latin America, see Ana María Bidegaín, "From Catholic Action to Liberation Theology: The Historical Process of the Laity in Latin America in the Twentieth Century," Working Paper #48, Helen Kellogg Institute for International Studies, Notre Dame, 1985. On the development of liberation theology, see Michael Löwy, *The War of Gods: Religion and Politics in Latin America* (New York: Verson, 1996). On the role of the Brazilian Catholic Church in the development of liberation theology, see Kenneth Serbin, *Secret Dialogues: Church-State Relations, Torture, and Social Justice in Authoritarian Brazil* (Pittsburgh: University of Pittsburgh Press, 2000). On Catholic Action's revolutionary implications, see Chávez, *Poets and Prophets*, 50–71.

33. Phillip Berryman, *Liberation Theology: The Essential Facts about the Revolutionary Movement in Latin America and Beyond* (New York: Random House, 1987), 15–28. Phillip Berryman, *The Religious Roots of Rebellion* (Maryknoll, NY: Orbis Books, 1984), 26–32. A similar movement occurred among Protestant churches. See José Miguel Torres's testimony in Margaret Randall, *Christians in the Nicaraguan Revolution*, trans. Mariana Valverde (Vancouver, New Star Books, 1983). Also see his interview in Baltodano, *Memorias*, vol. 1, 343–366.

34. As quoted in Heyck, *Life Stories*, 170.

35. Fernando Cardenal, author's interview, April 5, 2011.

36. Baltodano in Randall, *Sandino's Daughters*, 61. Fernando Cardenal, *Sacerdote en la Revolución: Memorias*, vol. 1 (Managua: Anamá Ediciones, 2008), 75–76.

37. Anna M. Peña, "Informe de la visita . . . ," August 6, 1971; IHNCA CME D9 G4, exp. no. 1: Asociaciones Estudiantiles.

38. Óscar Quijano, *Los del Reparto Schick: Memoria del Movimiento Juvenil Cristiano de los Años 70* (Managua: EDITARTE, 2015), 146.

39. Cardenal, *Sacerdote en la Revolución*, 74. Most of the participants were Catholic, although Protestants also joined. Following the lead of young religious activists, I use Catholic and Christian interchangeably here. On Protestant participation in the Sandinista struggle, see "Evangelicos y Educadores," in Mónica Baltodano, *Memorias de la Lucha Sandinista: Rebeldía e Insurrección en el Departamento de Carazo*, vol. 4 (Managua: Instituto de Historia de Nicaragua y Centroamerica de la Universidad Centroamericana, 2012), 167–174.

40. As quoted in Cardenal, *Sacerdote en la Revolución*, 143.

41. Vidaluz Meneses, author's interview, July 31, 2012.

42. Quijano, *Los del Reparto Schick*, 51–52, 57–67.

43. Ibid., 164.

44. Ibid., 89, 101.

45. See comments by Joaquín Cuadra, Luis Carrión, and Roberto Gutiérrez in Randall, *Christians in the Nicaraguan Revolution*, 127–129. See also, Manzar Foroohar, *The Catholic Church and Social Change in Nicaragua*, (Albany: SUNY Press, 1989), 127–135.

46. Flor de María Monterrey, author's interview, May 11, 2011.

47. Ibid. On the pressures facing young female activists in the sixties, see Carey, *Plaza of Sacrifices*, 87–89; Langland, *Speaking of Flowers*, 134–140.

48. As quoted in Randall, *Christians in the Nicaraguan Revolution*, 129.

49. On "leaving home" as a cultural phenomenon, see Manzano, *Age of Youth*, 97–157.

50. Enclosure one in airgram from US Embassy, Managua, to Department of State, Subject: Nicaraguan CASP, June 24, 1967; POL 1 NIC-US, Political and Defense, Box 2369, CFPF 1967–69, RG 59, NARA. On the FSLN activities in the early 1970s, see Black, *Triumph of the People*, 86–88.

51. Cabezas, *Fire from the Mountain*, 14–15. Zimmermann, *Sandinista*, 97.

52. Zimmermann, *Sandinista*, 95–98.

53. Millett, *Guardians*, 226; LaFeber, *Inevitable Revolutions*, 164. Airgram from US Embassy, Managua, to Department of State, Subject: Political/ Economic Developments, May 19, 1970; POL 2 NIC, Political and Defense, Box 2502, SNF 1970-1973, RG 59, NARA.

54. Zimmermann, *Sandinista*, 100.

55. Fonseca Amador, "Mensaje del Frente Sandinista de Liberación Nacional, FSLN, a los estudiantes revolucionarios." For a detailed analysis of this letter, see Zimmermann, *Sandinista*, 102–106.

56. Baltodano, *Memorias*, vol. 1, 495–496. René Núñez as quoted in Arias, *Nicaragua*, 53. Cabezas, *Fire from the Mountain*, 19.

57. Letter from Casimiro Sotelo R. and María Montenegro de Sotelo to FER, May 30, 1968; IHNCA, Fondo CUUN, F., no. 68, "FER Corespondencia." Telegram from US Embassy to Secretary of State, Subject: Tejada Case, Student Strike, May 17, 1968; EDU NIC, Culture and Information, Box 350, CFPF 1967–69, RG 59, NARA.

58. On JUC in Nicaragua, see the interviews with Marlen Chow, Bayardo Arce, Fernando Cardenal, and José Miguel Torres in Baltodano, *Memorias*, vol. 1. JUC has been well studied in Brazil. See Colin Snider, "Catholic Campuses, Secularizing Struggles: Student Activism and Catholic Universities in Brazil, 1950-1968," in *Local Church, Global Church: Catholic Activism in Latin America from Rerum Novarum to Vatican II*, ed. Stephen Andes and Julia Young (Washington, DC: Catholic University of America Press, 2016), 185–204. See also Bidegaín, *Participación y Protagonismo de las Mujeres*, 103–122, and Joao Roberto Martins Filho, "Students and Politics in Brazil, 1962-1992," trans. John Collins, *Latin American Perspectives* 25, no. 1 (January 1998), 156–169.

59. Airgram from US Embassy, Managua, to Department of State, Subject: Travails of a Leftist Student Politician, June 12, 1969; POL 23-8 NIC, Political and Defense, Box 2368, CFPF 1967–69, RG 59, NARA. Interview with Hugo Mejía Briceño in Baltodano, *Memorias*, vol. 1, 293–296.

60. Airgram from US Embassy, Managua, to Department of State, Subject: The

National University in Trouble, July 17, 1969; Culture and Information, Box 350, CFPF 1967–69, RG 59, NARA.

61. Cabezas, *Fire from the Mountain*, 21–23; Crawley, *Dictators Never Die*, 144; Millett, *Guardians*, 233. See Barbosa Miranda, *Historia Militar de Nicaragua*, 194–195.

62. Telegram from US Embassy, Managua, to Secretary of State, Subject: Student Unrest, July 18, 1969; POL 23–8, Political and Defense, Box 2368, CFPF 1967–69, RG 59, NARA.

63. Confidential telegram from US Embassy, Managua, to Secretary of State, Subject: Student Unrest, July 23, 1969; EDU NIC, Culture and Information, Box 350, CFPF 1967–69, RG 59, NARA.

64. Cabezas, *Fire from the Mountain*, 17 and 25.

65. Ibid., 25. Zimmermann, *Sandinista*, 103–104.

66. Interview with Omar Cabezas and Hugo Mejía Briceño in Baltodano, *Memorias*, vol. 1, 297–300.

67. Cabezas, *Fire from the Mountain*, 28–29, 32.

68. Bayardo Arce in Arias, *Nicaragua*, 63–64.

69. Jeffrey L. Gould, *To Die in this Way: Nicaraguan Indians and the Myth of Mestizaje, 1880–1965* (Durham, NC: Duke University Press, 1998), 102–133.

70. Cabezas, *Fire from the Mountain*, 36–38.

71. Interview with Bayardo Arce in Baltodano, *Memorias*, vol. 1, 495.

72. Núñez in Arias, *Nicaragua*, 65.

73. Interview with María Haydée Sequiera in Baltodano, *Memorias*, vol. 2, 406.

74. Carlos Tünnermann, author's interview, April 6, 2011.

75. "Informe del Rector Dr. Carlos Tünnermann" a la Asamblea General Universitaria, January 13, 1968, 4–5, cuadro no. 1, held at the library of the Universidad Nacional Autónoma de Nicaragua-León (hereafter, UNAN-León).

76. "Informe del Rector Mariano Fiallos Oyanguren" a la Asamblea General Universitaria, January 14, 1977, 19, UNAN-León.

77. In 1967 and 1968, the state contributed about 9 million córdobas to the university, which had 2,731 students. "Informe del Rector Dr. Carlos Tünnermann" a la Asamblea General Universitaria, January 13, 1968, 5, cuadro no. 1, 7; cuadro no. 2, 15; cuadro no. 3, UNAN-León. By 1977, the state was contributing 38 million to the National University, which now taught nearly fifteen thousand students. "Informe del Rector Mariano Fiallos Oyanguren" a la Asamblea General Universitaria, January 14, 1977, 7, 12, UNAN-León.

78. Airgram from US Embassy, Managua, to Department of State, Subject: Ramiro Sacasa and the University, May 20, 1969; EDU NIC, Culture and Information, Box 350, CFPF 1967–69, RG 59, NARA.

79. Suri, *Power and Protest*, 88.

80. See Pensado, *Rebel Mexico*, chp. 3; Markarian, *Uruguay, 1968*, 31–32.

81. Barbosa called this the "pipeline" between student activists and the professoriate. Barbosa, "Insurgent Youth," 183.

82. Airgram from US Embassy, Managua, to Department of State, Subject: Weeka No. 10, March 11, 1967; POL 2–1 NIC, Political and Defense, Box 2366, CFPF 1967–69, RG 59, NARA.

83. Félix Contreras, author's interview, May 19, 2011.

84. Michele Najlis, author's interview, June 9, 2011. Airgram from the US Embassy,

Managua, to the Department of State, Subject: Weeka No. 3, January 21, 1967; POL 2-1 NIC, Political and Defense, Box 2366, CFPF 1967–69, RG 59, NARA.

85. Airgram from US Embassy, Managua, to Department of State, Subject: The National University in Trouble, July 17, 1969; EDU NIC, Culture and Information, Box 350, CFPF 1967–69, RG 59, NARA. Airgram from US Embassy, Managua, to Department of State, Subject: Forthcoming elections lead to increased activity at UNAN, August 10, 1968; EDU NIC, Culture and Information, Box 350, CFPF 1967–69, RG 59, NARA.

86. Memorandum of conversation, participants: Carlos Tünnermann and Dan E. Turnquist, political/labor officer, US Embassy, Place: Rector's office in León, December 19, 1972; POL 13-2 NIC, Political and Defense, Box 2503, SNF, 1970–73, RG 59, NARA. "Dr. Carlos Tünnermann," Academia de Ciencias de Nicaragua, www.ciencias denicaragua.org/index.php/miembros/miembros-honorarios/dr-carlos-tuennerman -berhneim.

87. In the aftermath of the Cuban Revolution, young people throughout Latin America debated political strategies. See Pensado, *Rebel Mexico*, 155–167; Markarian, *Uruguay, 1968*, 62–101.

88. Baltodano, *Memorias*, vol. 1, 534.

89. Cabezas, *Fire from the Mountain*, 12.

90. Dora María Téllez, author's interview, February 21, 2014.

91. Baltodano, *Memorias*, vol. 4, 91.

92. Núñez in Arias, *Nicaragua*, 57–58.

93. César Aróstegui, author's interview, June 10, 2011.

94. Félix Contreras, author's interview, May 19, 2011.

95. Baltodano, *Memorias*, vol. 3, 447. Agustín Lara in Mónica Baltodano, *Memorias de la Lucha Sandinista: Rebeldía e Insurreción en el Departamento de Carazo*, vol. 4 (Managua: Instituto de Historia de Nicaragua y Centroamerica de la Universidad Centroamericana, 2012), 186.

96. Michele Najlis, author's interview, June 9, 2011.

97. Carlos Tünnermann, author's interview, April 6, 2011.

98. Airgram from US Embassy, Managua, to Department of State, Subject: Forthcoming Elections Lead to Increased Activity at UNAN, August 10, 1968; POL 12 NIC, Political and Defense, Box 2367, CFPF 1967–69, RG 59, NARA.

99. Serrano Caldera recounts this episode in his book *Desde la Universidad*, but he puts the date at October 1970. Serrano Caldera, *Desde la Universidad*, 115–120; telegram from US Embassy, Managua, to Secretary of State, Subject: Students Seize UNAN Medical School October 8, 1971; POL 23 NIC, Political and Defense, Box 2503, SNF 1970–73, RG 59, NARA; telegram from US Embassy, Managua, to Secretary of State, Subject: Student Strike at National University, October 19, 1971; POL 23 NIC, Box 2503, SNF 1970–73, RG 59, NARA; telegram from US Embassy, Managua, to Secretary of State, Subject: Student Strike at National University, October 20, 1971; POL 23 NIC, Political and Defense, Box 2503, SNF 1970–73, RG 59, NARA; telegram from US Embassy, Managua, to Secretary of State, Subject: Student Strike Ends, October 27, 1971; POL 23 NIC, Political and Defense, Box 2503, SNF 1970–73, RG 59, NARA.

100. Baltodano, *Memorias*, vol. 1, 335–337; Gould, *To Lead*, 263.

101. Baltodano, *Memorias*, vol. 1, 330.

102. Interview with Guillermo Parrales Medina in Baltodano, *Memorias*, vol. 1, 164.

103. Carlos Tünnermann, author's interview, April 6, 2011; Dora María Téllez, author's interview, February 21, 2014; and César Aróstegui, author's interview, June 10, 2011.

104. Universidad Centroamericana, *Informe Estadístico, Curso 1971–1972* (Managua: Departamento de Estadistica, October 1971), 3, UNAN-León.

105. Guadalupe Salinas Valle, author's interview, May 7, 2011.

106. César Aróstegui, author's interview, June 10, 2011.

107. Dionisio Marenco por el Centro Estudiantil Universitario de la Universidad Centroamericana, Comunicado, July 25, 1966; IHNCA CME, D9 G4, exp. 1.

108. Ibid. Guadalupe Salinas Valle, author's interview, May 7, 2011. Tensions between progressive and conservative clergy were a hallmark of the era. Robert Sean Mackin, "In Word and Deed: Assessing the Strength of Progressive Catholicism in Latin America, 1960s–1970s," *Sociology of Religion* 71, no. 2 (Summer 2010): 216–242.

109. Airgram from US Embassy, Managua, to Department of State, Subject: Strike at Central American University, September 13, 1970; EDU Nepal, Culture and Information, Box 395, SNF 1970–73, RG 59, NARA. Airgram from US Embassy, Managua, to Department of State, Subject: Political and Economic Developments, August 30, 1970; POL 2 NIC, Political and Defense, Box 2502, SNF 1970–73, RG 59, NARA.

110. Airgram from US Embassy, Managua, to Department of State, Subject: Political and Economic Developments, October 20, 1970; POL 2 NIC, Political and Defense, Box 2502, SNF 1970–73, RG 59, NARA. Telegram from US Embassy to Secretary of State, Subject: Cathedral Seizure, September 28, 1970; POL 23 NIC, Political and Defense, Box 2503, SNF, 1970–73, RG 59, NARA.

111. César Aróstegui, author's interview, June 10, 2011.

112. Protestors elsewhere in Latin America had used churches as sites for powerful symbolic protest. See David Fernández Fernández, *La Iglesia que Resistió a Pinochet: Historia, desde la Fuente Oral, del Chile que no Puede Olvidarse* (Madrid: IEPALA, 1996), 73–76. See also Chávez, *Poets and Prophets*, 151–152.

113. See articles in *La Prensa*, September 27, 1970. César Aróstegui, author's interview, June 10, 2011.

114. Bayardo Arce claims credit for organizing this campaign with other FSLN/FER leaders. Interview with Arce in Baltodano, *Memorias*, vol. 1, 497.

115. "Mensaje del rector de la UNAN al rector de la UCA," September 28, 1970, *Gaceta Universitaria* 5 (Septiembre y Octubre 1970), 3; IHNCA CC F, no 87.

116. César Aróstegui, author's interview, June 10, 2011; airgram from US Embassy, Managua, to Department of State, Subject: Political and Economic Developments, October 20, 1970; POL 2 NIC, Political and Defense, Box 2502, SNF 1970–73, RG 59, NARA. Telegram from US Embassy to Secretary of State, Subject: Cathedral Seizure, September 28, 1970; POL 23 NIC, Political and Defense, Box 2503, SNF, 1970–73, RG 59, NARA.

117. César Aróstegui, author's interview, June 10, 2011. Telegram from US Embassy to Secretary of State, Subject: Cathedral Seizure, September 29, 1970; POL 23 NIC, Political and Defense, Box 2503, SNF, 1970–73, RG 59, NARA. Airgram from US Embassy, Managua, to Department of State, Subject: Political and Economic De-

velopments, October 20, 1970; POL 2 NIC, Political and Defense, Box 2502, SNF 1970–73, RG 59, NARA.

118. Telegram from US Embassy, Managua, to Secretary of State, Subject: Trouble in the Universities, January 21, 1971; EDU Nepal, Culture and Information, Box 395, SNF 1970–73, RG 59, NARA. Airgram from American Embassy, Managua, to Department of State, Subject: Political Developments, February 9, 1971; POL 2 NIC, Political and Defense, Box 2502, SNF 1970–1973, RG 59, NARA. Airgram from American Embassy, Managua, to Department of State, Subject: Political Developments, March 2, 1971; POL 2 NIC, Political and Defense, Box 2502, SNF 1970–1973, RG 59, NARA.

119. Telegram from US Embassy, Managua, to Secretary of State, Subject: UCA Protest, April 20, 1971; POL 13–2 NIC, Political and Defense, Box 2503, SNF, 1970–73, RG 59, NARA. Airgram from US Embassy, Managua, to Department of State, Subject: Political Developments April 13–May 3, May 7, 1971; POL 2 NIC, Political and Defense, Box 2502, SNF 1970–73, RG 59, NARA.

120. Telegram from US Embassy, Managua, to Secretary of State, Subject: UCA Protest, April 22, 1971; POL 23 NIC, Political and Defense, Box 2503, SNF, 1970–73, RG 59, NARA. Telegram from US Embassy, Managua, to Secretary of State, Subject: UCA Protest, April 26, 1971; POL 23 NIC, Political and Defense, Box 2503, SNF, 1970–73, RG 59, NARA.

121. Octavio Rivas G. and César Aróstegui, "CUUN CEUUCA Desde la Cárcel"; IHNCA Colección CUUN F, no. 52.

122. César Aróstegui, author's interview, June 10, 2011. Airgram from US Embassy, Managua, to Department of State, Subject: Political Developments, April 13–May 3, May 7, 1971; POL 2 NIC, Political and Defense, Box 2502, SNF 1970–73, RG 59, NARA. Telegram from US Embassy, Managua, to Secretary of State, Subject: UCA Protest Broadens, April 29, 1971; POL 23 NIC, Political and Defense, Box 2503, SNF, 1970–73, RG 59, NARA. Telegram from US Embassy, Managua, to Secretary of State, Subject: UCA Controversy, May 4, 1971; EDU Nepal, Culture and Information, Box 395, SNF 1970–73, RG 59, NARA. Telegram from US Embassy, Managua, to Secretary of State, Subject: UCA Controversy, May 8, 1971; EDU Nepal, Culture and Information, Box 395, SNF 1970–73, RG 59, NARA. Airgram from US Embassy, Managua, to Department of State, Subject: Political Developments, May 4–May 24, May 30, 1971; POL 2 NIC, Political and Defense, Box 2502, SNF 1970–73, RG 59, NARA. Telegram from US Embassy, Managua, to Secretary of State, Subject: UCA/FSLN Controversy, May 13, 1971; EDU Nepal, Culture and Information, Box 395, SNF 1970–73, RG 59, NARA. Telegram from US Embassy, Managua, to Secretary of State, Subject: UCA/FSLN Controversy, May 14, 1971; EDU Nepal, Culture and Information, Box 395, SNF 1970–73, RG 59, NARA.

123. Núñez in Arias, *Nicaragua*, 76–77.

Chapter 7. Un Trabajo de Hormiga, 1970–1979

1. As quoted in airgram from Shaw to Secretary of State, December 21, 1948; BLAC, SDCF 1945–1949, Reel 5.

2. Fox Piven and Cloward, *Poor People's Movements*, 3.

3. Víctor Tirado López, author's interview, June 17, 2011.

4. Black, *Triumph of the People*, 169–170.

5. Ibid.; Gould, *To Lead*; Booth, *The End*; Zimmermann, *Sandinista*; Kampwirth, *Women and Guerrilla Movements*. On the student role in the revolution, see Traña Galeano, Avendaño Rojas, and Norori Gutiérrez, "Historia del Movimiento Estudiantil," and Barbosa, "Insurgent Youth." Orlando Núñez Soto's discussion of the "third social force" in revolutionary movements touches on the many ways that students and young people participated in the Sandinista Revolution. Núñez Soto, "The Third Social Force," 12–13, 16–20. This chapter expands on Núñez Soto's observations.

6. On the importance of cross-class alliances, see Wickham-Crowley, *Guerrillas and Revolution*, 8–9, 154–157, 262–277.

7. Randall, *Sandino's Daughters*; Kampwirth, *Women and Guerilla Movements*, 21–43.

8. Carlos Fonseca Amador, "Nicaragua Hora Cero," *Obras*, tomo 1, 149–169, cf. 164–165. Baltodano, *Memorias*, vol. 1, 501.

9. Baltodano, *Memorias*, vol. 1, 501.

10. Bayardo Arce, *El Papel de las Fuerzas Motrices Antes y Despues del Triunfo*, (Managua: Centro de Publicaciones "Silvio Mayorga," 1980), 22.

11. Interview with Arce in Baltodano, *Memorias*, vol. 1, 497.

12. Ibid., 497–503.

13. Ibid., 498.

14. Ibid.

15. The theory of weak ties is complex and requires a detailed analysis of individuals and their networks in order to fully establish that students function in this capacity, but, in general, I would argue that university students have many of the tendencies that Mark Granovetter describes in his pioneering study of weak ties. Chiefly, they operate in many different networks that give them access to a large number of acquaintances. Mark S. Granovetter, "The Strength of Weak Ties," *American Journal of Sociology* 78 (1973): 1360–1380.

16. Interview with Bayardo Arce in Baltodano, *Memorias*, vol. 1, 498, 503.

17. Patricia Orozco, author's interview, May 16, 2011. On FER membership drives see, Cabezas, *Fire from the Mountain*, 28.

18. Frente Estudiantil Revolucionario, "Normas Trazadas para el Reclutamiento," Julio 1978; IHNCA CC F, no. 71.

19. Airgram from US Embassy, Managua, to Department of State, Subject: Communist Wins Student Government Presidency at UNAN, December 7, 1969; POL 12 NIC, Political and Defense, Box 2367, CFPF 1967–69, RG 59, NARA.

20. Patricia Orozco, author's interview, May 16, 2011.

21. Interview with Arce in Baltodano, *Memorias*, vol. 1, 495–497.

22. Dora María Téllez, author's interview, February 21, 2014. Patricia Orozco, author's interview, May 16, 2011.

23. As quoted in Randall, *Christians in the Nicaraguan Revolution*, 156.

24. Interview with Luis Carrión in Mónica Baltodano, *Memorias de la Lucha Sandinista: El Camino a la unidad y al triunfo: Chinandega, Frente Sur, Masaya y la Toma del Búnker*, vol. 3 (Managua: IHNCA-UCA, 2011), 400.

25. Randall, *Christians in the Nicaraguan Revolution*, 159. Foroohar, *The Catholic Church*, 132.

26. Interview with Arce in Baltodano, *Memorias*, vol. 1, 503.

27. See for example, Ricardo Morales Avilés, "Charla al movimiento Cristiano revolucionario," *No Pararemos de Andar Jamás: Obras*, 2nd ed. (Managua: Editorial Nueva Nicaragua, 1983), 129–166.

28. On this process, see interview with Arce in Baltodano, *Memorias*, vol. 1, 507; Luis Carrión in Randall, *Christians in the Nicaraguan Revolution*, 162–163; interview with Carrión in Baltodano, *Memorias*, vol. 3, 402. On the Movimiento Cristiano Revolucionario, see Foroohar, *The Catholic Church*, 128–135.

29. As quoted in Randall, *Christians in the Nicaraguan Revolution*, 165.

30. Ibid., 166.

31. Morales Avilés, "Charla al movimiento," 151–152.

32. Interview with Agustín Lara in Baltodano, *Memorias*, vol. 4, 188.

33. Interview with Bayardo Arce in Baltodano, *Memorias*, vol. 1, 499.

34. Ibid.

35. Dora María Téllez, author's interview, February 21, 2014.

36. As quoted in Baltodano, *Memorias*, vol. 1, 317.

37. Doris Tijerino, *Inside the Nicaraguan Revolution* (Vancouver: New Star Books, 1978), 125–127.

38. Patricia Orozco, author's interview, May 16, 2011.

39. As quoted in Randall, *Christians in the Nicaraguan Revolution*, 137–138.

40. Randall, *Christians in the Nicaraguan Revolution*, 137–138.

41. As quoted in ibid., 147.

42. As quoted in ibid.

43. Cardenal, *Sacerdote en la Revolución*, 138, 140. Paulo Freire, *Pedagogy of the Oppressed*, trans. Myra Bergman Ramos (New York: Continuum, 2006).

44. Quoted in Randall, *Christians in the Nicaraguan Revolution*, 151.

45. Crawley, *Dictators Never Die*, 148–151; Gould, *To Lead*, 271–272; Millett, *Guardians*, 237–238; LaFeber, *Inevitable Revolutions*, 227; Zimmermann, *Sandinista*, 173.

46. Baltodano, *Memorias*, vol. 4, 128–129.

47. Cardenal, *Sacerdote en la Revolución*, tomo 1, 170.

48. Interview with Arce in Baltodano, *Memorias*, vol. 1, 507–508. Randall, *Christians*, 162.

49. Quoted in Cardenal, *Sacerdote en la Revolución*, vol. 1, 128.

50. Gould found that the Sandinistas did not reach out in earnest to these sectors until the mid-1970s. See Gould, *To Lead*.

51. Quoted in Baltodano, *Memorias*, vol. 4, 134.

52. Tijerino, *Inside the Nicaraguan Revolution*, 132–134.

53. Quoted in Arias, *Nicaragua, Revolución*, 85–86. For a brief discussion of the strike, see Gould, *To Lead*, 272.

54. Kampwirth, *Women and Guerrilla Movements*, 37.

55. Baltodano, *Memorias*, vol. 4, 242.

56. Baltodano, *Memorias*, vol. 2, 109. Humberto Román, a former FER activist, explained that the FER was the Front's urban organization. Humberto Román, author's interview, June 18, 2011.

57. Interview with José González in Baltodano, *Memorias*, vol. 2, 171.

58. Comunicado "Fuera Virgilio y el Prof. Rosales de la ENAC" from the Comité

de Estudiantes de la ENAC; Folder Especial el Huelga en Granada 1976, Caja 394, Fondo Educación, AGN. Letter to Carlos Huelva, Deputy Director of Educacion Media from Guillermo Rosales Herrera, Director, Escuela de Ciencias de la Educacion, September 3, 1976; Folder Especial el Huelga en Granada 1976, Caja 394, Fondo Educación, AGN.

59. "Paro de estudiantes triunfa en Jinotega," *La Prensa*, June 27, 1976.

60. AES pamphlet, March 1979; IHNCA CME D9 G4, exp. 6; undated and incomplete document, "Cronología de una huelga"; IHNCA CME D9 G4, exp. 6.

61. Undated and incomplete document, "Cronología de una huelga"; IHNCA CME D9 G4, exp. 6.

62. "Se agrava caso del Inst. Eliseo Picado," *La Prensa*, June 9, 1976.

63. "No hubo consenso en 'areglo' del Picado," *La Prensa*, June 12, 1976.

64. Humberto Román, author's interview, June 18, 2011.

65. Comunicado from various student associations in Managua, April 14, 1977; IHNCA CME D9 G4, exp. 1.

66. Comunicado from the Asociación de Estudiantes de Secundaria (AES), undated; IHNCA CME D9 G4, exp. 1.

67. Jonathan Smucker's ideas for creating what he calls an "aspiring hegemony" inspired this discussion. See Jonathan M. Smucker, *Hegemony How-To: A Roadmap for Radicals*, (Chico, CA: AK Press, 2017), 222.

68. Carlos Núñez attributed the FSLN's rapid growth in popularity after mid-decade to the various intermediary organizations that were producing flyers and painting pro-FSLN graffiti. Núñez in Arias, *Nicaragua*, 148–149.

69. On censorship and the "Journalism of the Catacombs," see the interview with Manuel Espinoza Enríquez and Carlos García in Baltodano, *Memorias*, vol. 1, 367–389, esp. 380–383. See also, Wickham-Crowley, *Guerrillas and Revolution*, 273–275.

70. *Novedades* attempted to discredit the rebels, but its status as the regime's organ limited its efficacy. On Chamorro and Fonseca, see Zimmermann, *Sandinista*, 85–86, 128. On the media's demonization of dissidents in Cold War Latin America, see Pensado, *Rebel Mexico*; David Carey Jr. and M. Gabriela Torres, "Precursors to Femicide: Guatemalan Women in a Vortex of Violence," *Latin American Research Review* 45, no. 3 (2010): 142–164.

71. Unless the students were protesting US policies. See chapter 5.

72. "Lista de oficiales GN que se esconden en el anonimato/pilotes asesinos," communiqué from the FER to El Pueblo en General, December 1977; IHNCA CC F, no. 77 "Comunicados FER."

73. "Introducción," FER, August 1975; IHNCA CME D9G4, exp. 4.

74. Communiqué from FER at the UCA, November 4, 1970; IHNCA CME D9 G9, exp. 4.

75. "Murieron Matando el Hambre," January 1971; IHNCA CME D9 G9, exp. 4.

76. CUUN, "Pueblo: Reclama a tus Hijos Encarcelados," undated; IHNCA CC F no. 84 "Comunicados CUUN 1970."

77. Asociación de Estudiantes de Ciencias Económicas, "Por una Información Hacia el Pueblo," undated; IHNCA CME D9 G4, exp. 1. Communiqué from Asocación de Estudiantes de Secundaria to Estudiantes y Pueblo en General, c. 1978; IHNCA CME D9 G4, exp. 6. Communiqué from Asocación de Estudiantes de Secundaria to Estudiantado y Pueblo en General, June 25, 1978; IHNCA CME D9 G4, exp. 6.

78. Zimmermann, *Sandinista*, 143–145.

79. Comunicado from AES to Pueblo Hermano de Mataglapa, undated; IHNCA CME D9 G4, exp. 6. Comunicado, February 1977; IHNCA CME D9 G4 G4, 1. FER comunicado, December 1978; IHNCA CC F. no. 77. Undated communiqué from the Movimiento Estudiantil de Secundaria to the Pueblo en General, undated; IHNCA CME D9 G4, exp. 6. "Introducción a Sandino," document reproducing Carlos Fonseca's writings on Sandino from the AEPS, undated; IHNCA CME D9 G4, exp. 6.

80. Communiqué from Movimiento Estudiantil de Secundaria to the Pueblo en General, no date; IHNCA CME D9 G4, exp. 6.

81. On Fonseca's writings on Sandino, see Zimmermann, *Sandinista*, 143–161. David E. Whisnant, *Rascally Signs in Sacred Places: The Politics of Culture in Nicaragua* (Chapel Hill: University of North Carolina Press), 359–365.

82. "Entrevista con 'Modesto,'" November 1978; IHNCA CC F, no. 74 "Entrevistas FER 1978."

83. For example, comunicado from the Asociación de Estudiantes de Secundaria to the Estudiantes y Pueblo de Corinto en General September 10, 1978; IHNCA CME D9 G4, exp. 6.

84. FER flyer commemorating the seventeenth anniversary of the student massacre, IHNCA CME D9 G4, exp. 4; "Homenaje póstumo Martina Alemán Chavarria" from the Asociación de Estudiantes de Ciencias y Letras; IHNCA CC F, no. 114.

85. "Mensaje del Frente Estudiantil Revolucionario en el Segundo Aniversario de los Mártires del 4 de Noviembre de 1967," November 4, 1969; IHNCA CME D9 G4, exp. 4. "Murieron Matando el Hambre," FER flyer, January 1971; IHNCA CME D9 G4, exp. 4.

86. Vrana, *The City*, 198–205. Markarian argues that the killings of students became a "call to arms." Markarian, *Uruguay, 1968*, 108–109.

87. Langland, *Speaking of Flowers*, 205–207.

88. "Pedimos o exigimos al regimen?" FER flyer, December 1977; IHNCA CC F, no. 77.

89. Félix Contreras, author's interview, May 19, 2011.

90. Article in *Juventud Patriótica*, the newspaper of the Federation of Youth Movements of Managua, no. 3, 1978; IHNCA CME D9 G4, exp. 3.

91. Humberto Román, author's interview, June 17, 2011.

92. Ibid.

93. Baltodano, *Memorias*, vol. 4, 327–329.

94. Article in *Juventud Patriótica*, no. 3, 1978; IHNCA CME D9 G4, exp 3.

95. Not all youth movements used cultural forms the same way. Markarian illustrates the ways in which culture as an "arena of struggle" constituted one "protest option" of many. See Markarian, *Uruguay, 1968*, 18–21, 103–150. See also Langland, *Speaking of Flowers*, 201–202.

96. On the counterculture movement in Latin America, see Zolov, *Refried Elvis*.

97. Whisnant, *Rascally Signs*, 28–29.

98. Interview with Sandra López in Baltodano, *Memorias*, vol. 2, 183.

99. Irving Dávila, interview with the author, May 18, 2011.

100. Interview with José Miguel Torres in Baltodano, *Memorias*, vol. 4, 170.

101. On the connection between Latin American protest songs and rock music, see Zolov, *Refried Elvis*, 225–233. On the Nueva Canción (New Song) movement in Nicaragua, see Whisnant, *Rascally Signs*, 174–179.

102. Baltodano, *Memorias*, vol. 1, 441. The Association of Secondary Students encouraged others to organize music festivals. AES, "La Poesía está en la calle," March 1978; IHNCA CME D9 G4, exp. No. 6.

103. Félix Contreras, author's interview, May 19, 2011.

104. Interview with Pancho Cedeño in Baltodano, *Memorias*, vol. 1, 433.

105. Some examples include Grupo Pancasán's "Hora Cero," "Canción para un Reo Político," "Requiém a la Muerte," and "Así Está la Cosa," and Arlen Siu's "María Rural." For a discussion of these songs, see Baltodano, *Memorias*, vol. 1, 427–449.

106. As quoted in Heyck, *Life Stories*, 152–153.

107. On the spectrum of allies, see Smucker, *Hegemony How-To*, 157.

108. Humberto Román, author's interview, June 17, 2011.

109. Interview with Sandra López in Baltodano, *Memorias*, vol. 2, 183–184.

110. Zimmermann, *Sandinista*, 164–184; Booth, *The End*, 144–145.

111. Black, *Triumph of the People*, 157–161; Zimmermann, *Sandinista*, 205, 209, and 212.

112. "Estudiantes de ENA firmes en demandas," *La Prensa*, March 29, 1978.

113. "Crece la huelga de hambre," *La Prensa*, March 30, 1978.

114. "En León: bombas y manifestaciones," *La Prensa*, April 4, 1978.

115. "Huelga estudiantil en Masaya," *La Prensa*, April 5, 1978.

116. "Se extiende paro estudiantil," *La Prensa*, April 6, 1978; "Toman tres colegios en Granada," *La Prensa*, April 8, 1978.

117. "Se extienden huelgas y tomas de iglesias," *La Prensa*, April 8, 1978; "Ocupación de los colegios se extiende," *La Prensa*, April 9, 1978.

118. Interview with Mario López in Baltodano, *Memorias*, vol. 3, 257.

119. "Ministra no quiere nada con 'contrarios,'" *La Prensa*, April 12, 1978.

120. Humberto Román, author's interview, June 17, 2011.

121. Interview with Victor Hugo Tinoco in Baltodano, *Memorias*, vol. 2, 110.

122. Humberto Román, author's interview, June 17, 2011.

123. Rodríguez Kuri, "Los primeros días"; Markarian, *Uruguay, 1968*, 139.

124. "Se extiende paro estudiantil," *La Prensa*, April 6, 1978.

125. "Problemas en educación con año escolar" *La Prensa*, May 4, 1978.

126. "Se extiende paro estudiantil," *La Prensa*, April 6, 1978; "Se organizan padres de familia," *La Prensa*, April 12, 1978; "Padres de familia apoyan a sus hijos," *La Prensa*, April 13, 1978.

127. "Sigue paro estudiantil," *La Prensa*, April 13, 1978.

128. "Demandan dimisión de Ministra de Educación," *La Prensa*, April 16, 1978.

129. "Desalojo en Jinotepe; rescatan estudiantes," *La Prensa*, April 18, 1978.

130. "Los estudiantes; ejemplo luminoso," *La Prensa*, April 20, 1978.

131. "En Jinotepe Igual: Hechos gravísimos," *La Prensa*, April 10, 1978; "Protesta popular a nivel nacional," *La Prensa*, April 10, 1978.

132. "Protesta popular a nivel nacional," *La Prensa*, April 10, 1978.

133. "Desalojo en Jinotepe; rescatan estudiantes," *La Prensa*, April 18, 1978.

134. "Profesor dispara a estudiantes," *La Prensa*, April 10, 1978.

135. "Sigue paro estudiantil," *La Prensa*, April 13, 1978.

136. "Conmoción en todos los departamentos," *La Prensa*, April 12, 1978.

137. *La Prensa*, April 11, 1978.

138. "Otro manifestante gravemente herido," *La Prensa*, April 8, 1978; "Huelga Estudiantil en Masaya," *La Prensa*, April 5, 1978.

139. "En Jinotepe Igual: Hechos Gravísimos," *La Prensa*, April 10, 1978.

140. "Desalojo en Masaya: Sangre y Capturados," *La Prensa*, April 20, 1978.

141. "Entregan colegios en León," *La Prensa*, May 4, 1978.

142. Humberto Román, author's interview, June 18, 2011.

143. Interview with Eva María Samqui Chan in Baltodano, *Memorias*, vol. 4, 230. Oyanguren secretly collaborated with the Sandinistas. Interview with William Ramírez in Baltodano, *Memorias*, vol. 1, 620–621. Leonor Álvarez, et al., "Último Adiós a Mariano Fiallos Oyanguren," *La Prensa*, June 26, 2014, www.laprensa.com.ni/2014/06/26/nacionales/200390-ultimo-adios-a-mariano-fiallos-oyanguren-ultimo-adios-a-mariano-fiallos-oyanguren.

144. Baltodano, *Memorias*, vol. 4, 317.

145. On the attack on the Carazo campus, see interview with Rodolfo Porras in Baltodano, *Memorias*, vol. 4, 247–248; Baltodano, *Memorias*, vol. 4, 342–344.

146. Booth, *The End*, 163–164.

147. Ibid., 111, 153–155, 164–167; Zimmermann, *Sandinista*, 212.

148. Interview with America Libertad Vidaurre in Baltodano, *Memorias*, vol. 2, 259; Baltodano, *Memorias*, vol. 4, 334.

149. Baltodano, *Memorias*, vol. 2, 278.

150. On these organizations, see the interviews with Mauricio Valenzuela, Daniela Lanza Solís, Sergio Lira, and Alma Nubia Baltodano, in Baltodano, *Memorias*, vol. 2.

151. Interview with Alma Nubia Baltodano in Baltodano, *Memorias*, vol. 2, 314. Mauricio Valenzuela called them "pre-combat units." Interview with Mauricio Valenzuela in Baltodano, *Memorias*, vol. 2, 453.

152. Interview with America Libertad Vidaurre in Baltodano, *Memorias*, vol. 2, 261–262.

153. Ibid., 258–259.

154. Baltodano, *Memorias*, vol. 2, 258. Interview with America Libertad Vidaurre in Baltodano, *Memorias*, vol. 2, 257.

155. Interview with Rodolfo Porras in Baltodano, *Memorias*, vol. 4, 246.

156. Interview with Mauricio Valenzuela in Baltodano, *Memorias*, vol. 2, 453.

157. Interview with America Libertad Vidaurre in Baltodano, *Memorias*, vol. 2, 260.

158. Interview with Eva María Samqui Chan in Baltodano, *Memorias*, vol. 4, 244.

159. "Llenan cárceles con jóvenes capitalinos," *La Prensa*, February 11, 1979.

160. "Ni combate, ni eran guerrilleros," *La Prensa*, February 5, 1979. "Detalles de la massacre de El Sauce," *La Prensa*, February 7, 1979.

161. "Continúan macabres denuncias campesinas," *La Prensa*, February 6, 1979.

162. "Reportan más desaparecidos," *La Prensa*, February 4, 1979.

163. "Desempleo crece a ritmo anonadante," *La Prensa*, February 7, 1979; "Comienzan ralas las matrículas," *La Prensa*, February 5, 1979; "Poca matrícula en la UNAN," *La Prensa*, February 6, 1979. On the violence wracking the nation in February 1979, see "Seis muertos más en terrible siege leonesa," *La Prensa*, February 6, 1979. Chester Alegría Icaza, "Muertos y Robos: Cuantos habrá hoy?" *La Prensa*, February 7, 1979. "Ola violenta sigue: Asaltantes se llevaron más de 30 mil córdobas," and "Para qué sirven las patrullas G.N.?" *La Prensa*, February 16, 1979.

164. Baltodano, *Memorias*, vol. 2, 413.

165. "Llueve solidaridad con hospitalarios!" and "Comunidad cristiana en apoyo a FETSALUD," *La Prensa*, February 4, 1979. "Angustia, conmoción, solidaridad," *La Prensa*, February 7, 1979.

166. Interview with Sergio Lira in Baltodano, *Memorias*, vol. 2, 413.

167. "Testigos: Única arma era 'guardia únete,'" *La Prensa*, February 16, 1979.

168. Interview with Sergio Lira in Baltodano, *Memorias*, vol. 2, 411.

169. "Testigos: Única arma era 'guardia únete,'" *La Prensa*, February 16, 1979.

170. Ibid.

171. "Indignación y vela en León!" and "Protestas en universidades de Managua," *La Prensa*, February 16, 1979.

172. "Arzobispo: 'Estamos en manos de Caínes,'" *La Prensa*, February 16, 1979.

173. "Toma pacífica en protesta por repression," *La Prensa*, February 17, 1979. On the National Patriotic Front, see Zimmermann, *Sandinista*, 214.

174. "Desde la curia: 'Extremos Intolerables,'" *La Prensa*, February 20, 1979. "Tomada iglesia donde murieron cinco jovenes," *La Prensa*, February 22, 1979.

175. "Mujeres se toman iglesia de la 14 de Septiembre," *La Prensa*, February 23, 1979.

176. Interview with Daniela Lanzas in Baltodano, *Memorias*, vol. 2, 417.

177. "Violencia en varias ciudadades," *La Prensa*, February 22, 1979.

178. Zimmermann observes that "the cities liberated themselves." Zimmermann, *Sandinista*, 216.

179. Booth, *The End*, 160–161.

180. Interview with Isabel Castillo in Baltodano, *Memorias*, vol. 2, 158–161.

181. Interview with Marcos Largaespada in Baltodano, *Memorias*, vol. 2, 158–161.

182. Katherine Hoyt, *30 years of Memories: Dictatorship, Revolution, and Nicaragua Solidarity* (Washington DC: Nicaragua Network Education Fund, 1996), 46–54; Zimmermann, *Sandinista*, 212–213.

183. Gould, *To Lead*, 284; Booth, *The End*, 165–167.

184. Carlos María Vilas, *The Sandinista Revolution: National Liberation and Social Transformation in Central America*, trans. Judy Butler (New York: Monthly Review Press, 1986), cited in Zimmermann, *Sandinista*, 217.

185. Booth, *The End*, 176.

186. Ibid., 174–182.

187. Manzano observed a similar gendered hierarchy of action at work within the Argentine guerrilla movement. See Manzano, *Age of Youth*, 209–210.

188. Kampwirth has argued that "within the Sandinista coalition there was a long continuum between unarmed and armed work. The armed guerrillas were very dependent on the unarmed revolutionaries for support for recruitment, and for the unrelenting pressure that would help to bring down the dictatorship." She suggests that there is no clear line between armed work and unarmed work. Kampwirth, *Women and Guerrilla Movements*, 36.

Conclusion

1. LaFeber, *Inevitable Revolutions*, 238.

2. Robert F. Arnove, *Education and Revolution in Nicaragua* (New York: Praeger Publishers, 1986), 19–20.

3. Ibid., 17.

4. Ibid., 19–22.

5. Arnove notes that the crusade strategically relied on the mass organizations that formed during the insurrection. Arnove, *Education and Revolution*, 21.

6. Pensado, *Rebel Mexico*. Recent scholarship on El Salvador and Guatemala has examined how the government attempted to use paid advertisements to demonize students, dissidents, and members of the armed movement as dangerous extremists. Virginia Garrard-Burnett, *Terror in the Land of the Holy Spirit: Guatemala under General Efraín Ríos Montt, 1982–1983* (New York: Oxford University Press, 2010), 61–64. Chávez, *Poets and Prophets*, 141–145.

7. Booth also observed the political diversity of the movement. Booth, *The End*, 111.

8. Gould, *To Lead*, 192.

9. Students made up the largest percentage (29 percent) in his sample of 640 cases from the Nicaraguan Institute for Social Security and Welfare's program for fallen combatants. There are 6,000 total cases. The next largest were tradespeople at 22 percent. Vilas, *The Sandinista Revolution*, 108, 112, 278, n10.

10. Moisés Hassan, interview with the author, June 21, 2011.

11. Irving Dávila, interview with the author, May 18, 2011; Patricia Orozco, interview with the author, May 16, 2011.

12. Father Fernando Cardenal told Robert Arnove that the campaign also served to promote a "revolutionary consciousness" among youth and integrate them into the revolution. Arnove, *Education and Revolution*, 18. Subsequent research has agreed with his assessment. See, Jan L. Flora, John McFadden, and Ruth Warner, "The Growth of Class Struggle: The impact of the Nicaraguan Literacy Crusade on the Political Consciousness of Young Literacy Workers," *Latin American Perspectives* 10, no. 1 (Winter 1983): 45–61.

13. Arnove, *Education and Revolution*, 27–28. As the Contra War took its toll on the nation's budget and reprioritized the Sandinista political agenda, the rate of illiteracy would rise again. See Andrew Kirkendall, *Paulo Freire and the Cold War Politics of Literacy* (Chapel Hill: University of North Carolina Press, 2010), 150.

Bibliography

Archives

Archivo General de la Nación (AGN), Managua, Nicaragua.
Benson Latin American Collection (BLAC), University of Texas at Austin, Austin, Texas.
Biblioteca de la Universidad Nacional Autónoma de Nicaragua-León, León, Nicaragua.
Instituto de Historia de Nicaragua y Centroamérica (IHNCA), Universidad Centroamericana, Managua, Nicaragua.
Firestone Library, Princeton University, Princeton, New Jersey.
United States National Archives and Records Administration (NARA), College Park, Maryland.

Magazines and Newspapers

Ahora	*Noticias de Nicaragua*
Avanzada	*Novedades*
El Estudiante	*La Nueva Prensa*
Excelsior	*El Nuevo Diario*
Flecha	*La Prensa*
Juventud Patriótica	*The Student*
La Noticia	*El Universitario*
La Verdad	

Interviews Conducted by Claudia Rueda

Danilo Aguirre, June 21, 2011.
Vicente Arsenio Álvarez Corrales, April 17, 2012.
César Aróstegui, June 10, 2011.
Jesús Miguel [Chuno] Blandón, April 11, 2011.
Fernando Cardenal, April 5, 2011.

Rafael Casanova, March 28, 29, and 30, 2011.
Ernesto Castillo, April 13, 2011.
Félix Contreras, May 19, 2011.
Irving Dávila, May 18, 2011.
Roberto Gutiérrez, May 10, 2010.
Moisés Hassan, June 21, 2011.
Iván de Jesús Pereira, June 22, 2011.
Eddy Kuhl, May 22, 2010.
Hugo Mejía Briceño, June 30, 2011.
Vidaluz Meneses, July 31, 2012.
Flor de María Monterrey, May 11, 2011.
Marisol and Irma Morales, June 9, 2011.
Michele Najlis, June 9, 2011.
Vilma Núñez, August 2, 2012.
Patricia Orozco, May 16, 2011.
Asalia Ortiz, May 23, 2011.
Humberto Román, June 17, 2011.
Guadalupe Salinas Valle, May 7, 2011.
Santiago Sequeira, June 29, 2011.
Alejandro Serrano Caldera, April 26, 2011.
Joaquín Solís Piura, June 29, 2011.
Dora María Téllez, February 21, 2014.
Víctor Tirado López, June 17, 2011.
Carlos Tünnermann, April 6, 2011.

Memoirs, Interviews, and Other Published Primary Sources

Arias, Pilar. *Nicaragua Revolucion: Relatos de Combatientes del Frente Sandinista.* Mexico: xxi, Siglo veintiuno editors, 1980.
Avendaña Sandino, Rolando. *Masacre estudiantil: 23 de Julio de 1959.* Leon, Nicaragua: Tipografico América, 1960.
Baltodano M., Mónica. *Memorias de la Lucha Sandinista.* Política y Sociedad. Managua, Nicaragua: Instituto de Historia de Nicaragua y Centroamérica de la Universidad Centroamericana, IHNCA-UCA, 2010. 4 vols.
Belli, Gioconda. *The Country Under My Skin: A Memoir of Love and War.* New York: Knopf, 2002.
Borge, Tomás. *The Patient Impatience: From Boyhood to Guerilla: A Personal Narrative of Nicaragua's Struggle for Liberation.* Willimantic, CT: Curbstone Press, 1992.
Cabezas, Omar. *Fire from the Mountain: The Making of a Sandinista.* New York, NY: Crown, 1985.
Cardenal, Fernando. *Sacerdote en la Revolución: Memorias.* Managua: Anamá Ediciones, 2008. 2 vols.
Chamorro Cardenal, Pedro Joaquín. *Estirpe Sangrienta: Los Somoza.* Buenos Aires: Editorial Triángulo, 1959.
Córdova Rivas, Rafael. *Contribución a la Revolución.* Managua, Nicaragua: Centro de Publicaciones de Avanzada, 1983.

Ebaugh, Cameron D. *Education in Nicaragua*. Bulletin 1947, no. 6. Washington, DC: US Government Printing Office, 1947.

Fiallos Gil, Mariano. "Carta del Rector a los Estudiantes." In UNAN, *Memoria Anual Presentada por el Rector 1958-59*. León, Nicaragua: Editorial Hospicio.

———. "El Dinero que Necesita la Universidad." In *A la Libertad por la Universidad y Otros Ensayos*. Managua, Nicaragua: Editorial Nueva Nicaragua, 1994.

———. *A la Libertad por la Universidad y Otros Ensayos*. Managua, Nicaragua: Editorial Nueva Nicaragua, 1994.

Fonseca Amador, Carlos. "Mensaje del Frente Sandinista de Liberación Nacional, FSLN, a los estudiantes revolucionarios." In *Obras*, tomo 1. Managua, Nicaragua: Editorial Nueva Nicaragua, 1985.

———. "Nicaragua Hora Cero." In *Obras*, tomo 1. Managua, Nicaragua: Editorial Nueva Nicaragua, 1985.

———. *Un Nicaragüense En Moscú*. S.l: s.n., 1961.

Fundis, Ronald Jay. *Población estudiantil, 1960-1967: Evolución Histórica de la Matrícula, Eficiencia del Sistema, Aspectos Demográficos, Proyecciones*. Managua, Nicaragua [Universidad Nacional Autónoma de Nicaragua], 1967.

Gordillo Cervantes, Fernando. *Obra*. Colección Letras de Nicaragua 32. Managua, Nicaragua: Editorial Nueva Nicaragua, 1989.

Guido, Clemente. *Noches de Torturas (Consejo de Guerra de 1956)*. Managua, Nicaragua: Editorial Artes Gráficas, 1965.

Heyck, Denis Lynn Daly, ed. *Life Stories of the Nicaraguan Revolution*. New York: Routledge, 1990.

Hoyt, Katherine. *30 Years of Memories: Dictatorship, Revolution, and Nicaragua Solidarity*. Washington, DC: Nicaragua Network Education Fund, 1996.

International Student Conference. *Nicaragua, 1963-64*. Report to the 11th International Student Conference. Leiden, Netherlands: International Student Conference, 1964.

———. *RIC Yearbook: Reports on Higher Education in Algeria, Cuba, Cyprus, Hungary, and Nicaragua*. Leiden, Netherlands: International Student Conference, 1957.

Morales Avilés, Ricardo *No Pararemos de Andar Jamás: Obras*. Managua, Nicaragua: Editorial Nueva Nicaragua, 1983.

Ortega Saavedra, Humberto. *La Epopeya de la Insurrección*. Managua, Nicaragua: Lea Grupo Editorial, 2004.

Partido Liberal Independiente. *Memoria*. León, Nicaragua: Partido Liberal Independiente, 1969.

Quijano, Óscar. *Los del Reparto Schick: Memoria del Movimiento Juvenil Cristiano de los años 70*. Managua, Nicaragua: EDITARTE, 2015.

Randall, Margaret. *Christians in the Nicaraguan Revolution*. Translated by Marianne Valverde. Vancouver, British Columbia: New Star Books, 1983.

———. *Sandino's Daughters: Testimonies of Nicaraguan Women in Struggle*. New Brunswick, NJ: Rutgers University Press, 1995.

———. *Todas Estamos Despiertas: Testimonios de La Mujer Nicaragüense de Hoy*. México, DF: Siglo Veintiuno Editores, 1981.

Randall, Margaret, and Floyce Alexander, eds. *Risking a Somersault in the Air: Conversations with Nicaraguan Writers*. San Francisco, CA: Solidarity Publications, 1984.

Serrano Caldera, Alejandro. *Desde la Universidad, 1957-1974: Un Enfoque de la Univer-*

sidad y la Sociedad Nicaraguense. León, Nicaragua: Editorial Universitaria, UN 2007.

Tijerino, Doris. *Inside the Nicaraguan Revolution*. Vancouver, British Columbia: N Star Books, 1978.

United States Army Reserve. *Nicaragua, an Area Study*. Edited by Sydney Cohe Providence, RI, 1962.

Universidad Nacional Autónoma de Nicaragua. *Guía Orgánica de La Universida Nacional de Nicaragua*. León, Nicaragua: La Universidad, 1963.

———. *Memoria Anual Presentada por el Rector 1958–59*. León, Nicaragua: Editorial Hospicio, 1960.

———. Oficina de Registro y Estadística. *Composición de la Población Estudiantil por Facultades, Escuelas, Años de Estudio y Sexo en la Matricula Inicial, 1950–1964*. León, Nicaragua, 1964.

Universidad Nacional de Nicaragua. *Memoria: Presentada por el Rector a la Junta Universitaria*. León, Nicaragua: Universidad Nacional de Nicaragua, 1957–1958.

Y Se Rompio el Silencio. Managua, Nicaragua: Editorial Nueva Nicaragua, 1981.

Dissertations and Theses

Barbosa, Francisco J. "Insurgent Youth: Culture and Memory in the Sandinista Student Movement." PhD dissertation, Indiana University, 2006.

Ochoa, Darling, and Yessenia Vergara. "El Movimiento Estudiantil Como Agente de Cambio (1914–1969)." Undergraduate thesis, Universidad Nacional de Nicaragua, 2002.

Sloan, Julia. "The 1968 Student Movement and the Crisis of Mexico's Institutionalized Revolution." PhD dissertation, University of Houston, 2001.

Traña Galeano, Marcia, Xiomara Avendaño Rojas, and Roger Norori Gutiérrez. "Historia Del Movimiento Estudiantil Universitario (1939–1979)." Undergraduate thesis, Universidad Nacional de Nicaragua, 1985.

Secondary Sources

Agnew, Jean-Christophe, and Roy Rosenzweig, eds. *A Companion to Post-1945 America*. Malden, MA: Blackwell, 2002.

Altbach, Philip G. "The International Student Movement." *Journal of Contemporary History* 5, no. 1 (January 1970): 156–174.

———. *The Student Internationals*. Metuchen, NJ: Scarecrow Press, 1973.

———, ed. *Student Political Activism: An International Reference Handbook*. New York: Greenwood Press, 1989.

———. "Student Politics in the Third World." *Higher Education* 13, no. 6 (December 1, 1984): 635–655.

Alvarado Martínez, Enrique. *La UCA: Una Historia a Través de La Historia*. Managua, Nicaragua: Universidad Centroamericana, 2010.

Álvarez A., Virgilio. *Conventos, Aulas Y Trincheras: Universidad Y Movimiento Estudiantil En Guatemala*. Guatemala: Facultad Latinoamericana de Ciencias Sociales, 2002.

las Fuerzas Motrices Antes y Despues del Triunfo. Managua,
Publicaciones, 1980.

. Brevísima Historia de la Educación en Nicaragua. Managua,
Nicaragüense de Cultura Hispánica, 1997.

ucation and Revolution in Nicaragua. New York: Praeger Pub-

Students on the March: The Cases of Mexico and Colombia." *Soci-
on* 37, no. 3 (April 1, 1964): 200–228.

co J. "July 23, 1959: Student Protest and State Violence as Myth
y in León, Nicaragua." *Hispanic American Historical Review* 85, no. 2
05): 187–221.

anda, Francisco. *Historia Militar de Nicaragua: Antes Del Siglo XVI Al XXI*.
Managua, Nicaragua: Hispamer, 2010.

Susan Fitzpatrick. "Knowledge Is Not Enough: Creating a Culture of So-
astice, Dignity, and Human Rights in Guatemala: Maryknoll Sisters and the
nte María 'Girls.'" *US Catholic Historian* 24, no. 3 (July 1, 2006): 111–128.

onte, Laura. *Selling the American Way: US Propaganda and the Cold War*. Philadel-
hia: University of Pennsylvania Press, 2008.

nales B., Enrique. *Movimientos Sociales Y Movimientos Universitarios En El Perú*.
Lima, Peru: Ciencias Sociales, Pontificia Universidad Católica del Perú, 1974.

Bernasconi, Andrés. "Is There a Latin American Model of the University?" *Comparative Education Review* 52, no. 1 (February 1, 2008): 27–52.

Berryman, Phillip. *Liberation Theology: The Essential Facts about the Revolutionary
Movement in Latin America and Beyond*. New York: Random House, 1987.

———. *The Religious Roots of Rebellion*. Maryknoll, NY: Orbis Books, 1984.

Bethell, Leslie, and Ian Roxborough, eds. *Latin America Between the Second World War
and the Cold War, 1944–1948*. New York: Cambridge University Press, 1992.

Bidegaín, Ana María. "From Catholic Action to Liberation Theology: The Historical
Process of the Laity in Latin America in the Twentieth Century." Working Paper
#48, Helen Kellogg Institute for International Studies, Notre Dame, 1985.

———. *Participación y Protagonismo de las Mujeres in la Historia del Catolicismo Latinoamericano*. Buenos Aires, Argentina: San Benito, 2009.

Black, George. *Triumph of the People: The Sandinista Revolution in Nicaragua*. London:
Zed Press, 1981.

Blandón, Jesús Miguel. *Entre Sandino y Fonseca: La Lucha de Los Pueblos de Nicaragua,
Centroamérica y el Caribe Contra Las Dictaduras y las Intervenciones USA, 1934–1961*.
Managua, Nicaragua: Segovia Ediciones Latinoamericanas, 2010.

Bonilla, Frank. "The Student Federation of Chile: 50 Years of Political Action." *Journal
of Inter-American Studies* 2, no. 3 (July 1, 1960): 311–334.

Booth, John A. *The End and the Beginning: The Nicaraguan Revolution*. 2d ed. Boulder,
CO: Westview Press, 1985.

Booth, John, and Patricia Bayer Richard. "Civil Society, Political Capital, and Democratization in Central America." *Journal of Politics* 60, no. 3 (1998): 780–800.

Borgwardt, Elizabeth. "FDR's Four Freedoms as a Human Rights Instrument." *OAH
Magazine of History* 22, no. 2 (April 2008): 8–13.

Brignardello, Luisa Amelia. *Movimientos Estudiantiles En Argentina: Historia-Vida Política Obra Gremial-Documentación*. Buenos Aires, Argentina: Editorial Dunken, 2007.

Buchbinder, Pablo, Juan Sebastián Califa, and Mariano Millán, eds. *Apuntes Sobre La Formación Del Movimiento Estudiantil Argentino (1943–1973)*. Buenos Aires, Argentina: Final Abierto, 2010.

Califa, Juan Sebastián. "La Militancia Estudiantil en la Universidad de Buenos Aires Entre Golpe y Golpe, 1943-1955." In *Apuntes Sobre la Formación del Movimiento Estudiantil Argentino (1943–1973)*, edited by Pablo Buchbinder, Juan Sebastián Califa, and Mariano Millán. Buenos Aires: Final Abierto, 2010.

Carey Jr., David, and M. Gabriela Torres. "Precursors to Femicide: Guatemalan Women in a Vortex of Violence." *Latin American Research Review* 45, no. 3 (2010): 142-164.

Carey, Elaine. *Plaza of Sacrifices: Gender, Power and Terror in 1968 Mexico*. Albuquerque: University of New Mexico Press, 2005.

Carpenter, Sara, and Shahrzad Mojab. "Adult Education and the 'Matter' of Consciousness in Marxist Feminism." In *Marxism and Education: Renewing the Dialogue, Pedagogy, and Culture*, edited by Peter E. Jones. NY: Palgrave Macmillan, 2011.

Carrillo, Justo. *Cuba 1933: Students, Yankees, and Soldiers*. New Brunswick, NJ: Transaction Publishers, 1994.

Caruso, Marcel. "La Amante Esquiva: Comunismo y Reformismo Universitario en Argentina (1918-1966)." In *Movimientos Estudiantiles en la Historia de América Latina*, vol. 2, edited by Renate Marsiske. México: Centro de Estudios Sobre la Universidad, Universidad Nacional Autónoma de México: Plaza y Valdés Editores, 1999.

de Castilla Urbina, Miguel. *Educación para la Modernización*. Buenos Aires, Argentina, 1972.

———. *Educación y lucha de clases en Nicaragua*. Managua, Nicaragua: Departamento de Filosofía, Universidad Centroamericana, 1980.

Chamorro, Amalia. "Estado y Hegemonía durante el Somocismo." In *Economía y Sociedad en la Construcción del Estado en Nicaragua*, edited by Alberto Lanuza, et al. San José, Costa Rica: Instituto Centroamericano de Administración Pública, 1983.

Chávez, Joaquín M. *Poets and Prophets of the Resistance: Intellectuals and the Origins of El Salvador's Civil War*. New York: Oxford University Press, 2017.

Choudray, Aziz. *Learning Activism: The Intellectual Life of Contemporary Social Movements*. New York: University of Toronto Press, 2015.

Clark, Paul Coe. *The United States and Somoza, 1933–1956: A Revisionist Look*. Westport, CT: Praeger Publishers, 1992.

Cowart, Billy F. "The Development of the Idea of University Autonomy." *History of Education Quarterly* 2, no. 4 (December 1, 1962): 259-264.

Crawley, Andrew. *Somoza and Roosevelt: Good Neighbour Diplomacy in Nicaragua, 1933–1945*. New York: Oxford University Press, 2007.

Crawley, Eduardo. *Dictators Never Die: Nicaragua and the Somoza Dynasty*. New York: St. Martin's Press, 1979.

Donahue, Francis. "Students in Latin-American Politics." *Antioch Review* 26, no. 1 (Spring 1966): 91-106.

Escobar, Edward J. "The Dialectics of Repression: The Los Angeles Police Department and the Chicano Movement, 1968-1971." *Journal of American History* 79, no. 4 (1993): 1483-1514.

Fernández Fernández, David. *La Iglesia que Resistió a Pinochet: Historia, desde la Fuente Oral, del Chile que no Puede Olvidarse.* Madrid, Spain: IEPALA, 1996.

Fitzsimmons, Tracy, and Mark Anner. "Civil Society in a Postwar Period: Labor in the Salvadoran Democratic Transition." *Latin American Research Review* 34, no. 3 (1999): 103–128.

Fleet, Michael. *The Rise and Fall of Chilean Christian Democracy.* Princeton, NJ: Princeton University Press, 1985.

Flora, Jan L., John McFadden, and Ruth Warner. "The Growth of Class Struggle: The Impact of the Nicaraguan Literacy Crusade on the Political Consciousness of Young Literacy Workers." *Latin American Perspectives* 10, no. 1 (January 1, 1983): 45–61.

Foley, Michael W., and Bob Edwards. "The Paradox of Civil Society." *Journal of Democracy* 7, no. 3 (1996): 38–52.

Foroohar, Manzar. *The Catholic Church and Social Change in Nicaragua.* Albany, NY: SUNY Press, 1989.

Fox Piven, Frances, and Richard Cloward. *Poor People's Movements: Why They Succeed, How They Fail.* New York: Vintage, 1979.

Frazier, Lessie Jo, and Deborah Cohen. "Defining the Space of Mexico '68: Heroic Masculinity in the Prison and 'Women' in the Streets." *Hispanic American Historical Review* 83, no. 4 (November 1, 2003): 617–660.

———. *Gender and Sexuality in 1968: Transformative Politics in the Cultural Imagination.* New York: Palgrave Macmillan, 2009.

Freire, Paulo. *Pedagogy of the Oppressed.* Translated by Myra Bergman Ramos. New York: Continuum, 2006.

Gamarra Romero, Juan Manuel. *La Reforma Universitaria: El Movimiento Estudiantil de los Años Veinte en el Perú.* Lima, Perú: OKURA, 1987.

Garrard-Burnett, Virginia. *Terror in the Land of the Holy Spirit: Guatemala under General Efraín Ríos Montt, 1982–1983.* New York: Oxford University Press, 2010.

Glijeses, Pierro. *Shattered Hope.* Princeton, NJ: Princeton University Press, 1992.

Gobat, Michel. *Confronting the American Dream: Nicaragua under US Imperial Rule.* Durham, NC: Duke University Press, 2005.

González, Julio V., ed. *La Revolución Universitaria, 1918–2008, Su Legado: Compilación de la Fundación 5 de Octubre 1954.* Buenos Aires, Argentina: Librería Histórica, 2008.

González-Rivera, Victoria. *Before the Revolution: Women's Rights and Right-Wing Politics in Nicaragua, 1821–1979.* University Park, PA: Pennsylvania State University Press, 2011.

———. "Somocista Women, Right-Wing Politics, and Feminism in Nicaragua, 1936–1979." In *Radical Women in Latin America Left and Right*, edited by Victoria González and Karen Kampwirth, 41–78. University Park, PA: Pennsylvania State University Press, 2001.

González-Rivera, Victoria, and Karen Kampwirth, eds. *Radical Women in Latin America: Left and Right.* University Park: Pennsylvania State University Press, 2001.

Goodman, Margaret Ann. "The Political Role of the University in Latin America." *Comparative Politics* 5, no. 2 (January 1, 1973): 279–292.

Gordon, Hava Rachel. *We Fight to Win: Inequality and the Politics of Youth Activism.* New Brunswick, NJ: Rutgers University Press, 2009.